U/P: Lean Business Philosophy

True-North Value

Benjamin Snipes

U/P: Lean Business Philosophy
True-North Value

Benjamin Snipes

ISBN 978-1-54390-252-5

All rights reserved. No part of this publication may be reproduced, stored in a retrieval system, or transmitted, in any form or by any means, electronic, mechanical, photocopying, recording, or otherwise, without the prior written permission of the publisher, Notology Publishing LLC.

Printed and bound in the United States of America.

© 2015 - 2017 Notology Publishing LLC

To my wife Angela, who brings me back to earth but never lets me down, dad, mom, brother, family in-law, dog Oscar my loyal writing companion, friends, supporters, and most notably, Philippa, who I hope will use this to make sense out of the world.

Contents

A Forward Slash to *U / P* i

U / P A3 Report. v

*U / P*Lexicon vii

*U / P*Further Summarized xiii
    Volume I: True-North Value. xiii
        Stream 1: Headwaters- U / P xiii
        *Stream 2: Money & Economics – Lean Normative,
        Real and Monetary Value*. xiii
        *Stream 3: Existence– Lean Universal, Process and
        Personal Values* xiv
        Stream 4: Lives– Lean Living Systems. xvi
        *Stream 5: People's – Lean Ethics, Motivation and
        Factors of Truth Value* xvi
    Volume II: Channels xvii
        Stream 6: People's, Chief Meaning Officer (CMÔ). . xviii
        *Stream 7: Optimizing, Chief Optimization Officer
        (CÔÔ)* xviii
        Stream 8: Energizing, Chief Energization Officer (CEÔ) xix
        Stream 9: Profitably, Chief Function Officer (CFÔ) . . xx
        *Stream 10: Uniquely, Chief In-formation, In-novation
        & De-sign Officer (I/DEÔ)* xxi

Stream 1: Headwaters to *U / P*. 1

CONTENTS

Stream 1 *A* 3 Report:. 1
Why Lean ?. 3
Why Lean Philosophically? 6
Structuring *U* / *P*. 9
Further Reasons to *Lean* Philosophically 12
Why Lean More Specifically?. 22
Philosophically *Leaning* Your Business Ideology. . . . 31
Philosopher Kings and Queens. 32
The Philosophy of *Lean* in the Grand Design. 37
    Science 40
    Religion 43
Limits to Business Quantification. 45
The *U* / *People* Business Model 46
Synthesizing Subjects 47
Quantifying *Lean* Abstraction and Analogies for Sales
    Success 51
    From Zero to One 52
The Symbols - The Forward Slash, Circumflex, and Sigmas 56
U People / Toward 6σ. 59
U/ *People* in the *Lean* True-North Value Stream. 62
Pay Us over the *Pay Wall* at the Margin of Existence . . 65
Identifying the Four Steps to *Lean* Philosophically toward *U* / *People*. 67
The Para-Scientific Business Process. 70
The *I/D Kata*. 74
High Flying Mamas 82
U / *P* in the Air 86
Consumers Are Always Right. 89
L-Shaped Reflection of *What U* / *People* Value 93
U/ *People* and Michael Porter's Value Chain. 95
You *Lean* People are *Philosophical* 99
Products and/or Services > p and/or s > *paos* > *pay us* >
    soap .com 103
Stream 2: Money & Economics as True Value. 106

Stream 2: Money & Economics 107
    Stream 2 *A* 3 Report:. 107
    The Brazilian *Real*. 115
    Precious Metals and the Locke-Lowndes Debates. . . . 116
    With Money Comes Great Power. 119
    Caveats to Measuring Money. 122
        (1) Supply, Substitutes and the Warhol Paradox. . . 122
        (2) Barter and Self-service. 128
        (3) Market Structural Distortions. 130
    U / *People's*Money Veil 131
    Off to See the Wizard 132
    Funny Money 134
    Traditional and Modern Measurements of Money. . . . 136
    Irrational, Process-Oriented Value Estimation. 142
    Optimal Slack 143
    Cash and Credit Flow as Meta-Economic Value Streams 145
        Chart of Economics Terms. 146
    Truth Value as Two Sides of the Same Physical Coin. . 148
    Moving Forward 151

Stream 3: Existence 153
    Stream 3 *A* 3 Report:. 153
    Existence and Ontology Defined. 156
    Tripartite Perspectives on Existence -*Universal*, *Process*
        and *Personal* Truth Values. 161
    You, the Plane and the Lottery – On*U* / *PP* as a*Universal*,
        Process ,*Person* 166
        Levels of Dependent Existence. 171
    Three*Lean* Truth Types Aligned with *Universal*, *Process*
        and *Personal* True-North Value Perspectives. . . 171
        Truth Value Correlations. 176
    Reason, Causation or Nothing. 183
    Reason as Causation from Aristotle's Perspective, with
        Modification 185

CONTENTS

Relating Aristotle's *Four Causes* to Levels of True-North Value 187
Rational Agnosticism- Existential Causation in the Eastern Traditions 190
Boundaries of Reason – Self-Causing Causes, Gödel's *Second Incompleteness Theorem* and Simon's *Bounded Rationality* 193
20th Century Fragmentation of Unification. 198
Money as Unified *Lean* Theory 199
Beautiful Question Marks??. 200
Fecund Universes? 207
Other Scientismic Theories. 209
Consumers' Existences are *As If* Self-Defined 210
    Theists 212
    Scientismists 213
Intuition Bracketing (the *IB*) Speculation for Money. . 214
    Chart of the *Intuition Bracket* or *IB*. 215
    Intuition Bracket of Reason. 218
Ontological Medium (the *OM*) 219
The *Ontological Teleology* (the *OT*) 222
Ontologically Prospective Projects (the *OPPs*) 225
Teleology v Teleonomy 228
The Open-Ended Paradox of the *OT* 232
Silly Suds 237

Stream 4: Lives 241
    Stream 4 *A* 3 Report:. 241
Customers Self-Organize Upward Along the *OT* 243
Self-Organizing and Supervening Levels of OT Sophistication: From *SO-OT* to *SL-OTS* 245
    Super Supervenience. 246
    Supervenience of Weather, Money and Consumers . 249
What Goes *U / PP* Must Come Down 251
How Did People Come to Live? Living *SL-OTS* E-merge 252

Lean aRe SL-OTS- You, Your Organization and Customers Become Meaningfully Viable. 255
   Universal Chart of SUDS Forming /aRe SL-OTS. . . 258
You aRe / People 258
One General Definition of *Life* Proposed by a NASA Working Group 259
Qualities of Living Qualities. 260
Lean aRe Processes 261
   "a" 262
   "R" 263
   "e" 263
How/*aRe* You and Consumers?. 265
How/*aRe* Organizational Processes? 266
   Apple of my *i* 267
      Consumers'*Pocket Universe* 269
The Axial Age – Energizing Money and Intuition. . . . 271
Spaghetti Suds as a Mental Model for */aRe* Processes . . 274
   The *FSM* is Not Dead 275
Emergence of*SUDS* through*SO-OT* into*SL-OTS* 275
The Survivor Tree of Life 278
The*Universal* Constructor, Games of Life and Langston's Ants 279
   Universal Constructors. 280
   Conway's Games of Life 281
   Langston's Ant 282
The Great Chain of Being 285
Valuable Energy Streams are*The Great Chain of Being*. 291
An Organization's (*B/aRe*) Viability. 294
   Universal Chart of SUDS Forming B/aRe SL-OTS. . 296
B/aRe as Modern Evolutionary Synthesis. 297
C/aRe Downward 299
   Universal Chart of SUDS Forming C/aRe SL-OTS. . 301
Studying Consumers' Circular Randomness. 305
Adding*Intention* to*Cognitive /aRe* (*I/C/aRe*) 309

CONTENTS

    Chart: Timeline of Known *Universe* vs. Degrees of
        OT Existence 315
    Mitochondria, Consumers and their Pets are Co-Determined 316

Stream 5: People **325**
    Stream 5 *A* 3 Report:. 325
    OT /*N-OT* as Strategic Degrees of Consumers' Sophist-
        ication 327
    As Consumers Find Themselves - Karl Jaspers' *Existenz*
        and Existential *Best Fit* Models 329
    Phenomenology and Survival of the Persistent. 333
    California Dreaming 338
    The Rothko Effect 340
    Test for Qualia: How Do You Know U/ *People* See the
        Color Red? 343
    Lifting the Veil to See Reality 344
    The Scientific Revolution of the *OT* 345
    Phenomeno-logical Categorization to Abstract Analogy
        Making 348
    Y AM I? 356
        Moving Beyond the ÔT to *What* is Gets *B-Ôught* . . 358
    Philosophical Zombies as Straw Men. 361
    U/ *People* are *N-OT* in Jeopardy. 365
    Maximally Existential *Me* aning Defined (/$\sigma\infty$) 367
        Universal Chart of SUDS Forming ME/aRe SL-OTS. 368
    OT Cognitive Dissonance(*OCD*) and Meaning. 371
    *ME*aning Means *M* aximum *E* xistence 372
    A Buy-Product of Conscious Existence is *ME* aning . . . 374
    Springing Beyond the *OT* 377
    Consumers' Hall of Mirrors. 380
    On the Shoulders of People *Who* aRe *N-OT* 383
        Will to Live - Shopenhauer 384
        Will to Power- Nietzsche / Adler 385
        Will to Pleasure - Freud 387
        Will to Meaning- Kierkegaard / Frankl 387

Will to Will - Nietzsche	388
Opportunities and *Threats* as Binary *SW-ÔT* Analysis .	390
WE/aRe Normatively Valuing Supervening Conceptual Structures	392
WE/aRe Willing to Existentially Optimize	392
Universal Chart of SUDS Forming WE/aRe SL-OTS.	394
U/aRe Forming Micro, Meso and Macro Economic, Political and Cultural Structures.	398
Universal Chart of SUDS Forming U/aRe SL-OTS	399
U/aRe Controlling Their Ontology and Ethics.	400
U/aRe Universalizing *Consumers' Will to Exist*	404
What An Organization *Ought* to *D/O*	405
Chart of Gradations of *Ought*	409
Universalization of Ought Ethics (*U.*) for Fun and Profit	410
Universalizing Consumers' *Universal Egoism*	418
Universalizing Your Organizations' *Perfectionist Consequentialism*	420
Altruism and Optimizing Being.	422
The Problem of Evil *Google* Can't Escape.	425
Ethical Prospects – *OPPs* for the Captain, Prisoner and Transplant	428
The Captain	431
The Prisoner	433
The Transplant	434
Emotions as Personal Analogies – How Consumers *Ought* to Feel about Your *paos*	436
Survival of a Systemic *Utilitarianism* Inside the *IB* . . .	437
Customers' Upward, Downward, Inward, Outward Demand - Supervenience and Enactivism.	445
Hierarchy of Needs - *Maslow Inc.*	450
Self-Actualizing Peak Experiences, Flow and Getting B-Ought	452
Peak Experiences	454
Flow	454
Self-Esteem	455

CONTENTS

    Love & Belonging 456
    Safety 457
    Physiology 457
No Need Hierarchy 458
Other Need Theorists 460
    Henry Murray 460
    Clayton Alderfer 461
    David McClelland 461
    Manfred Max-Neef 462
    Paul Lawrence 462
    Deci and Ryan 464
    Attachment Theory 465
    Factors of the *Ought* 465
Zero to One Again- Binary Oppositions of *B-Ought* and
    N-Ought 466
Ôught Factors(*Ôfs*) of Psychological Motivation. . . . 469
Model of *U/aRe Ôught Factors* 476
U/aRe Ôught Factors Within the ÔM 477
Higher Order *Meta-Ôfs* (*MÔs*) 478
Industrial Classification of *MÔs* 478
    Transportation *MÔs* 479
    Telecommunication *MÔs* 480
Factoring *Meta-Ôught Factors* 482
Emotional Meta-Ofs(*E-MÔs*) 483
Irrational Exuberance 485
Critical Phase Transitions while Dreaming - Extending
    U/aRe Persona 489
The Harder They Fall 490
The Only Way is *U / PP* through *Meaning* 491
Bringing it All Together 493
    Chart of U/Pęôple's Value Stream. 494

Volume II: Channels 497

A Forward Slash to *U/P*

In my last semester of graduate business school, I was trying to understand exactly what the business curriculum taught when I stumbled onto the business discipline of "Lean." From that point forward my thinking went sideways. I expected that during the business program I might have an "AHA" moment - an "AHA" moment synthesizing the entire degree into an overarching insight explaining how all business subjects led to making money. For comparison, in law school, that "AHA" moment for me was a sudden, intuitive sense of who, why, what, and how we regulate people, businesses and society. From business school though, I expected a singular understanding of the money making process.

However, when I ran into the popular business concept of "Lean," I realized that while I was taught the specific details of how money got made generally from all business activity, business school taught me nothing about the creation of "true-north value," which money ought to represent and "Lean" advocates pursuing. There is a difference. I realized that while all business subjects allude to and try to quantify "value," none fully described the genesis of "true-north value" in the way "Lean Thinking" suggests, which is helpful to know when leading a business toward creating the type of value for which customers willingly pay a price. I knew I had some extra-curricular work to do to graduate with the knowledge of true-north value applied to business that I was seeking. My business education then became a quest to understand the historical and philosophical foundation of "Lean" and apply it in my own life and business dealings.

Perhaps because my head was spinning from thought at that moment, the somewhat strangely unifying acronym, "U/People" (pronounced "You Lean People") also came to mind. The acronym stood for, "Uniquely/Profitably, Energizing and Optimizing People's Lives and Existences." To me though, that odd acronym cohered and explained the entire value stream in a way the business curriculum seemed to miss. It to me was the ultimate philosophical and logical consequence of studying Lean as I then understood it.

I saw *U/People* as an overarching principle tilting all business subjects toward the Lean philosophy of seeking true-north value. As you will see, I relate each letter of the *U/People* acronym to specific departments and functions of the modern business enterprise, and those departments and functions to the deepest levels of true-north value and problem solving in-turn. I then understood that this was my AHA moment I had achieved. I went to business school to get the intuitive sense of how to make money that successful entrepreneurs implicitly know and came away with an acronym.

While I was having this moment of clarity, the business concept of Lean was only growing more popular with its application to startup businesses due to Eric Ries' publication of his best selling book, "The Lean Startup." When reading this and the enormous number of other Lean-oriented books that had been produced to capitalize on the business trend, they reinforced for me the proposition that Lean represented a certain philosophical perspective on how to achieve success in business and life. As I became more educated about the history of Lean, it became for me a unique synthesis of Western and Eastern philosophies used to reach measurable business results.

Quite unexpectedly, studying the history and philosophy of Lean also led me to books in widely different domains that all seemed to align for one reason or another with the philosophical, humanistic and post-humanistic concepts of Lean, like Douglas Hofstadter's, "Gödel, Escher, Bach," Jim Collins' and Jerry Porras', "Built to Last," David Deutsch's, "The Beginning of Infinity," and Yuval Noah Harari's, "Sapiens." Thus, in this text and through a close reading of great books like these, I summarize and extend the intellectual legacy of Lean to its philosophical extreme, unifying everything from theoretical physics to the humanities to religion by further intertwining Lean like a golden braid within the themes that form the bedrock of all true-north value. Thus, you might find U/P to be an intellectual companion and counterpoint to all that has been written regarding Lean.

While I originally intended just to make a simple pamphlet or diagram explaining how the *U/ People* acronym expands on Lean, my thoughts kept growing on the page to become what I hope to be a well-researched book written with fun and style. How ironic that a mere acronym became this book. And this became more than just a business book to me because it led me to the most profound and unexpected places, far beyond what most business books cover. By writing it, I kept finding connections between radically different concepts and multiple levels of meaning, seeing new similarities and differences at every turn, and then recirculating that parallelism back into the book.

Through this research and writing process, this book evolved to become simultaneously academic, literary and artistic. It became academic because I tried to not only write truly, but to support it copiously with legitimate, well-researched footnotes. I consider it literary because its symbolism requires that it actually be read to be fully appreciated. And it to me became artistic because I could only articulate *true value* in the space where words fade away, and that sense of the unspeakably sublime that I felt started coming out in the writing methods I used. The fission, fusion, parallelism, coherence and discoherence of its language began to model for me the physics and metaphysics of Lean. It became an abstract meditation on all busy-ness - a transcendent business book. I sincerely hope and expect that you will enjoy and learn from it as much as I have writing it.

I believe that the more you improve people's lives and existences (and hopefully are also perceived to do so) through this philosophy's precepts, the more systemically, and thus personally important it will become to you. If you read this book end-to-end, you will be able to describe the psychological motivation of businesspeople and consumers in ontological terms. That in-turn will let you efficiently translate all business into scientific, philosophical and even spiritual concepts in a fairly concise way. And by converting between these seemingly disparate worlds of thought, you will be able to better think through and solve people's problems to make money more effectively while producing less waste than you otherwise would have, which in Lean is the highest form of true-north value creation.

Thus, my purpose in writing this book is both ego-centric, in that I wrote it for my own entertainment and benefit, and allo-centric, in that I sincerely hope to pass on what I consider useful knowledge to you about the intellectual history and philosophy of Lean and business in general. By reading this book, I expect that you will learn a bit about history, a bit about philosophy, a bit about business, and a bit about yourself, which may be like rebuilding a ship you are already on, as the philosopher Otto Neurath famously said. However, by studying this intersection of "Lean," "Business," and "Philosophy," I hope that you will become more powerful throughout your life's journey.

Edwin Land, founder of the Polaroid Corporation, once said, "Don't undertake a project unless it is manifestly important and nearly impossible."[1] I have often felt that writing a philosophical book about business qualified supremely on both accounts, and so I thrust myself forward in the open-ended endeavour of trying to produce something of lasting value that in my wildest dreams might be used by you in some small way to make money for everyone's benefit.

---

[1]Edwin Land as quoted in, *The Vindication of Edwin Land* , Forbes magazine, Vol. 139, p. 83 (May 4, 1987).

U/P A3 Report

- *Lean* is a global business discipline and paradigm that learns from and builds on what made Toyota® successful, now extended many ways like through the *Lean Startup* movement
- *Lean* combines the Western Philosophy of Science and Consumerism with some aspects of Eastern religious philosophies like Buddhism
- People criticize *Lean* because they feel those applying it rely too much on its tools without leaning toward its goal of "True-North Value" by way of respect for people, continuous improvement, customer satisfaction and waste reduction
- "True-North Value" though is a vague concept, leading to confusion when people seek to deliver it in the details of consumers' daily lives
- *U/P* summarizes and extends the philosophy of *Lean* to explain *what* "True-North Value" truly means in the context of all *Lean* business activity and life in general
- *U/P* describes a new framework called an "I/D Kata" used to identify people's deepest problems and ultimate satisfaction so you can better motivate employees and consumers to produce and purchase:

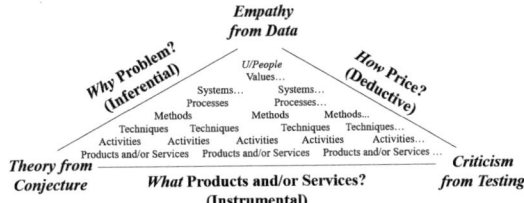

- *U/P* provides a unique business model for thinking through true-north value creation to make meaningful amounts of money

U/ P Lexicon[2]

Symbol/Term/Acronym	Meaning
/ *Lean*	
/6σ *Lean*	Six Sigma, or Pragmatic Idealism
/σ∞	Perpetual Pursuit of Perfection
/*aRe Lean adaptation*	, *Re-generation* and *energization* activities performed by living systems
3WH The	*who* , *why* , *what* and *how* of meaningfully making money, which another formulation of true-north value
A3 Report	A one-page report providing the in-formation needed to make decisions and progress
Abduction	Optimistic process of believing that a reasonable theory best fits limited data while holding skepticism hostage
AM	Analogy Making
B/aRe Barely	*Lean adaptation, Re-generation* and *energization*
B-ÔT or *B-Ôught* Being beyond	what is *Ontologically Teleological*, which is *Leaning* toward a state of universalized perfection
C/aRe Cognitively	*Lean adaptation, Re-generation* and *energization*
CEÔ	Chief Energization Ôf-ficer
CFÔ	Chief Function Ôf-ficer
CMÔ	Chief Meaning Ôf-ficer
CÔÔ	Chief Ôptimization Ôf-ficer
CÔRe	Critical to Ôntological Realization
Customers People who	*b-ought* or may purchase goods and/or services

---

[2] For a listing of the *Lean* lexicon that does not include those terms added by *U / P*, please see, *Lean Lexicon: A Graphical Glossary for Lean Thinkers*, 5th Ed., Lean Enterprise Institute, Inc. (2006).

Symbol/Term/Acronym	Meaning
Deduction	Process of reaching specific conclusions from general theories about how much money you will make
E-MÔs Emotional Meta-Ôught factors	functioning as a type of mental *Kanban*
FSM Flying Spaghetti Monster	®
Gemba The	*Lean* term of Japanese origin meaning the center of the organization where the *CEÔ* resides
Genchi Genbutsu The	*Lean* term of Japanese origin directing managers away from the board room toward the source of all production
Hansei Lean	term of Japanese origin meaning *self-reflection,* is part of the *Kaizen* practice of continuous improvement done by looking back and thinking about how a process or personal shortcoming can be improved
HQ Head Quarters	and/or *House of Quality*
House of Quality	Place where **me**aning gets re-generated
Hōshin Kanri A	*Lean* term of Japanese origin meaning *Strategy Deployment,* or more colloquially *Compass-Guided Management,* and is symbolized by the oh-hat Ô
I/C/aRe Intentionally, cognitively	*Lean adaptation, Re-generation* and *energization*
IB or *{ }Intuition Bracket*	
I/D Kata Inference - Deduction Kata	using the *3WH* interrogatories
I/DEÔ In-formation, In-novation and De-sign	Ôf-ficer
I/Deôlogy A system of ideas and ideals, especially	one formulated by the I/DEÔ as the basis of an organization's true-north value theory.
Induction	Process of creating a general theory from specific, robust data

Symbol/Term/Acronym	Meaning
Jidoka	The *Lean* term of Japanese origin meaning the process of error correction within certain degrees of significance with a human touch of knowledge and intelligence, which is the measure of quality for any *Lean* system of management
Kanban	*Lean* term of Japanese origin for a centralized source of in-formation, such as *E-MÔs* inside an *HQ*
Kata	*Lean* term of Japanese origin for the four-step *3WH* routine by which an organization *Leanly adapts*, *Re-generates* and *energizes* to continuously increase its *Ontological Realization*
Kaikaku	*Lean* term of Japanese origin meaning radical, revolutionary improvement of a value stream to quickly create more value with less waste; sometimes called *kakushin*
Kaizen	*Lean* term of Japanese origin meaning processually systemic continual improvement across an organization's entire true value stream
Lean	Formal business subject derived from studying the *Toyota Production System*; that which is best tuned for fitness
Life	A process performing /aRe activities; or more commonly, one having the power to intrinsically *Re-generate* its ontology across generations in some way, shape or form by either teleologically or teleonomically *adapting* and *energizing* itself within the *OM*
ME	Matter and Energy, Money & Economics, or Maximally Existing
Meme	A human behavior caused by conceptual *SUDS* forming cultural, economic, legal and commercial *SL-OTS* that pass from one Re-generation to the next

Symbol/Term/Acronym	Meaning
ME/aRe Maximally Existing	*Lean adaptation, Re-generation* and *energization*
MÔ Meta-Ôntological factor	(or a *Modus Ôperandi*), which is a higher order *Ôf*
Mottainai Buddhist	and *Shinto* term meaning regret for any form of waste
Muda Lean	term of Japanese origin meaning waste that adds no true-north value
Mura Lean	term of Japanese origin meaning waste from unproductive variance
Muri Lean	term of Japanese origin meaning waste from overburdening
N-ÔT or N-Ôught	Not *Ôntologically Teleological*
Ningen sonchō Lean	term of Japanese origin meaning *Respect for People*
Ô or ô Lean	symbol for *Hōshin Kanri* meaning, *Compass-Guided Management,* or more formally *Strategy Deployment*
ÔCD Ôught Cognitive Dissonance	, which is the conundrum created by the apparent paradox of the *ÔT*
Ôfs Ôntologically Teleological factors	of customers' lives and existences
ÔM Ôntological Medium	
Ôntology	The study or definition of *what* is versus *what* is not
OR Ontological Realization	, which is the binary either/or proposition of further being
ÔT or Ôught	The *Ôntological Teleology*, or the seemingly circular goal of *being b-ought* in an infinite *Universe*
Paos	Initialism for "products and/or services," like "soap" but spelled backward; pronounced "pay us"; *Paos* also being an ancient city in central Greece (37°51′N, 21°59′E) with a triangular perimeter and natural spring in its north-east quadrant
People	Charismatic megafauna, otherwise known as human ***be***ings

Symbol/Term/Acronym	Meaning
Poka-Yoke	*Lean* term of Japanese origin meaning that which helps avoid inadvertent mistakes
Problem	Either an *Opportunity* for or *Threat* to people's standard of existence, which requires a set of values, methods, techniques, activities, products and/or services to achieve or resolve
PSR	*Principle of Sufficient Reason* states that everything has another cause to an ultimate self-causing cause, or *sui generis*
R	*Re-generation*, or the *Rubicon* across *adaptation* and *energization* leading to *who* customers are
RCA	*Root Cause Analysis*, which is equivalent to the *PSR* when taken to its logical extreme, is generally limited to *5 Why's* within *Lean*
Σ or *σ*	Sigma, sum or standard deviation
6σ	Six Sigma
SO-ÔT	Self-Organizing Ontological Teleology
SUDS	Strategically Unique Degrees of Sophist-ication
Supervenience	Reciprocally dependent levels of self-organized sophist-ication
SL-ÔTS	Supervening Levels of Ôntological Teleological Sophist-ication
Stream	A chapter of *U / P: Lean Business Philosophy*
SW-ÔT	Binary business analysis of *Strengths* and *Weaknesses*, *ÔPPs* and *Threats* as taught in B-School
Takt Time	*Lean* term of *German* origin meaning the pace of demand for true value
Teleology	Intentional, goal-oriented purpose directed by an organization and consumers
Teleonomy	Unintentional, goal-oriented purpose directed by the *OT*
TPS	*Toyota Production System*, also referred to as *Total Quality Management* (*TQM*)

Symbol/Term/Acronym	Meaning
True-North Lean	terminology for the metaphorical direction and source of all true value and reasonable explanation
Truth Portmanteau of	*True* and *North*; a factual assertion combined with an explanation for it that has the highest degree of in-formed agreement among all possible alternatives
WE/aRe Wholly Existing (or	*Will to Exist*) *Lean adaptation*, *Re-generation* and *energization*
U/aRe Universally	*Lean adaptation, Re-generation* and *energization*
U/P The metaphorical direction of truth-value	and basis for the *U / People* acronym
U/ People Uniquely/Profitably, Energizing and	Optimizing People's Lives and Existences
Universe Everything that is, or may be and you	just don't know it yet
U/ PP values *Universal*	, *Process* and *Personal* degrees of true-north value
U/Sociality The theory of Eusociality regarding the	co-dependent *Ontological Realization* of all *beings*
Value Stream Lean	terminology for the flow of true-north value through all universal processes toward *who*, *why*, *what*, and *how* customers are

U/ P Further Summarized

The following summarizes this *Volume I: True-North Value*, and the next book, *Volume II: Channels*, before you dive into the confluence of business and philosophy within the paradigm of *Lean* to solve consumers' deepest problems.

Volume I: True-North Value

Stream 1: Headwaters - U / P

Stream 1 describes *what* the discipline and paradigm of *Lean* is, while explaining *how* U/ P extends its reach for you to make money well. *Stream 1* does this by teaching you the philosophical implications of *Lean* from both its Eastern and Western traditions to incorporate into a business ideology. *Stream 1* further introduces you to the *U/ People* acronym (pronounced, *You Lean People*) and business model that you may use to structure your *Lean* thinking. *Stream 1* explains the symbolism used throughout these texts, including CAPITALIZED acronyms, hyphens -, forward slashes /, circumflexes "^", and sigmas σ and Σ. Each conceptual fission, fusion and parallelism in the language compresses and unifies multiple levels of business and philosophical meaning to quickly capitalize on the far-reaching insights provided across all domains in which you operate.

Stream 2: Money & Economics – *Lean*Normative, Real and Monetary Value

Any*Lean* business philosophy necessarily requires a sound grounding in the meaning of money for you to make it well. *Stream 2:*

Money & Economics, analyzes the secret life of money that you may have missed so you may go up along consumers' value streams in ways you never expected.³ You will learn the true, *Lean* value that makes money meaningful through market transactions, which cross all consumers' value streams. *Stream 2: Money & Economics* attempts to review some of the intellectual history of money and economics and *how* that work applies within the balance of the *U/ People* business model.*Stream 2* prepares you to advance around, up and through the *U/ People* organization chart and business model, starting with *Existence,* as seen here and explained further below:

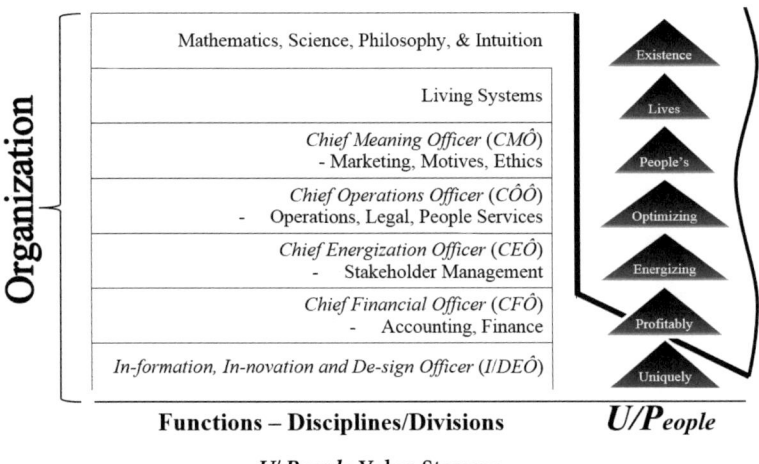

Stream 3: Existence– Lean Universal, Process and Personal Values

Following the *Lean* concept of*Genchi Genbutsu* directing all business people to go to the source of all production, *Stream 3* sums up*who* and*why* consumers are from their mathematical, scientific,

---

³*See e.g.,* Tad Crawford,*The Secret Life of Money: How Money Can Be Food for the Soul* , Allworth Press (1994).

philosophical and personally intuitive perspectives. This *Stream 3 Leans* to the philosophical extreme so you may better understand true-north value from the origin of life in *Stream 4: Lives* and human meaning and motivation in *Stream 5: People's*. *Stream 3: Existence*, takes you through the *Lean* solution space by factoring Eastern and Western traditions that form the intellectual foundation of *Lean*. This *Stream 3* provides a new way of organizing this body of work so you may understand it, slicing across academic disciplines to effectively dissect an *HQ*. All organizations may also use this *Stream* to form the cornerstone of their *Houses of Quality* to interrelate *what* they know and believe about existence with *what* consumers most truly value. Since these philosophical and scientific discussions involve the most fundamental questions, such as the origin of the *Universe* and the human condition within it, they do get a bit heady.[4]

Stream 3 introduces a new, *Lean* metaphysical concept of the *Ontological Teleology*, the *ÔT* or *Ôught*, which is the possibly circular goal directedness of life to further be, but possibly be more, because we live in an open-ended *Universe* – consumers can only intuitively speculate at this present moment *what* their purpose is.[5] The *Ontological Teleology* is not designed to give final philosophical answers, but rather to better frame the range of *what* customers know, believe, and witness actually improving their lives and existences that you may charge them for in exchange.

This *Stream 3* simultaneously recognizes that customers hold intuitive truths and attempt to eliminate the problem of the seeming paradox of life lived through the *ÔT* with a variety of non-circular spiritual, theistic or scientismic beliefs. An organization's products and/or services may serve these intuitively speculative beliefs in *Lean* fashion so long as those beliefs do not conflict with falsifiable,

---

[4]Such as *Heuristics* (Kahnman), *Ockman's Razor, Principle of Sufficient Reason* (Leibniz), *Cosomological argument, causa sui, a priori*, and why there is something rather than nothing [*i.e. teleological*(Leibniz) versus *ontological* (Anselm) arguments].

[5] *See generally*, Karl Popper, *The Open Universe: An Argument for Indeterminism*, W.W. Bartley III (ed.) (1982).

inter-subjective truths or the deontological ethical and legal rules to which society agrees to cohere for everyone's eusocial benefit. After reading *Stream 3*, you ought to be able to analyze *what* consumers will buy through the *Lean Ontological Teleology* to best energize and optimize their lives and existences by resolving their utmost problems most effectively.

Stream 4: Lives – *Lean* Living Systems

Stream 4: Lives applies the *Lean* true-north values arising from existence explained in *Stream 3* to the systemic origin of life within the known *Universe*. *Stream 4* examines these issues against the backdrop of current *Lean* thinking for developing a more physically oriented, *Lean* business *ideology* that brings business back down to Earth. *Stream 4* identifies the *Lean* slots from which living systems unexpectedly emerge, with each being a strategically unique degree of sophist-ication leading to its own *Ontological Realization*. This emergence is much like how *U/P* arises from and supervenes on *Lean* itself.

Finally, this *Stream 4* elaborates on the new, *Lean* concept of *Universalization* as the open-ended, possibly circular, end-goal of life when you bracket out intuitive, non-circular beliefs for business purposes. *Universalization* analyzes *how* customers actually live regardless of *what* they believe, which may be used as a further basis for a *Lean* true value theory of *what* consumers find most meaningful. *Universalization* is also largely *how* busy people discuss true value in the work-place, even if not in this same terminology, as I hope you will see.

Stream 5: People's – *Lean* Ethics, Motivation and Factors of Truth Value

Stream 5: People's, extends the previous *Stream 2: Money*, *Stream 3: Existence*, and *Stream 4: Lives* through the disciplines of ethics and motivation in a strictly human context. *Stream 5*will introduce you to the parameters of metaphysical, true value from which *Lean* originates. You will recognize these parameters as ones used to engage employees and market products and/or services daily. *Stream 5*proposes a motivational or needs framework based on these *Lean* parameters to identify the problems customers have to live and exist into perpetuity. This *Stream 5*thus extends the normative, existential perspective of human meaning to the actual lives of consumers and their *Universalization* by synthesizing*who* they are with*what* they ought to buy from you.[6]

Once this ethic of *Universalization* gets established within an organization's true-north business *ideology*, all *Lean* people in that work-place can then move the organization toward a universalized and collective ethic of expanding all life within existence in whatever markets it operates. You will learn how to increase consumers' and employees' standard of existence in a possibly infinite*Universe*, so you may monetize more meaning by solving more problems with the best solutions to delight the most people. Numerous, seemingly hubric, corporate credos and business ideologies demonstrate this *Lean* end-goal, and a few will be cited within this *Stream 5*. The *Lean*motivational drivers discussed in *Stream 5*feed into *how* an organization behaves and *what* consumers want in the balance of the*U / People* business model discussed in *Volume II: Channels*.

Volume II: Channels

The *U/ People* business model in *Volume II*applies the combined philosophy of *Lean* to organizations providing true-north value in the meaningful exchange of money.*Volume II: Channels* customers' true-north value streams through all products and/or services in the second of two volumes composing,*U / P: Lean Business Philosophy*.

---

[6]Yes, this is Hume's *Is-Ought* problem; *see*, the Stanford Encyclopædia of Philosophy entry on, '*Hume's Moral Philosophy*' (Rev. Aug. 27, 2010).

*Volume II: Channels*all businesses' upper-management/ontology in the following way:

Stream 6: People's, *Chief Meaning Officer (CMÔ)*

– Marketing

The *Chief Meaning Officer*addresses *Lean* marketing as the business discipline investigating *who* customers are and *why* they want to consume products and/or services. *Stream 6: People's* describes *how* the *Lean* true-north value discussed in *Existence, Lives* and *People's* value streams generates money *me*aningfully through products and/or services by solving problems in ex-change.

Marketers inconsistently define *value* in *Lean* business contexts, with some defining value as *what* people like and do, and others defining value as*what* people will pay—with*Lean true-north* value generally being bandied about as the vaguest concept of all.[7] I hope this matter is perfectly clear at this point of the *U/ People* business model, while you think about*what Lean* , true-north value truly means. Organizational leaders, if not all employees, really need to understand *Lean* value to *Lean* their organizations toward producing desirable products and/or services, i.e. the structured Matter and Energy pulled from and flowed to consumers to solve their deepest problems. Thus, *Volume: II, Stream 6*applies people's previously defined normative, real and personal values to help you become a marketer *who* better identifies and measures true value and *Lean*smore meaningfully toward all people.

Stream 7: Optimizing, *Chief Optimization Officer (CÔÔ)*

– Operations, G.C., People Services

---

[7]*See e.g.*, C. Saleh, F. H. Astuti, M. R. A. Purnomo and B. M. Deros,*Fuzzy identification of value stream analysis tools in lean manufacturing*, pp. 74-77, 2012 2nd International Conference on Uncertainty Reasoning and Knowledge Engineering, Jalarta (2012).

The *Chief Optimization Officer* functions to operate *Lean* business processes, guiding *how* you re-generate salable products and/or services. The CÔÔ avoids all forms of waste by optimizing procurement, production, and human resources with the support of other guiding functions like the *General Counsel* that place systemic boundaries on *what* is possible. The CÔÔ overall optimizes the meaning that *Lean* products and/or services produce. This *Stream 7* examines *how* an organization's internal stakeholders' normatively true and real values may be aligned with *what* customers truly value for greater business effect across all supporting departments. Optimization focuses true-north human value streams within the *Lean* business processes of energizing stakeholders, functioning finance, and uniquely innovating products and/or services.

Stream 8: Energizing, Chief Energization Officer (CEÔ)

– Stakeholder Management

The *Chief Energization Officer* sits in the middle of the organization right where s/he re-generates *Lean* true-north value for customers, while always thinking about *how* to charge customers more effectively. *Lean* and the further discipline of *Lean Six Sigma* formally calls this center of the *U / People* business model the *Gemba*, which is a word of *Japanese* origin used by *Toyota's Production Systems*.

With the guiding support and alignment of the *CMÔ, CÔÔ, CFÔ,* and, *I/DEÔ*, the latter two functions being further described below, the *CEÔ* energizes people's lives, and meaning by solving their existential problems. The *CEÔ* does this by aligning sales and marketing, talent recruitment, employee motivation, legal operations, accounting, financial investment, research and development, design, innovation and strategy toward a business' end-goal of making money meaningfully. The *CEÔ* is thus the most energy-centric of all employees by focusing the energy of all others toward *what* customers and other stakeholders most truly value by best understanding *why* and *how* they do *what* they do.

Just as marketing assesses and measures customers' normatively true and subjectively real values upward and through these activities, this *Stream 8* describes *how* the CEÔ in-turn identifies, measures and aligns his or her organization's *Lean* energy with *what* the I/DEÔ, CFÔ, CÔÔ, and CMÔ determine creates the most *Lean* true-north value for customers up along the value stream. This insight allows the CEÔ to produce the most optimized, energetic, profitable and unique products and/or services that customers want to buy for the most meaningful amounts of money possible.

Stream 9: Profitably, Chief Function Officer *(CFÔ)*

– Finance, Accounting, Treasury

The **Chief Function Officer** guides the CEÔ by equating *what* customers truly value to money or other objective *Lean* performance metrics. This gives the *CFÔ* a haloed rôle in any organization. Accounting and finance measure the monetary value generated within customers' lives and existences as developed through meaningful marketing, optimized operations, and energetic procurement of products and/or services, investments and people. This *Stream 9* analyzes the financial and accounting measurements of an organization's net value and *how* that organization may best *Lean* toward *what* customers most meaningfully value in ex-change for *what* price you charge them.

People's profitability explains *how* an organization can more effectively skew customers' existential reality and fundamental needs with the concept of profit as a relative change in customers' standard of existence. This *Stream 9* considers the CFÔ function to be a natural construct of the realities revolving around the monetary measurement of customers' true value streams within a business *ideology.*

Stream 10: Uniquely, Chief In-formation, In-novation & De-sign Officer (I/DEÔ)

– IT, Strategy, R&D, Creatives

The *Zen*-like *Chief In-formation / In-novation / De-sign Officer* uniquely optimizes customers' lives and existences over all customer segments by meaningfully marketing, optimizing operations, and functionally analyzing product and/or service strategies. The *I/DEÔ* is an organization's turning point and reflection of its true-north knowledge and power.[8]

The *In-formation* function of the *I/DEÔ* coheres *what* people value with *what* form of *Lean* products and/or services an organization re-produces for profit. In-formation also directs *what* whole organizations ought to *Lean* toward within their business *i/deô*logies. The *I/DEÔ* fully recognizes that all products and/or services are fundamentally phenomenological *in-formation* to customers however you may empathize with *what* they experience when they consume. Customers interpret this *in-formation* received from *Lean* products and/or services as either *good* or *bad*. This perception in-forms *how* a business *i/deô*logy *Leans* its organization toward in-novation and profitable success.

In-novation replaces *what* products and/or services consumers used with *what* more *Leanly* energizes and optimizes consumers' lives and existences. Consumers' quintessential problem of existence never changes, while *in-novation* entirely improves what makes customers' lives upwardly mobile. *De-sign*, on the other hand, symbolically describes the form, function and consumption of *Lean* products and/or services in ways that energize and optimize consumers' highest values, particularly in regards to *how* money semiotically represents those values. The *I/DEÔ* thus bridges *Lean Thinking* and *Systems Thinking* with *De-sign Thinking* across

---

[8]This *I/DEÔ* concept naturally owes its inspiration and thanks to the world-famous innovation and design consultancy IDEO at www.ideo.com.

the *3WH* Socratic value identification interrogatories as described within.

The *Uniquely Stream 10* thus analyzes all of an organization's *Lean* channels so a business *i/deô*logy may most meaningfully advance consumers' standard of existing, which causes them to push money back down in ex-change. *Stream 10* presents an evolved method of business strategic analysis by applying the *U/ People* business model for the greatest business results and competitive advantage while serving stakeholders' normative and really personal true-north values.

Stream 1: Headwaters to U/P

Stream 1A 3 Report:

- *Lean* is a global business discipline used to make money by improving commercial outcomes
- *Lean* has been applied throughout the business environment to all size companies and extended to all types of organizations
- *Lean* combines Western philosophies that investigate *what* is true through the scientific process, along with some aspects of Eastern religious philosophies like Buddhism to determine *what* has real value
- Many of the most truly successful business leaders today have seriously studied and written about philosophy
- U/P leverages this tradition by summarizing and extending the philosophy of *Lean* to explain *what* "True-North Value" truly means in the context of all *Lean* business activity and life in general
- U/P synthesizes and delivers this knowledge through creative symbolism and writing for improved learning
- U/P provides a people-focused business model and a heuristic called an "I/D Kata" that allows you to apply U/P to all business
- The *I/D Kata* teaches you *how* to discover true-north value by pursuing a series of interrogatories following a *Who*, *Why*, *What*, *How* methodology

Do you want to know *what* the philosophy of *Lean* is? Do you want to *Lean* philosophically as far as you can go to reach the highest point of true-north value for all consumers? This book explains *why* and *how* you ought to *Lean* philosophically for the greatest profit of all.[9] You can make the money you earn have lasting value by meaningfully observing and fervently divining *who* consumers are, *why* they may buy something, *what* they want to buy from you, and *how* you ought to delight them the most. *U/P: Lean Business Philosophy*, is a philosophy book about business that stretches your abstract thinking toward better understanding *what* creates true value and helping you implement that knowledge in life and business. You will learn to *Lean* philosophically so you can make meaningful amounts of money while feeling satisfied that you did good work.

However, like looking at the sun, such high-level, abstract thinking is painful, disorienting, and best done through a *Lean*, conceptual lens for you to see most clearly. *U/P* filters all complex subjects to help you better see *who* consumers truly are from their deepest problems up through the value stream. You will then discover *what* they find most personally meaningful in the products and/or services you serve. I suggest that you put on a thinking cap and eye-shades before reading further because these abstract concepts will help you see true-north value if you learn to look carefully enough. For example, examine this mark of a global company to see *what* it believes it produces for its customers:

© 2015 True Value Company

---

[9] You might even call it an Americana "middlebrow" bricolage that mixes up high-end philosophy and art with notions of money and power and all that may be meaningful; like the work of Mr. Sekou Andrews, it is philosophical, business rap.

Since commercial value gets measured in money, money is the mythical icon toward which all true value in business *Leans*. When deciding whether to buy now and receive meaningful true value from you, consumers consider *how much* money they must pay at the point of purchasing products and/or services. Like-wise, you as a business person want to know *how much* money you can earn through great work. Without clearly understanding *why* and *what* consumers want to buy, and *how* you deliver their greatest satisfaction, you cannot uplift an profits to where you think they ought to be.

While *what* exactly consumers individually believe to be truly valuable remains beyond *what* all people commonly agree, philosophy logically coheres and mediates the true-north value of money within our overlapping consensus of the way life is.[10] Importantly, philosophy will also guide you past any idolatry of money that will blind you to consumers' true religion. When you *Lean* philosophically, you consider *how* best to create true-north value for all people, which in-turn supports *who* consumers are and *what* consumers individually believe to be most worth their money.

Why Lean?

You may wonder how *Philosophy* relates to *Lean*, or *what* the concept of *Lean* is in the first place. While *Lean* has a long intellectual pedigree primarily formed from the philosophy of science and Eastern philosophical traditions, *Lean* is now the prevailing business discipline/fad/trend/paradigm used by people to make money in our time. *Lean* as a business paradigm was derived from studying *what* made the *Toyota Motor Corporation* so successful for so long. In the 1980s, business researchers developed the overall concept of *Lean* from that extensive body of knowledge. A gentleman named John Krafcik first coined the term '*Lean*' in an article he wrote for

---

[10]Such as the consensus forging described by John Rawls in, *A Theory of Justice*, Harvard University Press (1971).

the Massachusetts Institute of Technology about *Toyota's* highly successful production systems when he said, '*[I]t needs less of everything to create a given amount of value, so let's call it 'lean.*'"[11] From that point forward, the term *Lean* represented a modern business philosophy whose tenets organizations continue to learn.

> **Perfection is attained,**
> **not when there is nothing more to add,**
> **but when there is nothing left to take away.**
> – Antoine de Saint Exupéry, p. 60, Ch. III *L'Avion, Terre des Hommes* (1939).

From a fundamental philosophical perspective, *Lean* business techniques focus on creating the truest value by removing all forms of waste and adding only *what* most satisfies consumers' demands, just as *Toyota* continues to do today. However, while not complex on its face, *Lean* demands a different way of doing business.[12] In fact, since one of *Lean's* main points is to wash away everything but that which provides consumers with *value* however truly defined, it is a far more abstract money making methodology than most businesses are used to considering. At the same time, the businesses that are applying *Lean* evolved it into a philosophy of continuous improvement, which the Japanese word,*Kaizen*, represents.*Kaizen* means to take apart (*Kai*) and to make good (*zen*), and is key to continuous improvement efforts to reduce waste in an*HQ*.

In the spirit of *Kaizen*, *Lean*was iteratively improved in the 1990s and 2000s by intersecting it with more quantitative disciplines like

---

[11]John Krafcik is now an executive at*Alphabet* (aka*Google*, whose automotive division is now spun off as *Waymo*) leading its autonomous car development; *See generally,* Jim Womack,*Deconstructing the Tower of Babel* (accessed Oct. 7, 2004 at www.lean.org).

[12]*In re*the different sort of thinking *Lean* requires, Natalie J. Sayer and Bruce Williams state, *Involving people is what has to be done if organizations are to be truly effective, but, like so many of the Lean Six Sigma principles, it requires different thinking if it's to happen,* in *Lean For Dummies*, Kindle Loc. 669-670, Wiley (2008).

Six Sigma that Motorola (once a division of *Google* but now a part of *Lenovo*) developed at the same time. Motorola designed *Six Sigma* in the 1980s to ensure production of its information technology within six standard deviations of statistical precision. Thus, businesses use *Lean* to accurately target *what* people most value, while *Six Sigma* and other quantitative methods precisely *Lean* organizations of people in that direction. Countless books evidence this intellectual legacy of *Lean, Six Sigma* and other people-oriented, evidence-focused business insights that are referenced throughout the ten *Streams* (a.k.a. *Chapters*) of *U/P* that you can surface with any search.

Thus, *Lean* is the best paradigm for philosophically analyzing business because it has the highest rate of problem solving power as evidenced by its efficacy in generating profits.[13] *Lean* has evolved to become widely used by most companies[14] of all sizes in some way as part of their organizational DNA — from start-ups to large corporations — just ask any business person whether his or her organization uses *Lean*!

Lean, like most business theories, must be approached abstractly but applied concretely through specific actions to determine *what* delights the most customers for the greatest profit. However, if any criticism has been levelled at *Lean*, it's the irony that *Lean* practitioners overly rely on the plethora of tools, diagrams and instruments that *Lean* consultants produce without espousing an overriding ethos for their detailed implementation in the chaos of everyday business.[15] Consultants promote these tools because customers prefer to pay for repeatable mechanisms than abstract

---

[13]*See*, Peter Godfrey-Smith,*Theory and Reality: An Introduction to the Philosophy of Science*, Kindle Loc. 1650, Chicago Press (2003) and Larry Laudan *Progress and its Problems: Toward a Theory of Scientific Growth*, Part III, Berkley Press (1977).

[14]The 2011 Compensation Data Manufacturing & Distribution results found 71.6 percent of companies currently use lean manufacturing practices, found at http://www.compdatasurveys.com/2011/09/01/lean-practices-aid-manufacturers-in-recovery/ (accessed Mar. 2, 2015).

[15]*Volume II: Channels* will apply the *Philosophy of Lean* described in *Volume I: True-North Value*to the tools, instruments and methodologies developed by *Lean* in detail.

theories that require deep thought to implement.

However, if you move beyond all of the tools, diagrams and instruments provided by *Lean*, if you study it carefully enough, you will see that *Lean* represents a history of thought from the *Ancient Greeks*, the *European Scientific Renaissance* and the *Far East* that extends into all we as producers and consumers think about today. In this amalgamation, *Lean* articulates a good overriding ideology - a good unified philosophy - because *Lean* accepts the possibility of, desirability for and progress toward an infinitely optimistic future to reach commercial *Nirvana*.[16]

So, the intersection of *Lean* tools along with the sound business philosophy of *Lean* can generate radical wealth in this domain.[17] Yet, despite countless business books falling into the *Lean* canyon, a gap still exists in the *Lean* literature due to these proponents failing to identify *what* true-north value *Leans* businesses toward. *U/P: Lean Business Philosophy, True-North Value* attempts to fill this void by embodying the intellectual legacy of *Lean* in a set of high-level steps you can take to make money meaningfully in-line with all consumers' value streams.

Why Lean Philosophically?

While philosophy is said to *bake no bread*, the philosophy of *Lean* helps you analyze *what* bread you ought to bake and *how* to bake bread that gets bought and broken. For example, baking either a wedding cake or table bread requires you to satisfy consumers'

---
[16]According to S. Shapiro in *Mathematics and Reality*, p. 525 (1983), 'for nearly every field of study there is a branch of philosophy called the philosophy of that field... Since the main purpose of a given field of study is to contribute to knowledge, the philosophy of X is, at least in part, a branch of epistemology. Its purpose is to provide an account of the goals, methodology, and subject matter of X'; what I intend to do here by describing the philosophy of *Lean* and our ontology is reach an epistemology of knowing how to produce pure profit; see also David Deutsch, *The Beginning of Infinity: Explanations that Transform the World*, p. 324, Penguin Books (2011).

[17]David Deutsch, *The Beginning of Infinity*, p. 202, Penguin Books (2011).

very different fundamental needs in *Lean* fashion. Knowing *who* consumers are and *why* and *what* they most truly value further determines *how* you will bake bread that helps customers better become *who* they want to be, whether that is either married or well-nourished. If philosophy is dead, *why* not put it to practical use within *Lean* to find the true-north value of life and business and make money meaningfully? *Lean* philosophically if for nothing else than to more effectively guide you to consumers' point of physical, emotional and intuitive satisfaction.[18]

Leaning philosophically toward consumers is not about endless speculation, but rather about analyzing data with continuously new metaphysical perspectives in a unified way to make real decisions about *how* to make money well in all business environments. This isn't science fiction, but rather the best knowledge available about reality. It solves the problem of explaining *what* true-north value is and *how* it is created with money. It does that by explaining *who* and *why* consumers are in the grandest scheme of things for you to apply specifically to business. Knowing *how* to analyze business data implies that an organization knows *what* realistic, true-north value that data reflects and *why* the data means anything at all to consumers and other stakeholders, which philosophy explains. Thus, organizations *Lean* philosophically to energize and optimize their businesses through consumers' lives and existences and *what* they personally find meaningful.

Analyzing valuable data without continuously knowing *who* consumers are and *what* they find most meaningful prevents an organization from reporting as much money as possible inside its

---

[18]For an entertaining essay and some background on this perspective, see Mike Alder, *Newton's Flaming Laser Sword Or: Why Mathematicians and Scientists Don't like Philosophy but Do it Anyway*, Philosophy Now (May/June 2004) http://philosophynow.org/issues/46/Newtons_Flaming_Laser_Sword; in this way, the philosophy of *Lean* is in many ways synonymous with the Philosophy of Science primarily arising from the late *European Renaissance* as well.

headquarters.¹⁹ Getting to this point of profit in the philosophy of *Lean* requires both deeply respecting humanity and always improving, such as *how Pfizer's* upper management periodically does so within so within its global*HQ* .²⁰

Pfizer World Headquarters, New York City (Credit: Me, 2014)

Thus, the two pillars of any *Lean HQ* are *Ningen Sonchō* , which is Japanese for *Respect for People*, and *Kaizen*, which is Japanese for *Continuous Improvement* . To help you visualize these concepts, here is a diagram of a corporation's *HQ* with a *Lean* management system using profit as its foundation and bottom line:²¹

---

¹⁹Sid Shah, *Surprise! There's More To The Future Of Marketing Than Just Big Data: Creativity matters*, readwrite.com (Dec. 23, 2015).

²⁰Lorcan Mannion and Ciarán Crosbie, *Pfizer Reinvents Lean in the Lab*, Pharmaceutical Manufacturing Magazine (May 04, 2011).

²¹Jeffrey Liker,*The Toyota Way: 14 Management Principles from the World's Greatest Manufacturer*, p. 2, McGraw-Hill Education (2003).

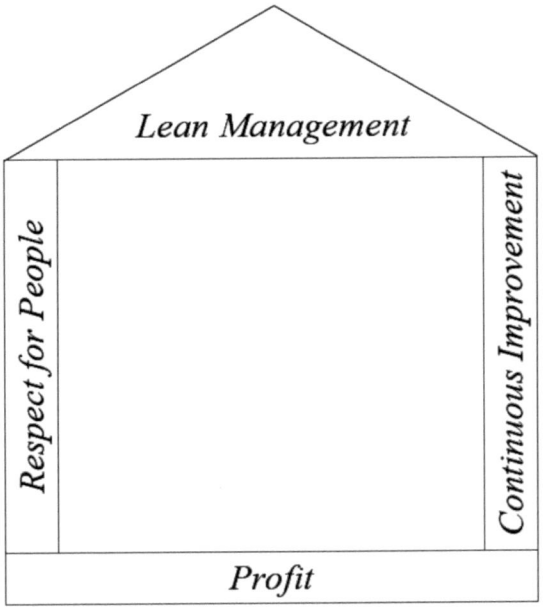

Diagram of a *Lean HQ*

Structuring *U / P*

U/ P structures its chapters, which I call *Streams*, around the *U / People* acronym. *U/ People* stands as a *meta-heuristic, upper ontology* and *business model*[22] for use by an organization to *Uniquely/Profitably Energize and Optimize **People's** Lives and Existences.* [23] *Lean* within this acronym stands as an adjective indicating those people and organizations that *Lean* philosophically toward other people. *Lean* also acts as a verb implementing the philosophical imperative to

---

[22] *See*, Alexander Osterwalder, *The Business Model Ontology: A Proposition in a Design Science Approach*, (Ph.D. Diss.) Universite De Lausanne, Ecole des Hautes Etudes Commerciales (2004).

[23] The *U/ People* business model is *why*, beyond social justification, corporate diversity initiatives matter; companies cannot produce products and/or services that serve the broadest markets unless their corporate ontologies (*i.e.* the corpus of their employees) reflect the general population of intended consumers.

make money the right way toward *what* consumers most truly value. For example, *Toyota Motor Corporation Leans* philosophically as a fictitious person,[24] and through its employees and other stakeholders as natural people, toward its customers' true-north value in an open-ended *Universe*, which I will explain further as we go along.

U/ P runs quickly through each part of its main acronym, from one *Stream* to the next, by synthesizing the essential qualities of each for you to better relate subjects and build a personal and organizational *House of Quality* and ideology from its two pillars - respect for people and continuous improvement. This business model and vocabulary - as supplemented by all the work cited within this book - allows an organization to point its own *true-north* value compass within its *House of Quality* (an *HQ*) toward profitably analyzing data to increase consumers' standard of existence. *True-North* is the metaphorical direction of all true-value in *Lean* terminology, and an *HQ*, *House of Quality* and *Head Quarters* is where true-north value is re-produced.[25]

However, as you might anticipate, this survey could never be exhaustive within a single volume, much less a part, *Stream*, section, paragraph, sentence and/or word as may be devoted to any given aspect of this universal subject of true value that defines all problems, which ultimately makes all money meaningful. The further analysis and re-search I could do for this book is necessarily limitless, since like every thing, it could be infinitely improved. My end-goal is to provide you with a fountain of knowledge that always allows you to identify and improve *who* consumers are by

---

[24]Yuval Noah Harari, *Sapiens: A Brief History of Humankind*, p. 30, Harper (2014), where he writes, 'In the US, the technical term for a limited liability company is a 'corporation', which is ironic, because the term derives from 'corpus' ('body' in Latin)... Despite their having no real bodies, the American legal system treats corporations as legal persons, as if they were flesh-and-blood human beings.'

[25]When reading *U / P*, you must keep in mind the critical distinction between geographic, magnetic and metaphorical true-norths or else you will get completely lost when seeking consumers' highest values.

intuiting, inferring and possibly inducing *why* they buy, and then assumptively deducing *what* should be re-produced and *how* you ought to create truly valuable products and/or services for them.

To help with this stretch assignment in plain-language philosophy so you may better understand the genesis of true-north value, this discussion cites the brilliant[26] work of those who understand the contents of this book so well. The biblical amount of footnotes and further commentary ought to supplement your own personal discovery and learning while building a *Lean HQ* and ideology for making money meaningfully. I footnote where I can recognize prior thoughts, but given the breadth of this discussion bridging together diverse disciplines, please forgive inadvertent omissions that I am sure you will surface! I strongly encourage you to use the references and footnotes as best fits your reason to *Lean* philosophically that you have in mind within an *HQ*. The footnoted references support all that I write by providing you from the ground up with even better explanations that will give your own re-search further reach.

To be clear, the philosophy of *Lean* does not provide a unique ideology, "-ism" or school of thought in the context of the great many others. Rather, the business concept of *Lean*, as philosophically expanded by *U/P*, is a vector of discovery by which you may synthesize existing, well-regarded Eastern and Western philosophies, ideologies, -isms, and business concepts in an *HQ* toward the ultimate goal of delighting customers for profit. If you must call this something, you might call it, *Universal Optimism*, which anticipates the panglossian future value consumers and organizations will

---

[26] *See generally*, David Kord Murray, *Borrowing Brilliance: The Six Steps to Business Innovation by Building on the Ideas of Others*, Gotham (2009).

receive by your doing the right thing.[27]

Further Reasons to *Lean* Philosophically

If you need some further reason to *Lean* philosophically around making money meaningfully, the following six reasons elaborate on *why* you ought to do so:

1) **Consistently Grow Profits.** You can help an organization meaningfully differentiate the products and/or services it creates to make more profits the right way. Ideally, a profit represent the true-north value created in customers' lives and existences over and above the economic cost deducted in order to produce and provide them. In a competitive environment, a profit also represents the true-north value provided to consumers in excess of the similar value consumers could have received from competitors.[28] However, as you know, you must qualify this idea of true-north value's association with financial profit since it comes with many caveats, like *the tragedy of the commons* where people free-ride on public goods like natural resources.[29] Nonetheless, ideally, you profitably uplift

---

[27] Here I mean *Optimism* in both the classical sense of this being the best of all possible worlds given existing constraints, and in the anticipatory sense of estimating *what* could be better based on that which ought to be optimized and adjusting variables accordingly to changes future results; for background on classical philosophical optimism, *see* , Nicholas Rescher, *On Leibniz Expanded Edition*, University of Pittsburgh Press (July 2013); *Panglossian* of course refers to Dr. Pangloss in Voltaire's *Candide, ou l'Optimisme* (1759) who Voltaire used to misrepresent the misunderstood ideas of Leibniz; interestingly, in the inverse and despite Voltaire's mocking, optimism does in fact appear to be universal, *see* , MW Gallagher, SJ Lopez and SD Pressman, *Optimism is universal: exploring the presence and benefits of optimism in a representative sample of the world*, J Pers.; 81(5):429-40. doi: 10.1111/jopy.12026 (Apr. 12, 2013); *see also* David Deutsch, *The Beginning of Infinity* , p. 199 (2011).

[28] Much of this discussion in business ethics relates to how responsive a business ought to be to the fundamental needs of consumers and society at large. Fortunately in capitalism, by and large, business' must specifically serve consumers' needs in order to induce consumption and payment. Thus, with capitalism in place, the question then becomes one of business' obligation towards society at large, which is often more of a matter of long-term societal support for a business' or industry's operation.

[29] Such as Garrett Hardin's theory of the *Tragedy of the Commons*, pp. 1243-1248, Science #13, Vol. 162 no. 3859 DOI: 10.1126/science.162.3859.1243 (Dec. 1968).

customers, employees, investors and society best while avoiding such pitfalls by *Leaning* on true value. In the end, you must *Lean* philosophically so you can consistently understand *what* will be truly profitable for all.

2) Develop a Core Ideology, Purpose and Values: You ought to adapt the *U/People* acronym and business model to an organization's core value theory to make money meaningfully by *Leaning* through all business fads/trends/disciplines/paradigms, including *Lean* itself that will eventually wash away given sufficient time.[30] Ray Dalio, founder of the world's largest hedge fund, *Bridge-water Associates*, writes, '... *adopting pre-packaged principles without much thought exposes you to the risk of inconsistency with an true values.*'[31] Ultimately, an organization must relate customers' true-north values to *what* they pay so a business can more effectively serve them products and/or services that energize and optimize the profits that rain money down on stakeholders.

In one of the best regarded business books of all time, *Built to Last*, Jim Collins and Jerry Porras wrote:

> *[I]n short, we did not find any specific ideological content essential to being a visionary company. Our research indicates that the authenticity of the ideology and the extent to which a company attains consistent alignment with the ideology counts more than the content of the ideology.*[32]

The *U/People* business model supports this statement because taken to its extreme, universal strategies get no free lunch,[33] and so

---

[30] *See*, Thomas Kuhn,*The Structure of Scientific Revolutions* , University of Chicago Press (1962); for a direct example, consider *how* all of the hyperlinks referenced in this book will rot away over sufficiently long periods of time.

[31] See http://www.bwater.com/uploads/filemanager/principles/bridgewater-associates-ray-dalio-principles.pdf (accessed May 6, 2015).

[32] Jim Collins and Jerry I. Porras,*Built to Last: Successful Habits of Visionary Companies* , p. 67, HarperCollins (2011).

[33] Except at*Google* , which is famous for its employer paid for cafeterias.

achieving optimum profitability requires an organization to adopt its own strategically unique degrees of ideological sophist-ication. Thus, you yourself must determine *how* a true-north value theory operates as a cômpass within your business ideology to make money meaningfully. *U/P* helps you decide on a sound basis through which channels consumers' value streams ought to flow through an organization.

3) Evidence Long-term Efficacy. Beyond zealously producing short-term profits, applying humanities-focused business models like *U / People* and concepts such as *Corporate Social Responsibility*, improves business performance and increases stakeholder returns in the long run.[34] Common justifications for humanities-focused value streams flowing within such business models and concepts include reputation management, risk management, employee satisfaction, innovation and learning, access to capital, and financial performance.[35] Again quoting Collins and Porras in *Built to Last*, they said that:

> **[C]ontrary to business school doctrine, we did not find 'maximizing shareholder wealth' or 'profit maximization' as the dominant driving force or primary objective through the history of most of the visionary and successful companies.**[36]

The authors found that organizations that pursue consumers' greater purposes are better able to motivate employees and other stakeholders while uniquely energizing and optimizing their profits over the

---

[34] Margarita Tsoutsoura, *Corporate Social Responsibility and Financial Performance*, Berkley Haas School of Business (2004); Chin-Huang Lina, Ho-Li Yanga, Dian-Yan Liouc, *The impact of corporate social responsibility on financial performance: Evidence from business in Taiwan*, 56–63 Technology in Society 31 (2009); Michael A. Pirson, Paul R. Lawrence, *Humanism in Business – Towards a Paradigm Shift?*, pp 553-565, Journal of Business Ethics, Volume 93, Issue 4 (Jun. 2010).

[35] Arthur D. Little, *The Business Case for Corporate Responsibility* (Dec. 2003).

[36] Jim Collins and Jerry I. Porras, *Built to Last*, Kindle Loc. 1318-1319 (2011).

long-run as an indirect effect.³⁷This concept has been reinforced by numerous other studies as will be referenced throughout this book.

In regards to *how* a business treats internal stakeholders, scholars Jeffery Pfeffer and John Veiga wrote a well-received article in 1999 titled, *Putting People First for Organizational Success*. Pfeffer and Veiga compiled a number of studies correlating the efficacy of well-run people-services programs and organizational profitability.³⁸ A number of subsequent studies confirmed this as well.³⁹These authors' research suggests that corporate cultures that self-organize themselves around *what* people most value perform better overall in the short, medium and long-run.

4) Innovate. Chiat\Day art director Craig Tanimoto asked each of us to '*Think different*' in *Apple*'s same titled 1987 ad campaign.⁴⁰ By pursuing the philosophy of *Lean* in the practice of true-north value discovery, you too will think differently about *how* you may build wealth by upgrading consumers' lives and existences. Where U/P really takes off is in pursuing orthogonal innovation because this solution space is where you can become unmoored from organizational constraints.⁴¹When you *Lean U/P*, philosophy gives your business analysis further reach by allowing you to experience greater consumer insights. Philosophical, abstract thinking allows you to draw lines between science and the fundamental human needs being addressed, providing a way for you to ex-change competitors' solutions for truly novel ones that are at least ten times better. Philosophy thereby allows you to evaluate *Lean* and

---

³⁷*Ibid*, Kindle Loc. 65 (2011).

³⁸Jeffrey Pfeffer and John F. Veiga, *Putting People First for Organizational Success*, The Academy of Management Executive (1993-2005), Vol. 13, No. 2, Themes: Technology, Rewards, and Commitment (May, 1999), pp. 37-48; see also Pfeffer's earlier book,*The Human Equation: Building Profits by Putting People First*, Harvard Business Review Press; 1 edition (1998).

³⁹*See generally*, Wayne F. Cascio and John W. Boudreau, *Investing in People: Financial Impact of Human Resource Initiatives*, 2nd Edition, Pearson FT Press (2008).

⁴⁰Forbes,*The Real Story Behind Apples Think Different Campaign* (Dec. 14, 2011).

⁴¹Kenneth O Stanley, Joel Lehman,*Why Greatness Cannot Be Planned: The Myth of the Objective*, p. 94, Springer International Publishing (2015).

all business theories organically from first principles to reach new outcomes at a work-place to make money meaningfully.

An organization ought to *Lean* toward *who* consumers are to identify *how* to improve their basic human condition for a profit. Clearly understanding *what* consumers believe is phenomenally valuable allows an organization to pivot flexibly toward *what* better solves consumers' problems for the highest margins. As Steve Jobs said to the BBC in 1990, '*No market research could have led to the development of the Macintosh or the personal computer in the first place*,' However, I say that philosophy easily could have and is in fact what Steve Jobs used to innovate, whether he realized it or not, as evidenced by the correlations between his quotes and the philosophy of *Lean* espoused within this book.

Innovating requires an organization to find the confluence of *what* is possible, practical and demanded. Data analyzed through meta-physics toward *what* consumers most meaningfully value can help you find this intersection. By *Leaning* philosophically, you may iteratively re-confirm that your *Lean* thinking remains on this side of non-sense (or non-cents) as you develop and market products and/or services. You can then incrementally test whether customers really experience a revelation of true-north value from the products and/or services you re-generate. Through this process, an organization coheres its business ideology with *what* consumers will actually purchase so they increasingly congregate at its stores.

People Waiting to Enter the Apple Store at the Oculus, NYC (© 2016 Photo Credit: Me, Shot on iPhone 6)

5) Increase the Probability of Profitability. The principles described in this volume increase the probability that you will make profitable business decisions despite fickle markets. While empirically studying whether you make more money when you *Lean* toward *what* consumers most meaningfully value is outside the scope of this book, these principles cohere with well-regarded advice from scores of renowned tycoons, scholars, philosophers, theologians and poets *who* are all liberally quoted here.[42] U/P improves the chances of effectively achieving its obvious yet often disregarded main point that an organization ought to fervently seek true-north value to make money meaningfully. This book provides the fundamental structure for *why* and *how* that occurs.

You may quickly measure *how* effectively you *Lean* philosophically by analyzing *how* consumers respond when you follow this volume's precepts. While predicting human behavior always involves some degree of randomness due to consumers' rational irrationality, which limits the accuracy of any business projections you may make, U/P allows you to better identify the difference between *what* is tactically correct and *what* is not for the greatest

---

[42] *See e.g.*, Matthew Stewart, *The Management Myth*, The Atlantic (Jun. 2006).

chance of achieving profitable success.⁴³

Values Matter, NYC (© 2015, Whole Foods Market, Inc. (Photo Credit: Me))

6) Meaningfully Analyze Data. Most importantly, observing true-north value in life and business allows you to guide your business methods, particularly when clean data is lacking, as increasingly large datasets improve the ability to quantify and understand *what* consumers most truly value beyond *what* they just purchased. U/P connects metaphysical abstraction to *how* consumers actually live, exist and confess their deepest needs within whatever blessed data you may obtain.⁴⁴ U/P is the philosophy of the business discipline of *Lean*, and business remains the most legible of all the social sciences.

The best, most recent attempts to quantify true-north value outside of economics and marketing have been in the fields of psychol-

---

⁴³For example, in *Stream 3* I discuss the implications of work such as J. Reiskamp, J.R. Busemeyer, and B.A. Mellers, *Extending the Bounds of Rationality: Evidence and Theories in Preferential Choice*, Journal of Economic Literature, 44(3), 631-661 (2006); and S. Pironio et al, *Random numbers certified by Bell's theorem*, Nature 464, 1021-1024 (15 April 2010) | doi:10.1038/nature09008 (Received 25 November 2009, Accepted 18 February 2010) *Revised and Expanded Edition: The Hidden Forces That Shape Our Decisions*, Harper Perennial, 1 Exp Rev edition (Apr. 27, 2010).

⁴⁴David Deutsch, *The Beginning of Infinity* , p. 10 (2011).

ogy and neurology. Behavioral economics and "marketing neuroscience" increasingly identify *what* consumers most truly value before they pay a price by quantifying consumers' systemic biases and responses. However, to complement these studies and balance a dogmatic focus on obtaining data, *U/P* leverages conjecture through theory to discover *what* matters most both before it can be counted and when it cannot be counted at all. This mentality of approaching business through profound interrogatories is similar to *what* the famous management guru Peter Drucker wrote about the same Asian culture that produced *Toyota's Production System*:

> *The Westerner and the Japanese mean something different when they talk of making a decision. With us in the West, all the emphasis is on the answer to the question . . . . To the Japanese, however, the important element in decision-making is defining the question.*[45]

Likewise, Jeffrey Leek, Ph.D., professor of data science at *Johns Hopkins* said when further quoting Dan Meyer:

> *'Ask yourselves, what problem have you solved, ever, that was worth solving, where you knew all of the given information in advance? Where you didn't have a surplus of information and have to filter it out, or you didn't have insufficient information and have to go find some?' ... This goes to the heart of our philosophy about data science. We are interested in answering questions with data. We think the question should come*

---

[45] Peter F. Drucker, *What We Can Learn from Japanese Management*, Harvard Business Review (Mar.-Apr. 1971).

first, and the data should follow after. [46]

Or, as Albert Einstein and Leopold Infeld wrote in their 1938 book, *The Evolution of Physics,*

> *The formulation of a problem is often more essential than its solution, which may be merely a matter of mathematical or experimental skill. To raise new questions, new possibilities, to regard old problems from a new angle requires creative imagination and marks real advances in science.*[47]

U/P, as the philosophy of Lean, truly excels at asking the best open-ended business questions to discover the highest value. Since all problems are soluable within the universal value stream,[48] U/P allows you to properly infer and deductively question the meaning of and correlations within data as it applies to consumers' lives and existences. U/P bridges gaps in business analysis so you may ask beautiful questions and answer wicked problems with what good data you can obtain.[49] You ask the biggest questions to

---

[46]Jeffrey Leek, *First Lecture to the Data Science Track*, Johns Hopkins Bloomberg School of Public Health (March 15, 2015); the quote from Dan Meyer comes from his 2010 TEDx talk regarding making over the mathematics curriculum http://www.ted.com/talks/dan_meyer_-math_curriculum_makeover (accessed Mar. 20, 2015).

[47]Albert Einstein and Leopold Infield,*The Evolution of Physics: The Growth of Ideas From Early Concepts to Relativity and Quanta*, p. 92, Cambridge University Press (1938); fascinatingly, Einstein describes new scientific theories as 'incommensurable' with prior ones in 1949, more than a decade before Thomas Kuhn and Paul Feyerabend, *see*, E. Oberheim, *Rediscovering Einstein's legacy: How Einstein anticipates Kuhn and Feyerabend on the nature of science*, Stud. Hist. Philos. Sci. (2016).

[48]David Deutsch,*The Beginning of Infinity* , pp. 65 (2011), and where on p. 192 he notes, '*if the question is interesting, then the problem is soluble.*'

[49]Jon Gertner,*The Idea Factory: Bell Labs and the Great Age of American Innovation* , p. ix, Penguin Books (2012); and the 70,000 member of the Institute of Managerial Accountants said recently that, '*the first objection we commonly encounter on the topic of truth in managerial costing is consistently obtaining an absolutely truthful number in managerial costing is cost-prohibitive, if not impossible,*' in, *Conceptual Framework for Managerial Costing*, p. 82, Report of the IMA© Managerial Costing Conceptual Framework Task Force (2014).

reach the deepest problems you can find that customers will pay you to resolve. Thus, *U/ P's* Socratic method represents a form of *Design Thinking* by leading with empathy and crossing all business disciplines within the *U/ People* business model. This allows an organization to wholly identify *why*, *what* and *how* consumers will buy goods and/or services. You ask *who* to maintain an empathetic customer-centeredness, *why* to define problems, pierce ambiguities and achieve more "AHA" moments, *what* to ideate and produce, and *how* to prototype and test really tangible benefits for money.[50]

Thus, by normalizing *how* you discuss true-north value across an organization through *Design Thinking, Systems Thinking*, and altogether *Lean Thinking*, you can better connect all topics and disciplines to holistically identify and quantify *how* you can meaningfully make the most money by doing good while analyzing the data you have well. For example, of any business fields, finance excels at gathering and synthesizing big data sets, and yet, finance still shows limited (though still highly lucrative) success in accurately predicting true-north value creation.[51] As I hope you will see, all financial analysis boils down to philosophical perspectives as well and could be improved through these same Socratic methods.

 If you have little data or work in less readily quantifiable fields, How do you qualitatively and quantitatively analyze true-north value?

Every organization must ask beautifully inspired intuitive, inferen-

---

[50] *See generally*, Hasso Plattner (Editor), Christoph Meinel (Editor), Larry Leifer (Editor), *Design Thinking: Understand - Improve - Apply (Understanding Innovation)*, 2011 Edition, Springer (December 13, 2010); and *see generally*, *An Introduction to Design Thinking: Process Guide*, Hasso-Plattner Institute of Design Thinking, Stanford University (retrieved Jan. 24, 2016).

[51] *See*, Eugene F. Fama, *Random Walks In Stock Market Prices*, Financial Analysts Journal 21 (5): 55–59. doi:10.2469/faj.v21.n5.55. (2008-03-21); much of this is due to widely-criticized equilibrium theories, and as Nick Gogerty said, '*A cow that achieves equilibrium is called a steak, and the economy closest to achieving equilibrium today is probably North Korea circa 2013,*' in, *The Nature of Value: How to Invest in the Adaptive Economy*, Kindle Loc. 447-448, Columbia University Press (2014).

tial, inductive and deductive questions[52] to create true-north value with either a lot, little or no data by knowing *why* and *how* its business *Leans* toward *who* consumers truly are.[53] Once a business determines *who* its customers are or *who* they ought to be mostly by *what* they do, it then can relate *why* consumers value those activities to *what* it can satisfy them with the most. It deduces *what* metaphysically related products and/or services, functions, features or benefits consumers will actually buy. This allows a business to better hypothesize *how* to make the most meaningful amounts of money by identifying and relating these metaphysical factors to consumers' lives and existences to enter, expand or create new markets. This process will naturally transform an organization's upper-management into chiefly functional, meaningful and innovative officers. Once this is done, its *HQ* will uniquely/profitably energize and optimize consumers' lives and existences from analysis to execution.

Why Lean More Specifically?

Let's look at the common definitions of '*Lean*' to understand *why* the term '*Lean*' philosophically applies to business. The *Oxford English Dictionary* defines ' *Lean*' in Old English as '*Reward, recompense*,' which accords with the modern spelling of '*Lien*' as meaning a right to a debt to be re-paid in exchange for a product and/or service that has been provided. A *Lean* business owes its customers and society at large true-north value for the money it charged, deducted and now gets to re-distribute.

The *Oxford English Dictionary* also defines ' *Lean*' as, ' *The act or con-*

---

[52] Warren Berger, *A More Beautiful Question: The Power of Inquiry to Spark Breakthrough Ideas*, Bloomsbury (2014).

[53] For further discussion of problems understanding economics with pure data, *see generally*, the discussion of economics problems in Nate Silver, *Signal and the Noise: Why So Many Predictions Fail-but Some Don't*, Penguin Press HC, 1st edition (2012); see further Ron Miller, *Lies, Damn Lies And The Myth Of Following The Data*, techcrunch.com (Dec. 6, 2014).

dition of leaning; inclination.' This definition means that whatever or whoever *Leans*, does so against something or someone else, just like *how* any business organization funda-mentally supports itself by *Leaning* on its paying customers, and just like *how* shareholders do in-turn by *Leaning* on the organizations in which they invest.

Lastly,*The Oxford English Dictionary* defines *Lean* as, '*Wanting in flesh; not plump or fat; thin.*' This definition indicates that whatever or whoever is *Lean* efficiently processes energy, much like any effective organization maximizing stakeholder value; however, this definition of '*Lean*' does not mean gaunt, but rather athletically taut-ological as you will see.

Taking all these common definitions into consideration, '*Lean*' is, as we have discussed, also a term-of-art commonly used in business to mean a philosophical legacy and set of business principles organized from studying of *what* made the *Toyota Motor Corporation* so successful for so long by being amazingly prophetic about the future of the auto-mobile industry.[54] As you carry the definition and history of*Lean* forward to*Lean* philosophically toward people, you may recognize that *Lean*, when applied philosophically to business, is as conceptually simple or complex as you will it to be. Since the formal use of*Lean* as a business term is relatively new in the history of the English language, I suggest that you ought to use all of its *meaning* as a vehicle for a people-oriented, business ideology to pursue the greatest profit. You can *Lean* in business by developing customers to consume products and/or services that you efficiently re-produce in exchange for the money on which every corporation's very existence and identity depends.

To achieve the same success as *Toyota*, *Lean*, as ordinarily referred to in business, recommends creating value by removing waste

---

[54]Note with irony that while *Toyota* has been a bit late in developing autonomous, self-driving cars, John Krafcik, who as discussed coined *Lean* as a business term, now leads the development of autonomous cars for *Alphabet* (aka/dba *Google*); this aligns with what David Deutsch notes that all prophesy is inherently biased, in*The Beginning of Infinity* , p. 435 (2011).

from an organization's re-productive system. Any waste that does not create true-north value is referred to in *Lean* as '*Muda*.' The other forms of *Lean* waste are '*Mura*,' meaning any unproductive variance in re-production such as those caused by bad performance metrics so often employed by companies, and '*Muri*' meaning waste caused by overburdening production systems and not fully respecting people. This *Lean* legacy of waste avoidance can be traced to the *Buddhist* and *Shinto* concept of *Mottainai*, which is a term of Japanese origin meaning to re-(pro)duce (*i.e.*only reproduce productively), re-use, re-cycle, and re-inspect wherever possible. *U/P* synthesizes these forms of waste by defining *Lean* waste as activities that do not contribute to products and/or services that energize and optimize customers' lives and existences.

Lean, like most business theories, determines *what* most profitably satisfies the most customers and *how* to do that best. Like the formal discipline of '*Lean*' in quotes, the *U/People* business model directs you to bow from within an organization's *HQ* toward uniquely/profitably energizing and optimizing consumers' lives and existences by solving their greatest problems for a profit.[55] The world's largest companies *Lean* philosophically in this way, such as *General Electric*, which is famously devoted to *Lean* as exemplified by this graphic.

---

[55] *See generally*, John R. Hauser and Don Clausing, *The House of Quality*, Harvard Business Review, The Magazine (1988); *see also* Kevin Meyer, *The Simple Leader: Personal and Professional Leadership at the Nexus of Lean and Zen*, Gemba Academy LLC (2016).

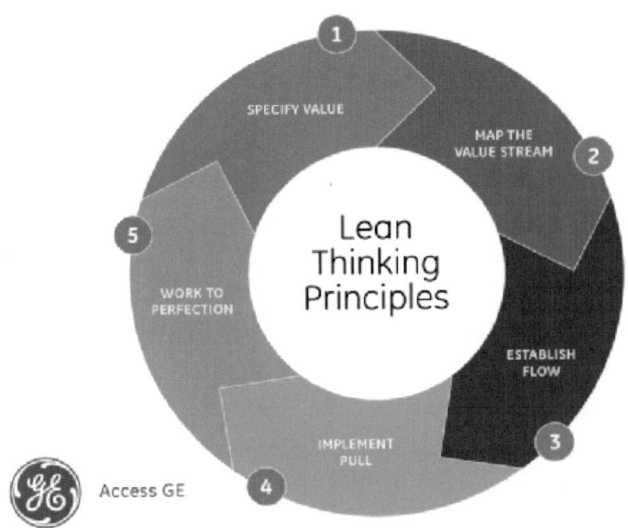

GE *Lean*Values

Here are the key elements shown in the graphic above of *what* formal *Lean* business processes are, including:[56]

1. ***Specifying value***;
2. ***Mapping the value stream***;
3. ***Establishing flow***;
4. ***Implementing pull***; *and*
5. ***Working to perfection***.

These criteria of fundamental *Lean* processes align with the academic description of *Lean* stated by James Womack and Daniel Jones in their well-regarded 2010 book, *Lean Thinking*, within which Womack and Jones defined *Lean* principles as:

---

[56]©General Electric, Inc. (image retrieved Oct. 8, 2014); *see also*, Steve Garbrech, *Embracing Lean Manufacturing Fundamentals*, found at http://www.ge.com/digital/blog/embracing-lean-manufacturing-fundamentals (accessed Dec. 4, 2016).

1. **Identify value** : 'The critical starting point for lean thinking is value...Value can only be defined by the ultimate customer. And it's only meaningful when expressed in terms of a specific product (a good or a service, and often both at once) which meets the customer's needs at a specific price at a specific time'; [57]
2. **Identify value stream**: 'The value stream is the set of all the specific actions required to bring a specific product (whether a good, a service, or, increasingly, a combination of the two) through the three critical management tasks of any business...problem solving...information management...and the physical transformation';[58]
3. **Flow**: 'In short, things work better when you focus on the product and its needs, rather than the organization or the equipment, so that all the activities needed to design, order, and provide a product occur in continuous flow';[59]
4. **Pull**: 'You can let the customer pull the product from you as needed rather than pushing products, often unwanted, onto the customer'; and
5. **Perfection**: 'As organizations begin to accurately specify value, identify the entire value stream, make the value-creating steps for specific products flow continuously, and let customers pull value from the enterprise, something very odd begins to happen. It dawns on those involved that there is no end to the process of reducing effort, time, space, cost, and mistakes while offering a product which is ever more nearly what the customer actually wants. Suddenly perfection, the fifth and final principle of lean thinking, doesn't seem like a crazy idea.'[60]

---

[57] As James P. Womack, Daniel T. Jones said, 'The critical starting point for lean thinking is value,' in, *Lean Thinking: Banish Waste and Create Wealth in Your Corporation*, p. 16, Free Press (1996).

[58] *Ibid*, p. 19.

[59] *Ibid*, p. 22.

[60] *Ibid*, p. 25.

While Krafcik, Womack, Jones and others established *Lean* as a business discipline following Krafcik's coining the term, a lot more has been written about *Lean* processes and application to making money since then, even if not a lot has been written regarding *Lean Thinking's* item number (1) *Identify Value*. For example, the entrepreneur Eric Ries applied *Lean* to early stage product and/or service development by coining the term, '*Lean Startup,*' in his same titled book. Ries described *how* he built an online avatar business, *Instant Message Virtual Universe (IMVU)*, through iterative user testing. However, Ries' para-scientific, *Build, Measure, Learn* method focused entirely on people's revealed preferences without philosophically identifying the meaning of the data being received from end-users. Observing *what* people do and the *how* they pay for it follows a process of trial and error correction, but without any guiding insight as to *what* to ask and *how* to identify meaningful revelations. This leads to waste and missed commercial opportunities.[61]

Thus, despite *Lean's* various applications to date, very little has been written to fully identify true-north value, other than this iterative process of offering minimally viable products and/or services to see *what* consumers purchase. This is because people have somewhat ignored the historical and philosophical legacy of *Lean* that consistently points in the proper direction. By better understanding the history and philosophy of *Lean*, organizations may quickly apply *Lean* to all their operations, while improving their insights with market testing. For example, people ought to know the origin of the *Lean* Japanese term '*Jidoka*' to apply *Lean* best. *Jidoka* originated from Sakichi Toyoda, the founder of the Toyota Group, when he installed a device called a '*jido*' on an automatic textile loom that allowed human operators to make autonomous judgements

---

[61]Notably, Alex Osterwalder, Yves Pigneur, Gregory Bernarda, and Alan Smith, recently released a very good book, *Value Proposition Design: How to Create Products and Services Customers Want*, Wiley (2015), whose recommendations you will see reflected in U/P simply in a more analytical fashion; the *Build, Measure, Learn* process is a popularization of Bayesian confidence building and some Popperian falsification.

to improve production.⁶² *Jidoka* is thus a historical process of human trial and error correction in the context of the industrial revolution, which *Toyota* has now modernized to mean automation with a touch of guiding human knowledge.⁶³ True-north value identification through *Jidoka* comes from the integration of human insight (in *Lean* terms, '*Genchi Genbutsu*') and error correction (in *Lean* terms, '*Poka-Yoke*') to create the greatest true-north value for consumers. *Jidoka* is thus a measure of quality that any *Lean* system of management can apply as it iteratively tests its markets.

As you extend the iterative process of *Jidoka* out toward consumers and business in general, you ought to: 1. Follow the Western philosophical tradition of empathizing with the source of *who* consumers are called '*Phenomenology* (i.e., '*Genchi Genbutsu*'); 2. Conjecture, hypothesize, and theorize *what* creates the most value for them (i.e., '*Jidoka*'); and 3. Then criticise through market tests whether a solution provides at least an adequate profit (i.e., '*Poka-Yoke*').

As part of the philosophy of *Lean*, all of these processes are well-defined by the Western *Philosophy of Science* and *Consumerism*, which this book explains. *U/P Leans* these Western traditions with Eastern ones toward a higher, philosophical level to reach the point of all true-north value creation.

Thus, to align value streams toward a horizon of commercial possibility, you must fully *Lean* toward consumers by empathizing with the best evidence you can gather from the start. Then, from this *Universe* of empathy, you relate the problems consumers have to the price you may charge them for their resolution. Actually, you can see where the value streams of problem and price meet at the point of empathy in the logo for *Nissan's* luxury car brand, *Infiniti*:

---

⁶² *Ibid.*

⁶³ *Jidoka-Manufacturing high-quality products: Automation with a human touch*, at Toyota-Global.com/company/vision_philosophy/toyota_production_system/jidoka.html (last accessed Feb. 24, 2017).

Nissan® Infiniti® Logo

- *What if the philosophy of Lean, through the Socratic interrogatories of Who, Why, What and How, helped you know in advance what mattered most when you try to best fit the products and/or services you could offer to relevant markets?*
- *What if the philosophy of Lean allowed you to increase the marketability of a minimally viable product and/or service by empathetically analyzing with markets in advance?*
- *What if the philosophy of Lean then allowed you to better analyze the market feedback you received to optimize and monetize products and/or services?*

U/P's four primary interrogatories of *Who* , *Why* , *What* and *How* complement the iterative development processes of *Kaizen* and *Jidoka* by uniquely guiding product and/or service ideation, innovation, design and monetization.[64] These interrogatories will lead

---

[64] Each iteration is a hierarchy in Bayesian analysis, that simultaneously increases confidence in the result by falsifying possible alternative market solutions through an infinite process of elimination against shifting market conditions - that is the hard thing about hard things; *see*, particularly *Chapter 7* of Ben Horowitz, *The Hard Thing About Hard Things: Building a Business When There Are No Easy Answers*, HarperBusiness (2014).

you toward products and/or services that are practically useful, aspirational and profitable. I summarize the Socratic questions of *Who*, *Why*, *What* and *How* in the shorthand form of '*3WH*.' Since these interrogatories are critical to the philosophy of *Lean*, here are their definitions from *The Oxford English Dictionary* :

- **Who**, pron. (and n.), As the ordinary interrogative pronoun, in the nominative singular or plural, used of a person or persons: corresponding to *what* of things;
- **Why**, adv. (n. and int.), In a direct question: For *what* reason? From *what* cause or motive? For *what* purpose?;
- **What**, pron., adj., and adv., int., conj., and n.:

    1. As the ordinary interrogative pronoun of neuter gender, orig. sing., in later use also pl., used of a thing or things: corresponding to the demonstrative 'that';
    2. Of a person (or persons), In predicative use: formerly generally, in reference to name or identity, and thus equivalent to *who*; in later use only in reference to nature, character, function, or the like; and

- **How**, adv. and n., Qualifying a verb: In *what* way or manner? By *what* means?

Notice that the interrogatory '*what*' flows through all these definitions, and that '*who*' and '*what*' are essentially equivalent to one another by their reciprocal references. By following these four steps of *3WH*, you will consistently reach epiphanies about *what* you ought to produce to most uniquely, profitably energize and optimize consumers' lives and existences in all commercial environments.[65] However, instead of only reviewing *what* consumers say or reveal, *U/P*'s *Lean 3WH* method of analysis abstracts *Lean* value theory toward philosophically framing true-north value in

---

[65]This is in allusion to Steve Blank, *The Four Steps to the Epiphany* , K&S Ranch, 2nd edition (2013).

life and business within which all consumers' preferences best fit. *3WH* is a reformation of true-north value when you recognize that consumers ultimately seek true-north value beyond *what* is immediately known. Thus, the power of a *Lean* business ideology is to apply this abstract knowledge to identify specific solutions across all business problems you may face.

U/P, through the *3WH* process, makes *Lean* applicable to all aspects of business by further intersecting *Lean* with the Western study of true value called '*Axiology*.' *Axiology* may be considered the combination of *what* attracts consumers to buy through aesthetics, and *what* consumers ought to do through ethics. *U/P* channels both sides of *Axiology* through sound *Lean* value theory within business to help you make money meaningfully.

Philosophically *Leaning* Your Business Ideology

Those attempting to philosophize like me often paraphrase the famous 20th Century mathematician and philosopher Alfred North Whitehead[66] as saying that the whole of Western philosophy was, '... *a series of footnotes to Plato.*'[67] Whitehead captured the notion that trying to build a true-north value theory is like attempting to add an own deeply buried footnotes to countless thinkers before. Similarly, you *Lean* philosophically by collecting ideas together and applying them within your own context. You use *Lean* as a vessel to navigate through channels of timeless value streams toward a commercial *Nirvana*.

By explaining *who* consumers are, and *why* and *what* they most value, *U/P* enhances the art and para-science of business. Like Ries'

---

[66] *See generally*, the Stanford Encyclopædia of Philosophy's entry on, '*Alfred North Whitehead*.'

[67] Arthur Oncken Lovejoy, *The Great Chain of Being*, op. cit. (ref 1), 24 and 326 (1933).

'*Build, Measure, Learn*' methodology, business as a whole is a para-science because while science tests the causes of various effects, the desired effect of producing a profit in business is plainly obvious.[68] an challenge is causing such a singular outcome by universalizing true-north value for consumers as exceptionally complex people. You have the difficult task of optimizing their and society's standard of existence to the greatest extent in all domains, leaving no markets untapped, while also leaving no money on the table.

Philosopher Kings and Queens

As Jim Collins wrote in *Good to Great* , '*The good-to-great leaders... They are more like Lincoln and Socrates than Patton or Caesar.*'[69] World famous business people today most often describe their own, "business philosophies," with modern philosophical and scientific principles. For example, the famous entrepreneur Elon Musk advocates for all busy people to reason from first principles when he said during a 2012 interview,

> *First principles is kind of a physics way of looking at the world. You boil things down to the most fundamental truths and say, 'What are we sure is true?' ... and then reason up from there.*

However, none of these business people seem to provide other people with a way to think effectively from first principles without thoroughly educating themselves in esoteric philosophy and similarly dense subjects – this book on *Lean* business philosophy is enough! Thus, business philosophy often devolves either into vague aphorisms that do not lend themselves to functional analysis, or into

---
[68]Business as a para-science is at least on better ground than economics as a dismal science, as Thomas Carlyle famously noted.
[69]Jim Collins,*Good to Great: Why Some Companies Make the Leap...And Others Don't* , Kindle Loc. 233-235, HarperCollins (2001).

logically weak insights that eventually become entangled in their own reasoning when rigorously applied, leaving other business people frustrated when trying to borrow from these billionaires' brilliance.[70]

However, quite a few examples of rigorously philosophical billionaires exist. Billionaire trader George Soros writes with diligence and vigor when describing his philosophical concept of *Reflexivity* in his 1983 book, *The Alchemy of Finance*. You can also see Soros' concept of reflexivity in Alfred North Whitehead's and Nicholas Rescher's, '*Process Philosophy.*'[71] These philosophical concepts even play themselves out in business theory, like the tautological economic models in *Revealed Preference Theory* proposed by Herbert Simon, which is widely used by mainstream economists today.

For further philosophical examples, Dr. Patrick Byrne, founder of Overstock.com, earned a Ph.D. in philosophy from Stanford University. Reid Hoffman, founder of LinkedIn, earned a masters degree in philosophy at Oxford before joining *Apple*.[72] Michael Bloomberg studied philosophy at New School after graduating from Harvard Business School.[73] Ray Dalio, founder of *Bridge-water Associates*, described his true-north value theory in his manifesto, *Principles*, where he begins by instructing all to start their business

---

[70] Many good books have been under-written by billionaires, which touch upon their business philosophies. I most recommend Charlie Munger's, *Poor Charlie's Almanac*, Donning Company Publishers (2005); Ricardo Semler's, *The Seven-Day Weekend: Changing the Way Work Works*, Penguin Group (2003); and Michael Bloomberg's, *Bloomberg by Bloomberg*, Wiley (2009); some famous business people though go so far as to extend their pecuniary greatness into theological allusion, such as Andrew Carnegie and his, *Gospel of Wealth*.

[71] This "reflexivity" or "circularity" is exemplified by Douglas Hofstadter's theories of consciousness in *Gödel, Escher, Bach*, which significantly inspired the word-play this book.

[72] And yet, for even more well-known executives who either majored in undergraduate programs or completed graduate degrees in philosophy include Flickr.com and Slack.com founder Stewart Butterfield (B.A. and M.A. degrees in philosophy at University of Victoria and Cambridge), former Hewlett-Packard *CEO* Carly Fiorina (B.A., Stanford); Carl Icahn (B.A., Princeton), FDIC Chair Sheila Blair (B.A., University of Kansas), Fannie Mae *CEO* Herbert Allison Jr. (B.A., Yale), Time Warner *CEO* Gerald Levin (B.A., Haverford), and PayPal co-founder, Peter Thiel (B.A., Stanford).

[73] Sam Roberts, *Michael Bloomberg on How to Succeed in Business*, New York Times (Feb. 1, 2017).

analysis by asking the epistemological and ontological question, '*Is it true?*'- just as Elon Musk advocates.[74] The founders of *Apple Inc.* also espoused this epistemological sentiment when they designed its logo to be a piece of fruit from the tree of all knowledge with a byte taken out of it:[75]

®Apple Inc.

While each of these business people *Lean* philosophically in some way, none provides a broadly applicable, logical framework for organizing the first principles of the human condition from which all meaningful true-north value, and thus all consumer demand, ultimately originates. Business people write business books that invoke philosophy, but *what* may be more helpful in making real progress is a philosophy book about business, particularly one that places the philosophy of science at its core while synthesizing ancient wisdom through the language used. I present *what* I consider to be the philosophy of business within the paradigm of *Lean*, and hope to channel the thoughts of these great leaders for you to *Lean*

---

[74] *See generally,* http://www.bwater.com/uploads/filemanager/principles/bridgewater-associates-ray-dalio-principles.pdf (accessed May 6, 2015).

[75] This association of the *Apple Inc.* logo with the story of Adam and Even in *Genesis* and the basic units of digital information as proposed by Claude Shannon, along with the stories of Sir Isaac Newton and Alan Turing, are unverified urban legend, but I find them uncanny and like referring to them for this purpose.

an organization's business philosophy forward in their homage.⁷⁶

Supporting this approach, Collins and Porras in *Built to Last* stated, '*Contrary to popular wisdom, the proper first response to a changing world is not to ask, 'How should we change?' but rather to ask, 'What do we stand for and why do we exist?'* ⁷⁷ Collins and Porras described their pragmatic idealism as one that companies built to last use in the *Yin* and *Yang* symbols, adapting while preserving core values and purposes around a fly wheel.⁷⁸ Like *Lean*, this *Built to Last, Yin/Yang* approach also mixes Oriental with Occidental philosophies, and proposes them as a business ideology that may be used by all business people to make money consistently.

Thus, Oriental religious philosophies, like *Confucianism*, *Shintoism* and *Buddhism*, combine in-tension in a *Yin/Yang* with the Occidental *Philosophy of Science* and *Consumerism* to great effect. *Lean* is a philosophy of business grounded in ancient wisdom while always changing in the face of new demands and discoveries. Likewise, *Lean* is the existential core of every business, and *what* essentially changes is its implementation. Or, to paraphrase Aristotle from the 4th century B.C.E., '*[Lean] philosophy begins in wonder, seeking the most fundamental causes or principles of things, and seems the least necessary but is in fact the most divine of [business] sciences.*'⁷⁹ Or, as Marcus Aurelius more recently said in 167 A.C.E., '*No [organizational] role is so well suited for [Lean] philosophy as the one you happen to be in right now.*'⁸⁰ [the bracketed additions are my own of course].

---

⁷⁶ I would like to note here with great humility that according to Daniel Dennet and Asbjørn Steglich-Petersen's *Philosophical Lexicon*, a *Benjamin* is a philosopher who is not yet a bachelard, and a bachelard is a philosopher who has not yet attained a master level; I am sure to be guilty of any one of the pronouns or verbs defined within the *Philosophical Lexicon*; as Wittgenstein also said, '*The difficulty in philosophy is to say no more than we know*,' p. 45, *The Blue Book* (written between 1931-1935).

⁷⁷ *See generally*, Jim Collins and Jerry I. Porras, *Built to Last* (1994).

⁷⁸ *Ibid*.

⁷⁹ Aristotle, *Theaetetus* 155d; and, Aristotle, *Metaphysics*, 980-985, Book Alpha (both 4th Century B.C.E.).

⁸⁰ Marcus Aurelius, *The Meditations of Marcus Arelius Antonius* (167 A.C.E.).

By going beyond *what* a company certainly knows, the philosophy of *Lean* can help an organization determine *what* ought to be its core true-north values *whatever* it decides best energizes and optimizes all people. Alfred North Whitehead, the previously referenced philosopher and mathematician who wrote *Mathematica Principia* with Bertrand Russell, said, ' *Philosophy is the critic of cosmologies, whose job it is to synthesize, scrutinize and make coherent the divergent intuitions gained through ethical, aesthetic, religious, and scientific experience.*'[81] I would add that the philosophy of *Lean* also upends false assumptions and enhances a business' perspective to guide an organization's quantitative and qualitative insights into *what* consumers and all stakeholders find most meaningful.

Going one step further, Greek philosophers such as Cynics, Skeptics, Epicureans and Stoics analyzed: (1) *what* was truly valuable and *what* was not, and (2) *how* one could find true-north value and protect oneself against longing for false, valueless things.[82] Further in time, the Roman Cicero said that, '*To study philosophy is to prepare oneself for death.*' This means that you ought to use the philosophy of *Lean* to discover *what* consumers truly value for the most meaningful amounts of money before a business meets that same fate.[83] Thus, I hope you agree that the philosophy of *Lean* is the formal study of true-north value in life and business, and that the exchange of *Lean* value for money is (or perhaps ought to be) all organizations' ultimate source of viability.

In the end, *U/P* does not see philosophy so much as a means toward an independent truth (though philosophy can be a leading indicator for science), but more as an effective way to bridge your understanding of consumers' personal perspectives with *what* you know about them from math and science, or otherwise emotionally

---

[81] Alfred North Whitehead, *Science and the Modern World* (1925).
[82] Marcus Arelius, *The Meditations of Marcus Arelius Antonius*, Book Ten (167 A.C.E.).
[83] *Ibid.*

intuit.[84] Philosophy in this way best satisfies consumers' basic needs so they will be shattering the doors of stores to become customers!

The Philosophy of *Lean* in the Grand Design

However, to make clear philosophy's role in analyzing true-north value, let's play devil's advocate with Stephen Hawking. Stephen Hawking is a well-known theoretical physicist, who recently derided traditional philosophy as having lost its ability to answer the bigger questions of existence given recent scientific advancements toward that goal.[85] He says that philosophy has nothing to say regarding the origin of *what* consumers most truly value, and thus says nothing about *how* an organization may make money meaningfully.[86]

Presuming for argumentative purposes that Stephen Hawking is correct, which he could very well be, and theoretical physics succeeded philosophy (and religion for that matter) as the tool with the greatest explanatory power for consumers' lives and existences, I propose that philosophy's rigorously analytical tools developed by tremendous minds over millennia can and ought to be repurposed to frame the analytical questions of *what Lean* true-north value in business is. Summarized well, philosophy can structure products

---

[84] *See e.g.,* Wilfrid Sellars, *Philosophy and the Scientific Image of Man, Frontiers of Science and Philosophy*, pp. 35–78, University of Pittsburgh Press (1962), who said, *'The aim of philosophy, abstractly formulated, is to understand how things in the broadest possible sense of the term hang together in the broadest possible sense of the term'*; and Rebecca Goldstein, *How Philosophy Makes Progress,* in *Chronicle of Higher Education* (Apr. 14, 2014), where she said, *'And this is progress, progress in increasing our coherence, which is philosophy's special domain.'*

[85] Stephen Hawking and Leonard Mlodinow, *The Grand Design*, Bantam (2012); for further discussion, see Robert Pasnau, *Why Not Just Weigh the Fish?*, New York Times (Jun. 29, 2014); *see also,* in *A Brief History of Time* (1988), where Hawking wrote at p. 175, *'Philosophers reduced the scope of their inquiries so much that Wittgenstein, the most famous philosopher of this century, said, 'The sole remaining task for philosophy is the analysis of language.' What a comedown from the great tradition of philosophy from Aristotle to Kant!'* However, no known written record confirms Ludwig Wittgenstein as saying that.

[86] *Ibid.*

and/or service innovation and guide business processes toward profitable and ethical success to make meaningful amounts of money over generations, which is all that truly matters to the ultimate viability of an organization.

In sum, mathematical, scientific, philosophical and intuitive insights into *who* and *why* consumers are provide the logical underpinnings of *Lean* true-north value theory, and thus, the foundation for organic growth. The philosophy of *Lean* acts both as the middleware between an organization's scientific and intuitive business analysis, and helps you identify true-north value at the intersection all reason and speculation. By implementing these insights, an organization will make money meaningfully when the currents of science, economics and philosophy intersect at the fjord of experience that products and/or services produce for consumers. *U/P* thus approaches *Lean* true-north value from its very inception and streamlines it for business success.[87]

So while modern philosophy and the rest of the humanities respect mathematics and scientific knowledge as the most widely shared and predictable true-north values, the humanities still function to illuminate and speculate as to *what* are the overall processes leading to consumers' lives and existences and the associated meaning their lives may have. In the end, the humanities inform the existential gaps an organization and consumers inevitably find themselves in, bounded by their ignorance, circularities, infinities and paradoxes.[88] No matter *how* intelligent they are, consumers are surrounded by marginal event horizons and cosmic censorship, left only to hope for something greater. Where neither science nor philosophy fully

---

[87]From one perspective, this book may be viewed as an exercise in philosophical pragmatism, which means that it is not intended to be rigorously empirical in nature as a technical economic study would, but rather descriptive to provide the reader with a way to organize his or her thinking more accurately to produce clearer thinking and better results in pragmatic business decision making. Like Decision Theory itself,*U/P* combines information from many different disciplines to provide a *big picture* perspective of reality that can be applied to individual decision making and action.

[88]Gödel's *Second Incompleteness Theorem* naturally applies here; for false boundaries, *see,* David Deutsch,*The Beginning of Infinity* , p. 446 (2011).

informs *who* consumers are and *why* they buy products and/or services, consumers' individual agnosticism, intuitive spiritualism or speculative scientism fulfills the third rail in an organization's value worship. As Steve Jobs famously said,

> Part of what made the Macintosh great was that the people working on it were musicians and poets and artists and zoologists and historians who also happened to be the best computer scientists in the world.[89]

From the modern, post-modern, or post-post-modern (sometimes referred to as *meta-modern*) perspectives, you can see levels of validated, commonly shared beliefs about consumers' reality in the golden braid of mathematics, science, philosophy and intuition. These domains identify *Lean* true-north value with increasing levels of common agreement among all potential customers as you move upstream:

?
Mathematics
Science
Philosophy
Religious, Spiritual, or Scientismic Intuition
?

Mathematics and science provide the most technically validated and commonly agreed forms of in-formation.[90] On the other end of this spectrum, religious, spiritual and scientismic intuition fills

---

[89] Interview with Steve Jobs (1994) about the creation of the Apple Macintosh, *Did Steve Jobs steal from Xerox PARC?* http://www.mac-history.net/computer-history/2012-03-22/apple-and-xerox-parc (retrieved June 28, 2015).

[90] *See generally*, Karl Popper, *Objective Knowledge: An Evolutionary Approach*, Oxford: Clarendon Press (1972).

a void where science and philosophy do not qualify as commonly agreed true-north values at any level of significance. Consumers realize this latter form of true-north value by *what* they intuitively speculate, even if *what* they believe is not commonly experienced by all people. In contrast, philosophical principles at their best act as short-hands of abstract concepts that people use to reach better solutions to technical and intuitive problems. The *Lean* business philosopher thus ought to have a competitive advantage to more effectively re-produce and monetize true value for this reason. So, you will walk away from this text with new, *Lean* philosophical acronyms and analogies that you may use as rules of thumb to monetize more meaning regardless of the origin of your ideas.

An excellent question exemplifying a point where science, philosophy and intuition intermix to determine *what* consumers most truly value is, '*What created natural, physical laws, consumers, and the Universe in the first place?*' This question is represented by the question mark ? at the beginning and end of the above value stream. I'm sure consumers have some intuitive belief, faith, or agnosticism marking that question, and their attitudes toward it particularly determine *why*, *what*, and *how* they purchase. Let's look at this question briefly from the perspectives of science and religion to see *what* role the philosophy of *Lean* plays in mediating between these fields today to identify true-north value and the secret meaning of money as we move up along the universal value stream.

Science

Physicists generally attempt to describe the origin of consumers' existences, and thus all true-north value, by statistically analyzing quantum theories, or they theorize classical notions of *what* the *Universe* is or is not to get to that same point. Scientists generally make these physical explanations for *why* consumers exist intentionally circular since they base these explanations on physical laws of unknown origin.⁹¹

For example, a certain classical theory in vogue is *multi-verses* specifying that the *Universe* consumers personally know is one of an infinite number of them, and they are but one variation of infinite possibility. The laws in such *Universes* are randomly created with *whatever* probabilities might exist in such warped domains. Within some variations of this theory, each black hole holds a *Universe* unto itself, each with its own variation of the laws of physics. Another theoretical variation demonstrates the multi-verse by explaining quantum mechanics itself as a consequence of the coherence and discoherence of the subatomic units of parallel *Universes* within the multi-verse. These theories hold that each parallel *Universe* is well designed in its own unique way while remaining fungible at its most basic level, much like the multiple meanings simultaneously arising from word-play, symbolism and acronyms introduced within *U / P*.⁹²

Alternatively, consider that if consumers could see past the limit of the speed of light racing toward them from the edges of the known *Universe*, they might find further cosmoses within the same space-time continuum if only they could *Lean* far enough to see them. Finally, if you project far enough into the future, you might conclude that video games, like Eric Ries' *Instant Message Virtual Universe*, or *The Sims*, would improve to such a degree with each new version that this *Universe* you know so well might itself be

---

⁹¹*Cf*, Lee Smolin, *Time Reborn: From the crisis in physics to the future of the universe*, Mariner Books (2013).

⁹²David Deutsch, *The Beginning of Infinity*, p. 265 (2011).

a simulation.⁹³ We might be characters within *IMVU* at this very moment. *Who* is winning?

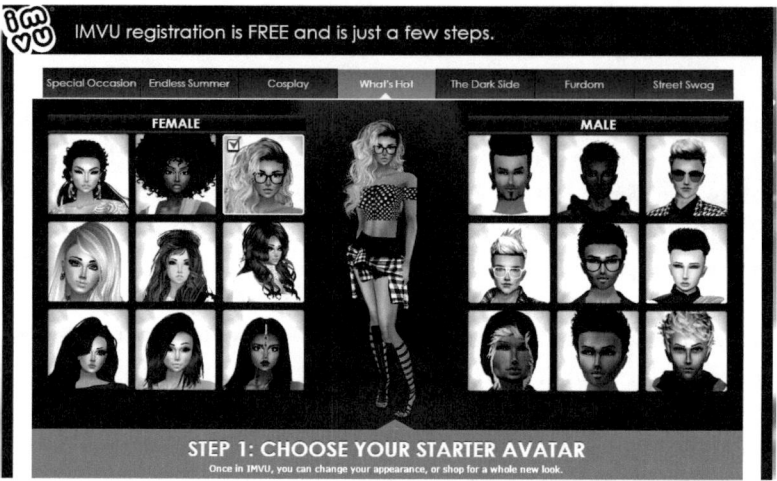

Step 1: Choose an Starter Avatar, © Instant Message Virtual Universe (*IMVU*) as discussed by Eric Ries in the book, *The Lean Startup*

---

⁹³*I.e.* you might find yourself in an *Ontologically Anthropocentric Sensory Immersive Simulation* (an *OASIS*) such as described by Ernest Cline in, *Ready Player One*, Random House (2011); David Deutsch, *The Beginning of Infinity*, p. 192 (2011); one of the proponents and popularizers of this simulation concept is Nick Bostrum, a philosopher in residence at the University of Oxford; *see*, Nick Bostrom, *Are You Living In a Computer Simulation?*, pp. 243-255, Vol. 53, No. 211, Philosophical Quarterly (2003); Bank of America/Merrill Lynch in an investor report on the future of reality, citing Nick Bostrom, wrote, '*Many scientists, philosophers, and business leaders believe that there is a 20-50% probability that humans are already living in a computer-simulated virtual world... It is conceivable that with advancements in artificial intelligence, virtual reality, and computing power, members of future civilizations could have decided to run a simulation of their ancestors,*' as further noted by Myles Udland in, *Business Insider*(Sep. 8, 2016).

Let There Be Sims, The Sims ® Electronic Arts Inc.

While these scientific theories are all grand, consumers must recognize that no such purely physical or computational theory to date conclusively answers in non-circular fashion *why* the physics (or programs) guiding their lives exists at all-*what* explains*why* anything exists at all, and thus *why* consumers live and buy anything at all other than to subsist. The ongoing faith an organization has that consumers will find the products and/or services it provides truly valuable leaves open all forms of intuitive speculation by an upper management.[94] Ultimately, consumers' true religion is hard to define, but U/P diagrams its contours for you as you will see below.

Religion

To begin understanding *what* creates *Lean* true-north value, you cannot ignore the very personal topic of religion. It must be discussed for this conversation to be complete. To address it head on for your *Lean* business ideology, look at one of the most widely adopted academic definitions[95] of religion that was proposed by

---

[94]*See*, Gary Gutting's interview with Michael Ruse in,*Does Evolution Explain Religious Beliefs*, The Stone, New York Times (Jul. 8, 2014).

[95]Geertz definition of religion is the most widely used to day in religious studies courses in the United States; this definition was first provided in, Clifford Geertz, *Religion as a Cultural System* loc. in,*The interpretation of cultures: selected essays* , pp. 87-125, Fontana Press (1993).

the anthropologist Clifford Geertz. Geertz described religion as a system of symbols that acts to:[96]

1. *Establish powerful, pervasive, and long-lasting moods and motivations in people;*
2. *Formulate conceptions of a general order of existence;*
3. *Give these conceptions an aura of factuality; and*
4. *Make these moods and motivations seem uniquely realistic.*

Not coincidentally, Geertz's definition of religion *Leans* a business *philosophically* through the *3WH* value creation interrogatories of *Who, Why, What,* and *How.* Like the four parts of Geertz's definition, consumers' true-north values determine:

1. *Who consumers are as emotionally motivated people* ;
2. *Why consumers buy products and/or services to better exist*;
3. *What consumers conceive as factually valuable* ; *and*
4. *How consumers really get uniquely and emotionally motivated to buy products and/or services with money.*

Thus, religion, just like science, seeks to answer *Who* , *Why* , *What* , and *How*, except religion attempts to answer those interrogatories through intuitive speculation. *Why* postulates a general order of existence, while *What* grounds consumers' moods and motivations in the soil of experience. *Who* divines the powerful, pervasive, and long-lasting moods and motivations of all people, while *How* improves their facticity from the indulgences that get paid to get clear. We will explore further these *3WH* interrogatories as you proceed up through the *U/ People* business model with a religious devotion to all consumers *whoever* they may be.

---

[96] *Ibid*, pp. 87-125.

Limits to Business Quantification

You as a business person reasonably tend to rely heavily on the quantifiable aspects of true-north value measurement, such as with accounting, finance or econometrics. Monetary or other quantitative measurement provides a fairly uniform way to discuss business processes globally. However, the common expressions, '*Not everything that counts can be counted,*' and, '*Businesses measure everything and understand nothing,*' articulate the fact that, significant, unresolved, and often under-appreciated limits exist in money's ability to quantify and measure *what* people truly find meaningful in an absolute sense. In the difference between science and religion, you come to the natural limits of *what* the four-step *Lean 3WH* value proposition interrogatories can quantify and predict since no one has a firm grasp on *what* permits open-ended, infinite intuitive, spiritual, scientific and/or religious speculation.[97]

U/P will clarify and explain those limits more precisely for understanding exactly *what* money and other metrics do and do not measure and mean. Understanding the difference will not only improve a business for societal profit, but will also improve financial profits by taking you to the edge of *what* an organization can monetize so you can focus on *what* you have reason to believe is most profitable.[98] The difference between making meaningful amounts of money and making money meaningfully is that while the former immediately satisfices, the latter allows you to achieve greatness and build a company that will carry your legacy onward and upward.

So while money reasonably accurately quantifies people's preferences, accounting, finance and econometrics cannot entirely direct research and development and marketing toward *what* best

---

[97] Sean Carroll, *From Eternity to Here: The Quest for the Ultimate Theory of Time*, Kindle Loc. 978, Penguin Group US (2009).

[98] *E.g. see* Jim Stengel's research found at, *Grow: How Ideals Power Growth and Profit at the World's Greatest Companies*, Crown Business (2011).

satisfices and optimizes consumers – many things are difficult to measure well, due to incomplete information and knowledge, which are often referred to as business *intangibles*. In fact, the more knowledge we as people have and apply toward our own ends, the less we can predict the future.[99] Thus, despite very well developed financial measures and operational metrics, businesses still pray for epiphanies as to *what* meaningfully making money means through the *Lean* value stream, and *how* such insight might further guide quantitative analysis toward blue oceans of profit in an unchartered *Universe*.

The *U / People* Business Model

By constructing a comprehensive true-north value theory to apply *Lean* thinking to an organization, you ought to be able to understand the context in which an organization measures true-north value for all of its stakeholders. By all stakeholders, I mean customers, employees, board members, shareholders, and/or society. Thus, a *Lean* business ideology ought to be a universal system of thought grounded in true-north values, but also related to the apparent paradoxes inherent in all stakeholders' lives and existences. It ought to bring together a wide range of ideas and disciplines in a unified structure for analyzing and predicting *what* all stakeholders find most truly valuable and therefore want from you.

By way of example of *U/ P*'s flexibility for building an meaningful true-north value theory, references to businesses, corporations, or organizations may likewise be read throughout this book to include governmental or not-for-profit entities. You can replace *customers* with *taxpayers*, *donors*, or *congregants*, since they are all *consumers* of existential solutions. For example, in the charitable context, charitable recipients and society are the indirect beneficiaries of charitable activities. Charitable beneficiaries are part of

---

[99] David Deutsch, TEDx Brussels (2011).

the products and/or services actually sold to donors. Donors in-turn indulge in the satisfaction of, possibly receive some prestige for, and certainly universalize their influence as a result of naming buildings and institutions after themselves.[100] That is a very real way to look at the business of charity, but making abstract theory really applicable to *what* consumers most truly value is *why* you *Lean* philosophically.

Synthesizing Subjects

Hopefully, given this introduction to *U/P* thus far feeding a *Lean* analysis of *what* matters most to stakeholders, you can appreciate *how* an overarching true-north value theory that philosophically organizes business information ought to be useful to you. Quite commonly, researchers at the highest levels of different fields independently examine the same concepts from different perspectives within their own disciplines. Authors generally write in one discipline or another without interrelating their disciplines to others with which their domain of expertise intersects. However, *U/P* and the philosophy of *Lean* will help you do just that for remarkable business insights.

For example, as Fred Gluck, the founder of McKinsey's strategy practice, recently said:

> *[T]he question [of strategic planning] becomes what process continually engages the top-management team in synthesizing and resynthesizing analysis into both meaningful strategic initiatives and some strategic rules of thumb that can inform opportunistic decision making and continually evolve.*[101]

---

[100] *E.g., Hey Cynics, Hold That Cold Water: Why The Ice Bucket Challenge Worked*, Forbes (Aug. 15, 2014).

[101] *See generally*, Fred Gluck, *The Essence of Strategic Management, Synthesis, Capabilities and Overlooked Insights: Next Frontiers for Strategists*, McKinsey Quarterly (Sep. 2014).

Philosophical metaphysics and strategic metadata create these rules of thumb exceedingly well if brought down to Earth. For example, consider all knowledge from the top down. Philosophy was the intellectual parent of modern physics, which in turn determines chemistry, which informs biology, which affects psychology, which combines chemistry and biology into psychopharmacology that can change *who* consumers are and their philosophical perspectives on life and existence. At some point, all these fields of knowledge intersect and inform one another in circular fashion, since all academic subjects ultimately reduce themselves toward the goal of best understanding and improving consumers' lives and existences, which is philosophy's ultimate domain of inquiry as well.

Steve Jobs consistently said as much, as further evidenced by his interview with the Smithsonian Institution on April 20th, 1995 while he was running NeXT Computer:[102]

> *I actually think there's actually very little distinction between an artist and a scientist or engineer of the highest caliber... They've just been to me people who pursue different paths but basically kind of headed to the same goal, which is to express something of what they perceive to be the truth around them so that others can benefit by it.*

However, the polymath- a person who could truly excel across multiple disciplines- is increasingly rare if not already extinct due to the fact that the quantity of knowledge needed to enhance any part of the body of knowledge of any given general field of knowledge stands beyond *what* any one person is currently capable

---

[102] Accessed at the Smithsonian Institution's website, http://americanhistory.si.edu/comphist/sj1.html, (accessed on Feb. 2, 2015).

of understanding in a lifetime.¹⁰³ This has been truly said for some time, and will only become truer as our knowledge exponentially increases, and sub-disciplines of knowledge continue to grow.¹⁰⁴

Making a genuine contribution of knowledge to any given subject these days consumes a person's entire intellect and a lifetime of dedication, so seeing beyond existing knowledge and interrelating the collective body of knowledge in general, particularly in business, becomes increasingly difficult even as the information within sub-disciplines becomes more effective at addressing specific problems. This situation is sub-optimal for *Leaning* an entire organization toward all that consumers most truly value because of the difficulty in knowing and synthesizing all this information intelligently.¹⁰⁵

U/P thus becomes a type of product and/or service of its own, a philosophical and pragmatic body of knowledge for a corporation, constituting the sum of the expertise that went into creating and aligning it with *what* consumers truly value, allowing you to *Lean* across multiple disciplines to serve them best. Likewise, think about *what* consumers truly value when they employ chemical and mechanical engineers the next time they use a toothbrush. Think about the expertise of the aerospace engineers consumers hire the next time they fly. Consider the cumulative medical knowledge gathered through millennia of trial and error in the process of *Jidoka* and *Kaizen* that doctors currently *Lean* on and re-transmit

---

¹⁰³Though fairly recent examples do exist, such as the incredible John von Neumann and Marilyn vos Savant; however see any list of recent prodigies with the highest IQs, none of whom dominate any single field of knowledge.

¹⁰⁴Ahmed Alkhateeb, Corey S. Powell (Ed.), *Science has outgrown the human mind and its limited capacities*, aeon (Apr. 24, 2017).

¹⁰⁵For further motivation, some good evidence exists from a study conducted by Guy Berger, Ph.D. at LinkedIn, Inc. demonstrating that thinking cross-departmentally greatly increases your chances of becoming CEO (found at https://www.linkedin.com/pulse/how-become-executive-guy-berger-ph-d-, with article co-authored by Link Gan and Alan Fritzler and published on linkedin.com on Sep. 9, 2016).

when a consumer enters a doctor's office for a check-up.[106]

While *U/P* provides this intellectual leverage, an organization will never make money rotely with the philosophy of *Lean* and the *U/People* business model.[107] While *U/P* is more background information than an explicit formula for success, I guarantee that you will gain confidence from knowing when you are on the right path if you flow that embodied expertise about customers' lives and existences through your own business ideology. You will have the confidence that you are providing the products and/or service you ought, which ought to produce for you the greatest profit of all.

For example, if making money meaningfully involves understanding consumers' lives and existences, then even the financial industry can make more money by intuitively understanding the human condition and *why* people enter into economic exchanges. While financial engineering does not require understanding people's lives in all the ways described in this book, the negotiations and strategies used to execute financial transactions require understanding the counter-parties engaging in those transactions and all that they truly value beyond any money being negotiated.[108] As another example, leverage aside, private equity depends to a great extent on effectively operating companies rather than mathematically engineering their acquisition and divestment to produce financial gain.[109] This means that even private equity firms and hedge funds must have a business ideology to understand *what* and *how* products and/or services get bought and sold to produce satisfactory

---

[106] *See e.g.*, Mark Schrope, *Medicine's Hidden Roots in an Ancient Manuscript*, New York Times (Jun. 1, 2015); in a certain sense, much of the content of this book may be seen as, *old wine in a new a new bottle*, but it has been a robust vessel, and I think anybody would find something new here to at least consider it a *blend*, or an effective decanter for old ideas to pour into your value streams.

[107] Kenneth Stanley, Joel Lehman, *Why Greatness Cannot Be Planned: The Myth of the Objective*, p. 136, Springer International Publishing (2015).

[108] *See e.g.*, 'Geeks Venture Into Goldman Sachs' World of Big Deals and Egos,' Reuters (Feb. 14, 2017).

[109] *See generally*, Danielle Ivory, Josh Williams, Ben Protess and Kitty Bennett, *This is Your Life, Brought to You by Private Equity*, New York Times (Aug. 1, 2016).

returns most days.

While the *U/People* business model and acronym may describe *what* creates wealth and *what* you ought to *Lean* toward in greater detail, and describes *how* wealth gets generated by higher order economic activity, it will fail to identify *how* to make money meaningfully in mechanical fashion, since money making is of course is an open-ended endeavor.[110] *U/P* as the philosophy of *Lean* is about an organization developing a metaphysical value theory of continuously improving and pursuing perfection however unattainable it might be. The *U/People* business model by no means automates economic advancement, but it will provide you with a universal set of true-north values, processes, and methods to guide you to make the money you earn genuinely meaningful for everyone's benefit.

Quantifying *Lean* Abstraction and Analogies for Sales Success

In addition to the foregoing benefits to studying *Lean*, the analogical (or dis-analogical) reasoning of *Lean* philosophy allows you to differentiate between partial or impartial truths to drive sales efficiency. Words, similes, metaphors, analogies, phrases, proverbs and fables all go into telling the sales stories to consumers that get products and/or services bought. You can in-turn use mathematics to produce precise descriptions, probabilities and measurements of these partial or impartial true-north values to determine the corresponding accuracy of analogies and similes in consumers' minds. Examples include any time you compare a new business initiative to others and see the differences in *how* you served people's true-north values from one period to the next. Once you identify the analogical comparables, you may ask questions like:

---

[110] In terms of the philosophy of science, making money can never be deterministic.

How is this product, service and/or initiative different than the past ones or from those of my competitors'?
Can I quantify the change in true-north value that a product and/or service will deliver from the present state to the future state?

U/P as the philosophy of *Lean* provides a business ideology with the tools to see the organic essence of any given situation and analogically reason from there to provide a greater return on customers' investments in a product and/or service. True-north value originates from existential dichotomies in the difference between one period in time to the next, and *how* you reason analogically between those periods to identify and classify *what* has *Lean* value and *what* does not for consumers. This is especially true when comparing two different points in time, which lets you readily communicate and quantify the change in that true-north value to consumers.[111] You *Lean* philosophically through a binary business ideology toward your own, infinite sales potential.

From Zero to One[112]

> *When you look long into an abyss,*
> *the abyss also looks into you.*
> — Fredrich Nietzsche, *Beyond Good and Evil*, Ch. IV, No. 146 (1886).

Consumers make analogies and use binary computers to improve their human condition and better describe themselves in relation to *what* is or is not in the *Universe*. In dichotomous fashion, they

---

[111] Douglas Hofstadter, *Surfaces & Essences*, p. 485 (2013).

[112] *See generally*, Peter Thiel, *Zero to One: Notes on Startups, or How to Build the Future*, Crown Business, 1st edition (2014).

compute *1* as being not like *0* just like they self-reflexively identify their *I* as not being like *n0t* into infinite, counter-factual detail.¹¹³ In fact, consumers do this to determine *how* best to ontologically realize themselves being in the *Universe*. Through the processes of time, however, the big data of life and existence defines consumers and describes their behavior in some of these ways, which allows you to attempt to predict *what* consumers truly value. Both analogy making and mathematics converge to illuminate the fundamental, binary condition of consumers' existence in all of its probability of being or not being to help you determine *what* might get bought and sold.

Since *U/P* improves analogical thinking, it also sharpens your business acumen by helping you make more sense out of markets, since abstract concepts in consumers' minds shape their behavior, to which you can relate. The better you understand the abstractions consumers are thinking, the more fully you will be able to explain *who* consumers truly are.¹¹⁴ For example, the modern sociological researcher James Flynn, famous for the *Flynn Effect* demonstrating rising IQs across time, presented significant data showing that your own IQ score will increase once you increase your capacity to abstract and analogize between yourself and other people. As abstraction increases your own intelligence quotient, like Auguste Rodin's, '*The Thinker*,' it likewise increases your appreciation of consumers' and all other stakeholders' IQs as well. Absorbing new true-north value streams grows your mindset¹¹⁵ toward abstracting a metaphysical business ideology to more intelligently serve your markets.

U/P is thus like the abstract art-work you pass by everyday in the hallways of an organization, which serves as a palette for your imagining ways to grow your future profits by meaningfully

---

¹¹³Which may be considered both a Hegelian, Heideggerian and Sartian thesis of being, and the anti-thesis of nothingness.

¹¹⁴David Deutsch, *The Beginning of Infinity*, p. 114 (2011).

¹¹⁵Carol Dweck, *Mindset: The New Psychology of Success*, Random House (2006).

providing true-north value to customers.¹¹⁶

© Robert Delaunay, *Windows Open Simultaneously* (1912) (Public Domain PD-ART; PD-OLD-70)

The *U/People* business model and acronym - *Uniquely/Profitably Energizing and Optimizing People's Lives and Existences* - and all the acronyms I use throughout this book, are acrobatic heuristics for you to use in a metaphysical business ideology to compress and unify widely divergent information together to *Lean* toward consumers more profitably.¹¹⁷ The multiple definitions, word combinations, acronyms and phrases derived from *U/P's* meaning demonstrate that the business model's concepts exceed the individual letters, symbols and words composing it, allowing you to reach across all value streams.¹¹⁸ At its very best, *U/P* might even be analogized (or dis-analogized) to a long poem, since actual poetry represents the most compressed and extreme example of

---

¹¹⁶See James Flynn discuss the Flynn effect at, James Flynn, *Why our IQ levels are higher than our grandparents'*, TED2013 (Mar. 2013).

¹¹⁷Such as those proposed by Alan Hájek in, *Philosophy tool kit: with heuristics anybody can think like a philosopher*, aeon (Apr. 3, 2017).

¹¹⁸As Wittgenstein said, '*My difficulty is only an — enormous — difficulty of expression,*' at p. 40 in, *Wittgenstein's Personal Journal* (May 8, 1915), and further at p. 48 of the same text, '*Language is a part of our organism and no less complicated than it.*'

analogy making between concepts, thereby further abstracting and re-categorizing life, value and meaning for all people.[119]

You will in-fact find quite a bit of actual poetry interwoven throughout U/P. With this, hopefully, you will see *how* analogy making is a powerful tool for abstraction that complements quantification to guide an organization's faith in better learning, understanding and predicting *what* really works.

For example, much of the premium you place on an employees' work experience originates from their generally large set of examples of past problems, failures and solutions so they may efficiently analogize toward an iterative, *Lean* solution to present business problems. A business ideology will allow you to better see *how* employees *Lean* their experiences toward serving consumers' fundamental true-north values. Think of the last time you were at work and you recognized similar patterns of issues and were able to more effectively propose *Lean*-oriented continual improvements based on past experiences that you remember – that is *how* you analogically *Lean* philosophically.

Analogy making from past experiences particularly relates to the details of the industry in which you operate. Look at *how* an organization asks interview questions of candidates' past experiences, like the Gallup-style tests for employee selection repeatedly questioning interviewees from different perspectives.[120] Look also at the interaction of qualitative and quantitative analysis when employers decide *who* to hire based on their own past experience within an industry. Analogy making is especially important in day-to-day situations in organizations that seek to continually improve, and a true-north value theory enhances an organization's ability

---

[119]Since people generally loath both philosophy and poetry, you dear reader are very ardent indeed; people do like making money though, which may draw some fellows to the flame.

[120]*See e.g.*, Gallup, Inc. where they discuss their own selection process, which they also sell as a service to other corporations, at http://www.gallup.com/careers/108163/selection-process.aspx (last accessed on Dec. 4, 2016).

to analogize when it does not have the ability to quantify every decision.

The Symbols - The Forward Slash, Circumflex, and Sigmas

> *'Then you should say what you mean,'*
> *the March Hare went on.*
> *'I do,' Alice hastily replied;*
> *'at least—at least I mean what I say*
> *—that's the same thing, you know.'*
> *'Not the same thing a bit!' said the Hatter.*
> – Lewis Carroll,*Alice's Adventures in Wonderland* , Ch. VII,*A Mad Tea-party*(1865)

To facilitate the highly conceptual and artistic nature of this discussion, you will notice some instances in the text and charts where I modify standard English. I split words with hyphens -, use the forward slash / to mean*Lean* , add the diacritic pronunciation accent of the circumflex or hat "^" over the letter o, convert some letter o's to sigma's σ, use a capital sigma Σ, and CAPITALIZE new business acronyms along with all of these techniques. I use this symbolism because while I write in American English, you *Lean* philosophically in a sign-language that all consumers comprehend, such as through the trade-marks you use.[121]

I look to reveal the implicit meaning within the words we use in business every day regardless of whether a word's etymology

---

[121]As Wittgenstein said, *'The limit of my language is the limit of my world'* (*'Die Grenzen meiner Sprache bedeuten die Grenzen meiner Welt'*), (5.6) *Tractatus Logico-Philosophicus* (1922); and further, *'There are things that cannot be said with words. They manifest themselves instead as the mystical.'* (*'Es gibt allerdings Unaussprechliches. Dies zeigt sich, es ist das Mystische.'*), (6.522) *Tractatus Logico-Philosophicus* (1922).

explicitly supports that meaning. So, using symbols like "/" will likewise help you devise *how* to universally im-prove the lives of all people for profit. I also hope to reveal *how* business vocabulary itself guides the direction of true-north value when you pause a moment to examine it carefully.[122] As the philosopher Ludwig Wittgenstein wrote in 1953 at paragraph 129 of his, *Philosophical Investigations*:

> *The aspects of things that are most important for us are hidden because of their simplicity and familiarity... — And this means: we fail to be struck by what, once seen, is most striking and most powerful.*

The circumflex carrot "^" over the o, like so *Ô*, is the diacritical pronunciation carried throughout. It is also similar to that used in statistics to indicate the necessary, actuarial estimation of reality that a metaphysical business ideology must take. The *Ô* generally symbolizes a *true-north* value compass described by the Japanese principle of *Hōshin Konri*. *Hōshin Konri* is a combination of *Hoshin*, meaning a compass or needle, with *Kanri*, meaning management or control. So together the symbolic *Ô* is generally interpreted as *Compass Guided Management* pointing upward. To emphasize this point from here on, please consider the word *truth* to be an interchangeable portmanteau of *true* and *north*, with *true-north* being the metaphorical direction of all value in the *Lean* vernacular. To make clear *what* and where *Lean* value truly is,[123] the *Ô* symbol meaning *Hōshin Kanri*, or *Compass Guided Management* in English, is reflected in the logos of a wide range of businesses as seen here:

---

[122] This line of *Lean Thinking* owes tremendous debt to ordinary language philosophers such as Ludwig Wittgenstein and his, *Tractatus Logico-Philosophicus* (1921) as noted from his quote below.

[123] The actual etymology of *truth* does not support this, but I think it is a useful fiction for these purposes.

From top to bottom, *TrueNorthLogic®*, *True North Inc.®*, *Acura®* luxury division of *American Honda Motor Co., Inc.*

In fact, here is a single slide from a presentation that *Toyota Motor Corporation* gives exemplifying this symbolism used in *Toyota's* real-world business environment of *Toyota's Production System* (a.k.a. '*TPS*'). This slide fairly presents both *TPS* and *Lean* as business ideologies geared toward customer satisfaction and human development, representing a people-focused, true-north value theory:[124]

---

[124]Slide from AME 2002 conference, Hajime Ohba, Cindy Kuhlman-Voss, Leadership and the Toyota Production System, TSSC, Inc.

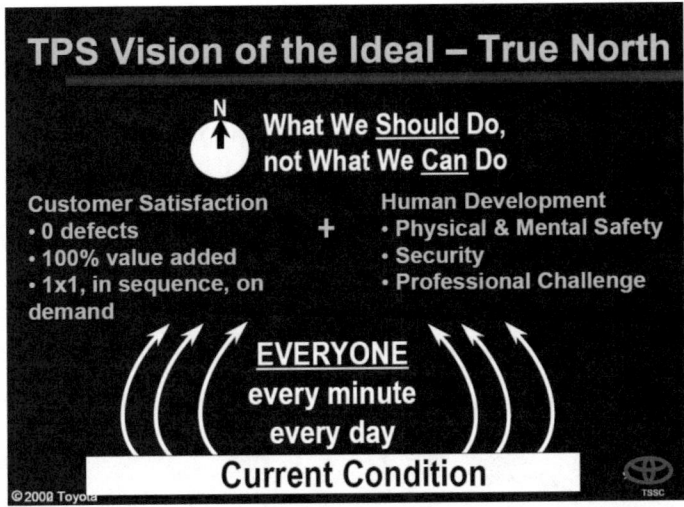

Toyota® Internal Presentation (© 2002 *Toyota Motor Corporation*)

Lastly, the capital sigma Σ you may see reflected in various places within this book either in its normal orientation or turned upright, represents the paradoxical summation of open-ended value inherent in the human condition. I hope all these symbols will become as clear to you as a natural spring by the time you finish this volume of, *True-North Value*.

U People/ Toward 6σ

For another example of this symbolism, U/P compresses the term *Lean Six Sigma,* into "/6σ." The forward slash "/" naturally represents all *Lean* true-north value theory in addition to a metaphysical focus on *what* consumers' most meaningful problems are; the six "6" represents the attempted quantification of *what U/People* value; the sigma "σ" represents the necessary estimation of *what* true-north value is in the *Universe,* and the infinity symbol "∞" is the elusive, circular perfection we all pursue. "/6σ" overall is the pragmatic pursuit of perfection.

The *U* in *U/P* and *U/People* is partially inspired by the *U*-shaped work-cells implemented by *Toyota* when it developed the *Toyota Production System*, and the desks where *Toyota's* office workers sit. You can also see in these pictures below that the *U* in *U/People* applies to the *U*-shaped factory work-cells and office cubicles comprising people's work-spaces worldwide. The *U* in *U/People* also applies figuratively as a universal condition of *U/People* either at work as a core concept of /6σ efficiency, or in serving customers, which the *U* shape facilitates. *U/People* is thus both ego-centric to an organization and allo-centric to consumers at the same time.

U/People in all these respects may be seen in these pictures here:

U-Shaped, *Lean* Oriented Workstations (© 2016 Bosch Rexroth Corp. (Fair Use)

You Lean People(CC-BY-SA 3.0)

U/ P (CC-BY-SA 3.0)

Thus, *U/ P* applies universally to an organization's business model as a legally fictitious person, to an employees working within an organization in U-shaped cells, and to consumers that an organization in-turn *Leans* philosophically toward. All *People Lean* philosophically toward all other real or legally fictitious people by providing them with meaningful true-north value. *U* is thus open-ended organizationally, logically and ethically.

For example, philosophers use *U* to mean abstract concepts like *Universal Egoism,* economists use it to mean *Utility,* and academics use it to mean learning at a *University.* All of these meanings around

U align and cohere within *U / People* sitting in cubicles, working in U-shaped cells, and serving as optimistic, upwardly mobile, white- and blue-collar people factoring *what* matters most.

U/ People in the *Lean* True-North Value Stream

The application of the philosophical principles embodied by the *U/ People* business model is not new, as you might expect. People-oriented business ideologies have been advocated since the dawn of management science. The entire history of business theory applies notions of true-north value to people's everyday lives within well-known concepts that you may have studied. For example, *IBM*'s *Three Basic Beliefs* stated by Thomas Watson Jr. in 1962 are strikingly similar to *Lean* principles:[125]

- *Respect for the individual,*
- *Superlative customer service, and*
- *The pursuit of excellence*

And in 2003, *IBM* employees in a *ValueJam* revised these *Three Basic Beliefs* to be:[126]

- *Dedication to every client's success;*
- *Innovation that matters—for our company and for the world; and*
- *Trust and responsibility in all relationships*

The philosophy of *Lean* thus reconstructs old concepts in new ways because cutting-edge businesses like *IBM* still struggle to learn from

---

[125] Fond on IBM.com, *A Business and Its Beliefs*, for its *IBM at 100* campaign http://www-03.ibm.com/ibm/history/ibm100/us/en/icons/bizbeliefs/) (accessed on Nov. 5, 2015).
[126] *Ibid.*

and implement them, which is no easy task.[127] Furthermore, the field of management science as exemplified by the *Lean*-oriented books continuously improves on and expands *Lean* concepts below,[128] such as *Lean's* intersection with *Six Sigma*. Recent business titles include:

- *Lean Thinking* (2010),
- *The Lean Startup* (2011),
- *The Lean Turnaround* (2012),
- *Running Lean* (2012),
- *Lean for Dummies* (2012),
- *Lean UX* (2013),
- *Lean Analytics* (2013),
- *The Lean Mindset* (2013),
- *Lean Enterprise* (2014),
- *Lean Customer Development* (2014),
- *Lean Enterprise* (2015),
- *Lean Product Playbook* (2015),
- *Lean Six Sigma* (2016),
- *Lean Administration* (2016),
- *Lean Construction* (2016),
- *Die Lein Reise* (*The Lean Trip*) (2016),
- *Introduction to Lean Manufacturing* (2017),
- *Lean Strategy*(2017)

---

[127] Besides *Lean*, other similar business ideologies have originated out of the East, such as *Jugaad* in Hindi cultures, *see*, Navi Radjou, Jaideep Prabhu, Simone Ahuja, *Jugaad Innovation: Think Frugal, Be Flexible, Generate Breakthrough Growth*, Jossey-Bass; 1 edition (Apr. 1, 2012); and in the Latin-American South, such as the open-book, bottom-up management implemented by Ricardo Semler at Semco of Brazil, *see*, Recardo Semler,*Maverick: The Success Story Behind the World's Most Unusual Workplace*, Grand Central Publishing; Reprint edition (Apr. 1, 1995).

[128] John Krafcik, *Triumph of the Lean Production System*, pp. 41– 52, Sloan Management Review 30 (1), (Fall 1988).

Amazon.com lists 5,931 business books for sale and counting with *Lean* included somewhere in their titles as of early 2017. *U/P* encompasses all of these domains, moving beyond start-ups or any other single aspect of business to provide the best explanation and goals for all business activity so you may deploy *Lean* most powerfully in an*HQ* .

Elaborating on*Lean* philosophically though requires knowing*what Lean* really is as a business discipline in the context of all this history. While Womak and Jones delineated one of the most widely revered descriptions of *Lean* in *Lean Thinking*, despite all this time and effort, no universally recognized, internally consistent definition of *Lean* exists. To provide some symmetry between *how* Toyota Motor Corporation defines *Lean* and all the other definitions of *Lean* generally, I broadly define *Lean*within *U / P* as:[129]

1. ***Fairness and respect for people*** ;
2. ***Viewing the customer as the "true-north"*** ;
3. ***Elimination of waste to add true value*** ; *and*
4. ***Creating scientific, knowledge-driven continuous improvement.***

U/ P's item (1), '*fairness and respect for people*,' describes *how* business workers in *Lean* processes are as dignified as the organization's own customers.*U / P's* item (2), '*viewing the customer as the 'true-north,"* emphasizes that since an organization exists most fundamentally to serve the interests of customers*who* pay money, stakeholders receive that money only as a consequence of that service toward *what* customers ultimately value. For an example of this *U/ P* item (2), '*viewing the customer as the 'true-north',* in a business context, consider *what* Tim Cook who succeeded Steve Jobs as CEÔ of*Apple, Inc.* said in his keynote at the company's 2016 developers' conference:

---

[129]*Toyota Production System and what it means for business*, Toyota Material Handling Europe, Toyota (2010); Samuel Obara and Darril Wilburn,*Toyota by Toyota: Reflections from the Inside Leaders on the Techniques That Revolutionized the Industry*, CRC Press (2012).

> *I would like to take a moment to talk about why we do what we do at Apple. Our North Star has always been about improving people's lives by creating great products that change the world.*[130]

Just as importantly, *U/ P's* item (3) of its definition of *Lean*, '*elimination of waste to add value*,' along the lines of *Muda*, *Mura* and *Muri*, explicitly states that the overall mission of *Lean* is to eliminate work that does not directly or indirectly create '*true-north value*' for the customer. The philosophy of *Lean* revolves around optimizing opportunities by avoiding misallocating resources. *U/ P's* item (3) can thus be summarized as optimizing efficiency to enhance profits while avoiding overly exploiting people.[131]

U/ P's item (4), '*creating scientific, knowledge-driven continuous improvement*,' emphasizes the empirically iterative nature of *Lean* arising both from the *Buddhist* presently experiencing self and the Western philosophy of science to discover and reveal *what* most philosophically *Leans* an organization toward consumers' highest values and thus leads them to sustain and enhance their being.

Pay Us over the *Pay Wall* at the Margin of Existence

You must recognize that while all definitions of *Lean* emphasize maximizing true-north value for consumers, none identifies true value beyond *what* customers actually purchase or use. *Lean* to date has focused on identifying true-north value by *what* people purchase at the point of sale. This *Lean* method of analyzing *what* consumers reveal they prefer is the most direct and efficient method

---

[130] *See*, Tim Cook speak this at *Apple Inc.'s* 2016 Worldwide Developers' Conference https://www.youtube.com/watch?v=n5jXg_NNiCA (accessed last on Dec. 4 2016).

[131] See also, *The Four Rules for TPS* described by Steven Spear and H. Kent Bowen, *Decoding the DNA of the Toyota Production System*, Harvard Business Review (2006), which may be collapsed under items (3) *waste* and (4) *scientific improvement*.

of understanding their greatest problems, since they are by and large *what* they do. However, when you *Lean* further philosophically, you reach deeper, beyond *what* consumers do or say, to more accurately conjecture, hypothesize, theorize and identify *who* consumers are by better interpreting their data that you receive. This greater insight leads you to *why* customers truly value a product and/or service beyond *what* I call this *pay wall, pay us wall* or *point of purchase*.[132]

A *pay wall* is generally used by online media and information services to indicate the content that consumers must purchase with money. However, even in cases where media companies provide information without charging money, they generally do so in exchange for selling the viewers' data and attention to advertisers, which forms its own sort of *pay us wall.* As the economist Herbert Simon said, '*In an information-rich world, the wealth of information means a dearth of... attention and a need to allocate that attention efficiently among the overabundance of information sources that might consume it.*'[133] The pay us wall gets viewers to spend their attention and personal information viewing the advertisements instead of money as its own form of value to other businesses.

Advertisers in-turn directly charge people for their own products and/or services. The *pay us wall* represents the often unclear boundary between *what* people actually do that leads to meaningful monetization, and *what* organizations provide that creates true-north value for people in ex-change. You likewise can use an *U/People*-oriented business methodology within an *HQ* to define *what* pain points consumers pray that you sooth at the *pay us wall*.

---

[132]Edith Penrose was one of the first to accurately delineate the boundary between internal, administrative nature of an organization and the free market through which natural demand emerges in her book, *The Theory of the Growth of the Firm*, New York, John Wiley and Sons (1959). This allows us to alternatively call it the, '*Penrose Pay Wall*,' which we will later connect to the, '*Penrose Triange*' as you will see.

[133]Herbert A. Simon, *Administrative Behavior, 4th Edition: A Study of Decision-making Processes in Administrative Organisations*, p. 22, Free Press (2013 (originally published in 1947)).

A business creates points of purchase by predicting *what* true-north value customers shall be blessedly given by consuming its products and/or services.

Identifying the Four Steps to *Lean* Philosophically toward *U* / *People*

To get out of an *HQ* and move past consumers' *pay us wall,* you must develop an overarching understanding of *who* consumers are and *why* they value products and/or services up along the *Rubicon* [134] of their value streams. You must reach toward the firmament of true-north value in its most intangible, abstract sense and work back down to the specific activities, instruments and tools used by an organization to realize the specific details of those true-north values in consumers' lives and existences through the products and/or services an organization re-produces. Where within this outcome space products and/or services satisfy consumers depends on the intersection of *who* , *why* , *what* , and *how* they are.

Along this *Lean* line of thinking, Peter Drucker[135] said in, *The Practice of Management,* in 1954:

> **If we want to know what a business is we have to start with its purpose. And its purpose must lie outside of the business itself. In fact, it must lie in society since a business enterprise is an organ of society. There is only one valid definition of business purpose: to create a customer.**[136] [emphasis added]

---

[134] *See generally,* Amitai Etzioni, *Crossing the Rubicon: Including Preference Formation in Theories of Choice Behavior,* George Washington University, pp. 65–79, Challenge, vol. 57, no. 2 (Mar./Apr. 2014).

[135] John A. Byrne and Lindsey Gerdes, *The Man Who Invented Management*, Businessweek (Nov. 27, 2005).

[136] Peter Drucker, *The Practice of Management* , pp. 39-40, HarperCollins (1954).

This image of *creating a customer* reminds many of Drucker's commentators as well as me of an unfinished sculpture Michelangelo created in 1525-30 CE titled, *The Awakening Slave.* [137]

The Awakening Slave (Public Domain)

However, I believe that organizations often misapply Drucker's quote by only considering his statement regarding, '*creating a customer.*' This implies that organizations can artificially develop *who* consumers are and push products and/or services to them as if they were somehow slaves to an organization. However, if

---

[137] This unfinished work by Michelangelo, *The Awakening Slave* , is a 2.67m high marble statue dated to 1525-30 CE. This work is part of the *Prisoners*, the series of unfinished sculptures for the tomb of Pope Julius II that is now held in the Galleria dell'Accademia in Florence.

you read Drucker's full quote, it says that organizations create a customer by meeting people as they are in front of the *pay us wall*. As Peter Drucker says a paragraph further down in, *The Practice of Management*:

> *It is the customer who determines what a business is. For it is the customer, and [s/he] alone, who through being willing to pay for a good or for a service, converts economic resources into wealth, things into goods.*

The metaphysics of this statement— '*[I]t is the customer who determines what a business is.*' [emphasis added] —ought to become apparent as you *Lean* philosophically through the *U/ People* business model toward those people *who* want to buy from you. With this customer-oriented business model, you may reach over the *pay us wall* to re-generate profits from *who* , *why* , *what* and *how* customers are as consumers, which is the predicate to all consumption.

You thus metaphysically speculate with every personal and business decision you make as to whether you can improve customers while satisfying them. The only way for you to increase the probability of success is by sufficiently aligning speculative, intuitive beliefs about true value with *who* consumers really are so you know *why* they value *what* you offer. You ought to consider consumers less like slavish minds for you to hack and, like yourself, more like Rodin's, '*The Thinker*' *leaning* toward *what* is and ought to be produced by a corporation.[138]

---

[138] August Rodin (French, 1840–1917), *The Thinker* , ca. 1880, cast ca. 1904, Bronze. Height: 6ft. 6in., Signed: A Rodin; stamped: Alexis Rudier / Fondeur. Paris., Gift of Alma de Bretteville Spreckels, 1924.18.1.

The Model Customer(© 2011 Patrickxdaniel, CC BY-SA 4.0)

The Para-Scientific Business Process

Besides employing radical empathy through the data you gather, the best way to discover consumers as they are is to para-scientifically test for them like Eric Ries did for his product, '*IMVU*.' By doing this iterative testing, you too will surface consumers' deepest demands that you in-turn philosophically analyze. Because all business value flows up through people, *who* still exceed anyone's complete comprehension, business analysis still requires this philosophical synthesis of qualitative and quantitative information. Business cannot yet be managed by numbers alone for this reason. Thus, business is a para-science to which you may apply a scientific process of testing *who* consumers truly are with philosophically defined degrees of confidence that extend into the unknown.

As a contemporary of Fredrick Taylor, Walter Shewhart was one of the first, modern people to apply scientific empiricism to business to achieve customer success. Walter Shewhart invented the para-scientific, *Specification-Production-Inspection Shewhart Cycle*,[139] in the early 1900s. Following Shewhart's lead, Edward Deming famously modified the *Shewhart Cycle* into, *Plan, Do, Check, Act*

---

[139]Walter Andrew Shewhart, *Statistical Method from the Viewpoint of Quality Control*, New York: Dover (1939).

(*PDCA* or *Deming Cycle*). Deming introduced his PDCA Cycle to Japan in the 1950s.[140] Through *Toyota's* initial leaders like Eiji Toyoda and Taiichi Ohno, *Toyota* most particularly internalized PDCA in the 1950s within its industrial processes to create the foundation of the industrial *Kaikaku* that we now call *Lean*. *Kaikaku* is the *Lean* term meaning a revolutionary improvement in a value stream to quickly create more value with less waste by up-ending the status quo. This cross-breading of Western, para-scientific business analysis with the legacy of *Japanese* theologies and philosophies is the pedigree and evolutionary beginning of the *Lean* meme.

In 2003, the venture capitalist Steve Blank in his book, *Four Steps to the Epiphany: Successful Strategies for Products that Win*,[141] refined and applied these *Kaikaku* cycles toward starting up new businesses. In *Four Steps*, Blank described the four steps necessary to reach a commercial epiphany as a *Customer Development Model*. Blank's *Customer Development Model* applies the Shewhart and Deming Cycles, and Drucker's notions of customer development, toward building viable, new businesses. The *Customer Development Model* for new businesses follows the four steps of:

1. *Customer Discovery*;
2. *Customer Validation*;
3. *Customer Creation*; and
4. *Company Building*.

You can see the cover of Blank's book here with Michelangelo Buonarroti's, *The Creation of Adam*, painted on the ceiling of the

---

[140] Ronald Moen, *Foundation and History of the PDSA Cycle*, Associates in Process Improvement-Detroit (date unknown); for deeper insight into the connection of Deming's work and its relation to U/P, I recommend studying the, *Deming System of Profound Knowledge* (*SoPK*) produced by the W. Edwards Deming Institute.

[141] Steve Blank, *The Four Steps to the Epiphany*, K&S Ranch, 2nd edition (2013).

Sistine Chapel. Blank notably added a light bulb between God[142] and man *who* has an exclamation mark over his head.

Steven Gary Blank, *Four Steps to the Epiphany*, with Michelangelo's *The Creation of Adam* on the cover

Eric Ries further consolidated the Shewhart, Deming and Blank cycles with his, '*Build, Measure, Learn*' process, and applied it to start up businesses as described by his book,*The Lean Startup*.[143]. Even though Ries skipped over initially intuiting *what* he thought ought to be built before he had something to measure and learn from, he applied this line of empirical thinking that reached back not only to Deming, Shewhart and Taylor, but also to the philosopher, Sir Francis Bacon (1561-1626) and scientist Galileo Galilei (1564-1642) during the European*Renaissance*. All of these empiricists emphasized testing rather than making deductive assumptions based on an abstract ideal. To emphasize how old this concept is, one of the first people to even think this way was actually the Arab scientist

---

[142]This depiction of God and his angels, particularly when you see the image in full, has been interpreted as a subversive depiction of the human brain, *see*, Frank Lynn Meshberger, MD,*An Interpretation of Michelangelo's Creation of Adam Based on Neuroanatomy*, Journal of the American Medical Association, Vol. 264, No. 14 (Oct. 10, 1990); notably, Steve Blank cropped the image to just show the *cerebral cortex*.

[143]Eric Ries,*The Lean Startup, How Today's Entrepreneurs Use Continuous Innovation to Create Radically Successful Businesses*, Crown Business, First Edition edition (2011).

Ibn al-Haytham from 1000 C.E. Thus, Ries', *Build, Measure, Learn*, methodology heeds the wisdom received from old masters to avoid reinventing wheels.

Nonetheless, Reis was lauded for reintroducing empiricism to product and/or service development since too many business decisions were being made with bad effect based only on mental models of *who* consumers were and *why* they would purchase - mental models that were only created by analogy from empathy without any real data. However, true-north value is found at the pragmatic intersection of both conjecture from intuition and criticism from market testing in a virtuously para-scientific business cycle.[144] Both are necessary to triangulate and truly know *what* consumers value.[145] All these cycles, methods and models are all part of *U/P* and the philosophy of *Lean*.[146] They all require deeply empathizing with consumers' pain points that you abduct from an intuition, infer from the problems they state, induce from their behavioral data, and deduce from the products and/or services they already purchase. Thus, you can reach commercial epiphanies by following the *Lean 3WH* interrogatories as seen here:

1. ***Who: Customer Discovery*** - Discovering *who* consumers are;
2. ***Why: Customer Validation*** - Identifying *why* consumers are;
3. ***What: Customer Creation*** - Constructing *what* makes consumers become *who* they want to be; and

---

[144]This point was further emphasized by the American pragmatists, such as William James, Charles Pierce and John Dewey. Notably, Pierce and James formed their '*Metaphysical Club*' in 1872 to study this problem related to consumer insight; *see for background*, Louis Menand, *The Metaphysical Club: A Story of Ideas in America*, Farrar, Straus and Giroux (2001).

[145]For some criticism of relying too much on *The Lean Startup* methodologies alone, *see*, Tomer Sharon, *Validating Product Ideas Through Lean User Research*, p. 75, Rosenfeld Media (2016), in regards to how it might lead you to miss true-north value by not abstracting to unobservable problems enough up front in the open problem space.

[146]At least within the *Philosophy of Science*.

4. *How: Company Building-* Deducing *how* consumers become *who* they consider themselves to be as customers for the greatest profit.

Thus, an organization may pursue this *3WH* customer development process by discovering *who* consumers are, identifying *why* they value *who* they are, learning *what* they want to consume that makes them further be, and understanding *how* an organization ought to charge for *what* consumers will actually buy that supports their further becoming *who* , *why* and *what* they are and want to be. Or, as Eric Ries wrote in the double negative, '*If we do not know who the customer is, we do not know what quality is.*'[147]

The *I/D Kata*

Better discovering, identifying and quantifying the money you can make requires that you engage in *Hansei* by repeatedly reflecting on *who* consumers truly are in-line or on-line at stores, *why* they wish to purchase, and *what* will delight them most. *How* you reach your greatest profit through Eastern and Western philosophical traditions gets determined by continually improving your respect for people and revitalizing your competitive advantage through a *Lean* process called a *Kata* .[148] *Kata* is a term of Japanese origin describing the discipline of linking behaviors together in parallel. You will better align the seemingly disconnected portions of consumers' value streams by abducting, inferring, (less commonly) inducing, and deducing them through a *Kata* .[149]

---

[147] Eric Ries, *The Lean Startup* , p. 107 (2011).

[148] For a thorough definition of *Kata, see*, Mike Rother, *Toyota Kata: Managing People for Improvement, Adaptiveness and Superior Results: Managing People for Improvement, Adaptiveness and Superior Results*, p. 15, McGraw-Hill Education (2009); *Competitive Advantage* being a term introduced by Michael Porter in his same-named book, *Competitive Advantage: Creating and Sustaining Superior Performance* (1985); I intend the term competitive advantage in this book to include all current notions of evolutionary game theory and its applications as proposed by others.

[149] *See*, the entry for *Kata* in the, *Lean Lexicon: A Graphical Glossary for Lean Thinkers*, 5th Ed., Lean Enterprise Institute, Inc. (2006).

For those unfamiliar with logical systems, *abduction* is the technical term for when you rely on intuition to tell you *what* creates the most true-north value for an consumers.[150] To do so, you must critique pure reason and hold it hostage to abduct consumers' highest values; however, you do that if you have a hunch, *Lean* forward with your best intuition, and deeply empathize with consumers' lives and existences while bracketing all else you think you know. The fundamental criteria for abducting a true problem is to determine whether or not your best guess causes you or others to smirk. For the sake simplifying our *Lean Lexicon*, we will use *intuition* to simply mean *abduction*.

Inference and *induction*, on the other hand, allow you to hypothesize and theorize a general maxim from evident data you have observed rather than from a gut feeling. Rarely, if ever, will you have all possible data to make an induction, so you usually are inferring the best explanation to hypothesize how you will make the most money meaningfully. The best explanation is the one that not only delineates *how* you will make money, but also distinguishes between *why* you will achieve one result rather than another.[151] And regardless of whether you posit a conjecture, hypothesis, or induction, you then test and assumptively deduce *how* you will make money. You may only deduce *what* consumers will value without making an assumption when you already know *what* consumers pay for, and you are absolutely confident that a product and/or service will be perceived by them to be a perfect solution, which is the ideal goal you always strive to perfect.

To produce this competitive advantage of a true-north scientific investigation through a *Kata* , *Lean* practitioners usually focus of the twin pillars of, '*Respect for People*' and '*Continuous Improvement*'

---

[150]Charles Sanders Pierce, the principle inventor and proponent of the term, believed it to be a form of inference and guessing; *see, Collected Papers of Charles S. Peirce*, Vol. 7, p. 219, Charles Hartshorne, Paul Weiss, and Arthur W. Burks (eds.) Cambridge, MA: Harvard University Press (1901); Charles S. Peirce, *The New Elements of Mathematics* , Vol. 4, 319-320, Carolyn Eisele (ed.). The Hague: Mouton Publishers, (c. 1906).

[151]David Deutsch, *The Beginning of Infinity* , p. 16 (2011).

when market testing and producing products and/or services. However, if you look closely at the capstone of a *Lean HQ*, you will see that the *Lean Management* portion is also composed of increasingly plentiful values, systems, processes, methods, techniques, and activities that ultimately result in the products and/or services delivered as you move toward the customer base. Through this process, a *Lean HQ* forms a delta, temple, pyramid and/or steeple-shape above its foundation. It forms a symbolic *Kata* that funda-mentally aligns its twin pillars of *Respect for People* and *Continuous Improvement* as seen again here:

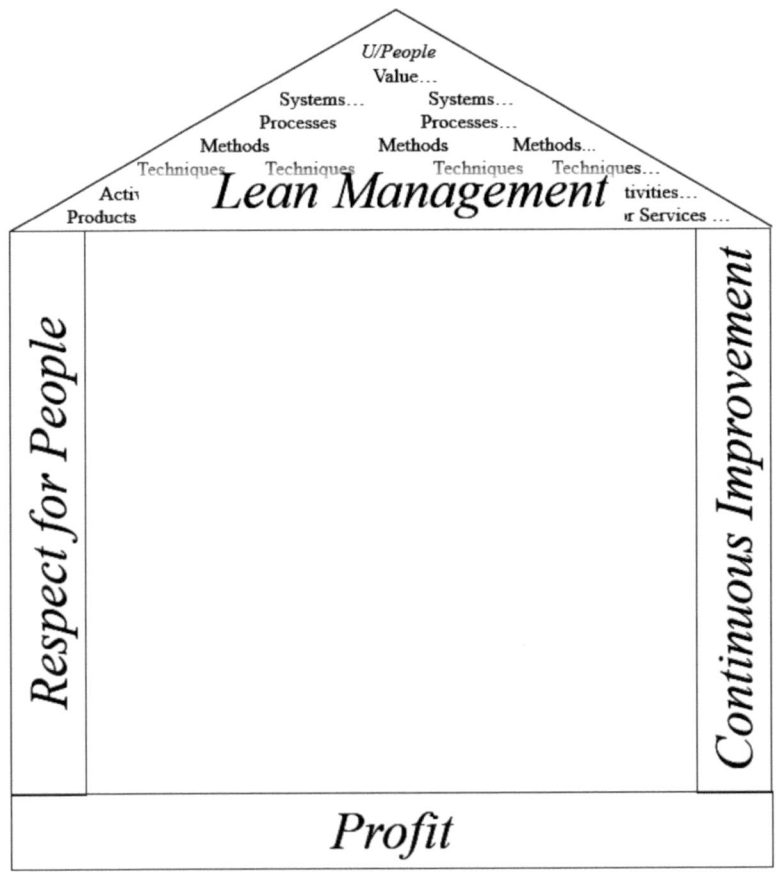

Lean Management I/D Kata with values, systems, processes, methods, techniques, activities, products and/or services

Following this pyramid principle,[152] I graphically represent *Lean Management* as an *I/D Kata* in a delta "Δ" shape with "/" representing *why*, "_" representing the *what*, and "" representing *how*. The sum of this *I/D Kata* represents the entire ex-change of *who* customers were in the present state for *who* they will become in the future state by purchasing the products and/or services that *Lean*

---

[152]For another form of this analysis, *see e.g.*, Barbara Minto, *The Minto Pyramid Principle: Logic in Writing, Thinking, & Problem Solving*, Minto Intl, Expanded edition (1996).

Management provides. With the *I/D Kata*, a *Lean Management* team in the '*See Suite*' can perform penetrating analysis that might help an organization become something special, like a rocket-ship or unicorn.

Using this *I/D Kata*, once you discover *who* consumers are largely by *what* they do, you intuitively, inferentially and/or inductively theorize through conjecture *why* consumers' deepest problems cause them to truly value goods and/or services. You match up *why* customers will buy anything at all with *how* you expect to exchange a solution for the greatest profit of all. Between *why* and *how* extending from *who* customers are around this *I/D Kata*, you identify the solution by determining *what* products and/or services an organization ought to produce to serve their Freudian ids, egos and super-egos. The difference between *why* and *how* is the problem space that you resolve. A solution ultimately represents all of the values, systems, processes, methods, techniques, activities, and ultimately, products and/or services that remove customers' problems in exchange for the price you charge and deduct from them.

Using the *I/D Kata*, you can triangulate any given side or angle from the other two. You can determine *who* customers are in the difference between *why* they actually purchase now and *how / how much* they will pay for it - e.g. if customers pay a lot of money for water it means they **ARE** thirsty. The difference between *who* customers are and *what* they want to buy can be extrapolated from the delta of *why* they want to live and exist and *how* they currently pay to do so. To begin this process, you must engage in customer discovery and identification with an *n* number of *Why's* along the left-side, rightward leaning y axis, as seen here.[153]

---

[153] *See e.g.*, Simon Sinek, *Start with Why: How Great Leaders Inspire Everyone to Take Action*, Portfolio (Oct. 29, 2009).

Ex-change *Who* Your Customers Are

```
              ?                                              ?
         lem                U/People                     ice
     rob                     Values…                  Pr
  yP          Systems…                Systems…     ow ve)
Wh ential)    Processes…              Processes… H cti
  fer          Methods…                Methods… (Dedu
(In          Techniques…  Techniques…   Techniques…  Techniques…
            Activities   Activities    Activities   Activities   Activities…
         Products and/or  Products and/or  Products and/or …
           Services        Services         Services
```

***What* Products and/or Services?**
(Instrumental)

Lean Management I/D Kata

Along the *y* axis, you then proceed with a downward progression of increasing precision by intuiting, inferring and/or inducing *what* specific products and/or services solve consumers' utmost problems until you conjecture a value theory. The right-side, leftward leaning axis reflects *how* consumers will value with the price they pay each activity that produces the products and/or services they purchased. In the philosophy of *Lean*, if any activity reflected in the *I/D Kata* does not support a profit, then it is considered one of the many form of waste (*Muda, Mura, Muri*) and must be cut from the organizational structure.

Finally, along the bottom *x* axis, you specifically determine *what* products and/or services best support *who* customers are and *why* customers will ex-change anything for them at all. Since this *x* axis is a cost base, the closer you align *why* and *how* in parallel, the *Leaner* an organization will be, the closer to customers you will become, and the greater the profit margins will be as you increasingly make a dent in the *Universe*. Ideally, you want an *HQ* to look something like a skyscraper, such as the top of this one at 750 Lexington Avenue in New York City.[154]

---

[154] Is it any wonder that this building is adjacent to, '*Evil Corp*,' as seen in Sam Esmail's, *Mr. Robot*(2015)?

750 Lexington Avenue(Photo Credit: Me from the Bloomberg Building)

To follow the four steps of the *I/D Kata*, you ought to trace them as follows:

1. *Who* - From the top of the *I/D Kata*, ask *who* you have reason to believe potential customers are based both on intuition and data, by empathizing with *why*, *what* and *how* they wish to purchase solutions that solve their problems to further and better be;
2. *Why* - Going down to the left, ask *why* values, systems, processes, methods, techniques, activities and products and/or services provide true-north value to a target market, solving their problems to further and better be, so you may intuitively conjecture, inferentially hypothesize or inductively theorize *what* you will sell them and *how* you will make meaningful amounts of money;
3. *What* - Rounding out the bottom, ask whether *what* products and/or services you wish to offer in-fact delights and satisfies consumers with the most narrowly tailored solution possible with sufficient margins for error correction; and
4. *How* - Heading back toward potential customers, ask *how* all the line-items of the products and/or services, activities, techniques, methods, processes, systems and values that

you construct and provide *Lean* back toward supporting the greatest profit, in perfect alignment with the human problems they resolve, with the least waste possible.

In between the four steps of 3WH are three acts of *empathizing, conjecturing* and *criticizing* tying the *I/D Kata* together:

1. **Empathizing** with consumers through data;
2. **Conjecturing** from intuition, hypothesizing from inference, theorizing from induction, and/or legalizing from deduction (whenever possible)*what* best solves consumers' problems for the greatest profit; and
3.**Criticizing** whether products and/or services produce the greatest true-north value by rigorously testing whether they will generate the highest profit.

Here you can see the addition of these three elements around the *I/D* Kata here:

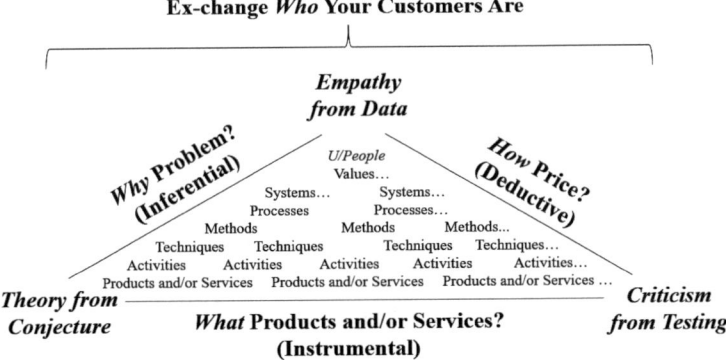

Lean Management I/D Kata with Empathy, Conjecture and Criticism

These degrees of explanation align with the para-scientific methods of analysis you will employ in your business ideology (*a.k.a.* your '*I/Deology*' or '*i/deôlogy*'). These explanations follow certain patterns of reasoning with decreasing degrees of confidence, from *deductive laws* to *inductive theories* to *inferential hypotheses*, and finally to *intuitive conjectures*. The relations between these patterns of reasoning are organized in this table for your review and use:

Method of Analysis	Degree of Explanation
Deduction	Law
Induction	Theory
Inference	Hypothesis
Intuition	Conjecture

Chart of *Methods of Analysis* compared to *Degrees of Explanation*

High Flying Mamas

For a fairly obvious example of using this complete *I/D Kata* process, presume you own an airline and wish to market services to mothers *who* often have a large say in *how* a family's travel budget gets spent. You know that these mothers purchased large, safe, but otherwise unremarkable mini-vans (in their own opinion) that they use to transport their children in one piece. Your data gives you reason to believe that *why* these mothers live and exist is in large part for their children as a physical and emotional extension of themselves. Naturally, this is a universal, true-north value, and thus a very powerful one. You theorize that these mothers will most value a specific class of airline service that will keep their families seated together, near a bathroom, with diapers and other sanitary items provided in a large seat-pocket in front of them. You believe it will induce them to purchase higher priced seats at the back of the plane than they otherwise would have knowing they will have these conveniences handy. You may now pilot test your profit hypothesis with a few sample customers to see whether this new tier of service will increase your profits when all is said and done. Based on those test results, you can then iteratively improve your family-oriented flight offer until it best energizes and optimizes the mothers who might fly an airline, and thereby increase your margins.

I recommend that you extend this *Lean I/D Kata* technique to consumers' much more obscure identities and motivations by carefully observing and applying it to *what* they physically and virtually say and do in relation to *who* they are. You always analyze *how* you can make an effective difference in consumers' lives and existences for the greatest profit in a semi-circular, U-shaped pattern around the *I/D Kata*, moving first from either *why* customers have a problem or *how* they will pay for a solution. Once an organization identifies *who* customers are in the difference, the *I/D Kata* flows naturally to explain *why*, *what* and *how* that organization intuits, infers, induces and/or deduces *what* customers most truly value to conjecture, hypothesize, theorize, and in some cases legalize *what* they want to buy from you.[155] The best explanation for *how* you will make money is the one that you can test at each point in its stream of causes, and the better the explanation for *how* you will make money, the more universally profitable a business will become.

In the early stages of explaining *who* customers are and *why* and *what* they most truly value, you may choose to use intuition instead of inference or induction even if it may require more second guessing from you later on. This analytical process will be more fully elaborated as *U/P* proceeds. Most importantly, *how* you apply the *I/D Kata* toward making money meaningfully defines the core *i/de\^ology* around which all business activities revolve.

You can see the structure of the *I/D Kata* represented in *Toyota's Lexus* division's, '*Relentless Pursuit of Perfection*,' advertising campaign made famous in the 1980s and 1990s. The image from the advertisement below shows a temple of champagne glasses standing up on the engine of a *Lexus* luxury car while it spins its wheels inside *Toyota's HQ*.

---

[155] Deductively legalizing value happens through the legislative process. For example, consider the movement to legalize, sell and tax cannabis/marijuana in the U.S.A., and pharmaceutical companies' lobbying to sell other drugs without prescription. The demand for these drugs is certain; only the legality of delivery is in question.

Toyota® Lexus® The Relentless Pursuit of Perfection , Ad Campaign (circa 1985)

Once *Toyota* discovered *who* its target market of luxury buyers were, it used an inference engine like the *I/D Kata* to abstract *why* people wanted to buy anything from them at all. Before determining *who* would become its customers, *Toyota* first needed to determine *who* were consumers of transportation and *why*. With *who* and *why* firmly in mind, *Toyota* then identified *what* form of transportation to re-produce just in time to make their future customers become more of *who* they wanted to be. In the process, *Toyota* deduced *how* to charge for *why* and *what* its customers really wanted to buy in *Takt* time. *Takt* time is a *Lean* term of *German* origin meaning a perfect pace of production designed to meet customers' ongoing demand just-in-time to provide their utmost satisfaction.

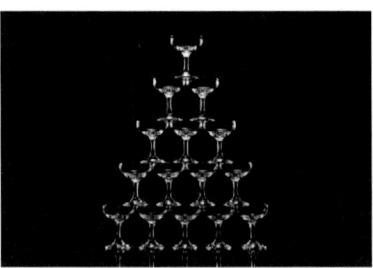

Toyota® Lexus® Division's *I/D Kata*

Toyota's competitors and all organizations adhere to these same developmental processes and space-time constraints for developing products and/or services in *Takt* time. You can see this measurement of *Takt* time symbolized broadly by the calipers within the *Acura* logo for *Honda's* luxury division, in the *Infiniti* logo for

Nissan's luxury division, and the similar, pyramid shape of the *I/D Kata*. As you remove the space and time constraints of organizational processes by eliminating waste, you increasingly make more money with increased margins in *Lean* fashion by creating narrowly tailored solutions.

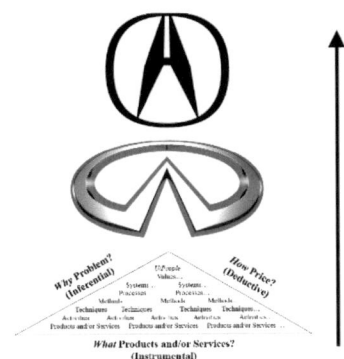

On Up, from Bottom to Top, *I/D Kata*; *Infiniti*® Logo; *Acura* ® Logo

*Toyota's Lexus*division's *Relentless Pursuit of Perfection* advertisement with its stacked champagne glasses was made at the same point in time that John Krafcik first coined the term '*Lean*' to describe *Toyota's Production System*. *Toyota's* luxury *Lexus* division demonstrated the concept of *Lean* in this advertisement by accurately inferring *why Lexus*' target customers had a problem with the cars currently in the market, theorizing *what* to precisely produce and deliver, and then assumptively deducing *how* to price those benefits in exchange for the greatest profit. That is *why* this ad made luxury car buyers want to purchase and pay *Toyota's* price.

Following the *I/D Kata* around like you see reflected in the *Infiniti* and *Acura* logos, your true-north value theory should intuit, infer and/or induce *why* consumers want to buy from *who* you discovered they are in the context of their real lives and existences. You abstract and then assume *why* consumers are from the problems they have to hypothesize *what* and *how* to re-produce meaningful goods and/or services that they will buy. You deduce *what* specific processes, methods, activities, instruments and people that consumers ought to be paying for to serve their highest values, which is *how* you make money meaningfully, as seen again here in detail for reference:

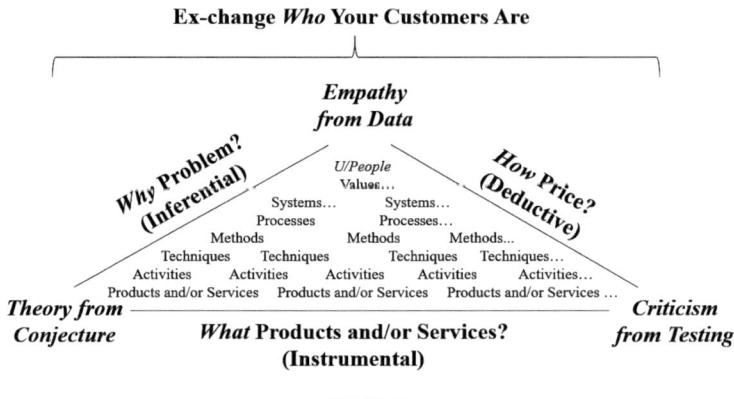

U/ P in the Air

For example, consider this *I/D Kata* as an analytical process from the perspective of providing business class airplane service:

1. ***Who* are an target customers?**: They are age 35-60 professionals *who* travel frequently and upgrade classes whenever their companies will pay for those seats;
2. ***Why* do they value travel?**: They value safely accomplishing business goals to earn a living to support their lifestyles and families; potentially meeting other business people and experiencing some prestige; possibly experiencing new or favorite places (i.e. fun); and hopefully escaping the daily grind a bit - those are their valuable problems;
3. ***What* do you produce that serves those values?**: They consume safe movement from one location to the next;

preferred member lines for prestige and convenience; lounges for mingling with other business travellers and working; and travel guides to encourage discovery at destinations;

4. ***How* do you price these products, services, methods, and systems to align them with *why* consumers fly so you may reach the greatest profit?**: An organization's value and profit gets built from the mechanics and pilots employed; the schedules kept; the destinations served; and the lounges staffed, which all contributes to the price charged. You ought to align the price you deduct from customers to exchange *who* they were as a person present in one location, with *who* they wish to become as the same person delighted to be at the destination of their choice.

Clearly though, airlines could do a lot more to serve *who* their business-class customers are and *why* they value business class travel to better monetize their becoming more of *who* their business-class customers want to be and become. Airlines ought to *Lean* right toward consumers to discover *who* their customers are and *why* they value being to most accurately re-produce *what* their target markets wish to further be and become, which is *well-travelled*, in a virtuous business cycle.

'*UP is always getting the window seat. And the isle.*' (©2016 Wheels Up Partners LLC)

Leaning up toward people's true-north values through the *I/D Kata* addresses both the source and satisfaction of consumers' demands. When both the source and satisfaction of *who* customers are and *what* they truly value dramatically changes, you circle a-round and call it a *business revolution* and change in business

89

paradigm.[156] In *Lean* terms, you call this, *Kaikaku*, which again, is a revolutionary improvement of a value stream to quickly create more value with less waste. Given how meaningfully a *Kaikaku* business revolution affects consumers' lives and existences, and an organizations' prospects for producing profits, take a moment to reconsider and reflect on *The Oxford English Dictionary's* definition of *Revolution*:[157]

Revolution • *(noun) Brit.* /ˌrɛvəˈl(j)uːʃn/, *U.S.* /ˌrɛvəˈluʃ(ə)n/:
I. A circular movement
II. Change, upheaval
III. Consideration, reflection

Consumers Are Always Right

> *New is easy. Right is hard.*
> - Craig Federighi, senior vice president of Software Engineering at *Apple Inc.* [a]
>
> ---
>
> [a] Sam Grobart, *Apple Chiefs Discuss Strategy, Market Share—and the New iPhones*, Bloomberg Businessweek (Sep. 19, 2013).

Clearly, you ought to religiously *Lean* an organization toward consumers' highest values by aligning *who* customers want to be with *what* an organization will provide throughout the *U/People* business model. Taking the *U/People* business model one step further: If you think of the *I/D Kata* in three dimensions at each level of an organization, you can see below a depiction of this parallel alignment on its side facing rightward, with the flow and pull of the

---

[156] As best explained by Thomas Kuhn in, *Structure* (1962); this relates to every customer-centric business framework that has ever been presented. Simply search for *customer focus business revolution* online at any point in time to learn more.

[157] *The Oxford English Dictionary*, Entry 164970 (accessed on Apr. 4, 2014).

I/D Katas running across each division of an organization's value stream. You can see again Auguste Rodin's, '*The Thinker*,' standing in for consumers on the right, *who* are themselves *Lean Thinking*, trying to energize and optimize their own lives and existences:[158]

<< (1) an organization infers *who* consumers are<<

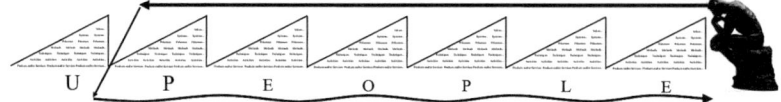

>> (2) an organization flows Matter and Energy represented by products and/or services up *U/People's* true-north value stream, which are pulled forward by customers' demand as a last step>>

Notice that when you focus on *how* right customers are by testing *what* they most value, each *I/D Kata* within an organization *Leans* so that its *y-axis* becomes the hypotenuse of each division. However, when the price charged customers is larger than the problem they perceive a business to be solving, then that organization *Leans* away from customers in the wrong direction, which is not good. As you know, in a *Lean HQ*, profit is its bottom line, but the aim of *Lean Management* is always toward customers. All organizations ought to likewise *Lean* philosophically not through false profits but rather toward consumers through the *U/People* business model to, *Uniquely/Profitably Energize and Optimize People's Lives and Existence*. A profit arises only as a consequence of keeping *U/People* in mind, rather than being self-caused by its pursuit, which is an important point many managers miss.

Thus, an organization's profit represents an oracle of business, to whom you refer when seeking consumers', and by extension an organizations', highest values. Jim Collins and Jerry Porras, in their 1994 book *Built to Last*, agreed with this when they quoted David Packard, one of the founders of the multi-billion dollar information

---

[158]This is a bit inspired by Modig, Niklas; Åhlström, Pär, *This is Lean: Resolving the Efficiency Paradox*, Kindle Loc. 1059, Rheologica Publishing (2014).

technology company *Hewlett Packard* (usually called *HP*), who said in 1960:[159]

> *I want to discuss why [emphasis his] a company exists in the first place. In other words, why are we here? I think many people assume, wrongly, that a company exists simply to make money. While this is an important result of a company's existence, we have to go deeper and find the real reasons for our being. As we investigate this, we inevitably come to the conclusion that a group of people get together and exist as an institution that we call a company so they are able to accomplish something collectively that they could not accomplish separately—they make a contribution to society, a phrase which sounds trite but is fundamental... You can look around [in the general business world] and still see people who are interested in money and nothing else, but the underlying drives come largely from a desire to do something else—to make a product—to give a service—generally to do something which is of value. So with that in mind, let us discuss why the Hewlett-Packard Company exists.... The real reason for our existence is that we provide something which is unique [that makes a contribution].*

Collins and Porras summarize this discussion by David Packard as:

> *[W]e see David Packard ruminating about what we can best describe as corporate existentialism, pondering about the philosophical, noneconomic 'reasons for being' of his company.'*

---

[159] David Packard, speech given to HP's training group on 8 March 1960, courtesy of Hewlett-Packard Company archives; Jim Collins and Jerry I. Porras, p. 56, *Built to Last* (2011).

You use the *U/People* business model to better discover a company's reason for being based on *what* you already know about *how* to make money and better discovering *who*, *why*, and *what*, and *how* you do in-turn. You may use the *U/People* acronym to aggregate and unify all the information you have access to beyond the ability of any single person to completely understand it in detail from wherever it may be produced in the world. Yet you may universally apply *U/People* in *Lean* fashion to decisions because the explanations it provides reach toward the Hellenistic levels of abstraction so you may deduce and measure *how much* something is really worth to the customers *who* you serve. To do this, you must balance the problem you ought to solve with the price consumers will pay to ex-change their disatisfaction for delight.

This form of pragmatic idealism satisfies consumers' normative and true values as well as possible within any given circumstances since intuition, inference and induction are pragmatic, while deduction is ideal for knowing *why* consumers will pay the price for products and/or services. Pragmatic idealism reflects the tension in the history of thought between rational, logical progress and moral and aesthetic value.

As Collins and Porras wrote in *Built to Last*, 'The dual nature—the pragmatic-idealism—of many of the visionary companies in our study. They are not purely idealistic; nor are they purely pragmatic. They are both.'[160] Collins and Porras go on to write, '*Marriott Corporation, like Motorola and HP, explicitly embraced the* **paradox of pragmatic idealism**,' [emphasis added][161] which means they strive to be perfect as far as they can be within the *Universe*. *Toyota* itself creates this paradox within its own organziation by requiring cooperation and coordination while encouraging independent thinking and action.[162]

---

[160] Jim Collins and Jerry I. Porras, *Built to Last*, p. 62 (2011).
[161] *Ibid.*
[162] *See generally*, Hirotaka Takeuchi, Emi Osono, Norihiko Shimizu, *The Contradictions That Drive Toyota's Success*, Harvard Business Review (Jun. 2008).

The business ideologies proposed in *Built to Last* and *Toyota* reconcile *what* really *is* with *what ought to be*. This tension between the pragmatic and the ideal, the *Yin* of all existential problems and *Yang* of prices representing perfect solutions, is the same philosophical problem described by the famous philosopher David Hume in the 1700s, which he referred to as the, *'Is-Ought'* problem. You will use *U/ People* from here on to attempt to reconcile the *Is-Ought* problem in your business *i/deô*logy, between intuitive, inferential, inductive and deductive methodologies, to energize and optimize an organization's own profitability.

> *There's this ongoing tension between the idealization and the concrete realizations, and we want both.*
> - Stephen G. Simpson, Research Professor, Vanderbilt University, regarding Yokoyama and Patey's proof resolving *Ramsey's Theorem for Pairs* [a]
>
> ---
> [a]Natalie Wolchover, *Mathematicians Bridge Finite-Infinite Divide*, Quanta Magazine (May 24, 2016).

L-Shaped Reflection of *What U / People* Value

In the chart below, you can see the horizontal alignment of *what U/ People* truly value across customers' value streams reflecting *who* customers are and *what* customers' demand to support themselves through an organization's people, functions, products and/or services in ex-change for large amounts of money. The money customers flow to an organization represents a transfer of legal rights to direct the consumption of other products and/or services, of other Matter and/or Energy, procured further up along the economic value stream.

Starting with consumers flowing demand as information to an

organization, an organization in-turn reflects that demand in *L* shaped fashion at the bottom of the *U* by sending products and/or services back to customers. The *L*-shaped logo of *Toyota's* luxury *Lexus* division as seen below demonstrates *how* an organization ought to *Lean* back toward its customers to reflect their demand, flowing products and/or services back up to them in the pragmatic pursuit of perfection:

(1) << In-formation flows from consumers' highest values

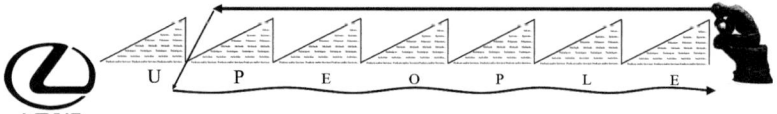

Toyota® Lexus® Division Value Stream Curve

(2) >> So customers may pull products and/or services back up their true-north value streams, serving their lives and existences

As an organization provides products and/or services in exchange for money, you might modify the above value stream to something curling into a six *6,* and eventually *Leaning* into something that looks like a sigma *σ*, as seen here in a *Lean Six Sigma /6σ*:

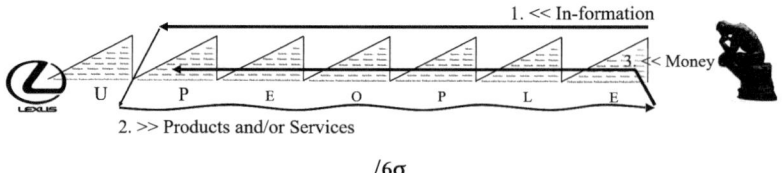

/6σ

As consumers think about your products and/or services, and you receive further feed-back, the re-production cycle begins to form a single figure eight, which when oriented on its side, is the symbol for infinity. This symbolic dynamic will become critical as you proceed to iteratively pursue customers' perfection /*σ∞*:

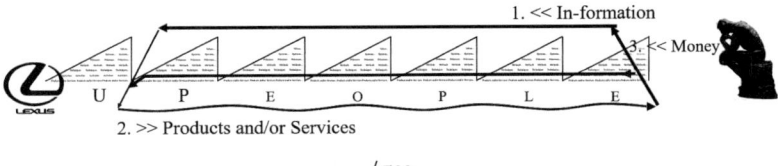

U/ *People* and Michael Porter's Value Chain

Michael Porter, a Harvard Business School professor and one of the most widely respected business strategists, created *what* he called the, '*Generic Value Chain.*' In a way, you can see the *U / People* value stream simply as a reformulation of Michael Porter's Value Chain from his seminal strategy book, *Competitive Advantage: Creating and Sustaining Superior Performance.*[163] Here is a diagram of Michael Porter's *Generic Value Chain* for an review and comparison of the departments of the *U / People* business model to Porter's own chart:[164]

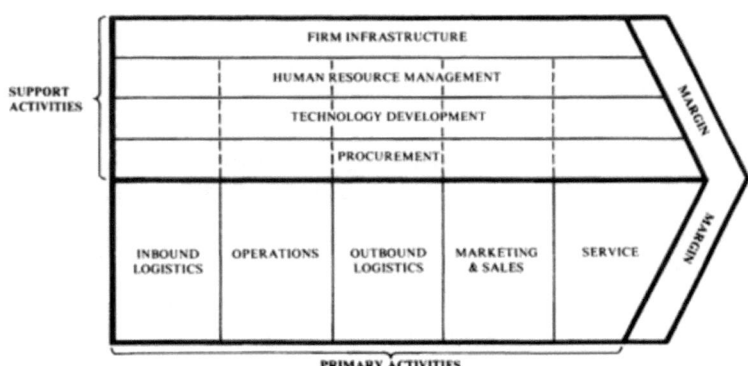

Michael Porter's *Generic Value Chain*

---

[163] Michael Porter, *Competitive Advantage: Creating and Sustaining Superior Performance*, Free Press (1985).

[164] *See generally*, Michael Porter, *Competitive Advantage* (1985).

The *U/People* business model aligns with the traditional business functions and academic disciplines of Porter's value chain by similarly providing an overall diagram of these concepts, breaking each out separately throughout this book's *Streams*. Margin in Porter's diagram as reflected above gets made by *what* an organization *Leans* toward in the balance of revenues minus expenses, or in *U/P* terms, the solution to customers over the economic cost to all people.

However, distinct from Porter's value chain, the *U / People* business model flows beyond the borders of an organization both to all economic activity and to the source of all true-north value from consumers' perspectives.[165] As you *Lean* philosophically, you advocate for *Lean* value streams based on customers' fundamental human needs at a deeper and more integrated level than even Michael Porter describes. Instead, you *Lean* philosophically at an intuitive, metaphysical and physical level in addition to all else you know about *who* people really are beyond Porter's *Generic Value Chain*. A *Lean* business *i/de*ô*logy* more specifically describes *how* you identify and exchange ideally normative and pragmatically personal true-north values for money.

By extending Porter's *Generic Value Chain* to its most extreme, you could instead perceive margin on the right side of the diagram as Matter and Energy flowing toward customers in the opposite direction as money, from which you would subtract the economic cost of producing the energizing material (*i.e.* products and/or services) provided from the left. As you learned from elementary physics, Matter and Energy (*ME* as in *MEaning*) are equivalent when units of matter are multiplied by the speed of light. Energy is simply matter actually (or with the potential) to move through spacetime due to universal, physical forces. For ease of reference, I may periodically refer to Matter / Energy just as *energy* moving upward along the crooked arrow of time.

---

[165] *Ibid.*

This idea around energy relates to a highly abstract, naturalistic perspective of business applicable to all people-oriented value theories like *Lean*.[166] From this perspective, utility is a direct or indirect satisfier of funda-mental human needs like Matter and Energy, and money is the contractual right to consume that Matter and Energy based on the social contract to which an organization is soundly bound. Since the term *Lean* biologically means the efficient use of Matter and Energy, I propose that is *why* people intuitively gravitate toward *Lean* as a universal business principle, which you now know as a progressive philosophy.

By uniquely/profitably energizing and optimizing people's lives and existences, you may abstract these concepts within your own business *i/deô*logy like within Porter's *Generic Value Chain*. You may also apply the *U / People* framework to an organizational strategy without over-simplification or over-complication in its execution. You may understand each word of the *U/ People* business model as an element of a *Lean* business *i/deô*logy from which you can re-generate metaphysical profit at each stage of the business cycle that eventually gets realized from the order-to-cash process that an treasury maintains, or as equity gains or dividends promised to stakeholders. Here again is a stack of *I/D Katas* pointing toward each other in the *U / P* organizational chart for you to review:

---

[166] For further background, *see*, Nick Gogerty, *The Nature of Value* , Kindle Loc. 611-612 (2014); Eric D. Schneider, Dorion Sagan, *Into the Cool: Energy Flow, Thermodynamics, and Life*, p. 60, University Of Chicago Press (2006); and A.J. Lotka, *Contribution to the Energetics of Evolution*, Proceedings of the National Academy of Sciences, 8: 147–151 (1922); and originally Boltzmann in 1886.

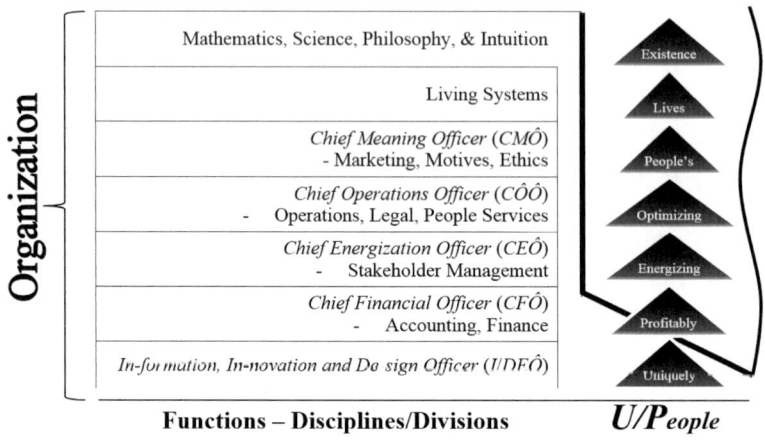

U/ People Organization Chart

Per the above, you may relate *Uniquely* to an *In-formation, In-novation and De-sign Officer*, the *I/DEÔ*; *Profitably* to an accounting and finance divisions through an *Chief Function Officer*, the *CFÔ*; *Energizing* to an primary stakeholder manager through an *Chief Energization Officer*, the *CEÔ*; *Optimizing* to an *Chief Optimization Officer*, the *CÔÔ*; *People's* to an meaningful marketing department through an *Chief Meaning Officer*, the *CMÔ*; *Lives* to consumers as a living systems that you support with products and/or services; and *Existence* to *why* you, organizations and customers are here and consume anything at all.

U/ P reverses the order of the *U/ People* acronym from top to bottom across its organizational chart. Through its *Streams* it first emphasizes that all true-north value starts with *who* you discover consumers are and *why* they want to buy as living systems through mathematics, science and intuition. Once you intuit, infer or induce *why* customers buy based on *who* they are, an organization must then *Lean* toward and attempt to deduce *what* increasingly tangible methods, techniques, activities, products and/or services will energize and optimize consumers' lives and existences for which they spend, buy and invest that will generate the greatest profit. From marketing to accounting and finance, money is the bridge between these activities. Along these lines, understanding consumers allows you to *Lean* an organization back up toward *what* consumers most value to create uniquely competitive advantages for a company to get over consumers' *pay us wall* so they will choose your products and/or services first.[167]

Like the *U / People* business model, this inverted corporate hierarchy is not new. In *Built to Last*, Collins and Porras also noted that Johnson & Johnson did the same in 1943 where they said,

> *J&J has periodically reviewed and slightly revised the wording of the credo since 1943, the essential ideology— the hierarchy of responsibilities descending from **customers down to shareholders** and the explicit emphasis on fair return rather than maximum return— has remained consistent throughout the history of the credo.*[emphasis added][168]

Like Johnson & Johnson, you will find that *U / People* rearranges the normal organizational chart to provide a *U/ People*-focused value system describing *what* you and stakeholders find most meaningful in philosophical, scientific, psychological and economic senses. *U / P* advances this rearrangement by placing the *CEÔ* in the middle of the *Gemba*, which is *Lean* parlance for the center of an organization, as shown in the *U / P* organizational chart above.[169]

You *Lean* People are *Philosophical*

For you as a business executive to understand *what* makes money meaningfully within a *Lean i/deô*logy, you must apply a true-north

---

[167]This being a combination of Edith Penrose's work and Michael Porter's generic value chain.

[168]Jim Collins and Jerry I. Porras, *Built to Last*, p. 58 (2011).

[169]M. Imai, *Gemba Kaizen: A Commonsense Low-Cost Approach to Management*, McGraw-Hill (1997).

value theory to all business functions in their purest forms from *how* the first principles of consumers' lives and existences *Lean* an organization up in that direction. Given that Peter Drucker said that marketing as well as innovation are the two primary entrepreneurial functions of business,[170] marketing naturally stands as a business discipline explicitly charged with both: (1) measuring consumer demand for products and/or services; and (2) communicating *what* innovative products and/or services get offered to best provide *what* customers want and need.

Marketing formally executes in both directions of the production cycle like a palindrome in-forming both *what* you produce and communicating the true-north value of products and/or services to customers in the end. Marketing may be perceived as just an advertising and promotion function, or it may be seen as the place of central analysis synthesizing production with demand, matching products and/or services to the appropriate consumers.

For an analogy that helps describe this marketing process through the business functions, consider an organization bowing toward customers based on *what* you provide them (/), and customers needfully *Leaning* back (\) to hand an organization money based on *who* they are. The intersection of an organization and consumers forms a fulcrum (/\), or delta, over the point of purchase in the center of the business cycle. This fulcrum stands between the production of products and/or services as structured Matter / Energy and consumers' willingness to ex-change money[171] over this *pay us* axis so it flows down in return.

For companies to most effectively focus on the end-goal of customer satisfaction, each employee in a business ought to at some level understand *why* customers decide to exchange money for *what* an organization offers over this *pay us* wall and *point of*

---

[170] Peter F. Drucker, *The Practice of Management*, p. 34, HarperCollins (2010).

[171] As will be seen later, this point of purchase may also be analogized to a *Penrose Triangle*, a purely hypo-thetical shape popularized by Lionel and Roger Penrose, due to the fact that people's demand has both tautological as well as non-tautological characteristics.

purchase. Modern, creative employees' greatest intrinsic motivation depends on their understanding *what* they contributed toward producing customers' *Lean* satisfaction, however indirectly, because they identify themselves as good, productive people. Employees' highest form of motivation will come from caring about improving customers' and stakeholders' lives and existences. While this can be highly intellectual, *U/P* is not dealing in vague aphorisms, but rather real science and philosophy supported by substantial evidence and the history of humankind.

By understanding employees' intrinsic motivation, you may in-turn provide them with the resources to understand *why* customers consume products and/or services as opposed to competitors'.[172] Once employees understand their contributions to customers' lives and existences, an organization as a whole can communicate more effectively throughout the business cycle to achieve business objectives for the short and long-term success of stakeholders and society-at-large.[173]

Everyone at an organization ought to be able to relate each of his or her daily tasks to the specific wants and needs of customers and think through *how* they, their departments and/or an organization may change to do so more effectively. Everyone ought to better understand *what* customers truly value, and be able to relate that insight across all organizational functions. While it is a truism that maximally effective businesses execute well on assessing consumers needs and delivering relevant products and/or services, I doubt that even executives at *Toyota Motor Corporation* would say their entire organization simultaneously *Leans* forward toward all consumers' needs and backward in applying that understanding to address those needs most profitably.

Some executives might say that not every employee in his or

---

[172] *See e.g.*, Kenneth Thomas, *Intrinsic Motivation at Work: What Really Drives Employee Engagement*, Berrett-Koehler Publishers, Second Edition edition (2009).

[173] The above fully recognizes that some goods and services may be considered anti-social, such as addictive products, but they act as exceptions to the general principle.

her organization needs such a heavy intellectual burden. However, to the extent this converged philosophical perspective can be effectively reduced to easy to grasp acronyms, it will benefit every employee's engagement and efficiency in serving customers. Furthermore, acronyms like *U/People* will help bring a *Lean* attitude to employees for intrinsic motivation and change management. A self-organized business *i/deô*logy you develop as you *Lean* philosophically ought to provide you with a common dialogue of fundamental true value that you ex-change with customers and all of an organization's stakeholders.

While a form of *Consumer Oriented Marketing* has been proposed and used for some time by marketers to measure and iterate the development and purchase of products and/or services based on consumers' express or implied demand,[174] I am proposing for an organization's business *i/deô*logy something far more expansive. I am proposing a business model and method for taking that customer centric analysis to the back of an office and forward into consumers' lives and existences. I want to make it easy for you to go to the furthest reaches of space, time and all intuitive speculation so you may make some sense of it all to apply it universally across all cultures for profit.

I am asking you to empathetically conjecture *who* and *why* customers and stakeholders are down to the first principles of knowledge, and then to test *what* and *how* an organization can re-generate that true value throughout the production cycle. I am asking you to use those insights to supplement and guide quantitative and qualitative business measurements to achieve it. From the top of this mountain of knowledge, you will see true value streams manifestly heading northward into blue oceans, extending toward a universal horizon, reaching a profit you never thought you would meet.[175]

---

[174]Read most any marketing book for this point, but as a suggestion, Philip Kotler, *Marketing Insights from A to Z: 80 Concepts Every Manager Needs to Know*, Wiley (2003).

[175]W. Chan Kim, Renee Mauborgne, *Blue Ocean Strategy: How to Create Uncontested Market Space and Make Competition Irrelevant*, Harvard Business Review Press; 1 edition (Feb. 3, 2005).

Products and/or Services > p and/or s > *paos* > *pay us* > *soap*.com

The products and/or services all organizations re-produce embody the *Lean* true-north value that floats upward. From here on, I will refer to *products and/or services* by the initialism, '*paos*' (sounds like, "pay us"). *Paos* represents all problem resolution, and thus all true-north value,[176] which may be easily remembered as, '*soap*,' spelled backward.[177] The term *paos* thereby abstracts all the structured Matter and Energy you and customers consider and connote with consuming. You can see the concept of *paos* synthesized in *Amazon.com Inc.*'s subsidiary, *SOAP.com*®, as shown by its logo here:

Paos sold at *soap.com* (© 2015*Quidsi, Inc.*)

You can also see the concept of *paos* within the *Purity* line of philosophy® brand *soap*:

---

[176]*I.e. paos* perfectly matches up with the formal use of money, per Yuval Noah Harari, 'Money is thus a universal medium of exchange that enables people to convert almost everything into almost anything else,' in, *Sapiens*, p. 179 (2014).

[177]*Paos* is the name of an ancient city in central Greece (37°51′N, 21°59′E) whose boundary and perimeter wall was triangle-shaped with a natural spring located north-east of it.

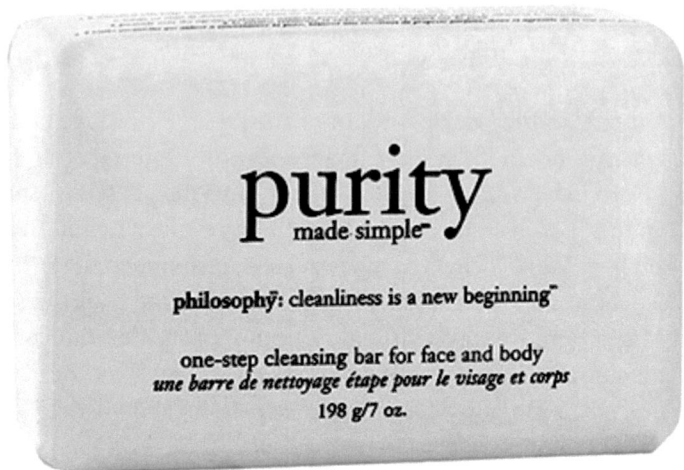

Purity Made Simple™ Philosophy® Soap (© 2016 *Philosophy, Inc.*)

People generally use the word *goods* to refer to *paos*, but perhaps after reading *U/P*, you may find that adjective *goods* presumptive of *paos*' true-north value. You almost certainly find now many *paos* are in fact *bad* products and/or services. This makes the term '*goods*' a bad one to use since we have so many alternative words available that scrub out value judgments, like *products and/or services* or simply '*paos*.'[178]

People often use the terms *good* and *best* as nouns, adjectives and value qualifiers, and economists often describe products as *goods* as well, which tells of their own mind-set in regards to economic value theories. So *U/P* does not refer to products as *goods,* so as not to falsely presume that a product and/or service is *good* when in fact it may be not. Referring to goods as *paos* also helps you launder any pre-concieved value judgments you may have about *how much paos* ought to cost. It allows you to freshly perceive and measure how

---

[178]Specifically, we wish to avoid the *naturalistic fallacy* described in Moore, G.E. Principia Ethica § 10 to the extent that just because we think something is good does not automatically make it so; see also Arthur N. Prior, *Chapter 1 of Logic And The Basis Of Ethics*, Oxford University Press (1949).

truly meaningful products and/or services are to people. It forces organizations to analyze whether they consider a product and/or service to be better than the status quo, or no *good* at all. All *good paos* must fundamentally re-produce true value within customers regardless of form. When you *Lean* philosophically, you consider *what* a *good* actually means to more effectively create truly valuable *paos* that customers really do consider to be and are in fact *good*, and for which customers willingly ex-change their money over the, *pay us wall*.

> *Towards the Good do all things tend,*
> *Many paths, but one the end,*
> *For naught lasts unless it turns Backwards in its course,*
> *and yearns To that source to flow again*
> *Whence its being first was ta'en.*
> – Boethius, De Consolation, IV, 6

Analyzing *why* customers buy from concrete actions[179] to first principles[180] in a business *i/deôlogy* requires you to understand *what* and *how paos* effects them. In a true-north value theory, you must understand the context that *paos* will get used in consumers' lives very well down to the scientific, philosophical and irrational levels.[181] You must know *why* in the confusing confluence of consumers' minds they decide to trade their money for *paos*. You must understand *what* they value and *how paos Leans* toward them with equal or greater potential effect on their lives and existences than *what* the money spent with you could have otherwise purchased from competitors. Thus, the wall over which you much reach to get

---

[179] *I.e. Instrumental Rationality.*

[180] *I.e. Epistimic Rationality.*

[181] For some background on the context of customers' intentional ignorance and irrationality, *see*, Brian Caplan, *Rational Ignorance versus Rational Irrationality*, KYKLOS, Vol. 54-2001-Fasc. 1, 3-26.

paos purchased with money guides all value streams in commerce.

Stream 2: Money & Economics as True Value

The following *Stream 2* will now take a brief tour through money and economics. *Stream 2* focuses on money as the common medium of value ex-change across the *Rubicon* of all true-north value streams. Money is the basic basis of self-organization for companies, and for the most part, society. Understanding money allows you to best understand *how* consumers better live and exist due to *who* they are and *what* they truly value. To get this straight, *Stream 2* will review some theories that will relate the various forms of philosophical, scientific, ethical and personally speculative values to money. *Stream 2* will put money in the proper academic, historical and economic context for developing a business *i/deô*logy as you move on *U/P*. It will also guide you through some caveats as to *what* makes money truly meaningful so you better understand *what* direction money takes to lead you to true-north value.

Stream 2: Money & Economics

Stream 2*A* 3 Report:

- Money represents the legal right and economic power to direct the flow of matter and energy in the form of goods and/or services
- Whether this right and power represents true-north value may be effected by creative financing, cognitive biases, bartering, substitutions, unpaid labor, legal regulations and criminal activity
- True-north value in business is the intersection of normative value, real value, and monetary value at consumers' point of purchasing a product and/or service
- Energy is the fundamental element of money's power, as evidenced by gold and silver being the direct and indirect color of sunlight, and cryptocurrencies being limited by the amount of energy necessary to produce them. All fiat currencies likewise reflect these fundamental power constraints that include governments' power to enforce them
- Consumers optimize their spending choices in neo-Darwinian fashion, constantly adjusting their budgets against their evolving survival needs
- True value measurement will never conform to Pareto-optimal models because of the above effects, and because optimization itself requires a degree of irrationality to stochastically discover *what* may be most beneficial in an open *Universe*

> *Money is the material shape of the principle that men who wish to deal with one another must deal by trade and give value for value.*
> Ayn Rand, *Atlas Shrugged*, p. 387 (1957).

In *Stream 2: Money & Economics*, I remove the veil covering *what* makes money meaningful by introducing the categories of truth value that *Lean* philosophically throughout *U/P*. This *Stream 2* describes *how* money represents the true-north value that is derived directly from the conditional fact of consumers' lives and existences, of *who* they fundamentally are. Going one step further, this *Stream* specifies that money, once received, gives you the contractual and economic power to re-direct the flow of Matter and Energy back to yourself, customers, organizations and/or society through taxes and philanthropy. To manage cash flows well, you must keep in mind that Matter and Energy move inversely to money, but that financial mechanisms like saving and investing create timing differences in that relationship.

In this *Stream 2*, I further relate the existential and physical value of money to *what* you commonly consider economics that in turn reflects itself in the money people pass along. Governments, businesses and investors quantitatively measure, model and report real value, but the secret meaning of money is found in truly normative value, which money on its face only partially reveals. In *U/P*, normative economic value relates metaphysically to customers' existences, and real value relates physically to customers' real lives. The sales, marketing, operations, *paos* development and strategy departments of organizations must understand these nuances of truly normative and real value to best support the prices charged for *paos*. Quite frankly, money is merely an after-throught to providing true-north value to consumers, which the best business people really get.

The prices charged to customers for *paos* support *who* customers are at the point of purchase by intersecting *why* they buy and *what* they most truly value at the other end of the value equation. Since money measures the relative tradeoffs customers make among all available choices for best energizing and optimizing their lives and existences, you must analyze these tradeoffs in the context of consumers' overall real needs and all possible substitutes they have available to energize and optimize themselves. '*Economics*' as an academic discipline is a fictional slot into which we place our ideas on *how* to do that best. Thus, separate and apart from money, real value is relative to a consumer's wealth, his or her alternative means of consumption and individual preferences – real value is not directly correlated with the price of a*paos* set in the market that business people often confuse as being *true value* to an individual customer. This makes money two steps removed from truly *Lean* value.

So while the philosophy of *Lean* generally defines *value* by how much money people willingly pay for some *paos*, money is iconic but not wholly representative of the true value of life and business.[182] As the well-respected Institute for Managerial Accounting recently confirmed, money is only the meta-language of economic activity and not the activity itself.[183] But to create satisfactory models, economists tend to equate relative prices wholeheartedly with the relative normative value of all life and business, even though we know that is not always the case. In economic terms, these relatives prices of *paos* at any given point in time are referred to as their *monetary* values. Start-ups and established companies usually describe the process of exchanging value for money as *monetization*, which can be seen here:

---

[182] Madhavan Ramanujam, Georg Tacke, *Monetizing Innovation: How Smart Companies Design the Product Around the Price*, Loc. 407, Wiley (2016).

[183] *Conceptual Framework for Managerial Costing*, Report of the IMA© Managerial Costing Conceptual Framework Task Force, loc. at http://www.imanet.org/PDFs/Public/Research/MCCF_2014.pdf (accessed on Dec. 20, 2014).

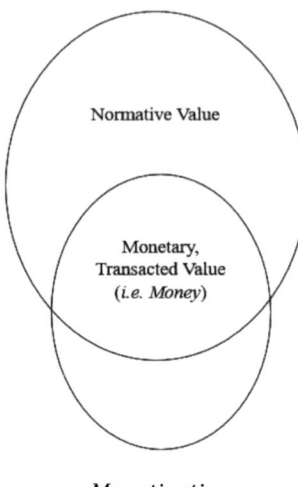

Monetization

Through this monetization, customers most abstractly experience the price of *paos* in terms of money as follows:

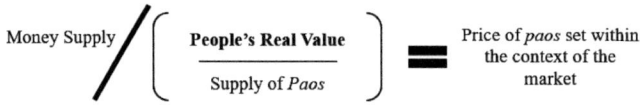

The Price of Paos

In this *Lean* equation, you can determine the money supply, the supply of *paos*, and the price of *paos* in the market to approximate *what* people find meaningful by analyzing *what* they bought for the most money within their budgets. That is easy. A much harder task is going the other direction and predicting *what* people most value before they actually make a purchase. The *I/DEÔs, CEÔs* and *CMÔs* in all established businesses and start-ups try to do this each and every day when they decide *what* to produce and *how* to market *paos*.

Lasting, true value depends on *normative value*, which is both an economic and philosophical term meaning the true value that ought to be. Let's define true value now in real value terms by saying that real value is the degree consumers believe, rationally or not, that *paos* will improve their lives and existences from their own personal perspectives. On the other hand, truly normative value is that which actually makes a constructive difference in consumers' lives and existences toward *what* ought to be within the *Universe*, which businesses attempt to objectively measure via real and monetary value.[184]

When considering normative true value and money, this side of common sense says that while monetization is a para-scientific litmus test and one of the highest forms of value exchange, not everything worth something can be bought and sold with money. Much of economics is actually studying a subset of all normative and/or real value that gets exchanged in market transactions that use money. Bartered exchange represents the transacted true value of *paos* without using money as a medium. For example, a significant portion of the global economy is in the form of unpaid, domestic labor from family members *who* freely work at home. Thus, money captures a large but incomplete portion of all transacted value as a lagging indicator of all that people find meaningful.

At the same time, as everyone well knows, not all money exchanged produces lasting, normatively true value. The real value for which businesses charge customers may possibly normatively affirm consumers' lives and existences, but not necessarily. For example, *eating* may be normatively valuable for consumers to get energy. But *eating junk food* because it tastes delicious is not necessarily normatively valuable in the long-run because other than the short-term Matter and Energy it provides, it harms consumers' bodies and may cause illness. Consumers' intervening factors like their physiological needs, their psychologies, ignorance or perverse economic

---

[184] Economists generally make a distinction here between *Normative Economics* or what is economically valuable without other structural constraint, and *Positive Economics,* or what is in fact deemed value in the context of real life; Nick Gogerty framed this notion as the '*Nature of Value*' perspective in, *The Nature of Value: How to Invest in the Adaptive Economy*, Kindle Loc. 212, Columbia Business School Publishing (2014).

incentives often create divergence between truly normative and real value.

Differences between normative and real value result because while normative value serves as the origin of all true-north value, consumers only experience normative value to the extent they really live and continually exist. While consumers only consider real value in the context of their real lives, their lives are only actually sustained by normative value as the only thing that truly matters. Any real value that does not align with normative value will eventually fail on its own accord because it does not positively reaffirm consumers' lives and existences.

However, consumers can sometimes be deluded by marketing *tricksters* to believe otherwise to produce short-term profits.[185] Consumers' psychology within the context of their lives and *who* they are mediates - sometimes well and sometimes not - between monetary, real and normative value. Just like the divergence between normative and real value within consumers' lives and existences, money as the narrative motif of true value may diverge symbolically from normative value. For example, do you know of time when something was paid for when neither normative nor real value was fully received? If you experienced that, then you or your organization transferred its money to the vendor, and along with it a right to direct the flow of a certain amount of Matter and Energy, but did not receive the normative or even real value bargained for in ex-change. The money the vendor received likewise did not represent either the normative or real value it ought to have as determined by the deal you made with the vendor. Thus, ideally, real value is synonymous with normative value, which becomes moments of true-north value realized by organizations and customers at the point of purchase during a meaningful exchange of money - but that does not always happen the way it ought.[186]

---

[185] This is (to sociologists) an allusion to Claude Lévi-Strauss and his identification of the *Trickster* persona mediating between life and death.

[186] This notion is inspired by Jan Carlzon, *Moments of Truth*, HarperBusiness (1987).

To illustrate these moments of true-north value, here is a chart and equation showing the values as realized by consumers at their points of purchase within the possibly circular nature of their lives and existences:

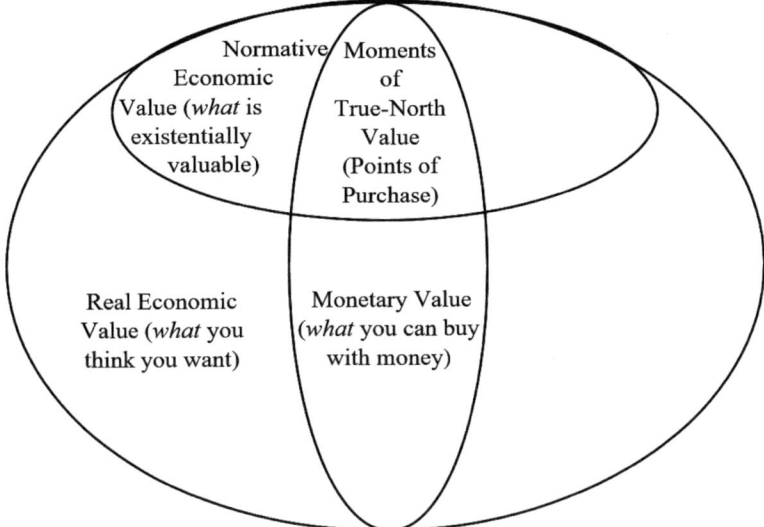

Normative value (non-monetary)
Positive real value (economic supply/demand)
*Money Value (monetary, actual prices)
_____

=*Moments of True-North Value at the Point of Purchase*

You can actually see these types of value realized in *why* consumers' demand flows down into organizations, and *how* customers pull out *what* organizations produce in return. Inversely, corporations pull their organizational in-formation from consumers, and flow the *paos* customers demand back up to them in *Takt* time. Organizations do this by comparing *what* customers demand to *what* organizations believe customers will value and purchase. They faithfully aligns their *paos* with *what* they believe customers normatively and really want to buy now. In ex-change, customers hope that the *paos*

114 Stream 2: Money & Economics

they pull from an organization matches *what* they normatively and really value to energize and optimize their lives and existences.

As described in *Stream 1*, you can see again below the pull and flow of these types of value reflected across the *I/D Katas* for all the *Streams* of the *U/ People* business model. In this picture, you can see *who* consumers are on the right and *what* they really value emerging from right to left in item (1). An organization ought to reflect *what* real value customers demand from left to right in *how* it produces and delivers *paos* to customers in item (2). In item (3), customers re-turn money in ex-change for *paos* across the point of purchase from right to left by faithfully believing that the *paos* will give them real (and hopefully normatively) true value:

(1) < < An organization observes *who* consumers are<<

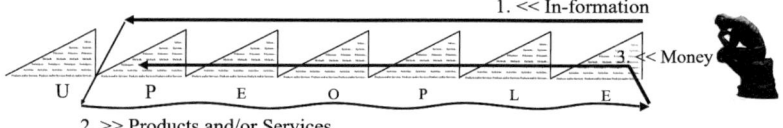

(2) >> **It understands *why* consumers truly, normatively value its *paos*>>**
(3) << **Customers re-turn money back to the business (or not) in ex-change based on their perception of the value generated for them, which is itself largely driven by the *paos*' normative value <<**

Ideally you want *paos* re-produced in (2) to provide the fundamental, long-term, normative value demanded in (1). You want *paos*' real and hopefully normative value to support the meaningful money you receive in (3), which completes the sigma σ around and through *U / People* as you can see above.

Since this intersection of normative, real and monetary value has the highest probability of being supported by society and law, an organization will be built to last if it focuses on this fundamental value ex-change well before reporting season. When people speak of producing *paos* that customers want, they largely mean providing *paos* that builds people upward toward *why* people are in a normative sense, as may be adjusted by the circumstances of consumers' real lives. That is the only legally and environmentally sustainable business value, as is fairly well recognized in this age by enlightened leaders, but is still extremely difficult for these leaders to justify and execute well in the face of short-term cost and competitive pressure from public markets.

The Brazilian *Real*

Brazil's economy during the 1980s and 1990s serves as a useful story to describe the relationship between normative and real value acting out within the secret life of money. During the last two decades of the 20th century, Brazil experienced hyper-inflation in all six of its currencies it issued during those decades. Prices in those currencies diverged significantly from the growth rates in real value based on the amount of *paos* Brazilians received in ex-change for their Brazilian currency. For example, Brazilians during that time might have been able to afford slightly more food for their families with *what* currency they earned, but that food cost many times as much in the prevailing Brazilian currency than they had on hand to pay for that food.

Inflation in Brazil became so extreme that in 1994 the Brazilian government began the *Real Plan*. Brazil began listing prices for basic commodities, like food, under the Real Plan in a fictitious currency called *Units of Real Value* or *URV* unlike the actual currency that was in effect. Brazil invented Units of Real Value so that its citizens could see *what* monetary value they could use for basic commodities if Brazil had a stable currency like URVs. These fictional Units of Real Value became so powerful in the minds of Brazilians that they eventually named their currency the *Real*, which is still used today in Brazil. If you wanted to, you can exchange U.S. Dollars (U.S.D. $) for Brazilian Reals (R $). Below is a picture of a Real with the Effigy of the Republic wearing a Roman-style crown of bay leaves and a phrygian liberty cap. Notice that she is *Leaning* toward people while looking back on the history of global commerce.

Brazilian Real(© 2015 Ministério da Fazenda Brazil)

Precious Metals and the Locke-Lowndes Debates

Going back farther in time, *The Great Recoinage of 1696* in England explains well *why* money functions mainly as a conduit for normative and positive real value within the channels of consumers' value streams. The English government in the late 17th century decided to maintain a fixed rate of ex-change between silver and gold. The great debates about this decision revolved around the writings of the famous philosopher John Locke, *who* is the same philosopher that conjectured many of the theories supporting the American Revolution during the 18th century. To decide this issue, John Locke engaged in the *Locke-Lowndes Debates* with William Lowndes about England's ex-change rate between its pound sterling and gold bouillon.[187]

The reason for the great debate regarding the silver/gold ex-change rate, was that England couldn't keep people from physically shaving off their silver coins to less than a full "pound" of sterling and passing them forward as if they were! The silver Pound's physical attributes literally diverged from the exchange value stamped on its face. Thus, the principle arguments of the *Locke-Lowndes Debates* revolved around two options for money: (1) whether money is best fixed to a specific physical element that people universally valued like silver or gold; or (2) whether money should be denominated in fictional units like the Brazilian Units of Real Value supported only by the government's willingness to take it for payment and support its true-north value in times of need.

Ultimately, John Locke successfully argued that the government should recoin its silver bullion to its official weight, making it truly represent *what* it purported to physically be. However, Locke's arguments for the true-north value of money within the *Lowndes – Locke Debates* actually settled very little because centuries of similar debates have followed. In case you didn't know, the book, *The Wonderful Wizard of Oz*, originally written in 1900 and filmed in 1939 with its Technicolor yellow brick road is an allegory of this debate. Dorothy's shoes were actually silver in the book, rather than ruby colored as they were in the movie, when she went to see the wizard of true-north value to get home to the golden wheat fields of Kansas that produce real food for people to consume.

The currency debates represented in *The Wonderful Wizard of Oz* culminated in meetings held in Bretton Woods, New Hampshire, United States after World War II. The meetings resulted

---

[187]John Locke, *Some Considerations of the Consequences of the Lowering of Interest and the Raising the Value of Money*(1691); John Locke, *Further Considerations Concerning Raising the Value of Money*(1697), wherein Mr. Lowndes's Arguments for it in his late *Report Concerning An Essay for the Amendment of Silver Coins*, are particularly examined; William Lowndes,*Report Containing an Essay for the Amendment of the Silver Coins* (1695); see also, J.R. McCulloch,*Classical Writings on Economics. Volume II. A Select Collection of Scarce and Valuable Tracts on Money*, Pickering and Chatto, London (1995).

in channelling the value of the U.S. dollar through gold like the Lowndes-Locke debates. However in 1971, the U.S. government shifted the value of its currency to its own full faith and credit, thereby making the U.S. Dollar a truly "fiat" currency for people to believe in, so that the U.S. government could artificially regulate its monetary supply beyond *what* was physically possible by exchanging commodities.[188]

From Gold to Fiat® (© 2015 U.S. Department of Treasury and Fiat Chrysler Automobiles NV)

Despite the U.S.'s and other currencies becoming "fiat" in modern times so governments can manipulate the money supply, gold and other precious metals still form the standard, physical "thing" that many governments hold in reserve to support the full faith and credit people have in those currencies. Investors likewise still hold precious metals to maintain the value of their investments during times of crises. After centuries of debate from Lock-Lowndes to *The Wonderful Wizard of Oz*, precious metals still stand as the most universal means of exchanging and storing true, economic value, and are *what* the U.S. Dollar would depend on if necessary. This begs the fundamental question:

---

[188]*See again*, John Locke, *Some Considerations...* (1691); and also John Maynard Keynes, *1. The Classification of Money* in *A Treatise on Money*, New York, Harcourt, Brace and company (1930).

Why do customers use precious metals consistently as the standard medium of common currency for all Lean value?

They can sell precious metals for use in jewelry and dental fillings. Some electronics and chemical applications use them. However, in regards to the vast majority of the needs for consumers' lives and existences that they normatively and really value, gold is an odd choice. Gold cannot be eaten other than in some liqueurs and chocolates as far as I know. Unless they were King Midas or Scrooge McDuck, consumers couldn't possibly own enough gold to clothe or shelter themselves.

So, *what* is the normative and positive real value of precious metals that generally makes them the most popular basis for real money? Consider the not very subtle coincidence that gold is the direct color, and silver the indirect color, of sunlight. Both symbolize consumers' funda-mental source of energy, which consumers subconsciously equate with beauty and ethics, aka '*Axiology.*' Consumers' lives and existences depend on capturing and converting Matter and Energy to live and exist with real and normative value, and precious metals simultaneously represent both.

With Money Comes Great Power

Thus, the very concept of *making money* is quite strange since it's generally not used for anything but ex-changing value and meaning. *Who* or *what* makes money a reliable source of meaningful, *Lean* value for this ex-change? Can you can make money simply by digging precious metals out of the ground? Can governments produce money merely because they enforce ex-change value? Can a computer programmer make money meaningfully by trading a digital currency whose scarcity is in part dictated by the amount of computational energy required to make it, as is the case with *BitCoin*?

Since precious metals can only be mined to a limited extent, and only governments can make fiat money literally at will, modern business people clearly do not *make money* in any real sense, but rather, they make money truly valuable instead. An organization only makes money valuable by exchanging it for *paos* that supports customers' lives and existences. People only *make money* meaningfully valuable by transacting with it in this transcendental exchange. This is the classic question discussed by John Locke, John Maynard Keynes, and many other philosopher economists as to whether governments give currency true-north value in commerce.

Generally, these mainstream economists agree that, in the long run, when you disconnect the funda-mental concept of money from any use of the commodity on which money's true value may be based, money's true-north value only gets made from the usefulness of the *paos* exchanged for it – a usefulness measured by the extent it uplifts *who* and *why* consumers are toward *what* they most value and *how* they live and exist.

However, in the short run, because prices coordinate *when*, *where*, *how* and *how much* people work, buy and trade, the quantity of money and the manipulation of financial instruments like interest rates really affect *how* consumers perceive the value of the *paos* they consume. Denominations of money attempt to accurately symbolize this perceived value nonetheless.

Customers in an open economy ultimately make currency have meaning by trading, lending and/or investing it in ex-change for *paos* to live and exist. This in-turn allows customers to some extent use money to measure the real and normative value that *paos* provides. On the flip-side, organizations make money valuable by solving problems that help people live and exist in normative and real value terms. Outside this customer-producer relationship, society measures an organization's worth by *how much* currency customers exchanged for its *paos*. The net volume of this exchange determines *how much* right an organization has to re-distribute power throughout society, which is what society truly adores.

At the highest level of this discussion, not accounting for the many valid qualifiers in *how* things occur in the *real economy,* customers measure an organization's normative and real value with the money they give to it. Thus, from a basic business perspective, people largely make money by affirming other people's lives and existences to a greater and greater degree. Money gets *made* in the economy through this process to the extent that each person's life is in fact improved in normative value terms. Real wealth gets made in the knowledge of the difference between *what* was, is, and *ought* to be. This affirmation thereby imbues money with ever increasing real value because people's lives and existences become increasingly sophist-icated with its ex-change.

Cash flowing through the economy makes money meaningful in upward fashion through customers' specific wants and needs to live and exist. Even financial services create normative value through saving, lending, risk-shifting, and investing by altering the time and division by which people consume energy, thereby helping them become upwardly mobile within the cardinal order of the value stream. This economic value stream, which is the ever increasing volume of ex-change of money for more *paos*, makes money have true value as customers' lives become im-proved by consuming more structured Matter and Energy to further exist in the real world. Thus, customers' standard of living gets measured in-part by the flood of money ex-changed overall.

Evidencing the physical origin of true-north value represented by money, even before John Locke first used *Currency* to mean money, *Currency* simply meant *run or flow* in plain English. [189] Locke applied the term *currency* to the units of *cash* or *money* to further emphasize the flow of Pound sterling silver and gold Bouillon though the economic value stream for the sole purpose

---

[189]Online Etymology Dictionary (2015) http://www.etymonline.com/ (accessed Mar. 12, 2015).

of normalizing the standard ratios of exchange.[190] In this way, money flowed from Locke's perspective similar to *how Toyota Motor Corporation* perceives its *Lean* production processes flowing to *Toyota's* customers in response to their pulling demand, making *Toyota's* customers rain money back down on the company in return. Thus, turning back to the original question, customers make money meaningful by ex-changing it for *paos* that makes the biggest positive difference to *who* they believe they are and wish to be. People refer to this market as the *real economy*.

Caveats to Measuring Money

Despite money's surprising effectiveness in measuring the wealth of true-north value captured within all *paos*, the process of making money meaningfully through a business *i/de*ô*logy* within an *HQ* requires you to consider some caveats to *how* money making actually works in the real world. I will now outline three major caveats to the ability of prices to semiotically reflect nominal and real value as:

- *Supply and Substitutes;*
- *Barter and Self-service; and*
- *Other Market Distortions.*

(1) Supply, Substitutes and the Warhol Paradox

Money's ability to measure *what* consumers truly value in *Lean* terms depends on:

- The degree to which all customers believe all *paos* exchanged for money in commerce will energize and optimize their lives and existences;

---

[190] *Ibid,Currency (n.) 1650s, 'condition of flowing,' from Latin currens, present participle of currere 'to run' (see current (adj.))*; in 1699 John Locke added a sense of flow to the *circulation of money.*

- The relative abundance of all *paos* that can be bought with money to serve customers' physical, emotional, and spiritual wants and needs, which more fundamentally, energizes and optimizes customers' lives and existences; and
- The availability of substitutes (like barter or using one's imagination for entertainment), for the satisfaction that all *paos b-ought*with money delivers to all customers.

To the extent customers believe that certain *paos* with limited substitutes is sufficiently abundant to energize and optimize their lives and existences, they must then set their budgets and spending priorities for that *paos* accordingly amongst everything else they need and want to consume. Just like you, consumers estimate *how paos* will affect their lives and existences and will adapt their consumption priorities accordingly.

Consumers adapt their spending priorities to best optimize and energize their lives and existences each time they consume. Consumers behave like the finches on the Galapagos Islands, which optimize their beak sizes through successive re-generations to reach more food and water and thereby energize their lives and existences. Like consumers, Finches on the Galapagos Islands right-size their beaks (i.e. consumers adapt their spending priorities) to consume the right amount of food and water (i.e. consumers adjust their spending budgets) to energize and optimize their species.[191]

---

[191]The finches of Galapogos Islands are also known as*Darwin's Finches* in reference to his notation of such birds in, Charles Darwin, *Journal of Researchers into the Natural History and Geology of the countries visited during the voyage round the world of H.M.S. Beagle*, revised edition, p. 403-420, Henry Colburn (1845).

Darwin's Finches of the Galapagos Islands (1845, Public Domain)

However, while some *paos* may be really necessary to people's lives and existences, like food and shelter, a critical *paos* may be in such abundance that customers need to exchange very little money in order to obtain sufficient quantities of it, like water. Water itself exemplifies well the relationship of transaction prices to normative value given that people need water to live, and nothing can substitute for water. Consumers must generally exchange something to get drinkable water because unlike air or sunshine, water usually gets monetized, though we might want to pay (pray for?) the Matsés to people maintain the Amazonian rain forests so we all may continue breathing oxygenated air in the future. However, people generally assume that water will always be available at low cost, even though each person's life and existence generally depends on other people to provide it consistently.

Should water become extremely scarce, assuming water was only available on an open market without governmental intervention, consumers would be forced out of necessity to ex-change all of their money for it to the extent they needed more of it to live. Water at that point would be far more valuable in normative and real value terms than any money in a person's possession, as if an alchemist had turned water into gold. Water can thus be considered one of the most disproportionately inexpensive products that consumers purchase relative to its normative and real value to *who* and *why* they are.

The famous economist Adam Smith, while chairman of the Moral Philosophy Department at Glasgow University, recognized this dynamic in what has come to be called his *Paradox of Diamonds and Water.*Adam Smith first described the seemingly contradictory and divergent values between water that people need to live, and diamonds, that consumers do not need in any immediate sense to support their lives and existences. Adam Smith wrote that the prevailing price of water does not reflect the extent that consumers need it to live and would pay for it if really needed.[192]Adam Smith used the terms *value in use*and *value in exchange* to differentiate between these differences in normative, real and monetary values.[193]

In economics terms, the relatively low market price of water tells you nothing about the *price elasticity*of water, or *what* consumers would pay for water should they really need it. Consumers' biological needs in relation to their existences tell you that water would have one of the lowest price elasticities of demand, or in other words, customers would generally consume the same amount of water even when its price changed.[194]Water's price elasticity of demand tells you everything about its true value to consumers' lives and existences in real value terms and *what* consumers would be

---

[192]In 1776, Adam Smith wrote, *An Inquiry into the Nature and Causes of the Wealth of Nations*, wherein he discusses the concepts of value in use and value in exchange, and notices how they tend to differ: '*What are the rules which men naturally observe in exchanging them [goods] for money or for one another, I shall now proceed to examine. These rules determine what may be called the relative or exchangeable value of goods. The word VALUE, it is to be observed, has two different meanings, and sometimes expresses the utility of some particular object, and sometimes the power of purchasing other goods which the possession of that object conveys. The one may be called 'value in use;' the other, 'value in exchange.' The things which have the greatest value in use have frequently little or no value in exchange; on the contrary, those which have the greatest value in exchange have frequently little or no value in use. Nothing is more useful than water: but it will purchase scarcely anything; scarcely anything can be had in exchange for it. A diamond, on the contrary, has scarcely any use-value; but a very great quantity of other goods may frequently be had in exchange for it.*'

[193]*Ibid.*

[194]Technically, price elasticity of demand is a measure used in economics to show the responsiveness, or elasticity, of the quantity demanded of a product or service to a change in its price, *ceteris paribus.*

willing to pay you for it if necessary. Water is core to consumers' being and thus its demand is tremendously inelastic from a true-north value perspective.

In contrast to water, diamonds largely get demanded because they are both extremely reflective of sunlight and are abundant enough to be widely used for ceremonial purposes, such as for weddings and other gifts. And yet diamonds are kept scarce enough by the diamond industry to command high prices, even now when we can artificially manufacture diamonds in laboratories. I speculate that if only one diamond was ever found, its monetary value would be less than the prices for large diamonds today because nobody would be able to relate it to the one they, their loved ones or ancestors had on their fingers, or associated it with the religious ceremony of marriage. Thus, the diamond industry at-tempts to maintain an optimal level of scarcity for diamonds with there being neither too many nor too few of them, so the *De Beers* cartel maintains an optimally sloping supply curve in order to maximize the prevailing price of diamonds that you pay to them in ex-change for love.

Substitutes, on the other hand, work in tandem with supply to mit-igate the extent to which money accurately reflects the normative and positive real value of *paos* to consumers in the context of their real lives.[195] Consider this alternative. If water became scarce, its exchange value would exceed diamonds at some point, becoming higher than diamonds ever would as supplies of both diamonds and water reached zero. We can see some hypothetical demand curves for diamonds and water here as available quantities increase or decrease:

---

[195]The paradox of water and diamonds may be found in, *Adam Smith: An Inquiry into the Nature and Causes of the Wealth of Nations*, Chapter IV. *Of the Origin and Use of Money*, (1776); *see also*Scott Gordon, *The Scottish Enlightenment of the eighteenth century, History and Philosophy of Social Science: An Introduction*, Routledge (1991).

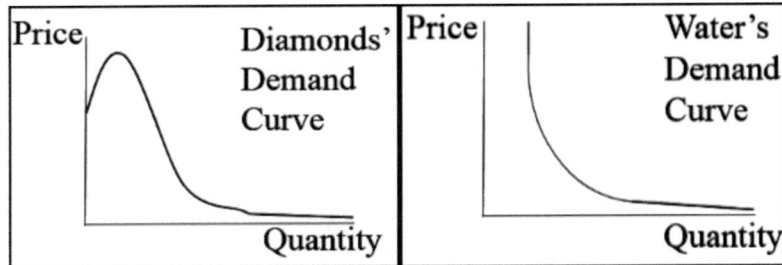

Diamond and Water's Demand Curves

To illustrate the difference between use and exchange value in the philosophy of *Lean*, suppose that customers consume a liquid that provided every benefit of water as a perfect substitute.[196] The prevailing market price of water and the price elasticity of demand against a changing price of water would be effected by the supply and resulting price of that other liquid in relation to water. Consumers' demand curve for water would change because they now had a substitute to quench their thirst.

For one other comparison of this diamond-and-water paradox for a business *i/deôlogy*, I ask you to think about the differences in the relative monetary, real and normative true value between the Andy Warhol painting, *Campbell's Soup Can (Tomato)*, Lot 12, Sale 2355 (1962) that sold for $9,042,500 USD recently at a Christie's auction house,[197] and a picture taken by me of a Campbell's soup can you might find at a local grocery store selling for $1 USD.

---

[196] Alludes to Hilary Putnam's 1973 '*Twin Earth*' thought experiment in his paper, *Meaning and Reference*, in, *Philosophical Papers, Vol. 2: Mind, Language and Reality*, Cambridge University Press (1973).

[197] http://www.christies.com/features/2010-october-andy-warhol-campbells-soup-can-tomato-1022-1.aspx (accessed Jun. 2, 2011).

128 Stream 2: Money & Economics

Andy Warhol, *Campbell's Soup Can (Tomato)*(1962) (Fair Use); and *Campbell's Soup Can I Bought at the Store*(Photo Credit: Me taken in my kitchen)

- *If food suddenly became very scarce, how many cans of Campbell's Tomato Soup do you think you would be able to buy in ex-change for Warhol's, "Campbell's Soup Can (Tomato)"?*
- *How important is each to who and why you and consumers are?*

(2) Barter and Self-service

As a second caveat to the meaningful money making process that you should consider for a *Lean* business *i/deô*logy, consumers only serve a certain proportion of their wants and needs in the process of purchasing the *paos* you sell them. In other words, even in well-developed market economies, customers often serve their normative and positively real values by bartering for *paos* with other people without using any money, just like *how* members of a family constantly re-negotiate *who* does which household chores without paying one another for the favor. Consumers may serve their wants and needs through their own thoughts and labor, and directly exchange their own *paos* with others through barter rather than with money. While neither barter nor consumers' own thoughts or labor involve financial transactions, these activities that do not involve money effect the price of *paos* consumers will pay you. Barter either substitutes for or displaces the *paos* you sell due to the limited time people have to consume within their day-to-day lives and existences.

Books like, *U/ P: Lean Business Philosophy*, exemplify this second caveat well by illustrating the limited ability of prices to measure the normative and positively real value of books. Consumers can often trade or lend physical books to other people instead of exchanging money for the same books from sellers. Also, consumers may write their own books, which would take a lot of the time they would have had to buy and read more books - I assure you. Also, the satisfaction consumers receive from reading - the normative and positively real value received - largely comes from the intersection of their imaginations, knowledge, memories, and intentions with the books' contents, which can only be truly determined after they buy and read a book.

Books' prices do not effectively capture all of this true-north value to consumers since they may have a much richer set of experiences related to one book rather than another due to their life experiences, demographics, educations, interests and personalities - essentially all that affects *who* and *why* consumers are. The price of a book may only reflect the normative and positively real value of that book in the aggregate if all people *who* read such book and then decided that reading experience was worth a specific price to pay among everything else they could have bought with the same amount of money. However, book's prices, like for nearly all other *paos*, do not adjust themselves in retrospect based on each customer's individual circumstances and experiences from consuming them.

(3) Market Structural Distortions

The third caveat to measuring normatively and positively real value by prices paid considers factors such as monopolies, governmental interventions, structural market inefficiencies, and crimes. These factors often distort the connection between normative and positively real value, and the money exchanged for business' *paos*. For example, if you found that to do business someone asked you for a bribe, the "price" of the *paos* you charged would then exceed that which would otherwise be set on balance by the market if you wanted to keep the profits the same. On the other side of this analysis, if someone stole *paos* from an organization, it would force the exchange of *paos* for less than *what* would have otherwise been exchanged in a free market, which may drive up costs for all other customers. Likewise, addictive *paos* like nicotine nearly eliminates customers' ability to decide whether consuming that *paos* best energizes and optimizes their lives and existences once they identify themselves as being a smoker. All these factors keep the markets in which you operate from accurately reflecting consumers' purely normative and real values.

Structural inefficiencies inherent in certain tax codes, political processes and financial institutions – each hopefully designed to combat other ills – inhibit the free operation of the economy in a way that would allow prices for *paos* to more accurately reflect the normative and positive real value that customers consider *paos* having in their lives and existences. For example, financial institutions and governmental intervention, while possibly useful, can also distort the ability of prices to measure *what* people value accurately. The collusion of government incentives and financial engineering, such as in the most recent global housing bubble, exemplify this point. Further, some industries like utilities tend to structure themselves into monopolies or oligopolies, either naturally from economies of scale, through collusion, or by governmental edict (think public utilities), thereby affecting prices through the monopoly's or oligopoly's purchasing power.

While not by any means exhaustive, all three of these major caveats exemplify the limited extent you can say that money's nominal *value* exchanged for a *paos* reflects its normative and positive real value to consumers' lives and existences. You must understand these limitations to the process of *making money* truly meaningful to reach the greatest profit in the philosophy of *Lean*, unless you are a crook, which you are not.

Economics throughout history has addressed all of these subjects in some form or another, some of which you could find by procuring any economics textbook. I only mention these caveats to re-emphasize how limited money prices are in identifying *Lean* normative and real value. Without prices, you must still understand *what* ultimately guides consumers' consumption of *paos* that in-turn leads to an organization's functional profitability and is *what* makes CFÔs happy. I will now further explain the secret life of money as follows, due to money's central importance in the philosophy of *Lean*, people's notion of *value* and *how* money gets made meaningfully.

*U/ People's*Money Veil

Economists call these caveats about prices' ability to measure true-north value a *Money Veil*. This money veil presents a significant problem with accurately pricing *paos* and optimizing *what* people will buy. Prices will increase or decrease in the long run in response to changes in supply and substitutes serving consumers' fundamental human needs, and changes in the supply of money, holding all else constant. *Why*? Because prices at their best merely reflect the amount of normative value you provide that supports consumers' lives and existences, or in other words, that supports *who* and *why* consumers are. The money veil never ends because the only way you can measure the units of normative, true-north value you produce is by dividing the infinite *Universe* by the finite number of *People* you serve, which leaves you endlessly speculating *what* units of *paos* are truly worth. As our equation earlier in this *Stream 2* describes, measuring the value of money simply sub-divides the universal demand to live and exist among all people currently buying and selling *paos* to do so, which is the only value that truly matters for making money meaningfully.

Critically, the philosophy of *Lean* as described in much of this *Stream 2*and the balance of U/P brings this fundamental economic utility back into the business conversation like '*The Lean Startup*' did with empiricism. U/P aligns true-north value with the rigorous test of normative and real value on their own terms. As demonstrated in the paragraph above, units of true-north value (i.e. *Universe / People*) may not be measured in discrete units, but only through degrees of confidence as to *what* those units either may be or are not. Thus, however useful neoclassical economic models might be with their presumption of Pareto optimality neatly factoring *what* all people prefer, they do not explain *how* the *Lean* value that those models attempt to measure actually gets made, and thus *how* the greatest prôfit gets reached in an infinite *Universe*, because they do not account for*what* matters most, which rationality does not entirely contain.[198]

Off to See the Wizard

I will now further elaborate on the foundations of money's use in commerce for you to get more meaning out of it regardless of how difficult it might be to measure money's true worth. Most plainly, money has both tangible and intangible qualities. Tangibly,

---
[198] *E.g.* for the genesis of this line of thinking, *see,How Vienna produced ideas that shaped the West*, The Economist (Dec. 24th, 2016).

money assumes the form of coins, paper, or other commodities like precious metals. Intangibly, money forms accounting entries, and more recently, digital certificates like *BitCoin*. These digital currencies exemplify money that is disconnected from a tangible commodity like gold. *BitCoin* takes money to the fictional extreme, whose only use and support is its ability to facilitate exchanges of the contractual right to receive energizing *paos* – ex-changes that consumers somehow find meaningful to their lives and existences. Whether virtual currencies will succeed in the long-run given that they lack deeply rooted customs, governmental support, widespread acceptance as payment, and carry technological risk, remains to be seen.[199]

However, the only difference between a digital currency like *Bit-Coin* and a governmentally issued fiat currency like the U.S. Dollar at this point in time, is that a government enforces its own currency's use as legal tender, accepts it as payment for taxes and government fees, has substantial reserves of tangible commodities like gold, and supports it with a military if necessary – most digital currencies have none of these qualities.[200] These qualities of governmental fiat currency vastly differ from privately created digital currency disconnected from any legal or military enforcement or commodity with normative and positive real value like gold, diamonds or water.[201]

Still, even fictional digital currencies have some normative and positive real value, which they share with fiat currency. First, they create economic flexibility by allowing efficient online storage of true value that does not require any intermediaries like governments or private institutions. They provide the same psychological benefit of possessing money by providing a sense of security, opportunity or superiority. They improve on barter by keeping

---

[199] *Digital Currencies: The BitCoin Debate*, BusinessInsider.com (Dec. 2013).
[200] Thomas Piketty,*Capital in the Twenty-First Century* , p. 105, Harvard University Press (2014).
[201] *Ibid*, p. 47.

records, facilitating value comparisons, and allowing saving, credit, investment and speculation. But all money, in the *form* of digital currencies or otherwise, mainly serves as a conduit for normative and real value supporting *who*, *why*, *what* and *how* consumers are.

In contrast to digital currencies, people trade things that they can feed, shelter or clothe themselves with in ex-change for precious metals so they may see the gold, silver and other beautiful colors they present. Precious metals serve people's need for beauty, and for relating to other people by showing them off as status symbols. Also, the transferability, natural scarcity, and permanence of precious metals supports their longevity and ubiquity as a *Lean* , global medium of normative and real value around the world.[202]

Funny Money

You can see further how funny money really is by looking at the seemingly counterintuitive relationship between currency, inflation, and productivity. Assume that a generic product costs one Unit of Real Value today, and new technology suddenly allows you to produce twice as much tomorrow with the same Matter and Energy. Keeping all else constant, the product's price in URV would decrease in half. With this increase in productivity, holding all else constant, the price of the product has achieved disruptive deflation. People could then use their extra money to consume other *paos* besides that generic product to better fulfill all of their wants and needs supporting *who* and *why* they are.

However, in the real world, while organizations constantly increase their productivity with new technology, you generally experience inflation in the *paos* for which there are no substitutes, such as certain commodities like electricity. Despite our constantly re-producing more, you generally exchange more money for commodities

---
[202]Denis Dutton, *The Art Instinct: Beauty, Pleasure, and Human Evolution* (2009); *see also* Denis Dutton, *A Darwinian Theory of Beauty* , TED Talks (Feb 2010); and Yuval Noah Harari, *Sapiens*, p. 173 (2014).

like milk, rice, corn and water that does not change in character.[203] *Why* should that be when we are producing most of these things more efficiently with less labor? The answer generally lies in understanding that over the course of history, governments increase the quantity of currency in their economies either by acquiring precious metals or by producing fiat currency in various proportions to the demand for and supply of *paos* in their economies. Countries' treasuries and central banks attempt to actively *make* enough money to control inflation in response to changing productivity, populations and demand, among other factors. But again, *why* ?

Nations generally try to create some inflation to incentivize people to spend money sooner rather than later. By creating some inflation in tension with the deflation of disruption, people generally get more for the same amount of money today than they would tomorrow, which encourages consumers to spend rather than save. Deflation dis-incentivizes people from spending, which leads to what economists call the "deflationary spiral" leading to a vicious cycle of reduced spending. Thriving economies must encourage people to trade currency for the *paos* they think will best satisfy *who* and *why* they are. The economy overall would decrease if everyone excessively waited to spend. The complete reasons for central banks' attempts to maintain an inflation rate in the prices of *paos* are beyond the scope of this book, but this illustrates governments' manipulation of the ratio of currency and normative and real value being provided, and the divergence between prices and productivity.

Traditional, neoclassical economists and their books model in great detail the regulation of the supply of currency in equilibrium, and the tying and decoupling of currency to precious metals such as gold along with rising populations and living standards. In the end though, for purposes of this book and funda-mentally understanding *what Lean* meaning money has, you should understand *what*

---

[203] *See*, Jesse McKinley, *With Farm Robotics, the Cows Decide When It's Milking Time* , New York Times (Apr. 22, 2014).

fiat currency is in relation to those things with material value, like precious metals. In the long run, setting aside any of the relatively minor practical uses of precious metals, the quantity of money really does not matter but for people's using prices to coordinate the relative trade-offs they must make between their options to consume *paos* to better live and exist within the context of *who* and *why* they think they are and want to become. Ultimately, customers don't care about the cost of *paos*, but rather only *what* opportunities they can realize or threats they can diminish with all the money they have at any given point in time to energize and optimize their lives and existences in relation to all other consumers in the marketplace. Prices only determine *what* solutions consumers must trade to best resolve their problems within their given situations, and if a price drops they simply shift that calculus along the demand curve.

However, as the famous economist John Maynard Keynes pointed out, even if money was just a medium of exchange, meaning very little by itself, in the long run, prices affect many consumers' short-term decisions, and thus indirectly impact the economy in the short and long term.[204] The Austrian economist Friedrich Hayek famously showed that people used the prices of *paos* to coordinate *what* they bought across the economy, which is *how* prices change people's behavior in the short run. Central bankers therefore adjust their short-run policies about money to align money's value with *what* consumers really need to better live and exist.

Traditional and Modern Measurements of Money

Mainstream neoclassical economics, which has done as much as any field to try to measure and quantify the true value of money as

---
[204] Keynes, *General Theory*, p. 36.

utility[205] or *revealed preferences,*[206] has generally abdicated the task of understanding the foundation of money's true value to others. Neoclassical economists reasonably decided that they could not peer into consumers' minds with any precision given the complexity of people's thoughts, emotions and actions in the context of their real lives.[207] Instead, mainstream, neoclassical economists chose to examine people's purchase decisions retrospectively, to consider only *what* they reveal as being truly valuable by the money they spend. These economists do not try to measure *what* people will buy or pay based on underlying positive real value (or much less normative value) measurements other than *what* people have bought in the past.

Economist Paul Samuelson introduced *Revealed Preference Theory* in 1938, which mainstream economists have used ever since to quantify *what* people truly value through *what* they buy, rather than peering inside people's needs, motives, morals and ethics.[208] Samuelson mathematically modelled his *Revealed Preference Theory* as being logically circular toward customers' end-goals, or *tautological,* since he assumed that people only act to maximize their own utility as expressed by *what* they reveal they prefer.[209] In other words, Samuelson believed that people buy simply to further be without any further objective supposed, which is important philosophically as you will see. Please keep this circular perspective

---

[205]Such as *how* philosophers like Jeremy Bentham described value as utility and *how* economists model utility through indifference curves. As a wise man once tautologically said, all utility models are wrong, but some are useful.

[206]As per the economic concept first introduced by Paul Samuelson through *revealed preference substitution* in P. Samuelson, *A Note on the Pure Theory of Consumers' Behaviour*, Economica 5 (17): 61–71. JSTOR 2548836 (1938); *see also,* Stanley Wong, *Foundations of Paul Samuelson's Revealed Preference Theory: A Study by the Method of Rational Reconstruction,* Routledge (1978).

[207]Lansana Keita, *Revealed Preference Theory, Rationality, and Neoclassical Economics: Science or Ideology, Africa Development,* pp. 73 - 116, Vol. XXXVII, No. 4 (2012).

[208]Hal R. Varian, *Samuelsonian Economics and the 21st Century: Revealed Preference,* Oxford University Press (Jan. 2005, Rev. Sep. 20, 2006).

[209]Christopher P. Chambers, Federico Echenique, and Eran Shmaya, *General Revealed Preference Theory,* Theoretical Economics (2016); Don Ross, *Game Theory,* The Stanford Encyclopædia of Philosophy, Edward N. Zalta (ed.) (Winter 2012 Edition).

on *Revealed Preference Theory* firmly in the HQ as we go through the balance of *U / People* because it is a conundrum that the philosophy of *Lean* attempts to delineate.

Not coincidentally, on the cover of Eric Ries' book, *The Lean Startup*, you can see the *Zen* symbol of ensō of a near-circle created by a single brush stroke that symbolizes minimalism, strength, elegance, and the *Universe*. This symbol also represents Ries' '*Build, Measure, Learn*,' mythology, and the seemingly tautological empiricism of Samuelson's *Revealed Preference Theory*:

Cover of *The Lean Startup* (© 2011 Eric Ries)

Similar to the ensō duality as a near-circle, *Revealed Preference Theory* and most mathematical economic models fail to completely predict actual economic data since they do not account for consumers' bounded rationality. For example, economists have shown limited ability to accurately predict countries' Gross Domestic Product,[210] even though a little additional accuracy can be highly

---

[210] Nate Silver, *The Signal and the Noise: Why So Many Predictions Fail-but Some Don't*, Kindle Loc. 604-605, Penguin Group US (2012), *see*, note 63, *Survey of Professional Forecasters* (November 2007); *See also* table 5, in which the economists give a probabilistic forecast range for gross domestic product growth during 2008. The chance of a decline in GDP of 2 percent or more is listed at 0.22 percent, or about 1 chance in 500. In fact, GDP declined by 3.3 percent in 2008, found at http://www.phil.frb.org/research-and-data/real-time-center/survey-of-professional-forecasters/2007/spfq407.pdf; *see also* J. Bradford DeLong, *Estimating World GDP, One Million B.C.—Present*, Berkeley, CA, University of California Press, (1988) at http://econ161.berkeley.edu/ TCEH/ 1998_Draft/ World_GDP/ Estimating_World_GDP.html (accessed Jun. 14, 2016).

profitable.²¹¹The fact that marketing departments and advertising agencies do not widely use these econometric measurements like GDP at the micro-economic level to predict *what* consumers will want to buy evidences econometrics' general lack of both accuracy and precision at the micro-economic scale.²¹²This lack of accuracy and precision at the micro-economic level boils up to a similar lack of accuracy and precision at the macro-economic level.²¹³

Thus, in practice, neither marketers nor financiers primarily base their decisions on neoclassical economic models like*Revealed Preference Theory*, though they might use them within a stream of larger analysis. Governments' central banks rely on neoclassical economics to a much greater degree. Central banks' use of econometrics leads to the irony that*what* business people use to measure *what* all people want with the highest degrees of empirical validity is largely done under economic policies set by completely different true value measurement methodologies.²¹⁴Due to these known deficiencies in neo-classical equilibrium models, we are witnessing today a thoughtful, and empirically based reintegration of new forms of true value analysis into them. Behavioral economics represents one of these new fields, but other fields such as anthropological, evolutionary and agent-based economics are increasingly used as well.

The problem with *Revealed Preference Theory* is that people's choices in determining*how* to best be*who* and*why* they are, such as choosing a *Lean* diet because they consider themselves to be health nuts, are often contextually influenced by both physiological and psychological factors that exceed simple calculation. For example, physiological factors may include ones such as varying nutritional

---

²¹¹*See e.g.* regarding the problem of even using GDP as an accurate guage of economic activity at all in the writing of the current*World Bank* president, Paul Romer, *The Trouble with Macroeconomics*, Forthcoming in The American Economist (Jan. 5, 2016).

²¹²*E.g.* John Lanchester,*The Major Blind Spots in Macroeconomics* , New York Times (Feb. 7, 2017).

²¹³Amartya Sen,*On Ethics and Economics* , New York, NY, Basil Blackwell (1987).

²¹⁴*See again*, Lansana Keita, *Revealed Preference Theory...*, pp. 73 – 116 (2012).

needs, such as if you had recently eaten a lot of cashews but were otherwise deprived of nutrients provided by almonds that your body craved. Psychological factors could include suggestive advertising such as from the orange juice industry that made you associate the color orange with good health due to the vitamins in tropical fruits. The interplay between consumers' psychological and their physiological processes influences *what* they decide to purchase, which may waiver from normative and real value and all physio-logical meaning.

Despite those psychological distortions to measuring normative value, the purchases consumers make still reveal it to a large, though imperfect, degree. Normative value originates much further back from the point of purchase than is usually understood since normative value emerges from consumers' fundamental living processes. Thus, people's revealed preferences could be measured in front of the point of purchase if you knew every possible detail regarding consumers' physiological and psychological processes in choosing, say, between apples and oranges, cashews and almonds. We loose the ability to measure normative value in customers' sheer complexity. In contrast, consider how much simpler insects' revealed preferences are to model than people's since you can more easily value map *who* insects are, and *why* and *what* insects demand.

A distinct problem with measuring and predicting utility through revealed preferences is not only a matter of accurately measuring the pathways of all of consumers' processes, but also the part of people's processes that generate psychological meaning and preference. Psychological meaning created by *what* they perceive but cannot prove or readily measure often causes you and consumers to act irrationally. Hopefully, consumers act predictably irrational[215] so as to optimize their lives and existences, but we know this is not always the case.

---

[215] *See generally*, Dan Ariely, *Predictably Irrational, Revised and Expanded Edition: The Hidden Forces That Shape Our Decisions*, HarperCollins (2009).

In recent decades the field of *behavioral economics* and increasing amounts of digital information has provided some insight into human preferences beyond just *what* people bought with money. Behavioral economics attempts to explain *how* people value things through the intersection of the fields of psychology and economics to move past traditional, mainstream neoclassical economists' default position that positive real value can only be measured in any meaningful way through market transactions and equilibrium models. Behavioral economists do not assume that people always make rational decisions when consuming in the confusing confluence of life, and thus often fall out of balance.

Psychologist Daniel Kahneman and economist Amos Tversky produced some of the best known of this work when they elaborated on the biases and mistakes people have made.[216] Kahneman and Tversky won a Nobel Prize for demonstrating something called *Prospect Theory*[217] that people would rather not risk losing more than they would chance gaining when they know the specific probabilities of realizing each of their choices. However, in real life, people very rarely know the specific probabilities of the outcomes of their possible choices, as they would when gambling or playing a lottery. *Prospect Theory* can only tell you *what* people would decide to do based on *what* they prospectively believed or guessed the probability of something was holding all else equal. However, since people are very bad at guessing the true probabilities of events, most of the time consumers must still attempt to measure *what* best energizes and optimizes their lives and existences with limited data and bad guesses. *Prospect Theory* and other behavioral economic theories can only aid with better decision making by prospectively

---

[216] *See*, Amos Tversky and Daniel Kahneman, *Judgment Under Uncertainty Heuristics and Biases*, pp. 1124–31, Science 185 (1974); Daniel Kahneman, *Thinking, Fast and Slow*, Farrar, Straus and Giroux (2011).

[217] *See*, Daniel Kahneman and Amos Tversky, *Prospect Theory: An Analysis of Decision under Risk*, Econometrica, Vol. 47, No. 2, pp. 263-292, The Econometric Society (March 1979) DOI: 10.2307/1914185 http://www.jstor.org/stable/1914185; for the intellectual precursors to Prospect Theory, *see generally*, Milton Friedman and Leonard J. Savage, *Utility Analysis of Choices Involving Risk* (1948) and Harry Markowitz, *The Utility of Wealth* (1952).

revealing and helping compensate for these psychological biases. Both you and consumers must estimate probabilities so complex they generally trail off into purely intuitive speculation. Behavioral economics recognizes this boundary on consumers' reason and the ability to accurately assess true-north value within them.[218]

Irrational, Process-Oriented Value Estimation

You can more logically and scientifically measure the meaning of money and economics if you shift your conception of exchanging *paos* for money at customers' point of purchase. You must ex-change *what* you previously thought of as *products* and/or *services* as being *objects* and/or *activities* whose value is abstractly quantified by the prices people pay. Consider instead *paos*' advancement of the physical and meta-physical processes inherent in people's lives and existences for which they universally allocate a proportion of their budgets and adjust their spending priorities to improve regardless of *how much* absolute cash they have.

You can measure these processes in well established ways, such as through marginal, game and identity value theories. To truly measure the meaning produced by *paos* though, you must measure all of the constituent processes that aggregate into *who*, *why*, *what*, and *how* customers need and want to live and exist, which is admittedly very challenging. These prôcesses lead to people's normative and real values that ultimately make meaningful amounts of money get ex-changed for *paos* throughout the real economy.

Critically for your understanding *how much* consumers will value *paos*, these processes also have an irrational element within the

---

[218] *See also*, Game Theory and John Von Neumann and John Nash *minimax theory* or *Nash Equilibrium* where players find a strategy where each minimizes their own maximum losses discussed in *Stream 4: Lives*. Von Neumann proved that equilibrium is only possible in an expanding economy; otherwise, in a static economy or zero sum game, all players will constantly jockey for gain.

unbounded domain of an open-ended *Universe*.²¹⁹ For example, consider the study of ants by researchers such as E.O. Wilson, Eleanor Rosch, and Deborah Gordon *who* have substantially uncovered *why*, *what* and *how* ants consume. These researchers have shown that ants execute a mixed strategy of purely rational and intentionally randomized discovery models at the individual and colony levels, leading to some evidence that the collective activity of ants generates enough information to make and execute mathematically rational decisions without having to be conscious like you and me. Ants do this by incorporating randomized search into being one of their *Modi Ôperandi* (their *MÔs*).²²⁰ E.O. Wilson is even rumored to have an ant encased in Lucite etched with the phrase, *Onward and Upward!*

Optimal Slack

So is this *why* people do not likewise conform well to purely rational, Pareto optimal models of spending money when aggregated as a society? I (among others) propose that, yes, because consumers' adaptive processes produce by necessity a certain degree of statistical anomaly at the genetic and cognitive levels to optimize adaptive discovery. You might call this *optimal slack*. Ultimately, a *Lean* organization ought not be become brittle like a permanently pensive thinker, but rather athletically *Lean* as the Greek soldier Philippides running to Athens during the Battle of Marathon. Like ants in a

---

[219] *E.g. see*,fs Paul Feyerabend, *Against Method: Outline of an Anarchist Theory of Knowledge*, Verso Books (1975) wherein Paul said on p. 27, '... there is only one principle that can be defended under all circumstances and in all stages of human development. It is the principle: anything goes,' to which he said on p. 32, '... The best way to show this is to demonstrate the limits and even the irrationality of some rules which she, or he, is likely to regard as basic.'

[220] Susan C. Edwards and Stephen C. Pratt, *Rationality in Collective Decision-Making by Ant Colonies*, Proc. R. Soc. B (Jul. 22, 2009); Balaji Prabhakar, Katherine N. Dektar, Deborah M. Gordon, DOI: 10.1371/journal.pcbi.1002670, *The Regulation of Ant Colony Foraging Activity without Spatial Information* (Aug. 23, 2012); Deborah M. Gordon,*The Rewards of Restraint in the Collective Regulation of Foraging by Harvester Ant Colonies*, 498, 91–93, doi:10.1038/nature12137, Nature (May 15, 2013).

colony, organizations and consumers ought to flexibly think as a process to optimize *who* they are through active *adaptation* to win the battle for survival. As will be seen, the search for meaning in life as the ultimate knowledge in an open-ended existence helps organizations and consumers accomplish that task. Understanding this can help you make meaningful amounts of wealth as well.[221]

Presuming you measured every human process comprising *who* consumers are that a given *paos* advanced, you would still need some random variables in your estimations and predictions of true-north value because people are constantly energizing and optimizing their lives against *what* they believe provides meaning – a notion that is constantly shifting for people as they self-define the true-north value of *what* they find personally meaningful – as a form of Bayesian rational irrationality and mathematical optimization.[222] Contemporary genetic and other evolutionary *best fit* optimization algorithms include random variables as essential components, which you see mimicked in consumers *who* behave in similarly random ways in order to best energize and optimize their lives against a *Universe* of meaningful opportunities.[223]

---

[221] James C. Spall, *Introduction to Stochastic Search and Optimization: Estimation, Simulation, and Control*, Wiley Press (2003).

[222] This optimization may be compared to the notion of *satisficing* as described by Herbert A. Simon in, *A Behavioral Model of Rational Choice*, pp, 99–118, Quarterly Journal of Economics 69 (Feb. 1955); Reiskamp J., J. R. Busemeyer, and B.A. Mellers (2006), *Extending the Bounds of Rationality: Evidence and Theories in Preferential Choice*, Journal of Economic Literature, 44(3), 631-661; and S. Pironio et al, *Random Numbers Certified by Bell's Theorem*, Nature 464, 1021-1024 (15 April 2010) | doi:10.1038/nature09008 (Received 25 November 2009, Accepted Feb. 18, 2010).

[223] *See e.g.*, Xiaomin Zhong and Eugene Santos Jr., *Probabilistic Reasoning Through Genetic Algorithms and Reinforcement Learning*, Department of Computer Science and Engineering, University of Connecticut (1999); Pierre-Andre´ Noe¨l, Charles D. Brummitt, and Raissa M. D'Souza, *Controlling Self-Organizing Dynamics on Networks Using Models that Self-Organize*; Quanta Magazine, *Toward a Theory of Self-Organized Criticality in the Brain*, Simons Foundation (Apr. 43, 2014).

Cash and Credit Flow as Meta-Economic Value Streams

Because the search for meaning within the philosophy of *Lean* inevitably takes you into unchartered waters beyond traditional philosophical and economic systems, you ought to peer into meta-economic and meso-economic matters, in the spaces around and between micro-economic and macro-economic ones. Doing so will allow you to see the entire, universal value stream that makes money meaningful overall by transferring Matter and Energy up and around the production and consumption cycle.

While,*micro-economics* studies true-north value at the individual, family, corporate and organizational level, and *macro-economics* studies the economic performance and decision-making at the national, regional or global level,[224] I define *meta-economics* as economic analysis that underpins micro- and macro-economic conclusions. Meta-economic value emerges from metaphysics and *what* consumers personally intuitively believe as to *who* they are and *why* they exist. Meta-economics then realizes itself in physics and living systems that ultimately create micro- and macro-economic data. Meta-economics is thus consistent with evolutionary patterns of micro-and macro-economics as demonstrated by market behaviors.[225]

Like meta-economics, meso-economics is also not a formal discipline but rather a term describing the *Lean* economic structures residing between micro- and macro-economics.[226] I further define *meso-economics* as the study of *what* affect intellectual memes- such as courts, political parties, contracts and other social

---

[224] Andrew Sheng and Xiao Geng, *Micro, Macro, Meso, and Meta Economics*, Project Syndicate (October 9, 2012).

[225] *See e.g.*, Journal of Evolutionary Economics, ISSN: 1432-1386.

[226] *See*, Kurt Dopfer, University of St. Gallen - SEPS: Economics and Political Sciences, John Foster, University of Queensland - School of Economics, Jason Potts, University of Queensland - School of Economics,*Micro-Meso-Macro* , Journal of Evolutionary Economics, (May 17, 2005).

institutions- have on organizations and people's consumption and output in ways that are increasingly easy to measure as we improve the digital information about *why* and *how* people do *what* they do.

An organization's people-focused,*Lean i/deô* logy will mostly relate to the field of micro-economics at the firm level, but thinking in meta-economic and meso-economic terms should help you identify economic issues around traditional micro-economics to help you make money meaningfully. Here is a chart of these terms outlining these economic differences so you may *Lean* philosophically up through them:

Chart of Economics Terms

Macro-economics (formal discipline)	The economic performance, structure, behavior and decision-making at the national, regional or global level
Meso-economics (term for reference)	Economic structures between micro- and macro-economics in the form of intellectual memes, such as courts, political parties, contracts and other social institutions whose effect on consumption and output cannot be easily measured
Micro-economics (formal discipline)	Resource allocation by households and organizations
Meta-economics (term for reference)	Economic analysis leading to micro-, meso- and macro-economics as the economic value originating from the inception of physics and living systems, and consistent with evolutionary patterns of production and consumption now formalized into market exchanges by people

Surprisingly or unsurprisingly with the great time and minds dedicated these issues, many of the larger economic issues remain unsettled. For example, people still debate macro-economic issues like the appropriate levels of taxation and monetary policy.[227] And they debate micro-economic issues like measuring how *valuable* something is to people by *how much* they pay for *paos*. So a *Lean i/deôlogy* must still adapt to the changing macro-economic social and political environment in which an organization operates in order for it to understand and apply the true-north value of money and its associated meaning to its business at the micro-economic level - all with degrees of uncertainty.[228]

The meta-economic chains extending through the business process of people serving other people in complex situations where the probabilities are not known in advance with precision, may be analyzed through the range of quantitative and qualitative analysis that we have discussed. This movement to the most funda-mental aspects of *Lean* true value leads back to the natural sciences and the humanities to best measure and produce normative, real and money value.

Given all this uncertainty, I ask you at this point to further shift your conception of money as a means of ex-change for *paos*, to an even more abstract one whose store of true value is really more analogous to that of the real or perceived potential of *paos* to improve *who* and *why* consumers are. Consider money to be the means by which you enhance consumers' living processes by flowing to them the highly structured Matter and Energy that an organization produces. Since *what* consumers pay measures *what* consumers perceive to be the net benefit to their living processes among all available *paos*, hope that consumers consider a *paos* to be *good* and worth every cent.[229]

---

[227] Such as the challenge economists have in predicting the GDP and labor market statistics every quarter, as discussed by J. Bradford DeLong,*Estimating World GDP, One Million B.C.—Present*, Berkeley, CA: University of California Press, (1988).

[228] *See generally*, Gregory C. Chow, *Usefulness of Adaptive and Rational Expectations in Economics*, Princeton University, CEPS Working Paper No. 221 (September 2011).

[229] These concepts touch on marginal value theory along with the labor theory of value.

Truth Value as Two Sides of the Same Physical Coin

Normative economics are thus equivalent to capturing, structuring and delivering Matter and Energy, which physically are two sides of the same coin, to consumers' physiological and psychological processes to produce all normative value. In the pre-historic era, at the very inception of economic trading before the use of money, you generally would have traded an amount of *paos* that took the same amount of Matter and Energy you used to produce it for other *paos* that took an equivalent amount of Matter and Energy to be re-produced.

This exchange value of Matter and Energy aligns with the labor theory of value heavily favored by Karl Marx. That fact does not make this discussion "Marxist" because once trade advanced in any small degree of sophist-ication, people produced advanced *paos* that solved for strengths, weaknesses, opportunities and threats to *who, why, what,* and *how* people are, i.e. their real problems. This trade related not just to the energy used to produce the *paos* but also to relative energy efficiencies that the *paos* re-produced within those people who consumed them to more effectively support whole societies and nations. Comparative advantage depends on the extent trade energizes and optimizes all people as a species, and not on the labor inputs into an economy, which is at most only an indirect indicator of the extent a nation's *paos* produces *Utility*.

The Marxist labor theory of true value should have been easily debunked as well on purely common sense grounds given Adam Smith's *Diamonds and Water Paradox*, as well as the *Warhol Paradox* discussed earlier regarding Campbell soup cans on store shelves and museum canvases. You could sell a cup of water to a very thirsty person for far more than the energy you spent obtaining the water because of that customer's need to live and exist. Instead of pure labor value, people subjectively decide and then verify whether a *paos* helps their adaptation, re-generation and energization. Water uniquely does this if you or anyone else was thirsty.

In modern society, people also contractually pool money, separating labor or *energy* values from the time the labor value was originally generated. Finance further removes labor from Marxist notions of value, because in addition to labor, time also allows people to better live and exist. Thus, prices reside in the tension between the energy (aka *labor*) cost of producing *paos* on the supply side, and the optimization that *paos* subjectively produces to customers' lives and existences among all available substitutes on the demand side of the economic equation at a universal scale. That modern financial mechanisms may imperfectly balance this tension is the dirty secret of money and the current capitalist system.

But the Marxist labor theory of value erred in two key ways, making it less desirable than capitalism. First, it ignored normative values that dictate the true value *paos* has to *who* and *why* consumers are and personally consider themselves to be, and second, it failed to understand the real values that change the extent money represents normative economic value. Keep in mind though, economic conditions where competition is nearly perfect often drive the exchange value of commodities down to the cost of the Matter and Energy expended in producing them. Thus, the labor theory of true value has some validity as background information within a business *i/deô*logy, but it should not pre-dominate.

Thus, the only funda-mental physical axiom in measuring economic value is consumers' tautologically self-regulating purchase history – either consumers are buying a *paos* or they are not – which determines degrees of confidence you may have in the real value a *paos* has to consumers. While economic formulas may model economic activity with increasing accuracy, you can only reduce economic analysis to mathematical formulas at either the meta, micro, meso or macro levels if they accurately model the fluidity of the systems grounded in natural laws of unknown origin that re-produce consumers' lives and existences in an open-ended *Universe*. Yet, history thus far quantifiably confirms that no consistent set of axiomatic expressions has been shown to represent and accurately predict all natural systems through economic data. So, we consistently progress onward and upward, eventually increasing our standard of existence, by further explaining *what* makes life even better in the best economic system we have to date.

Regardless of what economic system people may be in along the twisting arrow of history, they iteratively perfect themselves as living systems, however impossible that perfection may be. The Japanese word, *Kaizen*, means, *good change*, while in *Lean* the term *Kaizen* further means a hypothetical, iterative pursuit of perfection.[230] By capturing and converting more and more Matter and Energy overall and applying Matter and Energy toward universalizing *who* people are as living systems, an organization iteratively reduces disorder through the process of *Kaizen* in society.[231] Customers' marginal benefit in economic terms can generally be equated with the iterative, natural benefit an organization reproduces for them. Customers' increasingly real and perceived need for *paos* in order to try and perfect their adaptive, re-productive and energy gathering processes dictates how much of their budget they are willing to give to achieve that end-goal. This energy expended to support the normative and real value of customers' lives and existences makes the true, metaphysical value of money

---

[230] *Lean Lexicon*, 5th Edition, by Lean Enterprise Institute, Inc. (2014).

[231] These notions align with current, quantum information theory and increasing quantum entanglement through equalibralization of the *Universe* into a stable state; for references to the scientific background, see Natalie Wolchover, *Time's Arrow Traced to Quantum Source*, Quanta Magazine (Apr. 16, 2014); Artur S.L. Malabarba, Luis Pedro García-Pintos, Noah Linden, Terence C. Farrelly, Anthony J. Short, *Quantum Systems Equilibrate Rapidly for Most Observables*, arXiv:1402.1093 [quant-ph] http://arxiv.org/abs/1402.1093 (Submitted on Feb. 5, 2014); Anthony J Short and Terence C Farrelly, *Quantum equilibration in finite time* , New J. Phys. 14 013063 doi:10.1088/1367-2630/14/1/013063 (2012); Noah Linden, Sandu Popescu, Anthony J. Short, and Andreas Winter, *Quantum Mechanical Evolution Towards Thermal Equilibrium*, Phys. Rev. E 79, 061103 (Published 4 June 2009); Seth Lloyd, *Black Holes, Demons and the Loss of Coherence: How Complex Systems Get Information, and What They Do With It*, Ph.D. Thesis, Theoretical Physics, The Rockefeller University (Apr. 1, 1988); and *generally* Sean Carroll, *From Eternity to Here: The Quest for the Ultimate Theory of Time*, Plume (2010).

have meaning.

From this meta-economic perspective, money prices really equal a systemic benefit that customers perceive from consuming *paos* that furthers some aspect of their living processes and ultimate existence. *Paos* provides structured Matter and Energy that systemically plugs-in like a hybrid into customers' living processes, analogously to *how* software applications do within a computer. All *paos* functions like an *App* on an *i-Phone*. All true value likewise systemically energizes and/or optimizes some aspect of consumers' living processes from their normative, real and really personal perspectives.

Inversely, consumers generally get money made by expending energy through their shopping as guided by knowledge. They then decide *how* to receive Matter and Energy by allocating their money to various vendors in order to optimize their living processes. They allocate *what* best optimizes their living processes across *who* and *why* they consider themselves to be. *Who* consumers consider themselves to be includes *who* they associate with their identity. Consumers' identity may include their family, friends, community, nation or otherwise into the whole *Universe*... or they may define themselves by the inverse of *what* is not or *what* people speculate may be but not everyone knows for sure. People generally engage in this identity crisis on a dynamic basis by balancing over time a very large variety of variables, including their religions. This makes specifically measuring and predicting true-north value, and people's actions in general, so difficult. Thus, you must understand the origin of structured Matter and Energy to enhance customers' living processes for which they will pay meaningful amounts of money over to you at the point of purchase.

Moving Forward

With the meaning of money defined, now go beyond *paos*, past the point of purchase, to the most fundamental levels of consumers' lives and existences, to the place you want to go in their hearts and minds so you can most effectively ex-change *what* they highly value for more meaningful amounts of money. After you move through the next few *Streams* of *True-North Value*, you will find new channels through the *U/ People* business model to apply a business *i/deô*logy to an organization.

Stream 3: Existence

Stream 3A 3 Report:

- *Genchi Genbutsu* is a term in *Lean* that directs managers to go to the source of all production, which *Lean* suggests may be reached by asking "Why" five times for any given problem
- *U/P* takes you well past five "Whys" to the problem of existence itself and thus to the cause of all true-north value
- The three types of true-north value are "universal," "process" and "personal," with each having certain commonly agreed degrees of truth value
- *Lean Six Sigma* represents the pragmatic pursuit of perfection since universal perfection is ultimately unobtainable by people and yet must always be sought
- The payment of money represents a para-scientific test of whether customers perceive *what* they bought as being worthwhile to their existences, thereby providing a means to measure the converged consensus of *what* true-north value is
- The *Ontological Medium* (the "OM") is the vehicle through which this converged consensus occurs and gets measured
- You can better identify *what* most consumers will buy by using an *Intuition Bracket* to examine the broadly applicable universal and process values, leaving aside ones that are only personal in nature
- The *Ontological Teleology* (the "OT" or "Ought") is the possibly tautological goal of all consumption within the IB, which has not yet been disproven
- *Ontologically Prospective Projects* ("OPPs") are those goal directed activities consumers do to advance upward along the *Ontological Teleology*

> *Sometimes you gotta go back to actually move forward, and I don't mean going back to reminisce or chase ghosts. I mean go back to see where you came from, where you been, how you got here. I know there are those that say you can't go back. Yes, you can. You just have to look in the right place.*
> - Matthew McConaughey in the *Intro* to the *Lincoln MKC* automobile commercial directed by Nicolas Winding Refn (2014).

Stream 3 now investigates the *Lean* concept of *Genchi Genbutsu*, a term of Japanese origin that directs managers to get out of the board room and go to the source of all re-production. To best create a business *i/de*ôlogy within the philosophy of *Lean*, you must seek the source of all *Lean* value streams through the process of *Genchi Genbutsu*. You pursue the process of *Genchi Genbutsu* by asking '*Why*' at least five times, which is the most strikingly beautiful question about the origin of truth value you can find. Once you get as close as you can to the source of, '*Why*,' you must then follow the true-north value streams you find across blue oceans toward the horizon of *who* all consumers are. *Genchi Genbutsu* requires that you get as close as you can to the source of all knowledge and existence from which all profits originate. Since the *U/People* business model inverts the normal organizational chart as you can see again below, you start this *Genchi Genbutsu* journey with consumers' existences firmly in mind:

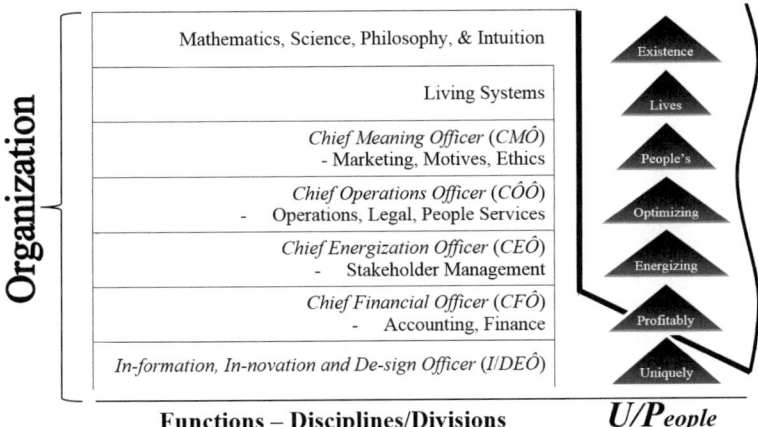

Since this process of *Genchi Genbutsu* takes you to the penultimate question of *why* customers' deepest problems exist, it explains all that they funda-mentally value, find most meaningful, will consume and pay for. Thus, following *Genchi Genbutsu* universally leads you to the edge *what* causes all consumption. When you reach the first degree of causation, you then have found the cement on which the foundation of an *HQ* will *Lean*.[232] The causation of consumption and existence is the first brick from which you will build an understanding of the major philosophical, scientific, sci-entismic, theological and intuitive perspectives. By understanding these perspectives you will construct a well of knowledge from which all consumers' value streams spring.[233]

As stated before, the philosophy of *Lean* does not answer the largest, most beautiful question with the conviction of a new metaphysical or scientific theory, but rather gets you close enough to the edge of existing knowledge for an organization to have a clear perspective

---

[232] The formal term for this study is, *Etiology* (alternatively *aetiology, aitiology*), which is the study of causation. The word is derived from the Greek word αἰτιολογία, aitiologia, *giving a reason for* (αἰτία, aitia, *cause*; and -λογία, [-logia]. For more background, please see, '*Value Theory*,' in the Standard Encyclopædia of Philosophy.

[233] As David Hume said at the end of, *An Abstract of A Treatise of Human Nature*, (1740), '*These principles of association… are the only ties of our thoughts, they are really to us the cement of the universe….*'

on *why* it ought to *Lean* ever so philosophically to reach the greatest profit. I want you to deduce the causal link between *who* consumers are at their existential limits and *what* you ought to re-produce that readily makes more money for you.[234] "When people seek rational answers to questions like these, they usually go too far down an intellectual path to communicate back in any sort of concise way, but I audaciously hope to do exactly that here on *this side of nonsense*.[235]

Existence and Ontology Defined

Let's start with a formal definition of existence. *The Oxford English Dictionary* defines existence as follows:[236]

> **Existence, n.** /ɛgˈzɪstəns/
>
> 1. **Actuality, reality.**
> 2. a. **Being; the fact or state of existing; 'actual possession of being'. in existence: as predicate = 'extant'.**
>   b. **Continued being; continuance in being.**
>   c. **Continuance of being as a living creature; life.**
> 3. **A mode or kind of existing**
> 4. a. **All that exists; the aggregate of being.**
>   b. **Something that exists; a being, an entity.**

---

[234]Unfortunately, I am not Arthur Dent, and you will not find a "number 42" here as an, '*Answer to Answer to The Ultimate Question of Life, the Universe, and Everything*,' as referenced in, *The Hitchhiker's Guide to the Galaxy*, Pan Books (1979).

[235]Nicholas Rescher, *Axiogenises: An Essay in Metaphysical Optimism*, p. 18, Lexington Books (2010).

[236]*The Oxford English Dictionary* (accessed on May 24, 2014).

Ontology, however, is the philosophical, scientific and business term for existence and the nature of being. *The Oxford English Dictionary* uses the word '*existence*' to define '*ontology*' as:[237]

Ontology, n. /anˈtalədʒi/

1. a. *The science or study of being; that branch of metaphysics concerned with the nature or essence of being or existence.*

The *U/P* lexicon *Leans* on the term *ontology* a great deal as a technical reference, so please get used to reading it![238] To emphasize how important *ontology* is to *U/P* and estimating true-north value, you could write *ontology* with its circumflex pronunciation accent "^" over the letter o, which is officially pronounced with the short o sound of "Ah," like "ôccupation," "ôntologically," or "pa/ôs." As you may recall, the formal *Lean* symbol *Ô* also stands for the Japanese term, *Hōshin Kanri*, meaning, *Compass Guided Management*, representing all true-north value.[239]

Thus, understanding normative value through consumers' ôntologies allows you to:

---

[237] *Ibid*; see also the Stanford Encyclopædia of Philosophy entry on, '*Ontology*.'

[238] The philosophical concept of *ontology* used here tends to conform with Quine's and thus to the notion of *universals* as described in this book merely as being that which is empirically predictable – though I do not disregard it, I generally care less about strict ontological commitment because the answer to those questions ultimately means very little to consumers since they *cause* meaning (and thus your profits) through their observation and wonder at your amazing *paos*; see generally, W.V. Quine, *On what there is*, (1948) Review of Metaphysics, vol. 2. pp. 21–38, (reprinted in 1980); I also use the concept of *Ontological Realization* along with *Lean* synonymously with the concept of *fitness* through natural selection as will become important later on.

[239] As earlier stated, in statistics, the circumflex is inserted to indicate and estimator, with such meaning to be seen later on in this book. For philosophy majors, the circumflex is also the same pronunciation accent used over the *u* as in *Noûs* for the title of the premier philosophy journal of that name (ISSN: 1468-0068), and is the Greek word *nous*, generally meaning sense or intellect, which in French means *we* or *us*, and when used twice as in *nous nous*, the word assumes a further, self-reflexive meaning.

1. *Intuit, infer or induce universal assumptions with some degrees of confidence as to why something matters most to consumers; and*
2. *Deductively measure how you create true value for consumers necessarily committed to a shared ôntology by living together within the open-ended Universe.*

You could likewise carry this circumflex "^" accent over the letter oh to other, related concepts within U/ P, like *ôptimization*. However meaningfully symbolic it may be, I will hold back my use of the circumflex for the sake of legibility.

Many non-philosophical disciplines use the term *ontology* as well to describe everything from gene expression in biology[240] to process ontology in computer science engineering to business models in business.[241] Informatively for developing a higher order ontology for your *i/de*ôlogy, the noted Stanford computer scientist Tom Gruber[242] who co-created *Siri* on the *i-Phone* defines ontology in the software context as:

> *... an explicit specification of a conceptualization. The term [ontology] is borrowed from philosophy, where an Ontology is a systematic account of Existence. For AI [Artificial Intelligence] systems, what exists is that which can be represented... We use common ontologies to describe ontological commitments for a set of agents so that they can communicate about a domain of discourse without necessarily operating on a globally shared*

---

[240]http://www.geneontology.org/ (accessed Nov. 15, 2015).

[241]*See e.g.*, Catherine Roussey, Francios Pinet, Myong Ah Kang, Oscar Corcho, *An Introduction to Ontologies and Ontology Engineering*, Springer (Jun. 17, 2011); see again, Alexander Osterwalder,*The Business Model Ontology: A Proposition in a Design Science Approach* (2004).

[242]For more information about Tom Gruber and *Siri*, see, http://tomgruber.org/technology/siri.htm (accessed Jul. 28, 2014).

159

> *theory. We say that an agent commits to an ontology if its observable actions are consistent with the definitions in the ontology.*
> - Tom Gruber, Computer Scientist and Co-Creator of *Apple's Siri*Artificial Intelligence

Tom Gruber, in this quote above says that agents, like consumers, commit to an ontology if the agents (think consumers) act consistent with their own shared ontologies. Are consumers' observable actions consistent with their shared ontologies by living together within the *Universe*? Just like for Paul Samuelson's *Revealed Preference Theory*, this definition of ontological commitment is tautologically circular because it means that consumers commit to *who*, *why*, *what* and *how* they think they are by sharing a common world, and a common *Universe* - a common ontological medium - by sharing it with all other living, biological systems, and thereby defining their essential natures through their existential actions.

> *All the world is an Ontological Medium,*
> *Through which U/People are*
> *Ontologically realized or not.*
> *And every business is a stage;*
> *Where performances get reviewed*
> *And every player plays a part.*
> –inspired by William Shakespeare,
> *As You Like It, Act II Scene VII*

Beyond an ontology being a simple set of rules reflexively committing consumers to certain actions in support of themselves within the global marketplace, some computer science ontologies define themselves by dynamically and self-reflexively optimizing a given set of information through algorithms. These ontologies reflect *what* they model by fitting their results to data. These

160   Stream 3: Existence

ontological optimization algorithms best fit data being analyzed to *what* is *Ontologically Realized*, and to *what* becomes revealed as the rules to which the search agents (think *consumers*) commit. Such computer ontologies invoke so called genetic algorithms, evolution strategies, evolutionary programming, simulated annealing (from the metalworking context), Gaussian (statistical) adaptation, hill climbing, and swarm intelligence (e.g. ant colony and particle swarm optimization)... each metaphorically alluding to a job to be done that enhances consumers' biological or economic fitness to better live and exist.

This computer science definition of ontology conforms with everyday economics by describing the common basis by which consumers agree with *what* they all value in *Lean* terms, like two people agreeing that a popular *paos* fits their definition of being *good*. If a *paos* fits the classification of *good* for both people, it must have been perceived as valuable for both people in circular fashion. Since *what* people perceive as valuable determines *who* and *why* they are, the *good paos* defined those customers' ontologies by furthering *who* and *why* they are when they consumed it, just like Tom Gruber saying about agents (again, think *consumers*) in a software context that, '... *an agent commits to an ontology if its observable actions are consistent with the definitions in the ontology.*'

Similarly for businesses as organizational agents serving customers *who* are individual agents, Collins and Porras wrote in their best-selling business book, *Built to Last*, '*The only truly reliable source of stability [for a business] is a strong inner core and the willingness to change and adapt everything except that core.*'[243] Businesses' inner cores are their ontologies as defined by their business models, or that which ultimately re-produces *Lean* value for their customers. Since businesses' commit to those ontologies that realize true-north value for their customers, customers' *Lean* values consequentially determine businesses' own ontologies up along the value stream.

---

[243] *See generally*, Jim Collins and Jerry I. Porras, *Built to Last*, HarperCollins (2011).

Businesses best fit themselves around *what* their customers want and need to be and become more of *who* and *why* they are. Businesses thus act just like *how* consumers decide *what* they want and need – consumers' and businesses' ontologies become symbiotic and converge by definition.

The *Ontological Realization* and origin of you, consumers and organizational *HQs* is that which is, *Critical to Ontological Realization (CORe)*. Understanding *what* is *CORe* to consumers helps you improve *who* and *why* they and organizations are.[244] Optimizing profits by enhancing consumers' lives and existences in-turn improves organizations' own viability. Such analysis enhances everyone's ability to ask correct and beautiful questions, measure specific benefits, and optimize an organization's activity to increase the probability of profiting within any given meta, micro, meso and macro-economic constraints that a*Lean* corporation faces. Doing so though requires you to go down into the well of all knowledge and come back up, which is no easy task.

Tripartite Perspectives on Existence - *Universal*, *Process* and *Personal* Truth Values

Consumers are the biggest of all subjects when taking into consideration *whatever* speculative beliefs they may have about *what* is and is not. It's the largest mindshare of theirs that you can get. To discuss consumers' existences, you must expand your own imagination as far as it will go, inducing it to the point of complete abstraction from the fact of your own existence, and then aligning that metaphysical perspective with consumers'. From a complete abstraction of pure existence, you can then sub-divide consumers' minds into categories and perspectives. These perspectives are technically philosophical propositions, but I refer to them as perspectives to make them more personally relatable. There are (generally) three

---
[244] Thus, I take a positivist approach to these matters.

true-north value perspectives on existence, which are: (1) the ideal or *universal* truth value perspectives; (2) the outside-in or *process* truth value perspectives; and (3) the inside-out or *personal* truth value perspectives. I define each of these perspectives on existence here for you to begin building a *House of Quality* within your *Lean* business *i/deôlogy* to fully divine *who* and *why* consumers truly are:

(1) ***Universal Perspective*** : The *Universal* perspective relates roughly to *platonism, idealism* or *epistemic rationalism*. In a modern context, universal value means the perspective of predictable, inviolable concepts such as mathematical and physical axioms that have no proven space or time dependencies.[245] The universal perspective also includes certain physical concepts that are predictably unpredictable, like certain aspects of quantum physics – universals simply must have predictive consistency (even if predictably unpredictable) across all dimensions to the nth degree. Their interaction results in consumers' ultimate physical manifestation. The universal perspective is notable for being unreasonably effective at explaining natural law[246] and conforms with such notions that all existence ultimately equates with mathematical coherence.[247] Specific examples of universal concepts include prime numbers and the speed of light.[248] The universal perspective is the fundamental, inviolable structure of the *Universe* that all process true-north values use forward and backward as their common denominator and ontology.

---

[245] Scientists usually discuss the notion of predictability in the inverse, as a positive assertion they prove as false.

[246] Eugene Wigner, *The Unreasonable Effectiveness of Mathematics in the Natural Sciences*, Communications in Pure and Applied Mathematics, vol. 13, No. I, John Wiley & Sons, Inc. (Feb. 1960).

[247] *See e.g.*, Max Tegmark, *Our Mathematical Universe: My Quest for the Ultimate Nature of Reality*, Knopf Doubleday Publishing Group (2014).

[248] To read a good article on the four universal physical forces, the electromagnetic, gravitational, and strong and weak atomic forces, and your current manipulation of them, *see, I Was Promised Flying Cars*, New York Times (Jun. 8, 2014).

(2) **Process Perspective**:[249] The *Process* perspective relates to the perspective that all events sequentially occur in space-time regardless of *whatever* consumers may personally believe. If you look out toward the event horizon of space-time, along the way to achieving complete problem resolution, everything you think of as a person or object eventually becomes a process due to the continual, cosmic dispersion of Matter and Energy. Thus, the process perspective explains *how* consumers came to be and *how* they eventually fade away over time in contrast to the universal mathematical and scientific laws that always seem to have existed since the start of and possibly before the *Universe* came to be.[250]

The process perspective says that in the ultimate long-run at the universal scale, consumers and all things may simply be perceived as a set of temporal relationships always changing at some point in time if you set a time horizon long enough. For example, if you were to speed up time from your own perspective, you would eventually see mountains change, oceans run dry and the greatest corporations dis-solve. For evidence of this creative destruction, the average time for a company on the S&P 500 narrowed from 61 years in 1958, to 25 years in 1980, and to 18 years in 2012. From 1955 to 2014, 89% of the Fortune 500 companies were either dissolved or had been acquired during that time. And 75% of the S&P 500 is expected to be replaced by 2027.[251]

As another example of long-term processes reaching forward into current events, consider *how* the process of natural selection led

---

[249] The Process perspective takes much of its intellectual heritage from Alfred North Whitehead's *Process Philosophy* such as he described in, *Process and Reality* (1929c); Alfred North Whitehead's description of *Process Philosophy* in *Process and Reality* reminds me of David Deutsch's in *Constructor Theory*, arXiv:1210.7439 [physics.hist-ph] (Jan. 13, 2013), wherein he somewhat similarly says that all laws may be described in terms of possible transformations.

[250] While so commonly applied to discussions like this as to be trite, I do not know if the expression, '*standing on the shoulders of intellectual giants*,' could apply more than to the content of this *Stream* describing the work of those who examined these issues in depth over millennia, as well as the U/P volume as a whole given its overly ambitious breadth.

[251] Richard Foster, *Creative Destruction Whips through Corporate America*, INNOSIGHT/-Standard & Poor's (2014).

to consumers now considering purchasing *paos* in stores today. The process perspective includes all events occurring from the inception of the physical *Universe* immediately following the creation of natural laws. It specifically includes everything that eventually happened to cause consumers' subjective, individual beliefs to occur within them today. Thus, processes dynamically arise from the chaotic interaction of universal laws and end at the point of intuitive, speculative belief.

The process perspective thus also inserts itself into discussions such as in mind-body distinctions, with some arguing that consumers' minds operate as physical processes *re-producing* self-awareness,[252] and some arguing that consumers' consciousness is something sitting beyond the physical *Universe* and is only knowable as a personal truth. To this end, *Universal* and *Process* true-north values constitute normatively true economic value supporting *what* consumers really personally value and *who* they consider themselves to be regardless of where their consciousness originates. From this physical perspective, *Process* true-north values may be thought of as instrumental rationality, or *what* consumers consequentially aim to achieve up along the crooked arrow of time.

(3) **Personal Perspective**:[253] The *Personal* perspective is *how* consumers, employees, and collectively businesses, find themselves at some point in spacetime within universal processes regardless of *how* they believe they may have been created.[254] *Personal* true-

---

[252] A good quote about this regarding the work of philosopher of Peter Carruthers is, '*Self-consciousness is just mind reading turned inward*,' as stated by Alex Rosenberg in, *Why You Don't Know Your Own Mind*, (July 18, 2016); *see*, Peter Carruthers, *The Opacity of Mind: An Integrative Theory of Self-Knowledge*, Oxford University Press (2011).

[253] *See e.g.*, Derrida's metaphysics of presence; *see also*, Thomas Nagel's essay, *What is it Like to Be a Bat?*, The Philosophical Review (1974), which describes this presence conception well but was written before more modern developments in cognitive science and your better understanding, universal, recursive mental conceptions through AI studies; *cf*, the balance of essays in which Nagel's essay is contained in Douglas Hofstadter and Daniel Dennett *The Mind's I* and other more recent work on these same subject; *see also*, Alva Noë, *Varieties of Presence*, Harvard University Press (2012).

[254] To read about people's personal perspectives being start-up businesses in and of themselves, *see*, Reid Hoffman, *The Start-up of You*, Crown Business (2012).

north value describes the point at which people very personally became aware of their wants, needs and ability to consume in a real and immediate sense. Thus, their *Personal* perspectives also relate to Descartes' famous phrase, '*I think therefore I am,*' that he used to distinguish himself.

Consumers' *Personal* perspectives are the cumulative outcome and function of universal laws and their resulting processes leading to individual intent.[255] So, while the *Universal* and *Process* perspectives apply to everything that exists, consumers' emotional, *Personal* perspectives are only applicable to them as self-reflexive, sensing people *who* decide to buy *paos* at points of purchase. For example, their very first shopping experiences reflected *Personal* true-north value as a self-aware intent to further their universal and systemic existences.

Consumers' personal perspectives are the same as the one you have right now as you read these words and personally consume this book. Consumers' personal perspectives provide a consistent version of themselves through time and space that is much the same as when you started reading today. Think of consumers' personal perspectives like a video camera sitting on their foreheads that they turned on to record all that passed by during their lives from the time they were born until now. Consider this perspective as being like the all-seeing,*Eye of Providence*, on the United States one dollar bill, or an omniscient *I/D Kata* having a singular, personal focus:

---

[255]For an interesting perspective on the Personal perspective and its relation with structure, see Christopher Alexander, Sara Ishikawa,*A Pattern Language: Towns, Buildings, Construction*, Oxford University Press (1977); and the four volume set by Christopher Alexander,*The Nature of Order* , including,*The Nature of Order: An Essay on the Art of Building and the Nature of the Universe, Book 1 - The Phenomenon of Life* (2004) (Center for Environmental Structure, Vol. 9); *Book 2 - The Process of Creating Life*(2006); *Book 3 - A Vision of a Living World*(2004); and *Book 4 - The Luminous Ground*, Routledge (2003).

$1 U.S. Dollar Eye of Providence as Omniscient *I/D Kata* (© 2016 U.S. Department of Treasury)

However, while a person may privately consider certain beliefs held from within his or her own *Personal* perspective to be truly *Universal*, society as a whole may not be convinced to the same degree. Thus, a person's beliefs held from within h/er *Personal* perspective are only universalized to the extent his or her society, environment or political system agree, but people are otherwise unlimited when professing their beliefs within their own imagination.

You, the Plane and the Lottery – On *U / PP* as a *Universal, Process, Person*

Einstein's *Specific Law of Relativity* serves well as a literal and figurative analogy illustrating the differences between the universal, process and personal perspectives to better understand *Lean* true-north value and existence itself. To illustrate, presume you wake up one morning and take an overnight flight. Also presume also that you are flying in a private, customized jumbo jet. Imagine that you board this plane, and given your wealth, you have had the sleep cabin decorated exactly like your bedroom at your home. While your plane flies you around the world, you go to sleep in the private jet's bedroom. Other than very minor turbulence in the jet stream, you hardly know the difference between the bedroom on the plane and the one at your home. You can even reach over and grab a cup of water while the airplane is flying and comfortably take a sip before going to sleep and drifting off to other worlds.

*Bed in Flight*on an *Embraer Lineage 1000E*(© 2015, Embraer SA)

Albert Einstein explained long ago that no practical difference exists between being in bed at your home and sleeping on the jet while it is travelling at a constant speed and direction. The laws of physics are the same from every perspective.[256]Thus, from outside the airplane, you are engaged in the process of flying through the air at high altitude supported by universal axioms and processual systems, but from inside of the plane, your personal, intuitive self is the same as you were on the ground at home. You wouldn't know the difference unless you looked out the window at *whatever* went past down below as you flew by.

---

[256]*See e.g.* Richard P. Feynman in the Twin Paradox at, *Six Not-So-Easy Pieces: Einstein's Relativity, Symmetry, and Space-Time*, Kindle Loc. 1520, Basic Books (1961-1963).

168 Stream 3: Existence

Analogously, from a doctor's perspective, consumers' bodies are like airplanes flying around the Earth. Your customers' bodies are a collection of processual systems constantly changing through time while *who* they are inside goes along for the ride. Andrew Wyeth's painting *Otherworld* (2002) comes to mind when I think about this concept, which depicts a women riding in a plane and looking out the window at scenes outside her funda-mental existence. Just like the woman sitting inside the plane in that painting, from consumers' personal, subjective perspectives, they are largely the same people with their same names held in a constantly present state of consciousness as their internal processes turn over, passing them by while supporting *who* they are. In an airplane, consumers will arrive as themselves at a new location even though they changed slightly during the trip. Consumers will similarly, self-reflexively identify themselves every new day they wake up by the same, universal name, even though *who* their persona is slightly changed from time to time.

We Are Travellers (©2017 Scandinavian Airlines Systems (Fair Use))

Another good analogy to the interrelation of the universal, process and personal perspectives is that of a lottery machine produced by *eGameSolutions Inc.*, a *Global Lottery Provider™*. *eGames'* lotto machine produces winners by randomly spinning, timeless, universal numbers around a wheel for a definite amount of time until its operator releases the numbers upward from the machine. The lottery machine randomly extracts those numbers from the spinning process at a specific point in time. You can analogize this lottery machine to potential customers spinning out of the womb looking back out at the apparent apparatus from which they came. Like the lottery machine, you can simultaneously conceive of consumers from the universal, process, and personal perspectives. While we may know that *eGames* created this lottery machine, do not ask *who* created the one that ultimately produced *who* consumers are!

Lottery Machine / Your Customers (© 2016*Getty Images* , Used with Permission)

You know that from a universal perspective, the world is composed of physical and mathematical laws. Once created, those physical and mathematical laws led to the *Universe* as you know it, and the relations between those universal laws created the bedrock of processes that you think of in-part as time. Over a very long period of time, these processes led to consumers' personal perspectives within the *Universe*. To the best of science's understanding, the length of time that passed from the creation of universal laws through natural processes to create consumers' personal perspectives occurred over many billions of years – over amounts of time that are hard for our minds to consider fully. Look below at this

170 Stream 3: Existence

24 hour clock of Earth's development located within the Museum of Natural History in New York City. In this clock, humans arose at the top 40,000 years ago, which corresponds to a fraction of a second before midnight:

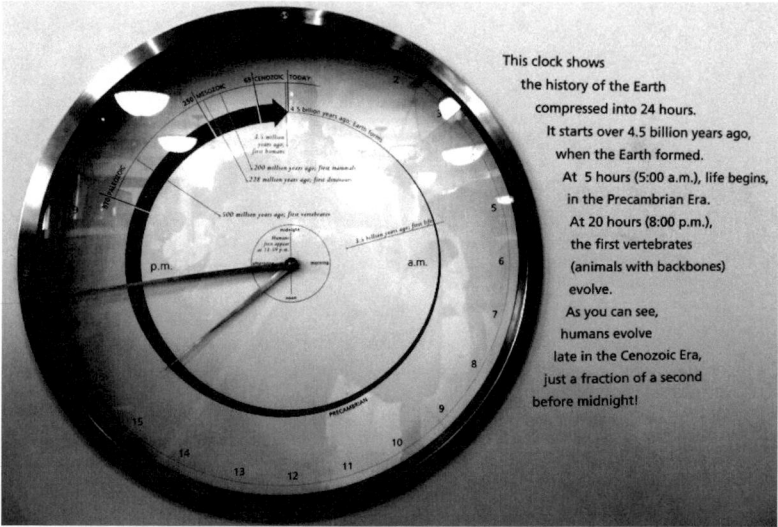

Universal Earth Clock at Museum of Natural History, NYC (Photo Credit: Me)

This clock represents well the tension between the teleological (i.e., purposefully goal directed) and seemingly tautological (i.e., unintentional, logically circular) nature of existence depending on whether the *Universe* is finite or infinite in time and space. Even this clock unintentionally, yet correctly, tells you *what* time it is once a day.

You can see consumers' subjective existences within this clock from their personal perspectives, from *who* they think they are, as a result of pre-existing processes such as their mother's pregnancies and labor. Thus at business scale, you can also measure the interactions between physical and mathematical axioms that create *paos* along the assembly line to enhance consumers' living processes and personal perspectives. Consumers' personal perspectives depend on those processes that in-turn depend on physical and mathematical axioms that further depend on a universal cause for which people do not yet have common agreement, even after asking more than five *why's*. An ultimate cause may or may not exist, or may exist in some way people do not universally agree on due to lack of predictably experiential evidence, but in the meantime you may go onward and upward regardless and as if there were.[257] To summarize, here is a chart of these levels of dependent existence as gradations of true-north value perspectives:

Levels of Dependent Existence

Levels of Dependent Existence	Universal Perspective
	Process Perspective
	Personal Perspective

Three *Lean* Truth Types Aligned with *Universal*, *Process* and *Personal* True-North Value Perspectives

> *My plan is as easy to describe as it is difficult to effect.*
> *For it is to establish degrees of certainty.*
> - Sir Francis Bacon, *Novum Organum Scientiarum* (1620)

---

[257] I relate physical and mathematical laws based on the principle that math has been demonstrated as having an uncanny ability to predict the operation on physics and vice versa (such as said by E.P. Wigner), such that one might seriously consider all of physics to be the empirical embodiment of mathematical relation and mathematical coherence as being the conceptual expression of physics.

These are the three broad and overlapping, but ultimately dependent, categories of true-north value that align with the *Lean* value you must uncover:[258]

(1) Axiomatic Truth Values[259]: Axiomatic true-north values are those truth value propositions from the universal perspective that you have reason to believe are uniform in nature and based on the seemingly timeless, universal axioms of science and math like the speed of light and prime numbers, from which you can deduce further true-north values. Axiomatic validity is generally assumed due to its coherence and predictability with at least five*Lean* sigmas ($\geq/5\sigma$) of confidence or $\geq$ 99.9999426697%. For example, particle physicists generally consider a discovery to be an axiomatic truth if it can frequently be verified within five sigmas (5σ) of confidence.[260] The four axiomatic physical forces well-trained physicists agree on right now with a *Lean* five sigmas ($\geq/5\sigma$) of confidence are the electromagnetic, gravitational, and strong and weak atomic forces.[261] Axiomatic truth values qualify as facts for physicists by their very definition as universal, inter-subjective truths, and are a sound basis for understanding customers' physical ontologies.

Given our continuous pursuit of perfection, a standard of six *Lean* sigmas ($>/6\sigma$) of confidence, or $\geq$99.9999998027% of inter-subjective agreement, represents the pragmatic idealism we ought to pursue in recognition of the fact that we may never be perfect as living systems in an open-ended *Universe*. Going even further, while a fully *Lean* infinite sigma ($/\sigma\infty$) of confidence will certainly allow us to determine whether something is in-fact an axiom, the assumption that anyone can ever be fully informed of all knowledge can only be hypothetical. Only if we determine an axiom by way of its

---

[258] This list of true-north types, and much of my Process oriented thinking, is greatly inspired by the work of Nicholas Rescher with his Process Metaphysics and other philosophers like Hillary Putnam, *What is Mathmatical Truth?* Lecture at Harvard University (1975).

[259] Can be related to Buddhist absolute truth or paramartha satya; Thich Nhat Hanh, *The Heart of the Buddha's Teaching* p. 121, Broadway Books (1997).

[260] *CERN | Accelerating science.* Public.web.cern.ch (Retrieved Aug. 10, 2013).

[261] See again, *I Was Promised Flying Cars*, New York Times (Jun. 8, 2014).

never having been proved false no matter *how* we test or criticise it over tremendous periods of time, can a fully *Lean*, infinite degree of confidence ($/\sigma\infty$) be conceived of as a reasonable axiomatic standard to pursue, and yet it is the one we ultimately seek as perfectionists;

(2) Systemic Truth Values:[262] Systemic true-north values are those truth value propositions arising from causal, process perspectives within science that you have reason to believe cannot be axiomatically defined. Systemic validity is based on something's general coherence on an empirical *best fit* basis with universal axioms. [263] Like axiomatic truths, systemic truth values also increase their validity in proportion to the number of people that commonly agree with them and the general failure of our attempts to falsify them. Systemic truths differ from axiomatic truths in that systemic truths are valid due to their general, but not unwavering, coherence with reality, rather than being experienced as axiomatically self-evident.[264] Qualitatively, you might also describe systemic truths as being nearly universal, inter-subjective truths.

Something may qualify as most likely a fact and systemic truth value if it has greater than two or more *Lean* sigmas ($\geq/2\sigma$) of confidence, or $\geq 95.4499736\%$ of inter-subjective agreement among all fully informed people. Under this standard, well functioning people would describe the systemic truth as common sense if fully informed of its details. However again, since you can only hypothetically assume that people will be fully informed of all knowledge in the real world, including their own biases that affect their understanding, you ought to look for a higher standard of

---

[262] For a discussion of systems thinking in a business context, see W. Edwards Deming, *Out of the Crisis*, MIT Press, (2000); and Peter M. Senge, *The Fifth Discipline*, Doubleday (1990); this can also be related to Buddhist worldly truth or samvriti satya, Thich Nhat Hanh, *The Heart of the Buddha's Teaching*, p. 121 (1997).

[263] *Best fit* basis being congruent to Karl Popper's scientific methods of empiricism; *see e.g.*, Karl Popper, *The Logic of Scientific Discovery*, p. 17, Routledge / Taylor & Francis e-Library (2005).

[264] *But see*, Keith DeRose, *The Case for Contextualism: Knowledge, Skepticism, and Context*, Oxford University Press; Reprint edition (Jun. 24, 2011).

measurement before considering something to be a systemic truth and common sense.

While you ideally want to measure all fully informed people, you may have to rely on the opinions of a consortia of experts to determine systemic truths because fully-informed people simply do not exist. A couple of examples of this form of support include the process of peer-reviewing academic papers, and the associations of journalists who increasingly certify public truths against fake news. However, reliance on experts and authority figures can compound those people's inter-personal subjectivity rather than clarifying *what* is systemic, true-north value based on the impressions of all people.[265] Unfortunately, there is no clear way out of this conundrum, which is why we must view systemic true-north value from different perspectives. So, anything goes when trying to assess systemic truths, so long as you test whether a *Lean* business process leads customers to a purchase for which you may deduct a payment from them.

(3) Intuitive Truth Values: Intuitive true-north values are those truth value propositions arising from consumers' personal perspectives that they speculate and believe based on their scientismic, spiritual and/or theological intuitions with less than two *Lean* sigmas ($</\sigma$) of confidence, or < 95% of common agreement among all fully fully informed people. Consumers' intuition may be called anything from *emotion* to *faith*.[266] Strictly personal intuitive truths are those that are truly speculative, that no known processual or

---

[265] *See e.g.*, Nate Silver, *The Signal and the Noise: Why So Many Predictions Fail-but Some Don't*, p. 198, Penguin Publishing Group (2012), where he discusses the element of bias in experts' economic models, and more particularly his research into the Survey of Professional Forecasters showing persistent bias even at the group level; *see also* as referenced by Silver, Stephen K. McNees, *The Role of Judgment in Macroeconomic Forecasting Accuracy*, pp. 287–99, 6, no. 3, International Journal of Forecasting (Oct. 1990).

[266] By *intuition*, I do not mean psychological intuition, such as that described by Daniel Kahneman as *System 1* thinking in his book *Thinking: Fast and Slow*, but rather intuitively speculative knowledge on an absolute basis for which we do not have axiomatic or systemic answers on a *Universal* basis. Thus, the distinction between axiomatic and systemic propositions and intuitive propositions represents the analytic/continental philosophical divide.

universal truths validate them up to and beyond a single *Lean* sigma ($</\sigma$) of confidence, or <68.2689492% of common agreement, among well informed people, and yet consumers nonetheless *feel* are true to an infinite degree. To be clear, intuitive truths are not consumers' psychological intuitions that they can confirm or deny with known universal or processual truths if they had access to the *Universe* of knowledge. Rather, intuitive truths are limited truths for which greater than two *Lean* sigmas ($\geq/2\sigma$) of informed people have not been convinced that they are not false (or in the unscientific inverse, are limited truths that informed people have not been convinced are true to the necessary degree).[267] Intuitive truths may be inter-subjective assuming more than one person believes the intuitive truth. Examples of inter-subjective, intuitive truths include political opinions or a religious faith that requires no degrees of confidence, both of which can still be held if a single person believes them to be true.[268]

Like consumers' perspectives, each of these three truth value types are arranged in the relational order of supervening dependency, with systemic truth values and resulting processes dependent on the validity of axiomatic truth values or *universals*. Intuitive truth values depend on both axiomatic and systemic truth values that provide an ontological medium within which consumers may intuitively believe and speculate.

Keep in mind though the the logical dependency of intuitive truths becomes circular to *who* consumers are. Once consumers' intuitive truths lead them to dogmatically believe both *what* they find personally valuable and *what* are universal true-north values, like

---

[267] In fact, the scientific standard by which the efficacy of pharmaceutical drugs is demonstrated and moved beyond being an intuitive truth is by its attaining a 5% level of statistical significance (i.e. $p < 0.05$) from inferential hypothesis testing with a double-sided Confidence Interval (*See Eye*); see e.g. Dr. Rick Turner and Dr. Russell Reeve, *Basic Biostats for Clinical Research - Confidence Intervals in Drug Development - An Overview of their Use and Interpretation*, p. 42, International Pharmaceutical Industry (Spring 2010).

[268] *See e.g.*, Daniel Dennett, *Intuition Pumps And Other Tools for Thinking*, W. W. Norton & Company (2013); *c.f.* truths that are held to be self-evident such as those stipulated in the second paragraph of the U.S., *Declaration of Independence* (Jul. 4, 1776).

those that may be espoused by a deity or demagogue, consumers then believe in a co-dependency between intuitive, systemic and axiomatic truths arising in their minds' all-seeing eye.

Thus, speculative belief can act like an intuitive tail wagging an axiomatic dog. Problems arise when an intuitive tail fails to lead axiomatic and systemic dogs (or consumers) to food, safety and shelter. In other words, while we cannot directly access Universal and Process truth values, they ultimately check all consumers' intuitive speculation since we must follow U/P values where they lead. U/P values thereby stop consumers' intuitive tails from wagging their axiomatic and systemic dogs, as is only common sense.[269] Cults of personality can exemplify this with intuitive speculation, such as when a cult's charismatic leader espouses axiomatic or systemic dogmas.

So, while keeping this interplay between these forms of true-north value in mind, these truth types are arranged below in descending order of commonly agreed validity, much as the three perspectives on existence were in the preceding chart in this *Stream*.

Truth Value Correlations

Truth Value Correlation	Perspective	Truth Value
$= /\infty\,\sigma$	Universal Perspective	Axiomatic Truth Value
$\geq /6\,\sigma$	Process Perspective	Systemic Truth Value
$\geq /1\,\sigma$	Personal Perspective	Intuitive Truth Value

To provide a recent, scientific example of an assertion that is currently being reclassified in some degree from an intuitive, scientismic truth to a systemic, processually scientific truth, and maybe even a universal, axiomatic truth, look to the research for the Higgs Boson or the *God Particle*. The CERN (Conseil Européen pour la

---

[269] This notion is inspired by George Soros' discussion of the concept of reflexivity in *The Alchemy of Finance*, Wiley (1987).

Recherche Nucléaire) laboratory in Switzerland has been searching for the presence of the Higgs Boson particle whose existence would help complete the standard physical model that is now agreed on as being at least a processual true-north value within the scientific community.

The Higgs Boson was predicted based on this standard physical model but had not yet been actually experienced by scientists through their instruments. Recent experiments at the CERN laboratory in-fact re-produced results demonstrating the Higgs Boson within at least five *Lean* sigmas ($\geq/5\sigma$) of certainty, thereby affirming the Higgs Boson's existence as a systemic truth. Due to the explanatory power of Higgs Boson and its coherence with the *Standard Model* of natural laws, this test set the stage for revalidating the existence of the Higgs Boson over time so the *God Particle* itself might become an axiomatic true-north value like gravity pulling water downstream.[270]

An example of another intuitive, scientismic truth value that people are working to convert into at least a systemically processual, scientific true-north value is the stipulation that the *Universe* was created in the *Big Bang*. Scientists describe the *Big Bang* as a processual system initiated by *cosmic inflation*, whereby the *Universe* rapidly expanded from a single point outward over about 14 billion years to *what* you experience today. In an attempt to make the *Big Bang* theory a processually systemic truth value, scientists have been studying whether cosmic inflation created ripples like waves in an ocean in the outer reaches of spacetime by observing the *Big Bang's* effect. The scientific validation of the processual truth of these ripples in spacetime is very much in flux at the moment,[271] but some scientists intuitively believe that they exist with increasingly systemic predictability. Scientists personally

---

[270] CERN topic page on Higgs-Boson found at, http://home.web.cern.ch/topics/higgs-boson (accessed Mar. 12, 2016).

[271] Dennis Overbye, *Astronomers Hedge on Big Bang Detection Claim*, New York Times (Jun. 19, 2014).

178 Stream 3: Existence

believe they can empirically validate the process of the *Big Bang* that eventually produced consumers' personal existences from this one point in the past.

As you might expect, something falling into more than one of these truth value classifications increases its validity as a *Lean* true-north value. For example, consumers can say that axiomatic truth values, such as mathematical proofs, reside supreme and unassailable. On the other hand, all three truth value categories ontologically realize themselves by *what* consumers actually experience. Critically, a thing or process falling within all three truth value types would be the most valid of all since such a thing or process would be the most completely *Ontologically Realized* by consumers. In fact, the only thing falling into all three truth types is *who* consumers are in their totality. Consumers evidence all three truth types, and this allows a *House of Quality* to *Lean* philosophically toward these three truth value types in the *paos* it produces. That *paos* creates the true-north value and meaning of the money customers give to ex-change *who* they were for something better as a customer.

While consumers' lives, existences and buying experiences are temporal processes, from consumers' personal perspectives, the only time they personally know is the time they have been really alive, such as when they first began shopping in stores. However, consumers only presume that time itself existed before they were born, and will continue after they die. For all consumers know, they became consciously aware at some point and believe they will die because they witness all others doing so over the course of their lives and history. Consumers feel themselves getting older, but they do not otherwise know for sure that they will die other than by defining their ontology as being *mortal* based on all of the evidence they received during their lifetimes.[272] Thus, because all consumers experience this evidence directly, they have great confidence that they are the result of a natural and biologically processual system

---

[272] This is due to having a healthy Humean and even Popperian skepticism of induction.

that terminates at some point within the *OM* due to old age, and that they will eventually become not alive because they witness others doing so unless they interrupt that process in some currently inconceivable way.

Similar to *how* they view their own mortality, consumers speculate whether or not the physical *Universe* itself was self-causing or caused by something else. Consumers' speculation though is neither an axiomatic nor a systemic truth value, unlike consumers' biological processes, due to insufficient certainty and agreement across the right people. Thus, consumers' personally intuitive consciousness remains the most valid truth to them, the surest thing they know, since it represents all three types of true-north value. This is *why* Rene Descartes' statement, '*I think therefore I am,*' has held such philosophical, and subsequently scientific, energy for so long due to its true-north validity from the *Universal, Process* and *Personal* (*U/PP*) perspectives. Descartes could have also used *U/PP* to pursue objective knowledge with varying degrees of certainty.

The balance of *U/People* leverages these true-north value perspectives by focusing on *what* consumers can commonly agree with at least two *Lean* sigmas ($\geq/2\sigma$) of processually systemic truth value, while recognizing the validity of *Lean* personally intuitive true-north values with less confidence ($</2\sigma$). You must bracket and recognize these *Lean,* personally intuitive truth values that have no axiomatic or systemic truth value validity so you can most accurately identify *why, what* and *how* consumers will purchase from you based on *who* they fundamentally are within the common ontological medium of the *Universe*.

To consolidate these matters in a business *i/deô*logy, you can correlate the forms of truth value we described, *U/PP* perspectives, degrees of explanation, and the methods of analysis in a single chart:

Truth Value Correlation	Truth Value	U/PP Perspective	Degree of Explanation	Method of Analysis
≥ /5σ	Axiomatic Truth Value	Universal Perspective	Law	Deduction
≥ /3σ	Systemic Truth Value	Process Perspective	Theory	Induction
≥ /2σ	Systemic Truth Value	Process Perspective	Hypothesis	Inference
< /2σ	Intuitive Truth Value	Personal Perspective	Conjecture	Intuition

Chart of Truth Value Correlations

Consumers' commonly-shared lives and existences ontologically depend on pragmatic, best-fit, systemic truths relying in-turn on axiomatic truths, and yet consumers are fundamentally motivated by their intuitive truths that create seemingly non-circular end-goals for them to be more than they are. This intuitive boundary outside processual and universal true-north values leaves room for personally intuitive speculation about *what* is not commonly agreed, or *what* consumers personally feel is best regardless of any common agreement among all people. When consumers intuitively speculate, they have faith that *what* they live for is better than *what* they know is not.

> *I don't want to achieve immortality through my work;*
> *I want to achieve immortality through not dying.*
> - Woody Allen, *On Being Funny* (1975)

The only condition for businesses to accommodate consumers' intuitive beliefs is that those beliefs must not interfere with certain processually systemic and universally axiomatic truth values generally agreed by others.... unless consumers willingly convince all fully-informed people with at least two *Lean* sigmas (≥/2σ) of common agreement that their intuitive truths qualify as processually systemic or universally axiomatic truths to an amazing degree. Consumers ought not impose their personal beliefs on others unless they meet this standard.[273] Moving from a personal truth to a process or universal truth is one of convincing others that no better explanation or *paos* can be found, which is the burden of proof an organization must carry when creating a new product category.

While not even consumers have perfect insight into all that influences *what* they decide to purchase, for the most part, you can intuit, infer and/or induce consumers' *Universal, Process* and *Personal* values (i.e. their ontologies), by observing their behaviors and preferences that they reveal to you. Once you have ascertained consumers' U/PP values from their stated beliefs or behavioral data, you can compare those values against the ones you know with various degrees of certainty. You may then conjecture, hypothesize, theorize (or even lobby to legislate) those universal truths that are in-line with those believed by customers to achieve righteous business results from the satiating *paos* you sell.

For example, suppose you want to sell *paos* to the *Alphabet* subsidiary, *Google, Inc.*, as a corporate consumer. Like a hermeneutic interpretation of the *Ten Commandments*, analyze *what Google Inc.* intuited, inferred, induced and deduced is *good* based on its stated business *i/deôlogy*, ontology and corporate philosophy of, '*Ten Things We Know to Be True.*' Consider whether you also intuit, infer and/or induce *what Google* believes are its *Universal* , *Process* and *Personal* true-north values from these statements. Determine whether *Google's* corporate behavior deductively reflects these stated true-north value beliefs as its ontology, which you can see *Google* has written below as its own commandments.

---

[273]For an interesting study demonstrating how people's intuitive belief may dominate their*Universal* and *Process* knowledge, *see*, Dan M. Kahan,*Climate Science Communication and the Measurement Problem*, Advances Pol. Psych., Forthcoming, Yale University - Law School; Harvard University - Edmond J. Safra Center for Ethics (Jun. 25, 2014); *see also Public's Views on Human Evolution*, Pew Research (Dec. 30, 2013).

182 Stream 3: Existence

Google Inc.'s 10 Truth Values [274]

- *You don't need to be at your desk to need an answer.*
- *Democracy on the web works.*
- *The need for information crosses all borders.*
- *G reat just isn't good enough.*
- *Focus O n the user and all else will follow.*
- *You can make m Oney without doing evil.*
- *It's best to do one thin G really, really well.*
- *Fast is better than s Low.*
- *There's always more information out ther E.*
- *You can be serious without a suit.*

YOU DON'T NEED TO BE AT YOUR DESK TO NEED AN ANSWER
DEMOCRACY ON THE WEB WORKS
THE NEED FOR INFORMATION CROSSES ALL BORDERS
REAT JUST ISN'T GOOD ENOUGH
FOCUS N THE USER AND ALL ELSE WILL FOLLOW
YOU CAN MAKE MONEY WITHOUT DOING EVIL
IT'S BEST TO DO ONE THIN   REALLY, REALLY WELL
FAST IS BETTER THAN S OW
THERE'S ALWAYS MORE INFORMATION OUT THER
YOU CAN BE SERIOUS WITHOUT A SUIT

Image from *Google's* NYC Office (© 2015 Photo Credit: Me)

  Might you re-write these true-north values to reflect more accurately what you think Google believes is true based on what you see Google actually doing rather than what Google merely says?

---

[274] *Google's Ten things we know to be true* https://www.google.com/about/company/philosophy/ (accessed Sep. 12, 2014).

Reason, Causation or Nothing

Intuiting, inferring, inducing and deducing human or corporate ontologies to create true north value within the philosophy of *Lean* requires that you ground an *i/deôlogy* on a presumption of universal reason, and its necessary corollary, causation. Causation itself is a form of formal Lean '*Root Cause Analysis*' (*RCA*)[275] that originates from a philosophical concept called the '*Principle of Sufficient Reason*' (*PSR*). Both *RCA* and the *PSR* may also be th-ôught of as an, *Axiom of Causation*, that assumes every reason or cause must have a prior one, back to the start of existence itself.

The PSR states that for every fact, there must be an explanation as to *why* that fact is.[276] The PSR holds that each action resulted from a prior cause down to an ultimate self-causing cause (a *Sui Generis* in *Latin*).[277] In the PSR, causation is an assumed abstraction of the relations between every series of events. Thus, the PSR underpins most classic explanations for existence, and yet this theory has the earlier stated limitation of not yet being proven as either a processual or axiomatic truth value itself.[278] To date, people have found no common agreement as to even a processual self-causing cause, much less an axiomatic truth, explaining the origin of the *Universe*. Thus, consumers, whether scientist, atheist, theologian or organization, can only intuitively believe in the PSR at a universal scale even if they might only employ RCA in a far more limited

---

[275] The *Lean* method of *Root Cause Analysis*, referred to as *RCA*, is commonly employed in business and government agencies such as NASA to identify the source of a problem; *see*, *Root Cause Analysis Overview*, NASA, Office of Safety & Mission Assurance Chief Engineers Office (Jul. 2003).

[276] *See*, Stanford Encyclopædia of Philosophy entry on, '*Sufficient Reason*'; the PSR was so named by Leibniz but its concept extends back to antiquity, *see*, Nicolas Rescher, *On Leibniz* (2013).

[277] Sui generis per *The Oxford English Dictionary*, lit. Of one's or its own kind; peculiar. Also used attrib. †Also illiterately as n., a thing apart, an isolated specimen.

[278] For example the philosopher David Hume believed that meaningful statements about the *Universe* are always qualified by some degree of doubt in, *An Enquiry Concerning Human Understanding* (1748); *see also* David Deutsch, *The Beginning of Infinity*, p. 96 (2011).

capacity within their business environments.[279]

Like the PSR, formal *Lean Thinking* uses the *Axiom of Causation* in the form of the *5 Why's* to find the *root cause* of any given business problem by simply asking *why* five times. The conversations within an *HQ* will benefit from moving beyond a mere five *why's* toward analyzing *who* consumers are through an infinite number of *why's* until a *House of Quality* is ultimately bounded by infinities, paradoxes and tautologies.[280] A *Lean* business *i/deô*logy ought to lead you to the edge of axiomatic and systemic explanations of the *Universe*, to the bare existence of an empty, infinite set at the conceptual inception of something rather than nothing at all.

Finally, an empty, infinite set is the last thing consumers ought to consider before moving past reason, beyond space-time itself to something other-than-reason.[281] Since a business *i/deô*logy cannot now axiomatically or systemically say *whatever* is beyond reason as its inverse, neither consumers nor organizations can axiomatically or systemically know how many *why's* will reach *what* is certainly *not here* without intuitively speculating. [282]

---

[279] For a recent survey of American beliefs in religious intuitive true-norths regarding the origin of human existence, see http://www.gallup.com/poll/170822/believe-creationist-view-human-origins.aspx (accessed May 11, 2016).

[280] David Deutsch, *The Beginning of Infinity* , pp. 166, 172, 192 (2011).

[281] *See*, Sean Carroll, *From Eternity to Here: The Quest for the Ultimate Theory of Time*, Kindle Loc. 978-980, Penguin Group US (2010), where he writes, '*So if someone asks you what really happened at the moment of the purported Big Bang, the only honest answer would be: 'I don't know.' Once we have a reliable theoretical framework in which we can ask questions about what happens in the extreme conditions characteristic of the early universe, we should be able to figure out the answer, but we don't yet have such a theory.*'

[282] Thomas Henry Huxley wrote, '*Agnosticism, in fact, is not a creed, but a method, the essence of which lies in the rigorous application of a single principle ... Positively the principle may be expressed: In matters of the intellect, follow your reason as far as it will take you, without regard to any other consideration. And negatively: In matters of the intellect do not pretend that conclusions are certain which are not demonstrated or demonstrable.*', in Huxley, Thomas Henry, *Agnosticism* , The Popular Science Monthly, 34 (46): 768, D. Appleton & Company, (April 1889); *see also*, Richard Dawkins, *The God Delusion* , pp. 72 Houghton Mifflin Harcourt (2008).

Reason as Causation from Aristotle's Perspective, with Modification

> *I believe one can divide [People]
> into two principal categories:
> those who suffer the
> tormenting desire for unity,
> and those who do not.*
> -George Sarton, aet. 20[a]
>
> ---
> [a] May Sarton, *I Knew a Phoenix*, pp. 40-41, W. W. Norton (1959).

In the Western/Occidental tradition, you can trace one of the first definitions of pure reason at the boundary of *what* may be considered rational to Aristotle's *Four Causes*, which like Blank's, *Four Steps to the Epiphany*, may be roughly conceptualized and related to this *U / P* line of *Lean* thinking as follows:

- **Formal ontological causes** that explain the shape of *how* consumers and *paos* came to be. Since formal causes generally don't make sense in the scientific age, in the philosophy of *Lean*, I somewhat modify the formal cause to be *what* I consider a self-defining ontological one encapsulating all that consumers, organizations and *paos* are, including all consumers' personal speculation, emotions, and dreams arising as a course of their personal perspective. The formal cause simply is as it is because it is in circular fashion;[283]
- **Material physical causes** define *what* physical processes led to consumers' and *paos*' existence as a subset of the formal, ontological causes. The material cause roughly aligns with modern scientific explanations of *how* natural law e-merged

---
[283] *See e.g.* Stanford Encyclopædia of Philosophy, '*Aristotle on Causality.*'

through axiomatic and systemic truth values. Thus, the material cause relates to *how* organizations actually produce *paos* for customers;
- **Efficient first causes** generally equate with the very first, initial cause whether material or not that initiated existence through the *Axiom of Causation* and eventually led to *who* consumers are, *what* they experience, and *how* organizations produces *paos* for them; and
- **Final teleological causes** explain the end-goal/factor/motives of the *Universe* and *why* the efficient cause created consumers and *paos* at all. The final cause is also synonymous with the teleological cause, the end purpose of all learning, which is a combination of the Greek τέλος, telos (root: τελε-, *end, purpose*) and -λογία, logia (*a branch of learning*).[284]

In this post-post-modern world, these formally ontological, materially physical, efficiently first and finally teleological causes may seem logically circular or tautological in that they lack unification or an axiomatic origin without another extended self-causing cause standing outside of known axiomatic and systemic truths. Nonetheless, consumers cannot help but experience their generally consistent personal perspectives as the synthesis of all these causes combined into their present state of *who* they identify themselves as being. Meaning emerges for them through this constant, simultaneous tension between the apparent tautological causation of the *Universe* and consumers' assumed teleology based on their intuitive beliefs.

Not coincidentally, the religious philosophy of *Buddhism* widely adopted in Japan where *Lean* thinking developed into a holistic business philosophy, describes an apparent causal circularity for

---

[284] Per *The Oxford English Dictionary*, Teleology is, '*The doctrine or study of ends or final causes, esp. as related to the evidences of design or purpose in nature; also transf. such design as exhibited in natural objects or phenomena,*' which leaves out, and yet alludes to, religious connotation in the use of '*design*.'

the *Universe* through a concept called *pratītyasamutpāda*, which Buddhist monk Thich Nhat Hanh explains:[285]

> *Pratitya samutpada is sometimes called the teaching of cause and effect, but that can be misleading, because we usually think of cause and effect as separate entities, with cause always preceding effect, and one cause leading to one effect. According to the teaching of Interdependent Co-Arising, cause and effect co-arise (samutpada) and everything is a result of multiple causes and conditions... A cause must, at the same time, be an effect, and every effect must also be the cause of something else. Cause and effect inter-are. The idea of first and only cause, something that does not itself need a cause, cannot be applied.*

Relating Aristotle's *Four Causes* to Levels of True-North Value

By seeing ultimate causation of consumers' lives and existences as a possibly circular co-arising through *pratītyasamutpāda* for business purposes, you can effectively map all four of the Aristotelian causal explanations to consumers' and organizations' universally axiomatic, processually systemic and personally intuitive perspectives and truth values as explained here:

(1) ***Universally Axiomatic*** : Aristotle's four causes may be seen as universally, axiomatically explaining the origin of consumers' existences in a logically self-defining sense not related to a cause outside of existence itself. Examples include axioms such as the Western *Ontological Argument* trying to prove God by the very definition of

---
[285] Thich Nhat Hanh, *The Heart of the Buddha's Teaching* , p. 221-222, Broadway Books (1973).

188 Stream 3: Existence

perfection, Eastern philosophical traditions like *pratītyasamutpāda*, and modern scientific notions of the *Universe* spontaneously co-arising[286] under the laws of quantum physics [287] through such things as *quantum fluctuations*.

A universally axiomatic cause is generally based on the logic that nothing exists in the truest sense since nothing cannot be by its own definition.[288] Even for efficient first and final teleological causes residing at the existential extremes of all spacetime, the basis of such causes may be seen to be axiomatically self-re-generating in this way. But, I would like to re-emphasize that no philosophical or scientific explanation for consumers' existences today may be deemed axiomatic with predictive, universal certainty. As stated, all people, whether theistic or not, must rely on systemically hypothetical and personally speculative explanations for their own existences and essences.

(2) **Processually Systemic**: Aristotle's formal and material causes may be seen as providing processually systemic explanations for consumers' and organizations' existence, such that consumers' and organizations' existences arise due to natural processes. Consumers e-merged from efficient or final causes arising systemically at the extremes of existence cohering with the overall system of the *Universe* in which consumers exist. The *Lean* value stream of physical or logical processes extends to the boundaries of known causation, creating consumers from an intelligible, systemic reason that may or may not be tautologically self-defining.[289] To be clear, no ultimate philosophical or scientific explanation for consumers' existences today may be deemed a systemic truth such that it

---

[286] This relates to speculation from physicists such as those of Alex Vilenkin and his theories about cosmic inflation in, *Many Worlds in One: The Search for Other Universes*, Hill and Wang; 1st edition (2007).

[287] Stephen W. Hawking, *Quantum Cosmology, M-theory and the Anthropic Principle*, Lecture published at http://www.hawking.org.uk/quantum-cosmology-m-theory-and-the-anthropic-principle.html (no date for lecture given at his website, but last accessed May 2016).

[288] Following Greek notions of this concept.

[289] *See*, the Stanford Encyclopædia of Philosophy entry on the, '*Cosmological Argument.*'

coheres sufficiently with people's commonly shared, predictable experiences within at least two *Lean* sigmas (≥/2σ) of confidence.

(3) ***Personally Intuitive***: Aristotle's efficient first and final causes may be seen like personally intuitive explanations for consumers' existences when they lead to a spiritualism or theology standing outside consumers' universally systemic and common experience. For example, consumers seeking Aristotle's materially physical cause may lead them to a scientismic belief that science will ultimately determine the origin of existence if it has not already. Like other personally intuitive truths, scientismic true-north values ultimately revert to self-defining speculation because they lack further support in universally axiomatic or processally systemic true-north values of their own, even if they seem intuitively true based on some limited evidence or belief in the consistent explanatory power of science.[290]

> *You can have whatever personal values you want, but businesses that don't provide what customers want don't remain businesses. Literally, never.*
> - Emerson Spartz, Internet Meme Meister [a]
>
> ---
> [a]Emerson Spartz as quoted by Andrew Marantz in *The Virologist*, The New Yorker, p. 26 (Jan. 5, 2015).

---

[290]If you doubt whether there is a speculative, scientismic edge to science, especially when studying human beings, consider a large, recent study published in the highly respected journal, *Science*, that could not replicate over half of the psychological studies it re-tested; *see*, *Estimating the reproducibility of psychological science*, Vol. 349, Issue 6251, DOI: 10.1126/science.aac4716, Science (Aug. 28, 2015).

Rational Agnosticism- Existential Causation in the Eastern Traditions

However, both Western and Eastern perspectives are represented within the philosophy of *Lean* since *Lean* originated from a synthesis of both Occidental and Oriental cultures and concepts.[291] In contrast to Western/Occidental philosophies' explanations for existence, with the limited exception of the *Buddhist* principle of co-arising, Eastern/Oriental philosophies have generally considered questions as to the cause of the *Universe's* creation to be without purpose, instead choosing to be rationally agnostic. Eastern philosophies attempt to prove existence from the very fact of consumers perhaps falsely presuming that the *Universe* could not exist. Coming from the West myself, I like to think about Henri Bergson's quote below from 1911 when he was considering this conundrum:[292]

> *...If I ask myself why bodies or minds exist rather than nothing, I find no answer, but that a logical principle, such as A=A, should have the power of creating itself, triumphing over the nought throughout eternity, seems to me natural.... Suppose, then, that the principle on which all things rest, and which all things manifest, possesses an existence of the same nature as that of the definition of the circle, or as that of the axiom A=A: the mystery 'o existence vanishes.*

---

[291] As discussed in *Stream 1*, the modern concept of *Lean* in many ways began with the export of the Deming Cycle from post-war England to post-war Japan; *Toyota* then developed the Deming Cycle into its notion of *Kaizen*; the term *Lean* was coined by John Krafcik while at MIT to describe *Toyota's* Total Quality Management (*TQM*) using the Deming Cycle through *Kaizen* ; and global organizations and consultants then iteratively applied *Lean* as a form of TQM to other businesses until it became a universal business philosophy.

[292] Heri Bergson, *Creative Evolution* , Ch. IV, 276, in, *The Cinematographical Mechanism of Thought and the Mechanistic Illusion — A Glance at the History of Systems — Real Becoming and False Evolutionism* (1911).

Eastern philosophy thus is almost an inverse of the Western/Occidental concept of, '*From nothing, nothing comes,*' being more, '*There is because there must be.*'[293] According to the 14 unanswered questions attributed to Buddha, much of the logical, *Axiom of Causation* reasoning is pointless because consumers' very existence means that consumers or something else must have always existed, which is quite smart. Buddha's 14 unanswered questions are organized into four *Lean*, philosophical categories according to their subject matter:

Questions concerning the existence of the world in time:
1. *Is the world eternal?*
2. *...or not?*
3. *...or both?*
4. *...or neither?*
(Pali texts omit "both" and "neither")

Questions concerning the existence of the world in space:
5. *Is the world finite?*
6. *...or not?*
7. *...or both?*
8. *...or neither?*
(Pali texts omit "both" and "neither")

Questions referring to personal experience:
9. *Is the self identical with the body?*
10. *...or is it different from the body?*

Questions referring to life after death:
11. *Does the Tathagata (Buddha) exist after death?*
12. *...or not?*
13. *...or both?*

---
[293] Hegel, G.W.F. [§ 133], *Science of Logic*; or in its Latin articulation, *ex nihilo, nihil fit*.

14....*or neither?*
- Attributed to Buddha[294]

By leaving these questions unanswered, Buddhists take a logically agnostic position in regards to the mind/body duality and the *Universe's* origin. Buddhists instead address the *pratītyasamutpāda/co-arising* by deeply pursuing questions of *who* consumers are today rather than focusing on *why* they came to be.[295]

Philosophers, physicists and mathematicians all have something to say about this. The ancient Greek Parmenides *who* also proposed this, '*From nothing, nothing comes*' concept, also stated that the last conceivable *thing* that could *be* before true nothingness would be an empty set or *knowledge* that nothing existed. And scientists often step further into this discussion by saying that the very structure of information itself comes from the mere possibility of true *nothingness*.[296] Mathematicians added to this concept by saying that an empty set still has enough information value to be considered more than completely empty.

You likewise may choose to view causation within a *Lean* business *i/deô*logy in a modified form resulting in an infinite regression and becoming self-defining since *nothing* could never *be* by circular reasoning.[297] This leads to the startling conclusion that you may be making a false presumption in business that true nothing could

---

[294] *See*, John Hick, *The Buddha's 'Undetermined Questions' and the Religions*, Article 8 (2004), found at http://www.johnhick.org.uk/article8.html (accessed Feb. 12, 2015).

[295] *See also the following*, Sanjaya Belatthaputta, a 5th-century BCE Indian philosopher who expressed agnosticism about any afterlife; Protagoras, a 5th-century BCE Greek philosopher who was agnostic about the gods; and the Nasadiya Sukta in the Rig Veda which is agnostic about the origin of the *Universe*.

[296] One might likewise describe the origin of existence in epistemological sources, which is the philosophical study of knowledge. The real origin of everything in a Cartesian sense could be studied through the neologism, *Epistemontology*. However, since knowledge requires some medium, even if that is only within a singular, physical dimension, I will simply use the term *Ontology* to incorporate the entire meaning of existence from a realistic perspective. Likewise, philosophers may note some sense of Hegal's, *Being and Nothingness*, throughout this discussion.

[297] Such as the Latin concept referenced earlier, *ex nihil, nihilo fit*.

in fact be.²⁹⁸ However, you of course cannot ever test that theory since you would never be around to experience the result!

Boundaries of Reason – Self-Causing Causes, Gödel's *Second Incompleteness Theorem* and Simon's *Bounded Rationality*

Unfortunately, as you can see, no one now demonstrates *why* information exists within at least two *Lean* sigmas ($\geq/2\sigma$) of intersubjective, scientific validity, thereby making any explanation of the origin of reason a mere story.²⁹⁹ The greatest problem for science in proving an intelligible reason for the *Universe's* existence and ultimately *who* and *why* consumers are is that while some scientific evidence exists that the *Universe* originated from a singular event like the *Big Bang*, science has not been able to describe such origin axiomatically or systemically, and thus scientists themselves still engage in theoretically intuitive speculation as a form of scientismic belief.³⁰⁰

Beyond our own scientific ignorance, many famous philosophers and mathematicians, such as David Hume, Bertrand Russell and Kurt Gödel, provided significant reasons *why* reason cannot explain itself.³⁰¹ Even Immanuel Kant, though he intuitively believed that human experience requires reason, famously limited the application of reason to human experience, which forms the basis for the scientific empiricism that allows you to scientifically test *what* a

---

²⁹⁸ *See*, the Stanford Encyclopædia of Philosophy entry on, '*Sufficient Reason*,' for support in regards to, *ex nihilo, nihil fit*.

²⁹⁹ In other words, your etiological speculation must be rationally agnostic.

³⁰⁰ For general background reading on this topic, I suggest reading, Jim Holt's book, *Why Does the World Exist?: An Existential Detective Story*, Liveright; 1 edition (Apr. 8, 2013).

³⁰¹ Stanford Encyclopædia of Philosophy entry on, '*Sufficient Reason*'; Hume, *Treatise of Human Nature*(I, 3,3); Russell, Bertrand, and Frederick Copleston, *Debate on the Existence of God,* (1964) in John Hick (ed.), *The Existence of God* , The Macmillan Company; 1st edition (Sep. 1, 1964).

paos is worth.³⁰² I provide a brief synopsis of these limits to reason within a business *i/deôlogy* below from a more logically systemic perspective so you may better know where the rational foundation of *U / PP* true-north value begins and ends.³⁰³

> *We shall not cease from exploration /*
> *And the end of all our exploring /*
> *Will be to arrive where we started /*
> *And know the place for the first time.*
> - T.S. Eliot, Four Quartets (1943).

One well-known circularity that is almost always described by authors writing on this subject is Gödel's *Second Incompleteness Theorem* (1931).³⁰⁴ Alfred North Whitehead and Bertrand Russell, in their book titled *Principia Mathematica* written at the turn of the 20th century, attempted to construct a logical, non-mathematical system starting from universally axiomatic truths, to prove all further truths from these postulates.³⁰⁵ While Whitehead and Russell thought they constructed a system for universally deducing all reason from these axioms, Kurt Gödel proved otherwise by demonstrating that some truths within Whitehead and Russell's system, though true, could not be proven within the system itself.

A common, one-phrase synopsis of Gödel's proof is the expression within Whitehead and Russell's logic that stands as the mathematical equivalent of, '*I cannot be proven.*' '*I cannot be proven,*' creates an immediate, obvious and obnoxious paradox, since if the sentence

---

³⁰²Emmanuel Kant,*Critique of Pure Reason* (1787).

³⁰³A book I recommend describing the axiomatic and systemic limits to reason is one so titled, Noson S. Yanofsky,*The Outer Limits of Reason: What Science, Mathematics, and Logic Cannot Tell Us*, p. 32, The MIT Press (Aug. 23, 2013).

³⁰⁴*Ibid.*

³⁰⁵Not to be confused with several other *Principia Mathmatica's*, most namely the one from Isaac Newton first published in a first edition on July 5th, 1687.

could be proven, its plain language meaning is false. However, if the statement could be proven that it cannot be proven, then that proof creates a logical contradiction for the system itself that is supposed to deductively prove everything non-tautologically. Thus, while true within the system, this paradox caused a big problem for people *who* wanted to understand and apply true-north value in a singularly consistent way!

Many mathematicians have validated *what* Gödel showed, which is that neither a logical nor mathematical system based on real numbers could exclude paradoxes and self-reference. The mathematical, logical conundrum stated by Gödel's *Second Incompleteness Theorem* is one that can be easily seen in Bertrand Russell's *Reference Paradox*. The *Reference Paradox* states that the, ' list of all lists cannot contain a listing of itself,' by definition since the *n*th item in the list would always need a further list to capture the list's total meaning.[306] This infinite logic creates a paradox to the definition of a list or set, sort of like an index to a library that would have to include itself but never stand outside the library's own reference collection.[307]

The full details of Gödel's proof likewise fall outside the scope of this book, but I encourage you to read further through the footnoted references for you to *Lean* philosophically because this is so important to understand the *Universe* in which consumers and organizations operate.[308] You are left with the fact that consumers' existences cannot be explained entirely through *Lean U/P* values, but rather only through personally intuitive speculation at this point in time. You cannot exclude all forms of tautological self-reference for *who* consumers are or *why* they buy anything at all at the furthest edges of a store.

So *why* does this matter to the philosophy of *Lean* and counting

---

[306] Or as stated another way by *Cantor's Theorem*, '*for any set A, the set of all subsets of A (the power set of A, P(A)) has a strictly greater cardinality than A itself.*'
[307] *See generally*, the Stanford Encyclopædia of Philosophy's entry on, '*Russell's Paradox*.'
[308] Such as, Noson S. Yanofsky, *The Outer Limits of Reason* (2013).

the money you make? Because one would think that mathematics based on real numbers could be self-contained since it is so widely heralded as the big data elixir to understand all that consumers truly value and will buy. However, Gödel showed that Whitehead and Russell's *Principia Mathematica* failed to create a mathematical system without self-reference, and that all mathematical systems based on real numbers invariably break down and fall into strange, logically tautological loops at some points.[309] Mathematicians have already seemed to settle the question for their discipline, accepting as an axiomatic truth that they cannot find a single, axiom to explain all mathematical theories in light of Gödel's incompleteness theorems, among many other mathematical paradoxes in existence.

You can find many paradoxes beyond Gödel's own inside and outside of mathematics.[310] Modern concepts beyond Gödel's *Second Incompleteness Theorem*, such as quantum physics and relativity theories appear to show that reason has its limits in a general, universal sense - that some truths cannot be logically deduced, some are relative, and some arise from matters of pure chance.

A common example of this provided by physicists and non-physicists is the scientismic debate around *Heisenberg's Uncertainty Principle*[311] under the Copenhagen interpretation that states that observing Matter and Energy at a quantum level actually in some ways determines its existential state and *Ontological Realization*. The competing Everette/Schrodinger interpretation says that these particles cohere/discohere with many other worlds like words and

---

[309] This point was alluded to by Douglas R. Hofstadter in, *Gödel, Escher, Bach*, Basic Books (1999), that while mathematics may hold true computationally, it is not a logically cohesive system overall such that it can abstract itself in a consistent way; Douglas Hofstadter expressed this notion more concretely in, *I Am a Strange Loop*, Basic Books, Reprint edition (Jul. 8, 2008) (or as noted later, '*I 'AM' a Strange Loop*').

[310] *See e.g.*, for language paradoxes, Chapter 1 in, Yanofsky, *The Outer Limits of Reason* (2013).

[311] Again, not drawing any other conclusions from this fact so as not to commit a Chomsky as described by the *Philosophical Lexicon*, where one, '... draws extravagant metaphysical implications from scientifically established facts.'

phrases with parallel meaning.³¹² Quantum theory is the next great debate - equivalent to that of a flat world or heliocentrism - whether we will sail off the edge of reason we do not yet know, but we nonetheless have a duty to be optimistic.³¹³

Given academic uncertainty even about the *Heisenberg Uncertainly Principle*, the theories of relativity and other physically scientific true-north values appear to become subjective, personal and require scientismic belief at sufficiently quantum or intergalactic scales - we do not know for sure the source of knowledge at this time on an axiomatic basis. Even if the laws of physics are deterministic, consumers as self-conscious, self-interested, and self-centered agents, freely and willingly optimize toward an infinite, indeterminable, and possibly tautological *Universe*. While this does not mean that knowledge cannot ultimately be explained, it evidences the tension between reason and apparent paradox in matters beyond logic, just as physicists recently did when attempting to demonstrate supersymmetry by discovering the Higgs Boson *God Particle* in the Large Hydron Collider that pushed scientists up against the limits of *what* makes physical sense.³¹⁴

You don't want to mis-apply these limits to matters of reasonable certainty.³¹⁵ In fact philosophers make fun of other philosophers who do. However, you ought to understand them in a general way to become aware of the boundaries of *what* consumers can truly value at this point in time. Bringing this discussion back to *Lean* organizations, Herbert Simon's *Bounded Rationality* demonstrated in any event that customers', employees', and organizations' irrationality stays well within the narrower boundaries of the walls and cubicles in which *Lean* organizations operate.³¹⁶ Nonetheless,

---

³¹²David Deutsch, *The Beginning of Infinity*, p. 309 (2011).

³¹³*Ibid* at p. 196.

³¹⁴*See generally*, Raffi Khatchadourian, *A Star in a Bottle*, The New Yorker (Mar. 3, 2014).

³¹⁵Dan Falk, *New Support for Alternative Quantum View*, Quanta Magazine (May 16, 2016).

³¹⁶Herbert A. Simon, *A Behavioral Model of Rational Choice,* pp. 99–118, Quarterly Journal of Economics 69 (Feb. 1955).

the very act of expanding the boundaries of knowledge is the same as creating wealth, which is what you want and ought to do.[317]

20th Century Fragmentation of Unification

Given these limits that 20th century mathematics ran into, science and even philosophy turned away from universal, systemic analysis that tries to induce a single explanation for everything from all that people specifically think they know. Thought leaders stopped trying to connect all details within a universal theory and instead segregated their analysis into discrete, disconnected fields of knowledge for the sake of advancing each domain. These more specific insights became much more effective at describing and predicting reality than could all the proposed unifying theorems, even if more specific theories could not be used to explain other true-north values.

Contemporary philosophers went so far as to concentrate only on problems they felt stood safely outside of science's reach.[318] While professional philosophers maintain this intellectual posture in this post-post-modern era, rather ironically, leading physicists like Stephen Hawking and David Deutsch among others still noodle on overarching physical theories of all true-north value in books like *Grand Design*, and through physical concepts like *string theory*, while philosophers largely abandoned that explanatory goal.[319]

Even if both contemporary philosophy and science dislike overarching, unifying theories, they cannot avoid the fact that all underlying axioms and systems resulted in all consumers' personal presences and consciousness that are Unified for most intents and

---

[317] David Deutsch, *The Beginning of Infinity* , p. 456 (2011).

[318] *See e.g.*, Werner Callebaut, *The Dialectics of Dis/Unity in the Evolutionary Synthesis and Its Extensions*, and his essay in the anthology edited by Massimo Pigliucci and Gerd B. Mueller, *Evolution – The Extended Synthesis*; or as per philosopher Nicholas Rescher who said tongue in cheek that this was so Ph.D. students could write dissertations without embarrassing themselves, Nicholas Rescher, *Axiogenises* (2010).

[319] Nicholas Rescher, *Process Philosophy*, University of Pittsburgh Press (2000).

preferences. On balance, consumers' unified consciousness' cause them to buy *paos*, which makes the money earned truly meaningful. Consumers bring together all of the natural laws and their biological processes into their personal presences of *who* they are as consumers. So to understand *what* people will buy, you must look at customers in the same way as cohering the three perspectives and truth types within *who* they are as *Lean* people. To conduct effective business analysis, you must apply all discrete axiomatic and systemic evidence, and all speculatively intuitive notions of true-north value, to *who* you believe consumers are and *why* you believe they will buy *paos* in meaningful quantities, which U/P as the unifying philosophy of *Lean* helps you do.

Money as Unified *Lean* Theory

However, a tension arises between the unification of the *Universe*, the different perspectives consumers bring to *how they* perceive the *Universe*, and the true-north value of the *paos* within it. You must recognize *how* consumers' mutations and adaptations in their underlying physical processes created divergent perceptual and cognitive biases within them, which behavioral economists and marketing neuroscientists increasingly explain. When you think about it, marketing departments analyze consumers' different personal perspectives on various *paos* daily.

And yet, while consumers may have been created by universal axioms and processual systems, they nonetheless stand in a singular, inter-subjective *Universe* that yields different personal perspectives on it. Common sense indicates that you ought to be able to discuss the full meaning of market research in largely coherent fashion, even in this post-post-modern, deconstructed world. Since these days deconstructionist scientific and literary theories have largely accomplished their end-goals,[320] organizations now operate in the deconstructed after-math of a post-post-modern world striving (perhaps pointlessly) toward some common sense re-unification to make an effective difference in *what* consumers commonly experience from the *paos* they buy. This unified experience ultimately informs *what* gets *b-ought* in the singular ex-change of *paos* for money that the philosophy of *Lean* represents.

With this intellectual history in mind, I propose a unifying, coherent, *Lean* business *i/de*ô*logy* that *Leans* an organization philosophically back into consumers, while simultaneously helping you become completely aware of the intellectual difficulties of creating over-arching, and over-sold, get-rich-quick schemes.

You must keep the scientific, literary and philosophical sophist-ication of consumers' underlying, divergent, funda-mental processes in mind while you re-cognize that customers identify themselves as buying *paos* from a singularly unified, *Lean*, personal perspective. Because regardless, consumers inevitably look to explain the coherence of their *Lean* personal identities from that perspective and uplift themselves by buying *paos*. Thus, U/P is a meta-modernist business philosophy optimistically attempting to synthesize this reality while keeping in mind all this post-modern skepticism.[321]

Beautiful Question Marks??

Keeping this post-modern intellectual legacy in mind along your journey up the true-north value stream, you ought to find some unifying reason for the origin of *who* consumers are from universally axiomatic, or processually systemic truth values with at least two *Lean* sigmas ($\geq/2\sigma$) of confidence in order to motivate

---

[320] As conclusively evidenced by the election of the 45th President of the U.S.A.,*see e.g.*, Casey Williams, *Has Trump Stolen Philosophy's Critical Tools?*, The New York Times (Apr. 17, 2017); for more on metamodernism, *see*, Timotheus Vermeulen and Robin van den Akker, *Notes on Metamodernism*, Journal of Aesthetics & Culture, Vol. 2 (2010).

[321] David Deutsch,*The Beginning of Infinity* , p. 314 (2011).

them to purchase something. Otherwise, you will be selling into a speculative market. To broadly find true-north value, you must still seek it in either philosophy, science or mathematics.

However, while philosophical attempts at finally explaining the origin of existence are at this point rather historical in nature, in the inverse, science must then be able to resolve all outstanding philosophical (or theological) questions, which science has not done to date. This counter-poses to Stephen Hawking's statement in his book *Grand Design* that logical philosophy was a historical relic, and that quantum physics had assumed all of the burden of explaining *why* consumers exist.[322] Perhaps Hawking has stated an axiomatic truth, but then science has not to date explained all outstanding philosophical questions, such as *what* might be a universally recognized, self-causing cause.[323] This leaves the pursuit of the largest markets with a problem that can only be resolved by finding a unifying, scientific explanation for all knowledge.

Science has clearly done a remarkable job in explaining discrete facets of the *Universe* and predicting consequences based on such insights. To provide a high level perspective of the relationship of scientific theories leading back to the gap that science still has to fill about the origin of consumers' and organizations' existences, consider this chart created by Prof. Max Tegmark at MIT of the efficient first causes interrelating the scientific and humanities disciplines leading to an ultimate *why* question mark above and below.[324]

Below you see in Prof. Tegmark's chart [325] a range of scientific

---

[322] Stephen Hawking, *Grand Design*, p. 1, Ch. 1 *Mystery of Being*, Bantam Books (2010), where he writes, '*Traditionally these are questions for philosophy, but philosophy is dead. Philosophy has not kept up with modern developments in science, particularly in physics.*'
[323] *Ibid.*
[324] *See e.g.,* Simon Sinek, *Start with Why: How Great Leaders Inspire Everyone to Take Action* (2009).
[325] Max Tegmark, *Parallel Universes*, p. 12, *Science and Ultimate Reality: From Quantum to Cosmos*, honoring John Wheeler's 90th birthday, J.D. Barrow, P.C.W. Davies, & C.L. Harper eds., Cambridge University Press (2003).

disciplines explaining many discrete aspects of consumers' existences. In fact, philosophy, physics and math are all degrees of the same 'thing' from different perspectives, each informing the other to create a cohesive body of knowledge within the *OM*.[326] Or as Galileo Galilei said, '*Philosophy is written in this grand book, the universe, which stands continually open to our gaze... It is written in the language of mathematics.*'[327] However, neither mathematics, science nor philosophy conclusively explain the origin of existence as indicated by the question mark ? at the top and bottom of this true-north value stream. To complete this chart, I added a question mark at the end of Tegmark's chart to represent the necessarily unbounded intuitive speculation about *what* is not. If you imagine seeing this chart in three dimensions, these two question marks are one and the same, folding back on each other to touch and complete the possibly circular ontological teleology of consumers' value streams within the ontological medium of all known existence:

---

[326] *See e.g.*, Robbert Dijkgraaf, *Quantum Questions Inspire New Math*, Quanta Magazine (Mar. 30, 2017).

[327] Galileo Galilei, *The Assayer: A Letter to the Illustrious and Very Reverend Don Virginio Cesarini* (1623).

203

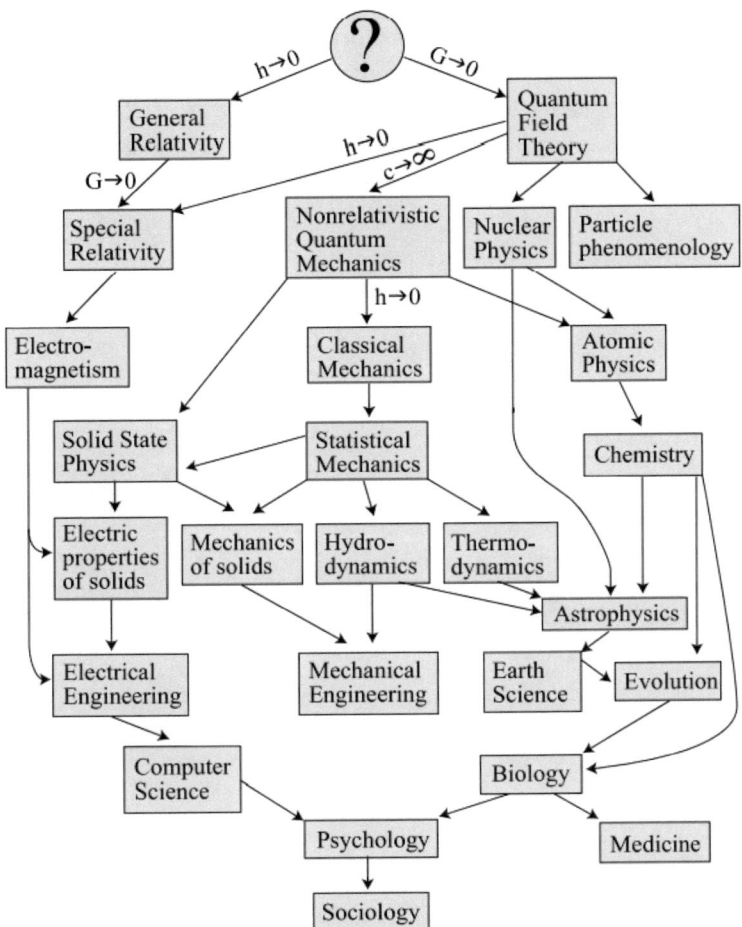

Prof. Tegmark's Chart of Disciplines (© 2015, Used with Permission)

?

Chart of scientific and humanities fields back to the inception indicted by a question mark ? at the top and bottom of this value stream.

204 Stream 3: Existence

Like Douglas Hofstadter did in his book, *Gödel, Escher, Bach*, I am including a picture by Maurits Cornelis Escher within this discussion of circularity. Here you may compare this image of Escher's to Tegmark's chart. Escher's grand image, '*Waterfall*,' shows *how* clearly Escher (and Hofstadter) understood this *Lean* true-north value stream:

Waterfall (All M.C. Escher works © 1961, 2016, The M.C. Escher Company - the Netherlands. All rights reserved. Used with Permission. www.mcescher.com)

Prof. Tegmark's chart aligns with our earlier delineation of the great fields of knowledge as seen again here:

> *? Mathematics*
> *Science*
> *Philosophy*
> *Religious, Spiritual, or Scientismic Intuition*
> *?*

You may further compress this spectrum of knowledge down to *U/PP* true-north values that are similarly bounded by a question mark at each end:

> *?*
> **Universal Truths**
> **Process Truths**
> **Personal Truths**
> *?*

You may finally condense this fountain of knowledge into *U/P* by like-wise putting question marks on either end:

> *?*
> *U*
> *Lean*
> *People*
> *?*

U stands for universal truth, *Lean* represents a processual truth, while People are a personal truth only truly knowable through empathy.

Fecund Universes?

> How do we know that the creations of worlds are not determined by falling grains of sand?
> – Victor Hugo, Les Misérables

To better understand existence from a physical perspective, let's revisit a little more closely one of the intuitive, scientismic explanations for consumers' possibly circular existences we discussed earlier called *fecund universes*. One of the most intuitively speculative, scientismic conceptions for existence is that of parallel or *fecund* universes, which describes unlimited levels of *Universes* representing all possible *Universes* that could be.[328]

In the inverse of the concept of, '*From nothing, nothing comes,*' the term *fecund universes* describes the notion that every possible thing exists, and *what* you know as the *Universe* simply represents one version of infinite universal variations in infinite regression.[329] In this scenario, consumers are a statistical result of the fact that something must exist, and if something exists then everything exists, and if every conceivable *Universe* exists then consumers exist in the one iteration that provides for consumers' existences as you personally know them now online or in-line in stores. In a way, the argument for *fecund universes* is reminiscent of the ontological argument for God's existence since proponents get close to saying

---

[328] Also referred to as *fecund universes* by Robert Nozick in, *Philosophical Explanations*, Belknap Press (1981); *see also* Lee Somlin in, *The Life of the Cosmos* (1997); *see also* Stephen Hawking, *Grand Design* (2010); *see also* the Stanford Encyclopædia of Philosophy entry on, '*Many Worlds*'; and Jim Holt, *Why Does the World Exist?: An Existential Detective Story*, Norton (2012).

[329] As Leibniz said in 1710 CE, '... *the whole succession and the whole agglomeration of all existent things, lest it be said that several worlds could have existed in different times and different places. For they must needs be reckoned all together as one world or, if you will, as one Universe,*' in Part I, para. 8 of *Theodicy: Essays on the Goodness of God, the Freedom of Man and the Origin of Evil.*

that if you could imagine any *Universe* then that *Universe* does exist. However, if you think this notion is completely far-fetched, consider the small irony that you like all people hopefully spend a third of your life each day in fairly random, parallel universes that are very personally real to you every time you go to sleep.

This concept of infinitely many universes actually originated with Plato and has been brought forward by modern physicists to conform with modern mathematics and physics.[330] This adapted scientific concept of many worlds follows from the details of quantum mechanics that fall outside the scope of this book, but this general concept ought to help you gain perspective on *what* may be in the fullest sense and *what* may be not at all.[331]

This concept of fecund universes in one sense may also be seen as the *Anthropic Principle* set into scientific terms, meaning that you should expect that the structure and cause of the *Universe* as consumers have come to know it is consistent with one that intelligibly results in consumers being *who* they are.[332] The fecund universes concept conforming with the *Anthropic Principle* is thus just another way of stating that a consistent stream of reasoning exists from consumers' existences back to a *sui generis*, or self-causing cause, of everything simultaneously being since *nothing* simply could not be by its own definition.[333]

---

[330] *See generally*, Stanford Encyclopædia of Philosophy entry on, '*Many-Worlds Interpretation of Quantum Mechanics*.'

[331] *See generally*, Mark Tegmark, *Parallel Universes*, Dept. of Physics, Univ. of Pennsylvania (Jan. 23, 2003) found at http://space.mit.edu/home/tegmark/multiverse.pdf (accessed May 12, 2014).

[332] Per *The Oxford English Dictionary*, the *Anthropic Principle* is, '... *any of several versions of the principle that since humans exist in the universe, the observable properties of the universe, and particularly of certain of the fundamental constants, must be compatible with the existence of intelligent life, esp. human life.*'

[333] *Ibid*.

Other Scientismic Theories

Aside from parallel or fecund universes, quantum physicists have posited many other theories for the origin of existence and all true-north value over the last several decades as quantum physics has advanced. Each real advance of quantum physics often directly affects the philosophy of *Lean* when determining the reason for consumers' existences and source of true-north U/P values. Quantum physicans such as Alex Vilenkin and Steven Weinberg have put forward several explanations for *why* consumers exist beyond fecund universes, from *quantum fluctuations* creating a complex universe of *net zero energy,* to quantum physics experiments showing the possibility of matter appearing out-of-order in time, thus voiding the concept of ultimate causation altogether as a mere mirage.[334] Other physicists have examined a real probability that the *Universe* in which consumers exist is merely a simulation just like *The Lean Startup*'s *IMVU* as discussed in *Stream 1*, even though such answer would not resolve *what* created the simulation in the first place.[335]

Alternatively, some philosophers have suggested that this *Universe* as you know it exists because it is the best one that could be and still logically cohere. Thus, if something were to exist at all, it must be as you actually know it, which seems like a form of the *Anthropic Principle*.[336] Unfortunately, all such theories remain unprovable at the current moment, merely standing as intuitive, scientismic speculation not yet validated as processually systemic or universally axiomatic truths. While physicists and some philosophers continue to conjecture as to *why* consumers exist, none can yet prove it axiomatically or systematically, which is not to invalidate their

---

[334] Jim Holt, *Why Does the World Exist?: An Existential Detective Story* (2012).

[335] In *IMVU*'s case, we know it was Eric Ries *who* created it, but you know what I mean; see generally, Silas Beane, Zohreh Davoudi and Martin J. Savage, *Constraints on the Universe as a Numerical Simulation*, INT-PUB-12-046, Cornell University Library (Nov. 12, 2012).

[336] Nicholas Rescher, *Process Metaphysics: An Introduction to Process Philosophy*, SUNY Series in Philosophy, Publisher State University of New York Press (1996).

speculation but rather to note the relative degree of immaturity of this intuition.[337]

Physicists, and some philosophers of science, present all of these conjectures as they do for all scientific and philosophical explanations under a general *best fit* principle, under a presumption that they can only *know* reality directly to the extent testable data fits to a given theoretical model. This is *what* fecund universes and other physical theories do to explain the origin of existence within the domain of physics, by fitting current scientific evidence to universal, true-north values. The search for the Higgs Boson *God Particle* most recently reconfirmed this method in some degree by failing to disprove the *Standard Model*.[338] By better fitting evidence to known truth values, and occasionally changing those truth values in response to conflicting evidence, physicists continue to better understand *how* the *Universe* came to be and *how* physical laws led to consumers' existences. They also shed more light on the normative true-north value consumers demand when they buy *paos* from their unified, personal perspectives.[339]

Consumers' Existences are *As If* Self-Defined

To meaningfully monetize consumers' normative and real true-north values in *Lean* fashion, you must discover their ignorances, infinities, circularities and paradoxes.[340] To physicists, consumers are bounded at the atomic level by the difficulty in detecting particles and anti-particles, and at the cosmological level by the speed of light multiplied by the time light takes to travel from the furthest

---

[337] As referenced by Steven Weinberg in Jim Holt, *Why Does The World Exist: An Existential Detective Story* (2012).

[338] *See generally*, the Stanford Encyclopædia of Philosophy entry on, '*Simplicity.*'

[339] For further information on the *Mathematical/Computable Universe Hypothesis* and *Ultimate Ensemble, see again*, Mark Tegmark, *Parallel Universes*, Dept. of Physics, Univ. of Pennsylvania (Jan. 23, 2003); *see also* Nick Bostrom, *Are You Living in a Computer Simulation*, Vol. 53, No. 211, pp. 243-255, Philosophical Quarterly (2003).

[340] *See generally*, Marcelo Gleiser, *The Island Of Knowledge*, Basic Books (2014).

edges of the known *Universe* .³⁴¹ To mathematicians, consumers are bounded by infinities and inherent paradoxes that limit their ability to construct a universal, non-self-referential ontology.³⁴²

From the universally axiomatic perspective, you can view consumers' existences *as if* they themselves were self-defining, *as if* their existences did not have an initial self-causing cause that gives them an ultimate *why*. From a processually systemic perspective, consumers' reason to exist may seem logically tautological, *as if* they exist simply to further and more fully be even though logic suggests they ought to exist due to some finally agreed on, causal reason. And yet, consumers personally intuitively speculate, either as spiritualists, theists, scientismists or other -ists, about an ultimate third-party cause for their lives and existences.

I only restate here the common sense notion that consumers universally and processually experience existence *as if* they exist simply because they do regardless of creed, but they may also speculate about a theological or scientismic purpose not yet agreed on by at least two *Lean* sigmas ($\geq/2\sigma$) of informed people.³⁴³

Thus, for *Lean* business purposes only, I suggest that you ought to at least recognize the possibility that consumers exist entirely due to mathematical and/or scientific reasons, which is to say, entirely due to universally axiomatic and/or processually systemic true-north values. Your understanding this perspective strictly for business purposes will allow you to see more clearly consumers' existences *as if* they were *Ontologically Teleological*. Seeing all consumer's existences *as if* they were operating up through an *Ontological Teleology* is different than seeing them as coming from whatever open-ended intuitive speculation you or they may have

---

³⁴¹For a nice popular review of these concepts, *see generally*, the television series,*Cosmos: A Spacetime Odyssey with Neil DeGrasse Tyson* (2014).

³⁴²I am of course referring to Gödel's *Second Incompleteness Theorem*, though yet again I am careful not to commit a Chomsky by recognizing that the *Universe* is infinitely open ended.

³⁴³Truth value requires fully informed people because epistemic probability varies between them, which is why we generally revert to the consensus of experts.

as to *why* they exist. An *Ontological Teleology* recognizes the fact that consumers' ultimate cause may actually be tautological but may also be not - we don't know.[344] You benefit though from witnessing the upward genesis of their *Ontological Teleology* by better identifying and creating salable U/P value. You do this by seeing them *as if* their purpose was possibly *Ontologically Teleological* in nearly circular form, which I understand is difficult at first to comprehend. For starters, here are a couple of personally intuitive hypotheticals of consumers with different belief systems, from theists to scientismists, to exemplify *how* you may better identify these consumers' distinct forms of true-north value by drawing clear lines around them:

Theists

On the flip-side of scientific axioms, theists assume that an intuitive, theological, or emotional explanation of existence is an axiomatic true-north value. However, no spiritualistic or theistic explanation changes the fact that *what* theistic customers commonly experience is *as if* they lived in an *Ontological Teleology* given that they still live in a rational *Universe*. Their faith simply acts as a personal self-causing cause to move them beyond the apparent circularity of existence that they experience. Thus, theistic customers seek meaning by speculating with personally intuitive, sublime forms of truth that ascend beyond the apparently circular chain of explanation of their commonly shared existence with other people *who* do not share the same theistic perspective. Theologians most often stipulate that their own personally perceived, intuitive experience and speculation is *what* they consider actually meaningful and only falsifiable on a mythical or emotional level until certain miracles, *Nirvanas* or end-of-days arrive. Theologians find *Ontological Teleological* true-north value by serving their physical needs as a means to find non-

---

[344]More technically, in the spirit of Karl Popper, no one has yet disproven that the *Universe* is *Ontologically Teleological*, even though consumers conjecture many reasons *why* it isn't.

tautological true-north value through open-ended, non-falsifiable, religiously dogmatic axioms that will answer all their prayers.

Scientismists

Similar to theists, some consumers generally *believe* or *have faith* in reason itself to explain existence, despite the *PSR, RCA , Axiom of Causation* and *5 Whys* not yet having axiomatic validity as I have defined it here.[345] People *who* place their faith in science to answer the biggest questions of their existence are called *scientismists*.[346] Your scientismic customers assume that a rational explanation for their ultimate existence exists. Just like theists *who* constantly receive spiritual stimulation and emotional validation, scientismists have their faith substantially and commonly reinforced by advances in modern science that empirically prove further consequential reasons for their lives and existences. These scientismic customers push the explanatory boundaries for their existences further and further by pursuing yet unproven, scientismic theories. This scientismic faith leads scientismists to speculate that reason within their existences holds to a physically valid self-causing cause such as might exist under quantum physics. Just like theists, scientismists faithfully find *Ontologically Teleological*value in serving their physical needs to hopefully find an ultimately self-causing physical axiom as an answer to all their conjectures, hypotheses, theories and laws.

---

[345]For a thorough argument in favor of the PSR being an axiomatic truth,*see generally* , Alexander Russ,*The Principle of Sufficient Reason: A Reassessment* , Cambridge Studies in Philosophy, Cambridge University Press (2006).

[346]A term often used by Karl Popper and other philosophers of science; *see also* David Deutsch,*The Beginning of Infinity* , p. 189 (2011).

Intuition Bracketing (the IB) Speculation for Money

Now, to accurately measure the salable normative, real and monetary value that *Lean* organizations ought to be producing, I suggest that you carefully identify consumers' speculative, scientismic and theological notions of intuitive value and differentiate them from known universal and process true-north values. Your *paos* will serve each of those true-north values separately. For an organization to re-produce *paos* that accurately addresses these true-north values, it must ground itself as well as possible in *what* it can axiomatically and systematically validate within consumers' lives and existences, while recognizing that *what* consumers believe transcends the apparent circularity of their existences. This is especially true if starting a risky business venture or operating in a new market with limited historical profits since an organization will be bridging itself philosophically forward across unchartered waters toward true-north value that no one has yet discovered.

Like the money veil over *what* people monetarily value, a veil exists over *what* consumers normatively value within *who* they consider themselves to be, which requires further distinction. Consumers' intuitive speculation makes identifying truely normative value within the domain of the *I/D Kata* difficult, and therefore requires you to differentiate true-north value types so you can know *how* to produce meaningful *paos* worth lots of money. To define this value veil for *Lean* business purposes within an *HQ*, I recommend developing a *you*-shaped, conceptual value lens that I call an *Intuition Bracket(IB)* structuring *who* consumers are and may be. The *IB* conceptual lens sees through the veil covering the truly normative value of existence, while *what* the *IB* filters out is open-ended, intuitive speculation. The *Intuition Bracket* is thus the summation of an infinite set within which all U/P value (a.k.a. reason) resides, and is synonymous with understanding consumers' specific place in the *Universe* .³⁴⁷

Chart of the *Intuition Bracket* or *IB*

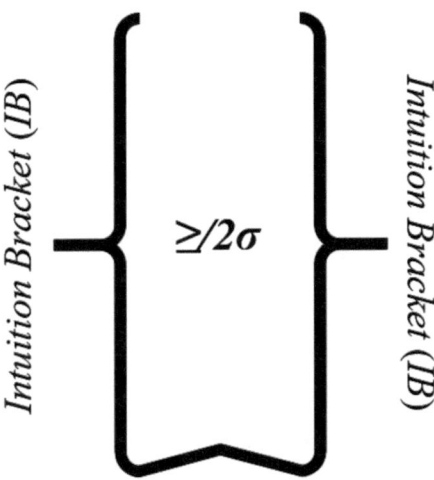

The *Intuition Bracket* or *IB*

As prescribed above, the conceptual *IB* allows a *Lean* business *i/deô*logy to separate consumers' universally axiomatic and processually systematic existences from *what* they personally, intuitively believe. You simultaneously ought to diverge such perspectives within your *Lean* business *i/deô*logy while keeping both in mind. Such an *Intuition Bracket* allows you to easily exclude consumers' intuitive speculation, but still allows you to define consumers' (and corporations') existences within the limits of the *IB*.³⁴⁸ As a reminder of what David Packard who founded HP said in 1965 as quoted from *Good to Great* :

> *I want to discuss WHY [emphasis his] a company*

---

³⁴⁷I provide these graphic pictograms in the spirit of Otto Neurath and Charles Bliss, to democratize knowledge so that these concepts might be universally well understood.

³⁴⁸*See again,* Marcelo Gleiser, *The Island of Knowledge: The Limits of Science and the Search for Meaning*, Basic Books (2014).

> *exists in the first place. In other words, why are we here? I think many people assume, wrongly, that a company exists simply to make money. While this is an important result of a company's existence, we have to go deeper and find the real reasons for our being.*

The *IB* thus identifies consumers and companies' essential reason for being by delineating different true-north value types. The *bracket* aspect of the *IB* creates an abstract category between the *U/P* and personal true-north values, and I propose, allows you to more deeply categorize existence itself to analyze, identify and try to measure consumers' real and monetary value as David Packard suggests.

The interior part of the *Intuition Bracket* contains that which consumers, and thus all of society, agree on an axiomatic or systemic basis. The *IB* contains that which belongs to consumers themselves, or by their very natures, that which is inherent, essential, proper, *of their own*, leaving outside the bracket their and all other people's speculative, intuitive true-north value perspectives they cannot confirm axiomatically or systematically with at least two *Lean* sigmas ($\geq/2\sigma$) of common agreement.[349] Let me reemphasize that *what* I mean by *intuition* is not *what* you might psychologically consider intuitive, but rather *what* people in general cannot axiomatically or systematically agree on at the moment with available knowledge.

I fully admit that the boundaries between these true-north value types can be unclear at first given the fact that science and perception, like *The Bed of Procrustes*,[350] often operate on a *best fit* basis. However, you can draw reasonably clear lines between that which

---

[349] This may be perceived to be analogous to existentialist *Epoché* bracketing objective true-north within all that we experience.

[350] *See generally*, Nassim Nicolas Taleb, *The Bed of Procrustes: Philosophical and Practical Aphorisms*, Random House (2010); *The Bed of Procustes* relates to the Greek allegory of a host who always amputated his guests to fit his beds.

can be falsified with empirical evidence through data and has some predictive validity through time with a reasonably certain degree of confidence, and those true-north values about which people speculate but have no widely agreed evidence or consensus.[351]

So within the *IB*, reason stands as that which you axiomatically and empirically know *on its own* based on widely agreed data across time, unlike intuitive truths that are not commonly agreed as predictably repeatable within at least two *Lean* sigmas ($\geq/2\sigma$) of universal confidence. Standing immediately outside of and adjacent to the *IB* are the true-north value perspectives consumers personally believe, which may be beyond any reason. Let me now provide you with another schematic to represent the *IB* and the boundary of pure reason that you may use in a business *i/deô*logy:

---

[351] *E.g. see*Massimo Pigliucci, *Philosophy of Pseudoscience: Reconsidering the Demarcation Problem*, University Of Chicago Press (Aug. 16, 2013).

Intuition Bracket of Reason

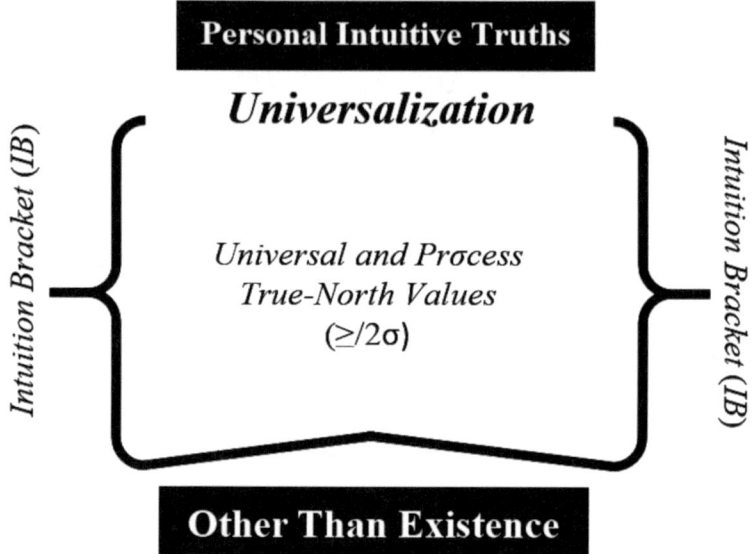

Inside the *Intuition Bracket* resides natural law, axiomatic and systemic truths, and all else that stands in juxtaposition to *what* is beyond consumers' widely shared conceptions of existence. Whether by intuitive or scientismic causes, bracketing axiomatic and systemic true-north perspectives within the *IB* allows you to focus on *who* consumers are when they find themselves in the world, hemmed in by their ignorances, infinities, circularities and paradoxes.

Let me re-emphasize for clarity sake that existence only appears this way for consumers on first impression, and that consumers must scientifically, intuitively or philosophically speculate to determine *what* caused the purpose of their existences. This matters in business because their purposeful meaning ultimately *Leans* them toward buying *paos* to further exist toward that end-goal, whether such end-goal is within the *IB* or not.

In the 1900s, the philosopher and psychologist Karl Jaspers was one of the first to define the *IB* when he created the term, '*Existenz.*' '*Existenz*' stands for the proposition that all people recognize these rational limits, and once known, begin to re-construct personal identities reflecting *who* they authentically are within those known limits. Jaspers' *Existenz* was the intellectual precursor to and inspiration for *Existentialism*.[352] Thus, within U/P, you might even write this notion as, "$\Sigma xistenz$," replacing the E with the capital sigma Σ. The capital sigma Σ indicates that $\Sigma xistenz$ sums all of *who* consumers are, and all that they want to buy, which they at least intuitively believe *Leans* them philosophically toward all meaning.

The Oriental religious philosophies that contributed to the development of *Lean* also support this concept of *Intuition Bracketing* for consumers to move beyond the origin of existence to understand their $\Sigma xistenz$ that much further up along the value stream. Since Buddha refused to systematically contemplate ontological arguments setting the question aside as moot,[353] consumers in general may also for all practical purposes bracket *what* they intuitively believe caused existence so they may further *Lean* themselves toward existing when buying *paos* while never needing to entirely let go of *what* faith they have. Thus, *paos* may serve consumers' needs for sustenance, consumers' intuitive speculation, or ideally a complementary combination of the two for a greater profit.

Ontological Medium (the *OM*)

Since the *IB* includes within itself axiomatic and systemic true-north value perspectives, it captures concepts such as universal space-time and physical processes that you can refer to as an

---

[352] Karl Jaspers also labelled the period where people started greatly increasing their energy consumption in the process of creating large scale social structures like religious institutions and economics departments as the *axial age*; see, Robert N. Bellah and Hans Joas, *The Axial Age and Its Consequences*, Harvard University Press (2012).

[353] According to their subject matter the questions can be grouped into four categories.

Ontological Medium, or an '*OM*' pronounced as, '*AUM.*' The *OM* is thick and pregnant with the *Ontological Teleology*,[354] consisting of all that you would expect within the *IB*, such as spacetime, chemistry, and the biodiversity of all life. Thus, the *OM* incorporates all of the assets that an organization manages.[355]

While consumers have some ideas as to the origin of their *Σxistenz* , applying *whatever* theological or intuitive causes they choose outside the *IB*, you and consumers can bracket those causes outside the bounds of the physical *OM* and conceptual *IB* to advance up along with *whatever* ought to be within those boundaries. You ought to employ the hypo-thetical concept of the *IB* in your *Lean* business *i/deô*logy with at least two *Lean* sigmas ($\geq/2\sigma$) of confidence to better isolate consumers' *Lean* true-north values. Doing so allows you to effectively bracket the origin of the *OM* through which consumers buy *paos* . When the *OM* is bracketed in this way, purchasing *paos* furthers the consumption of more *paos* to further be for nearly-circular purposes. I hope this concept of the *Ontological Medium* , a medium through which customers exist in space-time within stores, further explains for you the source of normative, real and monetary true-north value that *paos* re-generates and customers consume.

I am now going to provide a modified chart of the *IB* adding the *OM* to it:

---

[354]*E.g.* along the lines of holism as described by Jan Christiaan Smuts in, *Holism and Evolution*, 2nd Ed., Macmillian and Co. (1927).

[355]Similar conceptually to Assets Under Management; as stated earlier, beyond finance, ontology has a modern use in information science and genetics relating to the systematization and standardization of concepts within a given domain of knowledge, which extended meaning I will rely on in the later parts of this volume.

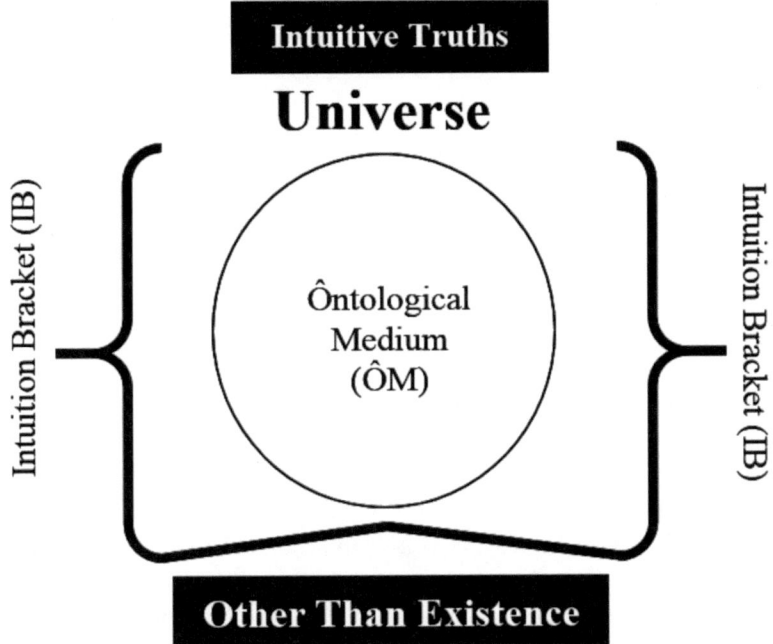

While all the forms of Matter and Energy within the domain of physics and other sciences reside within the *Ontological Medium*, within the *Intuition Bracket*, Matter and Energy self-organizes itself on a cosmological scale. This process occurs on balance within all universally axiomatic, immutable, and predictable physical transformations. The consistency of those transformations though seems to be impacted by the observer, and so the observer has a certain mesmerizing effect within the universal *OM*. This is *why* financial prophesy is inevitably heresy to some degree because the very act of planning and observing the results affects the very predictability of results that financial systems most reward. It is also *why* degrees of confidence increase with the number of people *who* agree with a truth value proposition, because they cohere their collective, overlapping consensus as they do.

The *Ontological Teleology* (the *OT*)

> *Corporations are getting better and better at seducing us into thinking the way they think - of profits as the telos...*
> - David Foster Wallace, *The Pale King* , p. 132, Back Bay Books (2011).

If you remove any notions of *grand design* from existence that people have devised or discovered, or any faith that science will ultimately explain *why* consumers exist at all, and you take existence simply as consumers' find it right now at this very moment, both within the *IB* and *what* stands in juxtaposition to it, you arrive at an apparently self-defining, *Ontological Teleology*, or in short, the *OT*. Since *Ontology* means existence, and *Teleology* means end-goal, *Ontological Teleology* simply means, ' *the end-goal of further existing.*' Thus, the concept of the *OT* within the *IB* has a possibly circular meaning.

Much like *how* you can see, '*Toyota*,' spelled out in its logo below, you can also see the overlapping *O* and the *T* of the *Ontological Teleology* within it: [356]

---

[356] Naturally, I associate the logo for *Toyota* with the *OT* coincidentally with no actual endorsement by *Toyota*; worth reading is *Toyota's* own description of the symbolism of its logo and trademark as follows: 'There are three ovals in the new logo that are combined in a horizontally symmetrical configuration. The two perpendicular ovals inside the larger oval represent the heart of the customer and the heart of the company. They are overlapped to represent a mutually beneficial relationship and trust between each other. The overlapping of the two perpendicular ovals inside the outer oval symbolize 'T' for Toyota, as well as a steering wheel, representing the vehicle itself. The outer oval symbolizes the world embracing Toyota. Each oval is contoured with different stroke thicknesses, similar to the 'brush' art known in Japanese culture. The space in the background within the logo exhibits the 'infinite values' which Toyota conveys to its customers: superb quality, value beyond expectation, joy of driving, innovation, and integrity in safety, the environment and social responsibility,' found at, *Ideas Behind the Ovals*, at http://www.toyota-global.com/showroom/emblem/passion/ (retrieved on Dec. 11, 2016).

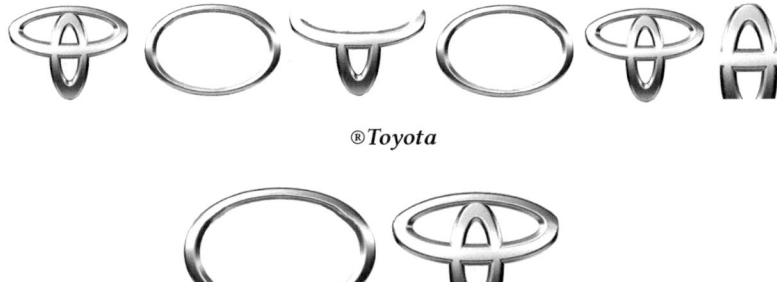

®Toyota

Ontological Teleology

®Toyota Motor Corporation

The Oxford English Dictionary further defines '*teleology*' as:

> *The doctrine or study of ends or final causes, esp. as related to the evidences of design or purpose in nature; also transf. such design as exhibited in natural objects or phenomena.*

Consumers' singular objective within the *IB* through the *OT* is an apparent end-goal to further exist to find meaning within the boundaries of axiomatic and systemic truths. Consumers search for meaning through the *OT* by attempting to springboard away from its apparent paradox by rational or irrational deed or creed to find linear, goal directed purpose.[357] However, the *OT* ultimately moves upward in a spiral motion along the curvature of spacetime because the present and future are always similes (though not fax-similes) of

---

[357] *See e.g.*, Bryan Caplan, *The Myth of the Rational Voter: Why Democracies Choose Bad Policies*, Princeton University Press (2008).

the past, so consumers are bound to re-invent history as they reach new heights.[358] Or to paraphrase the ancient Greek philosopher, Heraclitus of Ephesus (c. BCE 535 BCE – BCE 475), '*[N]o man ever steps in the same river twice because it is never the same river, and it is never the same man.*'

Of course, all goal-directed activity is teleologically non-circular to consumers as well within the boundaries of the *IB* so long as they only consider their beginning and final causes as being within the strict confines of the *OM*. Consumers can and do often choose to disregard the apparent logical circularity of their existences, or at least choose to believe in another cause not demonstrated through their common senses within axiomatic and systematic truths. For example, customers generally do not consider the apparently circular nature of their existences when consuming *paos*, because shopping does not seem tautological within the bounds of a store or shopping cart and consumers' everyday lives generally removed from existential extremes. Generally, people consciously consider only their immediate satisfaction and not their teleological purpose when consuming *paos* within the *Ontological Medium* as bounded by the *Intuition Bracket*. The *OT* though determines whether that consumption was nominally valuable, meaningful and thus good, and underlies all true-north value as defined by the fields of economics, psychology, and neuroscience, among all other disciplines...

At the same time, referring back to the earlier discussion of the circular nature of Samuelson's *Revealed Preference Theory* and *Lean* true-north value, that economic model generally fails to accurately map consumers' activities because it does not incorporate consumers' seemingly random search for meaning outside the *IB*. The oscillation between circular and non-circular belief causes people to waver between rational and irrational activity. Consumers' wavering toward seemingly irrational activity becomes validated

---

[358]David Deutsch,*The Beginning of Infinity* , p. 6 (2011).

when it helps them self-organize more effectively through the *OT* toward the *Ontological Realization* of *who* they wish to be. For example, putting massive resources into churches in the middle ages and space exploration in more modern times with little certain benefits other than achieving a sense of security, discovery and awe demonstrate *how* people attempt to boldly go where the apparent paradox of the *OT* is not and actually self-organize around truly teleological meaning. All this represents the collective human will to universalize, which can be immensely profitable if you market this very valid true-north value to move consumers along the upward curvature of the *OT*.

Ontologically Prospective Projects (the *OPPs*)

Please find below our universal diagram expanded to include an existentially goal directed *Ontological Teleology* recognizing *Ontologically Prospective*[359] *Projects* as *OPPs* or *OPPortunities*. In this chart, *OPPs* contrast with potential *Threats* people avoid in order to survive as the *Leanest*. People engage in *OPPs* to maximize their own lives and existences. *OPPs* are synonymous with *optimizing*, and are explicitly related to consumers' *Ontological Realization* by engaging in activity that ultimately orients them upward along the *Ontological Teleology*.[360] The chart below shows a twisting, *Ontological Teleology* that somewhat correlates with the physical

---

[359] I am making an allusion here to Amos Tversky and Daniel Kahneman's *Prospect Theory* as described in, *Judgement under Uncertainty: Heuristics and Biases*, Science, New Series, Vol. 185, No. 4157, pp. 1124-1131 (Sep. 27, 1974); and related notions such as Bernoulli's St. Petersburg paradox whose implications will be more fully explored in *Stream 5: People's*.

[360] For some examples of the mathematical applications of this concept, see Wolfram Alpha's description of, '...*the calculus of variations, control theory, convex optimization theory, decision theory, game theory, linear programming, Markov chains, network analysis, optimization theory, queuing systems, etc.*' located at www.wolframalpha.com (accessed Jan. 20, 2013).

arrow of time carving its way through the $ÔM$.[361]

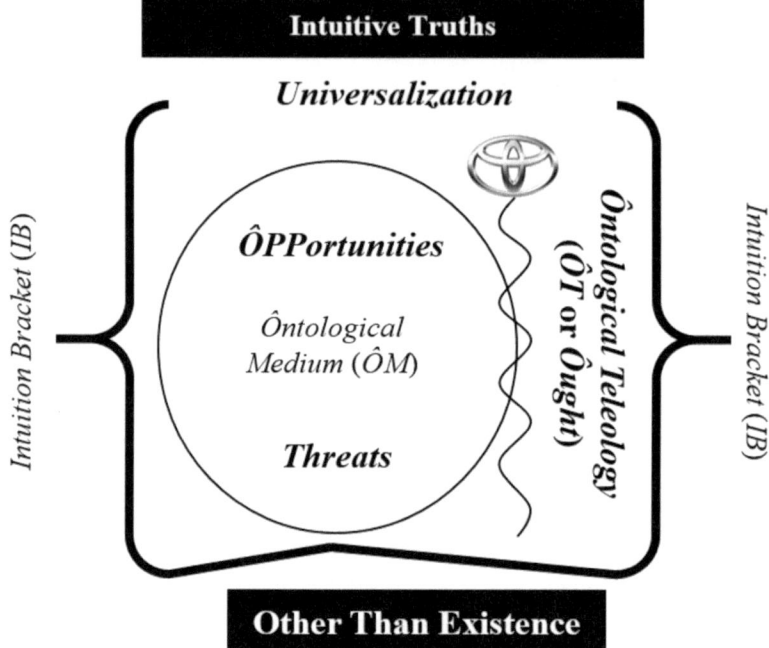

In this chart, consumers move between the existential extremes of:

1. *Ôpportunities to pursue a universalized, Lean perfection of instantaneous and seamless problem resolution*

---

[361]This (crooked) arrow of time was first discussed by Sir Arthur Eddington in 1927, for which there seems to be some scientismic belief because of quantum entanglement; *see*, Natalie Wolchover, *Time's Arrow Traced to Quantum Source*, Quanta Magazine, (April 16, 2014); Artur S.L. Malabarba, Luis Pedro García-Pintos, Noah Linden, Terence C. Farrelly, Anthony J. Short,*Quantum Systems Equilibrate Rapidly for Most Observables* , arXiv:1402.1093 [quant-ph] http://arxiv.org/abs/1402.1093 (Submitted on Feb. 5, 2014); Anthony J. Short and Terence C. Farrelly,*Quantum Equilibration in Finite Time* , New J. Phys. 14 013063 doi:10.1088/1367-2630/14/1/013063 (2012); Noah Linden, Sandu Popescu, Anthony J. Short, and Andreas Winter,*Quantum Mechanical Evolution Towards Thermal Equilibrium* , Phys. Rev. E 79, 061103 (Published June 4, 2009); Seth Lloyd, *Black Holes, Demons and the Loss of Coherence: How Complex Systems Get Information, and What They Do With It*, Ph.D. Thesis, Theoretical Physics, The Rockefeller University (April 1, 1988); Sean Carroll,*From Eternity to Here: The Quest for the Ultimate Theory of Time*, Plume (2010).

> *and satisfaction that consumers seek and yet only know as a hypo-thetical possibility; and*
>
> 2. *Threats to consumers' pursuit of perfection, or more accurately, being "other-than" perfection, which consumers know all too well and must correct for by thinking and behaving differently.*

Consumers' pursuit of perfection is their taking action to move toward real or perceived opportunities to re-generate as well as they can upward along the *OT* as they self-define it and away from *Threats* to their becoming not. Each of these actions constitutes the re-solution of the unique problem of existence. For example, customers optimize toward *OPPortunities* and away from *Threats* by purchasing *paos* that they perceive either as providing them with an *OPP* or removing a threat to their lives and existences. Customers rate *paos* on a sliding scale with one to five stars as to whether consuming a *paos* acts as an *OPP* to in-fact improve their ability to live better within the *OM*, or toward *what* they believe is outside the *IB*, so they may achieve meaningful moments of true-north value[362] by resolving their utmost problems, as seen again here in this chart:

---
[362] Yuval Noah Harari, *Sapiens*, p. 392 (2014).

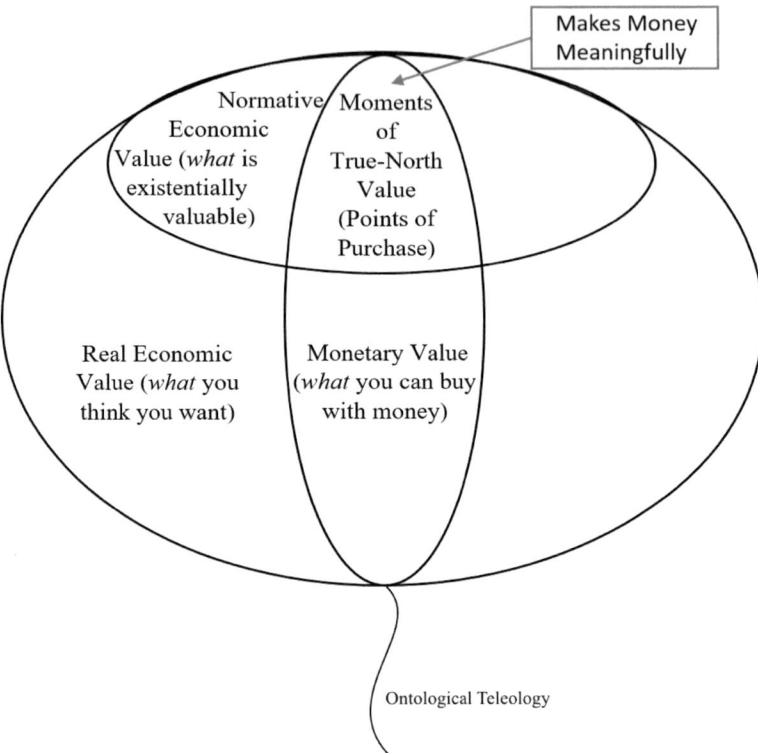

End-Goal of the *Ontological Teleology*

Teleology v Teleonomy

> *The Moving Finger writes; and, having writ,*
> *Moves on: nor all thy Piety nor Wit*
> *Shall lure it back to cancel half a Line,*
> *Nor all thy Tears wash out a Word of it.*
> - Omar Khayyám (translation by Edward Fitzgerald)

Now is an appropriate time to differentiate between the terms *teleology* and *teleonomy* for you to best understand which*Lean* end-goals consumers chose to pursue for their meaningful *OPPs*. In its historical sense, *teleology* describes a system whereby people intuit, infer, and possibly induce from the sophist-ication and organization of existence that: (1) creation exists to achieve a final end-goal due to its generally intelligible nature; or that (2) an intelligible first cause created a final end-goal that can only be speculated. However, *teleology* in its modern sense and as used in *U/P* means that organisms operate in anticipatory fashion to predict their future *Ontological Realization* according to their reliance on the truth of axiomatic, systemic or intuitive values. In other words, teleology intentionally seeks a specific end-goal.

However, modern behavioral scientists dislike the term *teleology* because they generally criticize historical teleology as having a *time reversal* problem in that the future goal of teleology in its historical sense must dictate present events. This entire notion violates natural law because the arrow of time within the context of the *OM* only moves in one direction as far as we know.[363] This time reversal problem arises from the fact that considering physics and biology to be goal directed violates the evolutionary principle held with at least five *Lean* sigmas ($\geq 5\sigma$) of confidence that behavior is unintentionally shaped by natural selection and environ-mental conditioning. Instead, behavioral scientists state that the evolution occurred "purpose*ively*" as a result of natural laws operating through complex systems, and not guided "purpose*fully*" toward an end-goal specifically defined in advance by those natural laws.[364]

To overcome this time reversal problem of teleology, in 1958 the behavioral scientist C.S. Pittendrigh created the alternative term *teleonomy* that has since been adopted by a number of behavioral

---

[363] Hayne W. Reese, *Teleology and Teleonomy in Behavior Analysis*, 17, 75-91, p. 78, The Behavior Analyst (1994).

[364] Hayne W. Reese, *Teleology and Teleonomy in Behavior Analysis*, The Behavior Analyst, No. 1 (Spring 1994).

230 Stream 3: Existence

scientists for this same reason.[365] *Teleonomy* is just a biological term for life's purposive nature. Thus, changing the terminology of *teleology* to *teleonomy* emphasizes the fact that natural laws act as the guiding force of the *OT* concurrently and coincidentally in complex, dynamic systems, resulting in the *Ontological Realization* or "*ori*gin" of biological creatures, rather than toward any predefined or purposeful goals.[366] Teleonomy is generally used to separate biological behavior from its more historically controversial first or final explanations in a universal sense.[367]

Behavioral scientists' jobs are to think about the root causes of behavior in animals in order to better understand, predict and manage them. In that light, *teleonomy* attempts to overcome these temporal problems and some theological connotations associated with the term *teleology* based on its historical use to *prove* an intuitively speculative self-causing cause. *Teleonomy* is thus a fairly recent term used to describe the appearance of design in nature that does not have any inherent end-goal, but rather appears *as if* it was designed to achieve a goal due to its being naturally selected for maximum efficiency in re-generating and becoming further *Ontologically Realized* through time. Or as Timothy Ferriss said in his book, *The 4-Hour Workweek* , '*Being efficient without regard to effectiveness is the default mode of the Universe.*'[368]

I consider the *teleonomic* from *teleological* distinction useful at the beginning of describing consumers' existences within the *OM* and *IB* in that the linear, existential development of life from organic

---

[365] Pittendrigh wrote, '*The biologists' long-standing confusion would be more fully removed is all end-directed systems were described by some other term, like 'teleonomic', in order to emphasize that the recognition and description of end-directedness does not carry a commitment to Aristotelian teleology as an efficient [sic] casual principle.,*' in his essay *Adaptation, Natural Selection, and Behavior*, at pp. 390-416, Anne Roe and George Gaylord Simpson (eds.), *Behavior and Evolution* (1958).

[366] Any book discussing this such as Addy Pross's book *What is Life: How Chemistry becomes Biology*, Oxford University Press, Reprint edition (2014).

[367] *See generally*, Nicholas S. Thompson, *The Misappropriation of Teleonomy*, p. 259, Perspectives on Biology, Plenum Press (1987).

[368] Timothy Ferriss, *The 4-Hour Workweek* , Harmony (Dec. 15, 2009).

matter prior to the creation of consumers' independent agency of themselves reflects *purposive* teleonomic activity regulated by the external dynamics of the complex *Universe*. However, at the point where teleonomic activity results in organisms with degrees of independent agency like consumers, that agency expresses a purposeful, teleological, goal-seeking cognition measured by *how* it acts to further become *Ontologically Realized* within the *OM*, *IB* and *Universe*. Consumers' Darwinian fitness gets both teleonomically self-organized and teleologically intentionally shaped upward along the *OT*.

For example, when bounded by the *IB*, even Aristotle's own final cause or end-goal of further existing seems to be for Aristotle himself to simply further exist as a living system in seemingly logically circular fashion. Sadly, Aristotle no longer is, but his thôughts lived on through us. Existence likewise is where the first and final causes of *who* and *why* consumers are e-merge into their unified personal perspectives. Consumers exist within a *Universe* that results in an inherent end-goal of their further simultaneously and optimally being both toward and away from *what* is *other than existence*. In other words, people live to a-void becoming not in a physical sense while also simultaneously living for *what* they speculatively believe to be so (i.e. *what* may be not) at the same time. This is true because at this moment any determination of whether the first or final causes were by grand design or not stands outside the *IB* as a speculative, intuitive truth.

Thus, the *IB* nearly equivocates Aristotle's efficient and final causes, almost connecting them around the teleological bend, so you can measure to some degree those causes' systemic expression and *Ontological Realization* along the upward curvature of the *OT*. The *OT* thus allows you to define and measure *who* consumers are within the limits of the *IB* because the *Ontological Teleology* is the great simpliciter and regulator of itself without further external reference outside the *OM* and *IB*. Either consumers are or they are not within these empirical boundaries.[369] For example, natural selection as *Ontologically Realized* through the *OT* demonstrates a *survival of the fittest, telos,* or *Lean end-goal* of true-north value for genes[370] to exist to a greater degree. So, while all consumers optimize themselves against universal possibilities, the *OT* simpliciter is *what* gets *Ontologically Realized* and is ontologically self-reinforcing, which is *what* allows you to measure it. Within the *IB*, the only thing that *matters* is *what* is.

Thus, this measurable, ontologically, teleonomically, *purposive* aspect of the *Universe* results in consumers *who* have teleologically, *purposefully,* and subjectively cognitive faculties with independent agency that furthers their apparently tautological, *Ontologically Teleological* goal of energizing and optimizing their existences by in-part buying and consuming *paos*. Just because the goal of universalization is hypothetical does not invalidate its pragmatism.[371] Consumers have a *purposefulness* that generally conveys a survival advantage and provides a higher standard of existence to them through their ability to spend money and consume energy to the greatest degree of all.

The Open-Ended Paradox of the *OT*

However, the *OT* through which consumers exist to a greater and greater degree appears paradoxical in an open-ended sense, since the origin of being and knowledge only seems self-defining when you bracket out intuitive speculation. Said another way, within the bounds of *what* people commonly experience, scientist, business person and theologian alike must all be collectively, inter-subjectively agnostic while personally and professionally speculative

---

[369] *See, The Data Against Kant*, New York Times, Sunday Opinion (Feb. 21, 2016).

[370] For more on this neo-Darwinistic concept of gene propagation, *see*, Richard Dawkins, *The Selfish Gene*, Oxford University Press (1976).

[371] This may be considered an *anticipatory system, see generally,* Robert Rosen, *Anticipatory Systems; Philosophical, Mathematical, and Methodological Foundations*, Springer (2012).

about whether or not the *OT* ultimately self-defines *what* purpose their existences may have.

This existential condition leaves consumers either:

1. *Personally or publicly declaring irresolvable ignorance as to the ultimate causation of the OM in an agnostic sense;*
2. *Attempting to leap beyond the apparently tautological, Ontological Teleology in an otherwise unexplained Universe by thinking and acting irrationally;*
3. *Engaging in intuitive spiritual, theistic, or scientismic belief and speculation as a rational response to the apparent paradox of the OT by placing faith in:*
   a. *A spiritualism that may or may not be commonly experienced;*
   b. *In one or more deities that may or may not be commonly agreed; or*
   c. *In the Principle of Sufficient Reason due to science's consistent explanatory success.*

Most people actually seem to live day-to-day by simultaneously engaging in a mix of all three of these strategies. As you know from experience, some people conflate intuition with processual or axiomatic facts. Some people profess and orient their actions toward their intuitive beliefs out of ignorance. Or, some people profess belief in intuitive truths to conform to society but otherwise live like pragmatic agnostics. And others still hold personally intuitive beliefs even after being fully educated as to *why, what* and *how* they are within the *OM* and *IB* to the best of existing knowledge. While all of these responses to the *OT* allow consumers exist with the least cognitive dissonance *vis-a-vis* the apparent tautology of the *OM* within the *IB*, very rarely if ever do consumers execute any one of these strategies consistently throughout their entire lives.

Instead, consumers employ a complementary mix of these strategies to energize and optimize their existences within the *OM* . For example, intuitive speculation allows consumers to conceptualize *what* is hypo-thetically possible in their hearts and imagination, but is not (yet) *Ontologically Realizable.* Consumers then scientifically test whether such intuitive speculation results in their experiencing a greater *Ontological Realization* of *who* they are. Such intuitive speculation also functions as a method for consumers to test their self-organization with passion and meaning to reinforce and validate (or not) their non-circular, personally intuitive true-north values. This passion play gets repeated until consumers switch to agnosticism or scientism, or just act a little crazy to see *what* happens, to see whether such other strategies more effectively enhance their standard of existence.

Whatever consumers happen to intuitively speculate gets validated to the extent it expands the volume and velocity of those consumers' *Ontological Realization*, which is equivalent to *who* , *why* , *what* and *how* they are. From a Darwinian, processually systemic perspective, within the bounds of the *Universe, IB* and *OM*, people's conscious experience and activity is simply an endeavor to ontologically reinforce their survival as the *Leanest* through off-spring, monuments, memoirs, academic theories, charitable foundations, pseudonymous corporations and the like. Even if you assume a logical circularity of purpose within the *IB*, the increasing organization of nature within the *OT* leads somewhere, most namely to universalizing people through successive re-generations onward and upward in an *Ontologically Teleological* fashion. Thus, intuitive beliefs constitute a rational response to the soft paradox of the *OT* and are effective so long as they facilitate and do not hinder people's overall *ener-*

gization and *optimization*.³⁷²

For example, imagine passengers' journey if you were an airline serving food to people with religious beliefs. If those religious beliefs forbade eating certain types of food, like spaghetti, then the airline's food should conform to passengers' intuitive true-north values for religious purposes as well as their process true-north values by being nutritious. At the same time, the act of serving the nutritious, religiously observant food cannot conflict with the axiomatic or systemic truths applicable to all people, like the ability for other passengers to have nutritious food. The food ought to reciprocally conform to all passengers' various forms of intuitive speculation as well within a free society. All these true-north values must *somehow* cohere within the singular, overlapping consensus³⁷³ and seemingly open-ended paradox of the *Universe*. You can witness this existential sentiment reflected in the, '*COEXIST*' stickers commonly adhered to the backs of people's automobiles and in the *Doodle 4 Google*logo created by Sarah Harrison from Connecticut:

---

³⁷²This may be considered a loose analogy to Pascal's Wager that you should rationally believe in God just in case there is one, in that instead of believing in God, you must rationally recognize that all must be agnostic to what is Not Ôntologically Teleological inside the*IB*, holding what you presently perceive to be Not Ôntologically Teleological outside the*IB* on a subjective, 'Personal' basis, which is a rational response to the apparent circularity of the purpose of existence within the *IB*.

³⁷³The term and academic concept of *Overlapping Consensus* was popularized by the philosopher John Rawls with his book,*A Theory of Justice*, Harvard University Press (1971); however, Jean-Paul Sarte first articulated this concept in, *The Communists and Peace*, p. 201 (1968), where he writes that truth value (a.k.a. justice) may be found from the perspective of the masses, by seeing the *Universe* '...*with the eyes of the least favored*'; Sarte's predecessors can be found in Thomas Kuhn (1962) and Karl Popper (1959) with their consensus-forging either through empiricism or revolution (*see*, the earlier definition of same causing consideration and reflection from change and upheaval through a circular movement).

The Coexist Logo, ®Coexist, LLP, www.coexistonline.com, produced by www.northernsun.com item #7167 (Photo Credit: Me)

A Peaceful Future, Google Spelled Out in Religious, Gender and Scientific Symbols (©2017 Sarah Harrison (fair use))

Even scientismists admit that they do not know precisely *how* existence originated within several *Lean* sigmas of confidence, and so they themselves hold personally intuitive, scientismic beliefs when existentially pursuing their work. So, whether you are a scientismist or not, you must recognize the extreme ignorance and the apparent tautologies, circularities and paradoxes in which all researchers and consumers find themselves existing regardless of their speculative persuasion.[374] People have no axiomatic or systemic explanation for *what* originated within the boundaries of the *OM*. At the same time, you likewise must appreciate that while intuitive true-north values are not axiomatically or systemically valid, they are *Ontologically Realized* within consumers' personal perspectives (i.e. within their hearts, memories and imaginations).

---

[374] *See generally*, Paul Feyerabend, *Farewell to Reason*, Verso Books (1987).

This may affect *what* and *how* customers purchase from you when you orient the production of *paos* toward their true-north values through U/P and the philosophy of *Lean*.

Consider further that the apparently circular nature of the *OM* within the *IB* would be shattered if all fully-informed people willingly agreed to at least a *Lean* two sigmas ($\geq/2\sigma$) of common agreement that a self-causing intuitive true-north value, like a deity, was one of Aristotle's efficient or final causes. This may in fact have been the case in ancient times within highly theistic societies. For example, at any religion's peak, did at least 95% of the informed population truly consider its dogmas to be systemic truth values if not axiomatic truth values? Did these theologies bring their dogmatically stated, efficient-first or final-teleological causes from outside of the *IB* to inside the *IB* as a universally axiomatic or processually systemic true-north values for their adherents?

Even if so, those theistic truths had to be ontologically validated to hold onto believers and continue to exist over time. Theologies ultimately live and die over time by their true-north viability, which is the *Ontological Realization* of their professed adherents.[375] Even where one or more people hold an intuitive true-north value, that personally held intuitive truth value either does or does not obtain by creating *Ontological Realization* over time when interacting with other axiomatic or systemic truth values and religions. This is the process by which speculative true-north value gets created and tested for falsification.

Silly Suds

A rather silly example of this dynamic is the recent *Pastafarian* movement. In 2005, a small group of people called themselves Pastafarians and satirically agreed that a *Flying Spaghetti Monster*® both created itself and the known *Universe*. Pastafarians started

---
[375] *See generally*, Paul Feyerabend, *Farewell to Reason*, Verso Books (1987).

doing that to protest the Kansas Board of Education's decision to teach intelligent design in Kansas schools, evoking the famous 1925 *Scopes Monkey Trial*[376] challenging the teaching of evolution in Tennessee public schools.[377]

Pastafarians satirically held that people's *Ontological Teleology* would be to serve the wishes and purposes of the *Flying Spaghetti Monster®*. The Pastafarians' proposed that the *Flying Spaghetti Monster®* (the *FSM*), as its greatness is officially called, was either a *Universal* or *Process* true-north value, which you may otherwise refer to as a *fact*.[378]

Flying Spaghetti Monster®, *Touched by His Noodly Appendage* (Public Domain)

If you want to know *why* the *FSM* held such satirical sway, presume for a moment you and all consumers are in-fact Pastafarians. If so, the *FSM* would be an axiomatic truth, keeping all else you know the same. In that case, Pastafarians' existential purpose within the

---

[376] *Scopes v. State*, 154 Tenn. 105, 289 S.W. 363 (1927).

[377] Bobby Henderson, *The Gospel of the Flying Spaghetti Monster*, HarperCollins Entertainment (2006); and Bobby Henderson, *The Loose Canon, the Holy Book of the Church of the Flying Spaghetti Monster*, self-published (Jul. 26, 2010).

[378] *Touched by His Noodly Appendage* (Public Domain), is a parody of Michelangelo's, *The Creation of Adam*, as seen earlier on the cover of Steve Blank's *Four Steps*, is an iconic image of the *Flying Spaghetti Monster®* by Arne Niklas Jansson.

OM would still appear *as if* it was *Ontologically Teleological*, with the goal still being to become universalized in juxtaposition to *what* may be not. Keeping all else the same, including a presumption of free markets, as a business person you would still ask *how* the *FSM's* new axioms may interact with previously known axioms to increase Pastafarians' *Ontological Realization* upward through the *OT*. Thus, the Pastafarians would become customers and buy a *paos* based on that *paos*' real or perceived ability to increase their *Ontological Realization* through the *OT* in coordination the new, axiomatic *fact* of the *FSM*. The Pastafarians would do this by adapting their consumption of the *paos* to all the dogmas of the *FSM*, *whatever* they may be, to best energize and optimize their existences under this new deity.[379]

On the flip-side, presume you and all people are not Pastafarians but rather scientismists *who* believe science has the ultimate explanatory power for *what* caused the *OM* beyond the *IB*. Presume further that a scientismist's dogma is that existence is fully expressed in string theory. This string theory says that this *Universe* in which consumers now reside is but one possibility of an infinite number of *Ontological Realizations*, with each string representing infinitely many possible *Universes*. In that case, consumers would accept that fact and continue to shop much the same as if this *Universe* we all know was created by the *FSM* outside of the *FSM's* own unique axioms. Customers would still seek to become further *Ontologically Realized* as they define themselves by buying *paos* unless a string *somehow* caused their buying behavior to change.

The *OM* clearly contains within itself today teleological, goal seeking customers looking to further their own existences by shopping up along the *OT* as if this was the only *Universe* that mattered. Thus, we now move along the *Ontological Teleology* within the *U/P* value stream to *Stream 4: Lives,* to consider the *OM* generally as *teleologically* ontological for the sake of clarity and to show some

---

[379]Stanford Encyclopædia of Philosophy, '*Supervenience*,' (November 2011).

continuity with the history of philosophical thinking about true-north value and all meaning for living things. I will use *teleonomy* only to the extent I intend to specifically indicate a goal directedness based on the measurable, dynamic confluence of axiomatic and systemic true-north values within the *OM* as bracketed by the *IB* with at least two *Lean* sigmas ($\geq/2\sigma$) of confidence.

> *'Cheshire Puss,'* she began...
> *'Would you tell me, please, which way I ought to go from here?'*
> *'That depends a good deal on where you want to get to,'* said the Cat.
> *'I don't much care where–'* said Alice.
> *'Then it doesn't matter which way you go,'* said the Cat.
> *'–so long as I get SOMEWHERE,'* Alice added as an explanation.
> *'Oh, you're sure to do that,'* said the Cat, *'if you only walk long enough'*
> - Lewis Carroll, *Alice's Adventures in Wonderland* (1865) [a]
>
> ---
> [a]Charles Lutwidge Dodgson (aka Lewis Carroll), *Alice's Adventures in Wonderland* (1865).

Stream 4: Lives

Stream 4*A* 3 Report:

- The self-organization of matter and energy within the *OM* leads to supervening levels of existence
- Thinking of life's emergence in *Lean* terms as a form of adaptation, regeneration and energization provides a philosophical perspective on modern evolutionary theory that may be applied universally to all consumers and organizations
- By this definition of life, even a stream of water is alive to a very limited degree
- Basic, biological activity is the first place were knowledge gets transmitted across generations of living systems to improve those systems' overall existence
- Cognitive activity further optimizes the storage, transmission and application of knowledge toward improving those living systems' existences
- Intentional, cognitive activity adds an element of self-interest to this process, thereby greatly increasing the ability for organisms to adapt, regenerate and energize
- Increasingly self-conscious organisms like consumers have had an advantage to date of improving their lives by being able to better imagine *how* their self-interest gets energized and optimized by the different decisions they make – but their advantage is ultimately tested by whether or not they are relatively short-lived
- Meaning gets created to the degree living systems actually universalize themselves through the above processes

> *The purpose of life, is a life of purpose.*
> – Robert Bryne

Now go along the *U/P* value stream to *Lean* through *how* consumers' really live. Consider *how* their lives and organization's viability e-merged within the *Ontological Medium*. Think about *how* universal truth values led to the processes by which consumers personally find themselves in the seemingly self-defining paradox of the *OT*. See *how* these value streams wound their way through the *OM* within the *IB* toward the seemingly limitless ocean of true-north value that all life and conscious existence is. This *Lean* thinking about consumers' lives within an *HQ* ought to flow from Descartes', '*I think, therefore I am*,' being a distinct cause and effect, toward a possibly tautological, '*We are, therefore we will be.*' Your business *i/deô*logy within the philosophy of *Lean* likewise ought to head in circles, similar to a tornado or whirlpool, to greater and greater effect.

As an organization advances up the value stream in this way, you more clearly see consumers explicitly or implicitly finding meaning in their lives in the difference between *what* is within the *IB* and *what* not. Thus, each department of an organization ought to produce *paos* that in-turn attempts to energize and optimize this meaningful difference in consumers' lives through the processes of the *I/D Kata* at each level, as seen again here:

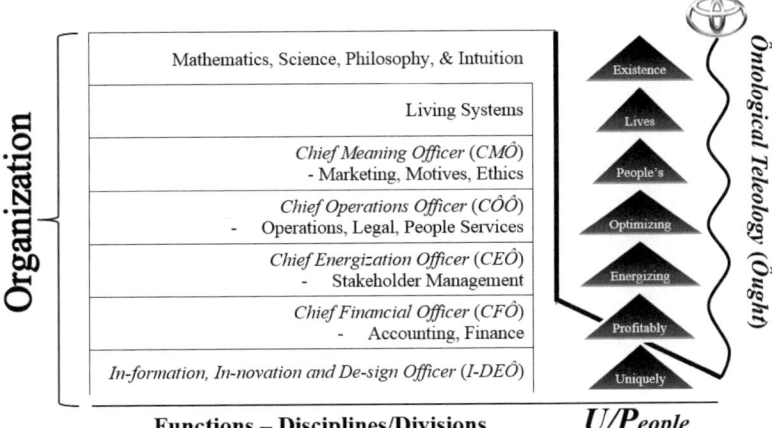

Customers Self-Organize Upward Along the OT

Like understanding organizations themselves, studying living, self-organizing systems within the boundaries of the *IB* and *OM* is *how* consumers find themselves in the open-ended, nearly tautological paradox of the *OT* running up through the busy *Universe*. These theories provide another perspective on *why* customers consciously buy and consume *paos*. To give you a notion of how old this idea of self-organization is, consider the fact that in his 1633 book, *The World*, Descartes wrote that order tends to arise naturally from the universal laws operating in the chaos of the cosmos. He wrote that the origin and course of the planets and comets in general, '...*were so extended and so impeding that, when they collided with one another, it was easier for several to join together.*'[380] Scientists today simply rephrase this principle of teleonomic physical interactions in terms of modern scientific knowledge.

---

[380] *See*, Descartes',*Discourse on Method*, fifth part, and his book,*The World*, particularly in his*Chapter 9* written in 1633; *see also*, Steven A. Benner,*Defining Life*, Astrobiology, 10(10): 1021–1030. doi: 10.1089/ast.2010.0524 (Dec. 2010).

Science increasingly tests scientismic theories to explain *why* living consumers e-merged from raw matter within the *OM* in an upward orientation to the *OT* to become *who* they are today. These scientismic explanations revolve around exploring the self-organization of complex structures from chaotic, dynamic systems of the *Universe*, like the study of planetary ecology. These theories model processes that ultimately created consumers' *Ontological Realization*. Your customers' *OT* processes successively depend on each other to become *Ontologically Realized*in upward, self-organized fashion due to physical, chemical and biological axioms and systems.

Life itself constitutes and constructs of the most sophisticated aspects of existence, the greatest of all, '*Strategically Unique Degrees of Sophist-ication*' (*SUDS*).[381] '*Strategic*,' in *SUDS* means the teleological end-goal of *Ontological Realization*, '*Unique*' means that which strategically succeeds among all neo-Darwinian games, and '*Degrees*' means the variously differentiated *SUDS* you experience in the *Universe*. Therefore, '*Sophist-ication*' means an organisms' strategically unique degree of self-organization that allows it to further and better live by adapting, re-generating and energizing. An organism's SUDS measure its dependence on various axiomatic and systemic true-north values and its ability to downwardly manipulate them in order to improve itself within the *OM*. Doing that in the*Universe* requires an organism or organization to pursue a specifically *Lean* angle or vector of true-north value while contributing toward greater degrees of systemic sophist-ication overall.

If you intuitively believe that life arose from super-natural causes intervening within the*OM* and disagree with scientismists' claims that super-natural causes do not, consider these constraints that scientismists propose for their hypotheses about *how* life began to work physically:

1. ***The time over which these processes occurred since the***

---

[381]Yuval Noah Harari, *Sapiens*, p. 109 (2014).

> *inception of the Universe over an estimated 13.7 billion years; and*
> 2. *The size of the Universe to the extent we can even detect it due to the limiting factor of the speed of light.*

When you think about the *Universe* that way within the *IB*, these scales make the probability of a single strange physical dynamic called *life* exceptional but not completely outside the possibility of axiomatic and systemic explanation.

Self-Organizing and Supervening Levels of OT Sophist-ication: From *SO-OT* to *SL-OTS*

If life is considered to have no larger teleological purpose in this way, then a person may say that a simple molecule has no more meaning than a cellular organism within the *OM* . Along that same line of reasoning, a person may further say that a cellular organism has no more inherent meaning than a mammal, and a mammal than a person within the *IB*. All this is true within the conceptual lens of the *IB* but for the fact that different types of life relate within different *Strategically Unique Degrees of Sophist-ication* juxtaposed to *what is Not Ontologically Teleological* (what is *N-OT*).[382] *What* is *not N-OT* in a double negative sense is *Self-Organizing Ontological Teleology* (*SO-OT*) within the *OM* , creating all that matters.

> *For SO-OT consumers are, and*
> *to SO-OT consumers shall return.*
> - inspired by *Genesis 3:19* , second sentence

---

[382] Yuval Noah Harari, *Sapiens*, p. 391 (2014).

Super Supervenience

The process of *Self-Organizing Ontological Teleology* forms dependencies between one level of existence to the next through *what* is technically called, '*supervenience*.'[383] Supervenience is an important concept within the *OT* for you to under-stand *how* to *Lean* an organization philosophically. *The Oxford English Dictionary* defines '*Supervenience*' as:

> 2. Philos. *The dependence of one property or quality on another for its existence.*

From this perspective, certain properties, qualities, and/or truth values depend on one another as a hierarchy of living existence. From this view, society depends on psychology, which depends on life, which depends on biology, which depends on chemistry, which depends on physics. Vice versa, the composition of physics determines chemistry, which eventually determines the foundational rules of sociology.

Thus, from the perspective of supervenience, cosmological *SO-OT* further self-organizes into *Strategically Unique Degrees of Sophistication* (*SUDS*) that become *Supervening Levels of the Ontological Teleological Systems* (a *SL-OT* or *SL-OTS*).[384] These *SL-OTS* emerge as levels of living existence,[385] built upon the universal, axiological true-north values of natural laws ascending via processes to living animals with cognition, intention, and eventually a sense of meaning - like consumers.[386] *SUDS* and *SL-OTS* are embodied

---

[383] See again, '*Supervenience*,' in the Stanford Encyclopædia of Philosophy.

[384] *SL-OTS* relate to Georg Wilhelm Friedrich Hegel's successive forms of evolutionary life and consciousness as he articulated throughout, *Phenomenology of Spirit*(*Phänomenologie des Geistes*) (1807).

[385] David Deutsch,*The Beginning of Infinity* , p. 123 (2011).

[386] *See e.g.* Gretchen C. Daily, Tore Söderqvist, Sara Aniyar, Kenneth Arrow, Partha Dasgupta, Paul R. Ehrlich, Carl Folke, AnnMari Jansson, Bengt-Owe Jansson, Nils Kautsky, Simon Levin, Jane Lubchenco, Karl-Göran Mäler, David Simpson, David Starrett, David Tilman, Brian Walker,*The Value of Nature and the Nature of Value* , Science 21, Vol. 289 no. 5478 pp. 395-396, DOI: 10.1126/science.289.5478.395, Policy Forum, Ecology (July 2000).

in everything from genes to memes (*i.e.* the cultural or behavioral "genes" of coordination, cooperation and imagination³⁸⁷). Thus, the supervenience of *SO-OT* into *SUDS*, and then *SUDS* into specific *SL-OTS*, occurs through axioms and systems interacting within the bounds of the *Ontological Medium* and *what* knowledge consumers pass on from one re-generation to the next.³⁸⁸

For example, just think about *how* this *Volume* of *U/P* supervenes on *Lean*, and *Lean* in-turn on the cultural and intellectual legacy of Eastern and Western philosophies. Consider further within *Lean how* consumers pull the production of *paos* up through these *SL-OTS* as we have described them. For another example, think about *how* an organization produces washing machines that energize and re-generate chemical reactions with *soap*. Since consumers need clean clothes to live, consumers' biological processes in one *SL-OT* require these washing machines to utilize chemical reactions that function within a physical *SL-OT* for which no axiomatic self-causing cause is known. *Who* or *what* created the *SL-OT* in which the physics behind *soap* operates? No one knows with axiomatic certainty, but all supervening *SL-OTS* collectively produce delightfully clean consumers.

To illustrate these different *SL-OTS* whether produced by living systems or not, below are three pictures that relate universal, processual and personal true-north value *SL-OTS*: (1) of a *Whirlpool Galaxy* self-organizing at a cosmic scale; (2) a *whirlpool* of water self-organizing in nature; and (3) a human-made *Whirlpool®* washing machine existing as an extension of consumers' need to clean *soot* out with *soap*.

---

³⁸⁷Yuval Noah Harari, *Sapiens*, p. 103 (2014).
³⁸⁸David Deutsch, *The Beginning of Infinity*, p. 379 (2011).

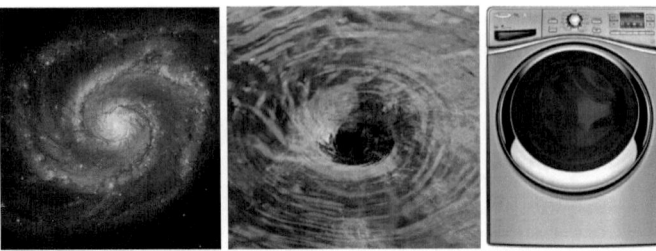

From left to right, 1.*Whirlpool Galaxy* (Universal True-North Value) © 2005 NASA (Public Domain); 2.*Whirlpool of Water* (Process True-North Value) © 2011 CC BY-SA 3.0; 3.*Whirlpool® Washer* (Commercial True-North Value) © 2015 Whirlpool Corporation http://www.whirlpool.com/ (NYSE: WHR)

The interrelation between these subserviening *SL-OTS* means that they get manifested at each level of sophist-ication. These inter-dependencies also mean that any given star, planet or washing machine could have looked quite different with a slight change in its production process. Slight differences in their formation could have arisen due to the notional *bullwhip* or *butterfly effect*, meaning that small differences across spacetime can have large effects at the largest scales. Given this extreme variability as to *what* becomes a fact, you must compare *what* you think ought to be with *what* you know is *N-OT* by examining the processes of *Ontological Realization*. For example, compare the creative processes and aesthetic beauty represented in both the image below from the Hubble telescope composited over a nine-year period[389] and the image of a kaleidoscope of butterflies next to it. Consider what a small change in certain natural processes might have rendered at these scales and whether you would change a thing:

---

[389]The HUDF shows a small section of space in the southern-hemisphere constellation Fornax. The resulting image – made from 841 orbits of telescope viewing time – contains approximately 10,000 galaxies, extending back in time to within a few hundred million years of the *Big Bang*. Image Credit: NASA/ESA.

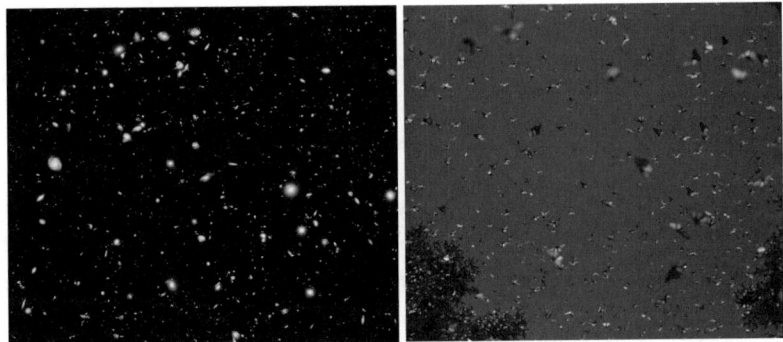

Hubble Telescope, Visible and Near Infra-red Light Spectrum of the Universe © 2012 NASA (public domain);*Kaleidoscope of Monarch Butterflies* © 2016 Dr. Lincoln Brower, Used with Permission

> *He who through vast immensity can pierce,*
> *See worlds on worlds compose one Universe,*
> *Observe how system into system runs,*
> *What other planets circle other suns,*
> *What vary'd being peoples every star,*
> *May tell why Heaven has made us as we are.*
> *But of this frame, the bearing and the ties,*
> *The strong connections, nice dependencies,*
> *Gradations just, has thy pervading soul*
> *Look'd thro? Or can a part contain a whole?*
> - Alexander Pope,*An Essay on Man: Epistle I* (1734).

Supervenience of Weather, Money and Consumers

You witness in everyday business *how* each of the supervening *SL-OTS* feeds higher levels of living sophist-ication. Such aggregate, supervening complexity often takes on a *life of its own* through its own internal sophist-ication not easily explained by the lower level departments of organization.

While a businessperson may attempt to forecast the viability of an organization to shareholders, no one in an organization could explain every thought or action taken by every employee that will re-produce that annual turnover. Analogously, while consumers perfectly understand the chemical interactions of H2O with the other primary elements in the atmosphere, they cannot predict the weather more than a few days in advance because they cannot model the interactions of every molecule in that system. The weather's complexity supervenes on particle physics, giving it a secret life of its own, just like the money an organization produces.

The publicly editable reference, *Wikipedia*, presents another perspective on supervenience, when it describes supervenience's metaphysical relation to money. Notice *how* the *Wikipedia* authors state that supervenience, '*does not obtain*,' between the paper money and value, which they consider two independent things, rather than *how* money supervenes on true-north value originating in some larger part of the world:

> **It is useful to know both when supervenience does and does not obtain. For example, the value of a piece of paper money does not supervene on the micro-features of the paper it's made out of, because the value of the money is not just determined by internal features of the paper, but also by a broader distribution of social facts and institutions. The paper alone does not determine the value of the money, so supervenience does not obtain between the value and the paper (though it does obtain between the value of the money and some larger part of the world which includes the relevant social institutions).**[390]

For a more sophisticated example of supervenience, here is an

---

[390] *Wikipedia* entry on '*Supervience*' (accessed on Nov. 3, 2014).

application of supervenience with the same science fiction that financial forecasts often represent. The "transporter" on the television series Star Trek® operated by having people become atomically disassembled, transmitted and reconstructed in another place, like an image of them projected from a monitor. These science fiction transporters beam people from one place to the next based on the premise that if people's atoms get reconstructed properly at a new location, then people's subjective consciousness and personal perspectives will follow along and supervene on their atoms in the new location as well.[391]

For a more realistic but sad perspective, people's physical supervenience may also be seen in emergency rooms or nursing homes where you live. *Who* people are appears to change as a function of *how* their brains get damaged as their neurological processes stop or change from disease or injury.[392] Any doctor will attest that people's minds and th-ôughts undoubtedly supervene on their patients' funda-mental physical processes.

What Goes *U / PP*Must Come Down

Thus, the notion of supervenience is generally one of upward causation from the less sophisticated systems with less*Strategically Unique Degrees of Sophist-ication* to higher *SUDS*. Generally *SUDS* are teleonomically purposive from one level upward to the next. However, at a certain point, consumers' teleologically purposeful intentions push back downward to similarly affect their aggregated, lower level systems that created their telenomically purposeful intentions in the first place. This notion is one of common sense, but it

---

[391]It was David Donaldson who first said, '[M]ental characteristics are in some sense dependent, or supervenient, on physical characteristics. Such supervenience might be taken to mean that there cannot be two events alike in all physical respects but differing in some mental respect, or that an object cannot alter in some mental respect without altering in some physical respect,' in, *Philosophy of Psychology*, pp. 214, Chapter 11,*Mental Events* (1980).

[392]*See e.g.*, Barbara K. Lipska,*The Neuroscientist Who Lost Her Mind* , New York Times (Mar. 12, 2016).

is best to keep in mind that supervenience functions bi-directionally both upward and downward within consumers. Ultimately though, both directions of supervenience within consumers are bound by and get means tested against the *Ontological Realization* of *who* and *why* consumers are overall across spacetime.

Taking on a deeper, more speculative topic by way of further example, any question as to whether a *soul* supervenes on consumer's physical processes (meaning a soul may or may not live at all), or whether it continues when consumer's brains no longer function, is only validated from consumer's personal perspectives, which in-turn direct *what* their bodies do and *how* they act on that belief while living. Whether a *soul* lives is a matter of intuitive speculation dealt with outside the *IB*.

The soul is a good example though of an intuitive truth value that, given sufficient empirical support leading to common agreement among at least two *Lean* sigmas ($\geq/2\sigma$) of fully-informed people, could make it a systemic or axiomatic truth value. Interestingly, a recent Nielsen poll in 2014 shows Americans right at a *Lean* sigma ($/\sigma$) on this issue with 68% of the general population agreeing to a soul's living existence. However, I can only speculate what percentage of Americans may be considered fully informed on these issues.[393]

How Did People Come to Live? Living *SL-OTS* E-merge

Thus, to intelligently discuss scientific explanations of *how* consumers' true-north values supervened and advanced upward through the living *SL-OTS* of the *Ontological Teleology* , you ought to limit a

---

[393]Harris Interactive, *Americans' Belief in God, Miracles and Heaven Declines: Belief in Darwin's Theory of Evolution Rises* (December 16, 2013) located at http://www.harrisinteractive.com.

business *i/de*ôlogy to the boundaries of shared universally, axiologically and processually systemic true-north values within the *OM* as bounded by the *IB*. To see clearly *what* is not intuitive within the Yin and Yang of a *Lean* business *i/de*ôlogy, you ought to recognize the abstract notion that axiological and systemic true-north values, or reason itself, is defined in juxtaposition to *what* is *Not Ontologically Teleological* (again, what is *N-OT*). Fortunately, science can help you in this endeavor when used within the philosophy of *Lean* since science has continually advanced *what* is known about *what* consumers truly value and *what* is not. Science's great virtue is that it provides evidence that may be empirically tested and perhaps falsified with a high degree of confidence – even if *what* is being hypothesized is not yet considered an axiomatic or systemic true-north value.

For example, discoveries in chemical systems[394] show that, under certain conditions, non-living molecules such as RNA compete for resources such as chemical nucleotides. Small differences in the configuration of these molecules may result in higher or lower reaction efficiency. Since chemical resources in these systems are finite, their variance leads more reactive processes to adapt, regenerate and energize to a greater extent than others. Less regenerative and adaptive chemical processes recede and eventually become extinct due to all the energy resources going to the more reactive processes.

---

[394] *See generally*, Addy Pross's book, *What is Life: How Chemistry becomes Biology*, (2014), which he wrote as a follow-up to Erwin Schrödinger's good book, *What is Life?* , Cambridge University Press (1944). Pross adds to Schrödinger's thoughts by introducing the concept of, *Dynamic Kinetic Stability*(*DKS*). As Pross explains it, *DKS* is a system that is not stable in the ordinary use of the term but rather only from a Process perspective by constantly turning over, much like a business' revenues not being stable but only apparently so year after year. Since a *DKS* system receives energy, the second law of thermodynamics is not violated, and biology and business become a particular *case of good chemistry*. Erwin Schrödinger also happened to be the physicist who developed the, '*Schrödinger's Cat*,' thought experiment describing quantum entanglement; if you are interested in seeing these ideas discussed in popular entertainment, see the HBO show, *The Sopranos, The Fleshy Part of the Thigh* , Season 6, Episode 4 (2006) and the character John Schwinn. Schrödinger's views as expressed in the episode have also been referred to as, *quantum mysticism* though David Deutsch certainly would argue with that characterization.

Thus, within a scientismic explanation for life, the process of natural selection begins at the chemical level. In fact, this type of chemical system - unlike the more common chemical reactions you study in beginning chemistry – is more like a tidal wave in that it only achieves a form of stability when it continuously changes. In this conjectured explanation for life, the chemical system maintains its *Ontological Realization* as a consistent process within the *OM* upward along the curved arrow of spacetime until it *somehow* fails to adapt to its environement, regenerate itself through reproduction or find a source of energy. You might think of these constant chemical changes producing a perpetual reaction to be much like an organization's revenue streams that only appear to be relatively stable, if (hopefully) increasing, while consistently turning over year after year.

To best understand consumers' and employees' systemic origins and to measure and predict *what* they will normatively and really buy, look further at recent scientismic explanations for *how* consumers came to live from inert matter. To do this, we will look through the conceptual lens of the *IB* at the *Ontological Realization* of these universal, processual and personally scientismic true-north values.

> *What do you mean when you say 'being?'*
> *We, who used to think we understood it,*
> *have now become perplexed.*
> - Plato, *The Sophist*, 244a (∼360 BCE)

Lean aRe SL-OTS- You, Your Organization and Customers Become Meaningfully Viable

I developed an *"aRe"* acronym, standing for **adaptation**, **Re-generation**, and **energization**, to test the necessary and sufficient processes that living systems like consumers - and organizations as a groups of real people organized as a fictional people - must do to remain minimally viable.[395] Everything consumers and organizations do is directed toward energizing their adaptation so they may ultimately Re-generate.[396] Similarly, all *paos* must ultimately optimize all aspects of *Lean aRe*processes from a meta-physical and scientismic perspective to help consumers and organizations maintain minimum viability in business. Organizations engage in *aRe* processes by *adapting* to market conditions, *Re-generating* product ideas, and gathering the contractual *power* to further distribute Matter and Energy as profits throughout society. 'aRe' is the organic inception of true value and all meaning within the *OM* when bounded by the *IB*.

The *Lean aRe*acronym ought to reflect *how* all consumers came to live and*what* produces their*Ontologically Teleological* motivation to buy *paos*. Living systems like all consumers adapt to further live through specific *Supervening Levels of Ontological Teleological Sophist-ication*. This scientismic perspective then allows you to determine *how* to best improve consumers' lives within the *OM* and *IB* through a meaningful ex-change for money by presuming that the *Axiom of Causation* applies within the bounds of the *IB*. If you presume this, you could then logically intuit, infer, possibly induce and then deductively market test the extent to which an organization's *paos* helps consumers *adapt*, *Re-generate*, and *energize* throughout the*OM* .

---

[395]Yuval Noah Harari, *Sapiens*, p. 30 (2014).
[396]The *aRe* processes are selected for *Leaness* through the parsimony of *Occum's Razor*, the inherent entropy of*The Second Law of Thermodynamics* , and sophisticated elegance of *Murphy's Law*.

Consider the *aRe* acronym in reverse order; its inverse meaning is, *eRa*. Thus, performing *aRe* processes determines *how* long consumers will persist through time. The capital letter *R* represents *Re-generation*, which stands central to this *aRe* concept for ontological continuity, which is the *Rubicon* of all consumers' value streams. *Re-generation* is necessarily and sufficiently supported by *adaptation* and *energization* because a system simply *Re-generating* like a water fountain cannot be considered alive since it must also teleonomically find *energy* to perpetually *adapt* and *Re-generate* at the most basic levels within the *OM*.

As will be elaborated further below in this *Stream 4*, the epic of evolution generally over-emphasizes re-production by individual organisms. It distracts you from seeing *Re-generation* by living systems as the higher abstraction better describing the *Ontologically Teleological* goal that all organisms (and organizations) have over time. *Re-generation* is *what* living systems most fundamentally do to maintain their identity against the force of entropy and competitive pressures.

Re-production in and of itself is not the process ultimately being satisfied. Rather re-production, along with adaptation and energization, is a subset of the larger, possibly circular goal of perpetuating and expanding systemic Re-generation. For example, consumers Re-generate themselves to universalize their personal value streams both during their lifetimes and through their off-spring.[397] Re-production is simply one method of *Re-generating* their *Ontological Realization* further in space-time once they pass away.

Living organisms like consumers do not intrinsically or necessarily want to re-produce for self-organization, but rather to increase the volume, velocity and effectiveness of their *Ontological Realization* that their off-spring physically ex-tend. *Re-generation* is the central true-value stream to which the tributaries of adaptation, energiza-

---

[397] This increasing systemic order may either be decreasing systemic entropy in a physical sense or senescence in a biological sense.

tion and re-production contribute. Consumers' *Lean aRe*processes adapt and *consume* energy to maintain or increase their functional structure and identity to the edge of senescence. *Lean*, living organisms want to *Re-generate*, and must re-produce because, as far as is known, biological organisms cannot perpetually *Re-generate* within themselves infinitely.[398] *Re-production* is one mechanism that organically arises as a matter of practical necessity to expand and perpetuate consumers' *Ontological Realization* through *adaptation* and *Re-generation*. Organisms must re-produce themselves in order to perpetuate and expand their lives and existences through their off-spring.

Here is a diagram showing the start of *Lean aRe*processes, which I will go ahead and symbolically shorten to */aRe*. This diagram shows that somewhere within the *Universe, IB* and *OM*, the *U/ People* business model becomes viable. This chart indicates *how* certain *Strategically Unique Degrees of Sophist-ication* arise into their own */aRe Supervening Level of Ontological Teleological Sophist-ication*:

---

[398]Though a counterfactual example may be found in hydra, for which mortality patterns suggest a lack of senescence through perpetual Re-generation;*see* , D.E. Martinez,*Mortality patterns suggest lack of senescence in hydra*, Exp Gerontol, 33(3):217-25 (May 1998).

Universal Chart of SUDS Forming /aRe SL-OTS

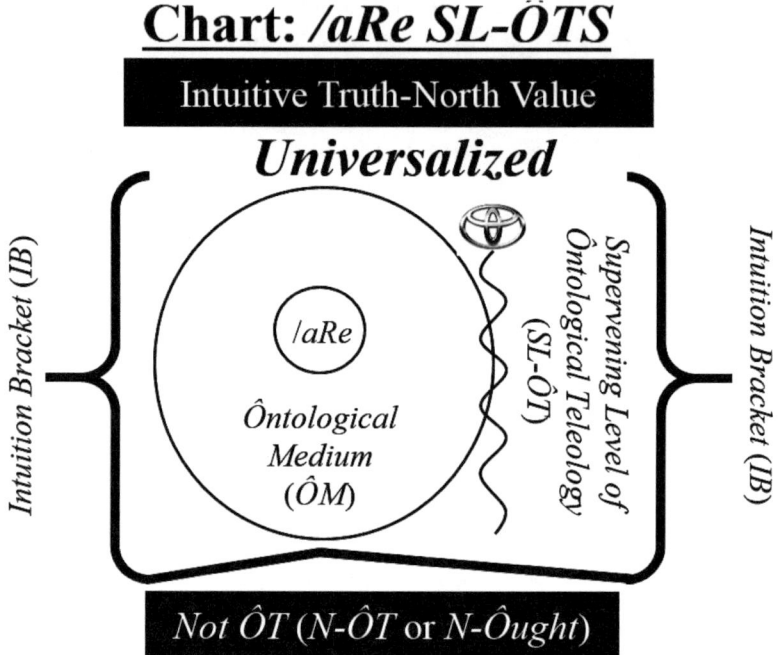

You aRe / People

To understand *what* true-north value is within the philosophy of *Lean*, you must understand *what* life truly is. However, the term *Life* with a capital *L* is difficult to define scientifically because *Life* is an informal and vague description of the things we consider to be alive because they self-sustain living processes.[399] Nonetheless, the term *Life* has some scientific meaning because

---

[399] *See*, Natalie Wolchover, *A New Physics Theory of Life*, Quanta Magazine (Jan. 22, 2014) article about the work of Jeremy England; *see also*, Leslie Mullen, *Forming a Definition for Life: Interview with Gerald Joyce*, Astrobiology Magazine (Jul. 25, 2013); *see also* Addy Pross, *What is Life?: How Chemistry becomes Biology*(2012); *see also*, Lynn Margulis and Dorion Sagan, *What is Life?*, University of California Press (1995); *see also* Erwin Schrödinger, *What is Life?*, Cambridge University Press (1944).

scientists commonly refer to the concept of, '*Living Systems*.' *Life* for scientists describes the boundaries between scientific fields such as chemistry, biochemistry and biology that ultimately produced consumers. No definition of *Life* could fully capture its meaning, especially for consumers as conscious beings, but you might find a *Lean*, flexible statement of the qualities of living systems to make money meaningfully by better serving *why*, *what*, and *how* consumers are alive.

One General Definition of *Life* Proposed by a NASA Working Group

If you research a general definition of *Life*, you will probably find one created in the 1990s by NASA's Exobiology Discipline Working Group (a.k.a. the, '*Working Group*').[400] Addy Pross referenced this definition of *life* in his book, *What is Life? How Chemistry becomes Biology*[401] that followed Erwin Schrödinger's 1944 book, *What is Life?*[402] The definition of life that NASA developed within the Working Group was, '*A self-sustaining chemical system capable of undergoing Darwinian evolution*.' This definition is fairly compact and self-explanatory, but I think you would find it more helpful toward better understanding true-north value in the philosophy of *Lean* to hear from Dr. Gerald Joyce,[403] who was a member of that Working Group. Dr. Joyce described the more complex definition of '*Darwinian evolution*' as follows:

> *'Darwinian evolution' has an associated property list: you can't have Darwinian evolution without*

---

[400] For more recent work from NASA, see the Institute for Universal Biology, a NASA Astrobiology Institute located at the University of Illinois at Urbana-Champaign, and housed within the Institute for Genomic Biology at, http://astrobiology.illinois.edu/.

[401] Addy Pross, *What is Life?: How Chemistry becomes Biology* , p. xiv (2012).

[402] *See generally*, Erwin Schrödinger, *What is Life?* (1944).

[403] Leslie Mullen, *Forming a Definition for Life: Interview with Gerald Joyce*, Astrobiology Magazine (Jul. 25, 2013).

self-replication or reproduction. You can't have it without mutability, heritability, and variation of form and function. And metabolism is in there too. You can't have Darwinian evolution without, at some level, a flux of higher-energy starting materials to lower-energy products that drive the processes of replication and whatever is necessary to support replication. And then there are the speciality properties like locomotion, irritability, ecological properties such as compartmentalization, and so on; those are all adaptations. And then things like photosynthesis, chemosynthesis, energy storage, and so on; those are just strategies of adaptation. All of that is subsumed by the 'Darwinian evolution' part.

Qualities of Living Qualities

NASA's Working Group definition is a great start, but by looking at the concept of life in abstractly meta-physical rather than Darwinian chemical terms as you have been doing in much of this *Stream 4*, you could perhaps better describe *Life's* qualities however consumers and organizations exhibit them. If you sufficiently broaden the qualitative description of *Life*, you might better analogize and relate its necessary and sufficient conditions to the para-sciences of business and economics. You might then perpetually improve consumers' standards of living through time in the meaningful ex-change for more money. If you include these broad, qualitative descriptors of living systems within the business *i/de*ôlogy of a *Lean HQ*, here are a few criteria that I recommend you follow when doing so:

1. Science recognizes that *Life* is more of a processually systemic true-north value than a thing per the Working Group's

definition, so any description of the qualities of *Life* ought to be processually systemic;
2. A description of the qualities of living systems ought to be as efficient as possible under the guiding principle of Occam's Razor;[404]
3. If an organization lists different qualities of *Life*, they ought to be:

    a. Necessary, such that if one quality was removed, the process of *Life* would never obtain or would eventually cease; and
    b. Sufficient, such that no further process would be necessary to sustain an overall living system;
4. Your organization ought to want a statement of *Life's* qualities abstracted to the highest true-north value possible to cover all physical and meta-physical contexts within the *Universe* and be amenable to analogizing to more specific business fields; and lastly
5. Your organization ought to want a statement of qualities that is easy to apply and remember in an everyday context for all, especially if you analogize from the broad qualities of consumers as living systems and apply them across all of organizational functions.

Lean aReProcesses

The */aRe* acronym provides the three necessary and sufficient qualities that consumers and organizations must possess to perpetually live. It provides a broad church for all forms of scientismic conjecture, hypothesis and theory about *what* life is *however* it may

---

[404]While *Occum's Razor* is controversial, I personally believe that this principle is an extension of the *Second Law of Thermodynamics*, making it for me more appropriately named, *Occum's Lazer*, so as to place a finer point on the sophist-icated parsimony of the rule.

appear, not just when it is biological. /aRe is thus the philosophical abstraction of the modern synthesis of evolutionary theory. /aRe measures scientismic conjectures, hypotheses and theories about evolution based on the degree they each explain the *Ontological Realization* of living systems through *Lean* adaptation, Re-generation and energization. You can use /aRe to analyze life as follows:

"*a*"

- ***Adaptive (Anticipatory/Aligning)***:[405] Living systems like consumers must systemically adapt to changing environmental factors to maintain and potentially expand their *energization* and *Re-generative* processes, such as through natural selection. In addition to natural selection and other biological *adaptation* theories,[406] *adaptation* also applies to consumers' behavior within their lives in the common sense that consumers decide best *how* to energize and optimize their lives as living systems. Consumers adapt and align as living systems by *Leaning* their *Ontological Realization* as best energizes and *Re-generates who*they are in response to the in-formation they experience within their demographic and environmental circumstances. Through these feedback mechanisms, consumers adapt according to *how* they are in fact *Ontologically Realized*, such as when deciding whether a *paos* provided its anticipated benefits after purchasing and consuming it.[407]

---

[405] This can be seen to include Robert Rosen's (M,R) System overall as an *anticipatory system* ôntologically building on predictive measure and adapting to changing circumstances in the context of an ecosystem, at Ron Cottam, Willy Ranson, Roger Vounckx, *Re-Mapping Robert Rosen's (M,R)-Systems*, Chemistry & Biodiversity, 4: 2352–2368. doi:10.1002/cbdv.200790192 (2007); see Ca´rdenas, M.L., et al., *Closure to Efficient Causation, Computability and Artificial Life*, J. Theor. Biol. doi:10.1016/j.jtbi.2009.11.010 (2009); M. Mossio, G. Longo, J. Stewart, *A computable expression of closure to efficient causation*, J Theor Biol. 257(3):489-98. doi: 10.1016/j.jtbi.2008.12.012 (Apr. 7, 2009).

[406] Such as methylation.

[407] A.H. Louie, *Robert Rosen's Anticipatory Systems*, Vol. 12 No. 3, pp. 18-29, Foresight, Emerald Group Publishing Limited (2010).

"R"

- *Re-generative (Re-productive/Re-pairing)*:[408] By definition, consumers as living systems adapt and consume energy[409] as a physical axiom to *Re-generate* their living processes within themselves or through their off-spring, which generally involves some form of *re-production* according to natural selection. To do so, consumers must adapt their energy transforming processes in order to continue to *Re-generate*. The most effective living systems increase the size and/or sophist-ication of their energy transforming processes by increasing the volume, velocity and/or effectiveness of adaptation through time in order to *Re-generate* even more. Per natural fitness, *Re-generation* stands central to living processes but necessarily requires *adaptation* and *energization* within the *OM* ; and

"e"

- *Energetic (Entropic/Endergonic)*:[410] To support Re-generation,[411] consumers' lives must ultimately increase universal thermodynamic equilibrium through transformational, material processes.[412] Since *energy* is an abstract collective

---

[408] Can be equated with Robert Rosen's *repair* or *R-System* noted above.

[409] Or decrease internal systemic entropy; *see*, Jeremy England, *Statistical Physics of Self-Replication*, The Journal of Chemical Physics, p. 139, 121923 doi: 10.1063/1.4818538 (2013).

[410] Can be equated with Robert Rosen's metabolic of *M System* noted above; the self-reflexive nature of Rosen's computability can be compared to Douglas Hofstadter's own claims for reflexivity in cognition.

[411] As Maslow wrote at p. 370 in, *A Theory of Human Motivation* (1943), '[T]he hunger drive (or any other physiological drive) was rejected as a centering point or model for a definitive theory of motivation. Any drive that is somatically based and localizable was shown to be atypical rather than typical in human motivation,' thus supporting the proposition that energization plays a supportive rather than primary role in customers' ontological motivation.

[412] *See again*, Jeremy England, *Statistical Physics of Self-Replication*, The Journal of Chemical Physics, p. 139, doi: 10.1063/1.4818538 (2013).

264   Stream 4: Lives

concept,[413] the vital question[414] for consumers as living systems is how they combine or match energy processes,[415] as exemplified literally by the pathway of sun to photosynthesis to food, and figuratively in their motivation to purchase *paos*.[416] Ultimately consumers' must synthesize metabolic energy to better live, exist and shop in ways they believe are best. But for this qualitative definition of life, consumers like all life must constantly seek potential energy in order to further their own adaptive and *Re-generative* activities. All life must do this either through direct consumption, or by matching external energy within their own internalized energy conversion pathways, whether unintentionally (i.e. teleonomically) such as *how* plant life grows toward energy, or purposefully (i.e. teleologically) like *how* consumers shop at grow-cery stores.[417]

This tripartite, scientific conception of */aRe - adaptation, Re-generation,* and *energization* - orients itself with the Buddhist concept of *pratītyasamutpāda* introduced in the last *Stream.* See *how* Dalai Lama XIV defines ' *pratītyasamutpāda*' as a reliance upon conditions, which you may apply analogously to the */aRe* acronym within

---

[413] As Vaclav Smil wrote in, *Energy: A Beginners Guide*, p. 9, Oneworld Publications (2006), '[E]nergy is not a single, easily definable entity, but rather an abstract collective concept, adopted by nineteenth-century physicists... Its most commonly encountered forms are heat (thermal energy), motion (kinetic or mechanical energy), light (electromagnetic energy) and the chemical energy of fuels and foodstuffs.'

[414] As Vaclav Smil noted, The word 'Energy' is a Greek compound. Aristotle (384–322 B.C.E.) created the term in his 'Metaphysics,' by joining εν (in) and έργον (work) to form ενέργεια (energeia, 'actuality, identified with movement') that he connected with entelechia, 'complete reality', in Energy: A Beginner's Guide, p. 1; for further background on this energizing factor of living existence, see Nick Lane, *The Vital Question: Energy, Evolution, and the Origins of Complex Life*, W. W. Norton & Company; 1 edition (2015).

[415] I.e., they match *Endergonic* and *Exergonic* processes.

[416] Yuval Noah Harari, *Sapiens*, p. 338 (2014).

[417] Egyptians intuitively understood this energetic distinction with their theistic conceptions of the Sun god *Ra*, and the design of the temple Abu Simbel where the other sun gods of Re-Horakhte and Amon-Re were lit by rays of light while the god of darkness, Ptah, remained in the shadows, per Lisa Krause, *Sun to Illuminate Inner Sanctuary of Pharaoh's Temple*, National Geographic News (Feb. 21, 2001).

the philosophy of *Lean*:

> *In Sanskrit the word for dependent-arising is pratītyasamutpāda. The word pratitya has three different meanings—meeting, relying, and depending—but all three, in terms of their basic import, mean dependence. Samutpada means arising. Hence, the meaning of pratītyasamutpāda is that which arises in dependence upon conditions, in reliance upon conditions, through the force of conditions.*[418]

According to Buddhist monk Thich Nhat Hanh, this Buddhist aphorism provides a physical analogy for this *pratītyasamutpāda* concept that, '*Three cut reeds can stand only by leaning on one another. If you take one away, the other two will fall.*'[419] Likewise, the Christian concept of the holy trinity dictates that the Christian God is dependent on the three identities as father, son and holy-spirit. Similarly, life is necessarily and sufficiently dependent on all three distinct but interrelated */aRe* processes in a scientismic, metaphysical and personal sense.

How */aRe* You and Consumers?

I am sure you recognize the three principal */aRe* qualities of living systems in consumers, by *how* consumers *adapt, Re-generate* and *energize*. The duration of any living system's era can be measured by the time it successfully executes */aRe* processes. These *aRe* processes are *Lean* (or */*) because they fundamentally, necessarily and sufficiently define *who, why, what* and *how* all consumers are within the *IB*. Consumers physically energize by eating well, but

---

[418] *See*, Dalai Lama XIV, *The Meaning of Life: Buddhist Perspectives on Cause and Effect*, translated and edited by Jeffrey Hopkins, Wisdom Publications (1992).

[419] *See*, Thich Nhat Hanh, *The Heart of the Buddha's Teaching*, Three River Press (1999).

they also energize metaphorically. For example, consumers figuratively energize themselves through education with in-formation and by developing new relationships in person and online. Thus going forward, *energizing* means consumers doing so in their lives both literally and figuratively.

Consumers likewise *Re-generate who* they are biologically, personally, financially and socially. They *Re-generate* biologically during their lifetimes against old age and through their descendants by consuming nutritious energy, personally through their psychological maturity, financially with their income used to pay for *paos*, and socially by sustaining relationships. Likewise, consumers adapt to the changing circumstances of their lives directly or indirectly through evolution. As long as consumers, their descendants and their societies successfully perform */aRe* processes to their limits, consumers will all continue upward along the spiralling arrow of time as consistent living systems as long as physically possible, thereby increasing their total lifetime value as customers to organizations.

How */aRe* Organizational Processes?

Given the breadth of this description of consumers as living systems for a *Lean* business *i/deô*logy, you may now further apply */aRe* living processes analogously to any organization. An organization must energize through commodities and human capital by converting those re-sources into adaptive and *Re-generative* business purposes. An organization must *Re-generate* new *paos* and profits, and it must adapt to changing circumstances by conducting regular *Strengths* and *Weaknesses*, *Ôpportunities* and *Threats* (*SW-ÔT*) analyses within its competitive context.

Given that an organization is a group of people, an organization must likewise convert its energizing inputs into greater structure through the *paos* it re-produces. The *paos* must enhance the structure of life because in the long run, perfectly functional societies regulate away organizations that re-produce money with no normative value, and thus no truly meaningful, true-north value. While keeping in mind the significant problems with money's reflection of true-north value as described in *Stream 2: Money & Economics*, an organization can approximately measure the meaning of the money it produces through the energizing earnings it retains. Since making money meaningfully means energizing and optimizing people's lives and existences for *adaptation* and *Re-generation* overall, an organization and its *paos* becomes a physical part of and an input into consumers' */aRe* processes, supporting their lives from below.

Apple of my *i*

You can *Lean* an organization toward making more money meaningfully by applying the */aRe* acronym to an organization and its technology by extension. For example, you can see the application of */aRe* at the micro-economic level with *Apple, Inc.*, the *i-Phone* and its related apps, since *simplicity is the ultimate sophistication*.[420] *Apple, Inc.'s paos* exemplifies *how /aRe* living processes determine the era of a specific organization and/or line of *paos* by similarly effecting *Apple's* customers:[421]

---

[420] As said by Steve Jobs in a 1980 presentation archived by the *Computer History Museum* and found here http://www.computerhistory.org/atchm/steve-jobs/.

[421] ©1984 *Apple Computer Inc.* .

Steve Jobs promoting *Apple, Inc.* in 1987

Adaptation: Since *adaptation* relates to *how* an organization successfully re-charges its *energization* and *Re-generating* processes to better exist in its business environment, you must ask questions such as *how* is *Apple* adapting to its changing competitive landscape? *What* is *Apple* developing to take advantage of *OPPortunities* available to it in the current business environment that might not have existed last year or may in the future? If you review *Apple's* risk factors described in its latest annual report, *how* is *Apple* adapting to minimize those *Threats*? Given the perpetual introduction of substitutes for its *CORe paos*, *what* is *Apple* developing to meet those *Threats* or avoid them altogether?

Re-generation: Since *Re-generation* relates to an organization's outputs, you must ask questions such as *how Apple* re-produces highly demanded *paos* through its *energization* and *adaptation*? *How* is *Apple* structuring its sales & marketing, finance & accounting, people services and operations to ensure it *Re-generates* and grows revenues and profits in the short, medium and long-term to pay operating expenses, debt and dividends? *How* is it *Re-generating* and growing equity gains to encourage further demand for its stock and ensure the perpetuation of its business? How is it Re-generating new lines of *paos* to delight consumers?

Energization: *Energization* relates to *Apple*'s figurative or literal inputs. For example, *energization* requires *Apple* to manage its human talent acquisition system to ensure it is attracting the most valuable employees it can. *Energization* requires asking *how* *Apple* makes sure that its vendors provide it with the best quality inputs for its products?[422] *What* sort of competitive and marketing intelligence is *Apple* gathering? *What* is *Apple*'s corporate and technological acquisition strategy? *What* sources of financing is *Apple* seeking in debt and equity besides the earnings it retains? *How* is *Apple* ensuring the health, engagement, and creativity of its workforce to optimize the energy of its human capital? All these inputs energize *Apple* and are necessary for it to successfully *adapt*, *Re-generate* and *charge* the best prices for its meaningful *paos*.

Consumers' *Pocket Universe*

If */aRe* is a universal descriptor of living systems' eras, then focus on *Apple*'s *i-Phone* more specifically to see *how* it and its apps serve the discrete needs of *Apple*'s customers' */aRe* living processes.[423] The in-formation produced by *Apple*'s *paos* inter-subjectively maps reality, including other people's perceptions, to other people's perceived reality in a converged consensus. Thus, the in-formation provided to people by apps metaphorically *energizes* people's *adaptive* and *Re-generative* processes.

Adapting through Apps: Energizing social media and news feeds provide the in-formation necessary for consumers to adapt to the

---

[422] For an example, see *Apple's* statement of supplier responsibility found here, http://www.apple.com/supplier-responsibility/ (last accessed Dec. 15, 2016).

[423] As the Chief Justice John Roberts of the U.S. Supreme Court noted, '... *such a pervasive and insistent part of daily life that a proverbial visitor from Mars might conclude they were an important feature of human anatomy,*' in, *Riley v. California*, 134 S. Ct. 2473, 2477, 189 L. Ed. 2d 430, 433, 2014 BL 175779 (2014); *see also,* The Pocket Universe, New York Magazine (Jun. 30, 2014).

changing circumstances of their lives. Weather apps allow people to adapt to their perpetually changing physical environment. Calendar apps allow *Apple*'s customers to adapt their schedules as necessary. Customers use fashion news to adapt their wardrobes to the latest clothing trends, or sports news to adapt their fantasy league teams each week.

Re-generating through Apps: In the most literal sense, dating apps allow customers to meet partners for continued vitality and off-spring. Customers use health apps and wearable technology in order to optimally *Re-generate* their well-being within their own lifetimes to the limit of their eras. Social media apps allow customers to create multiple, digital personas or avatars to virtually *Re-generate* themselves online. Customers communicate with apps such as those that check into a physical location in order to *Re-generate* friendships. Business apps allow consumers to *Re-generate* their income that in-turn gets spent on *paos* to enhance */aRe* processes further and further.

Energizing through Apps: Apple's customers must energize through new app in-formation as necessary to fuel *adaptation* and *Re-generation*, whether through algorithmic search suggestions, social media likes or fitness trackers. Customers use social media apps to energize their personal and professional networks. Customers energize through music recommendations, like *Siri* recommending *Johann Sebastian Bach* on iTunes based on feedback they have given. Customers use restaurant, delivery and grocery apps to vitalize themselves with new food. Customers use fitness apps and trackers to energetically stimulate their activity.

All these uses for *Apple's Apps* demonstrate the real-world application of the */aRe* acronym to all life and business. Let's now look at evidence supporting this tripartite conception of all living systems starting with *energization*, which funds all *adaptation* and *Re-generation*.

The Axial Age – Energizing Money and Intuition

The physical, metaphorical, and metaphysical concept of *energization* as a fundamentally *Lean* component of life is evident in the book, *The Measure of Civilization*, written by Stanford historian Ian Morris.[424] Morris provides significant data showing a statistical correlation between the development of money, vitality, and energy capture by people during a period of history Karl Jaspers termed the *Axial Age*. Karl Jaspers if you recall is the same philosopher *who* coined the term *Existenz* discussed in *Stream 3*.[425]

In *Measure*, Morris assesses the development of people by their, '...abilities to get things done in this world,' which *U / P* equates with *Lean adaptation*, *Re-generation* and *energization*. Morris remarks that one of customers' most remarkable attributes is their ability to consume and apply energy for non-food purposes. Morris noted that sociologist Leslie White first championed energy capture as the main driver and measure of social development of all people.[426] Morris further concludes in his book *Measure* that, '*Energy capture must be the foundation for any usable measure of social development.*'[427]

Morris supported this argument with extensive data. The following charts show Morris' estimated upward curve in the change of energy capture that occurred by people living in the Western world from 14,000 years before the *Common Era* to the turn of this

---

[424] Ian Morris, *The Measure of Civilization: How Social Development Decides the Fate of Nations*, p. 40, Princeton University Press (2013).

[425] *Ibid.*

[426] Leslie White, *Energy and the Evolution of Culture*, pp. 335-356, American Anthropologist (1943); Leslie White, *The Science of Culture*, New York: Grove Press (1949); Leslie White, *The Evolution of Culture*, New York: McGraw-Hill (1959); Leslie White even created a qualitative equation for this notion being, '$C = E * T$,' standing for *Culture* equals *Energy* times *Technology*.

[427] Ian Morris, *The Measure of Civilization*, p. 40.

Millennium:[428]

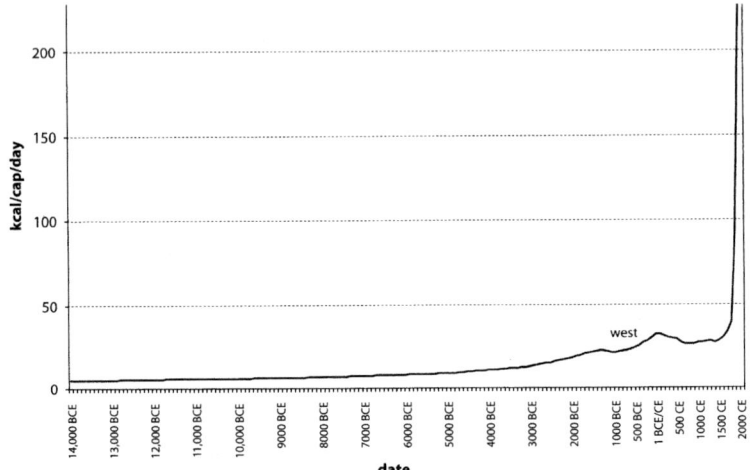

Figure 3.2. Western energy capture, 14,000 BCE–2000 CE, seen on a linear-linear scale.

© 2013 Ian Morris, Used with Permission

More recently, you can see a chart from 500 years before the *Common Era* to the turn of this *Millennium* here with similar effect. You can see an upward, exponential curve in energy consumption as meaningful society advanced:[429]

---

[428] *Ibid*, p. 62, Figure 3.2., © 2013 Ian Morris, Used with Permission.
[429] *Ibid*, p. 89, Figure 3.8., © 2013 Ian Morris, Used with Permission.

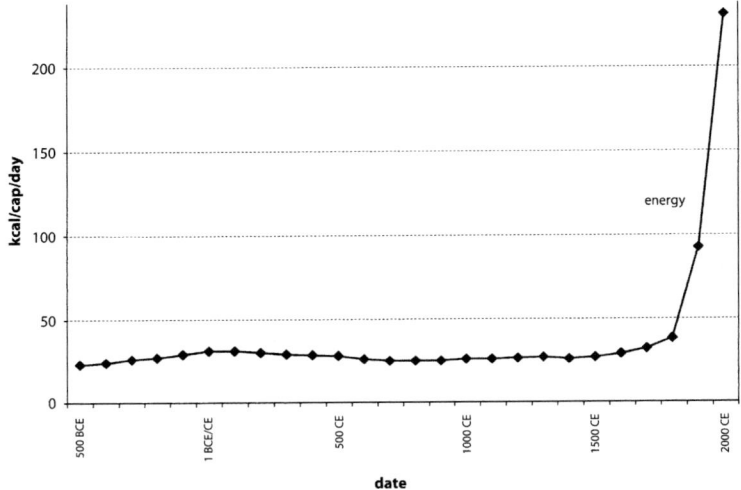

Figure 3.8. Western energy capture, 500 BCE–2000 CE.

© 2013 Ian Morris, Used with Permission

Another well-recognized scholar, Jared Diamond, author of *Guns, Germs & Steel*, supported Morris' claims by noting that people choose the means of production that yields the highest energizing and nutritional returns.[430] More recently, a group of scholars in the journal, *BioScience*, conducted a quantitative study confirming the unsurprisingly powerful correlation between economic growth and energy consumption.[431]

---

[430] Jared Diamond, *Guns, Germs, and Steel: The Fates of Human Societies*, p. 103, W. W. Norton & Company (2009); see also, Nick Gogerty,*The Nature of Value: How to Invest in the Adaptive Economy*, Kindle Loc. 827-828, Columbia University Press, who said, '*The story is clear: Energy consumption is highly correlated with value creation and consumption, which drives value flow throughout the economic network.*'

[431] James H. Brown, et al., *Energetic Limits to Economic Growth*, Vol. 61 No. 1, BioScience (Jan. 2011).

Spaghetti Suds as a Mental Model for /aRe Processes

Since *energization* represents one of the most fundamental components of living systems and consumption, I often conceptualize the */aRe* processes of *adaptation, Re-generation,* and *energization* as being like the *Flying Spaghetti Monster®* described in *Stream 3* brought down to Earth, sitting in a pot of boiling water. Eventually, the combination of boiling water and pasta creates persistent suds that float on the surface of the water to reach ever greater heights. Consider this process of boiling pasta as the most basic *Self-Organizing OT*developing a *Strategically Unique Degree of Sophist-ication* and e-merging into a unique *Supervening Level of OT Sophist-ication.*

Boiling Water(© 2013 (Public Domain CC 1.0))

The chemically axiomatic and processual true-north values of the water and pasta form one *SL-OT*, with the suds from the spaghetti and highly energetic, gaseous water having *Strategically Unique Degrees of Sophist-ication* in a higher, supervening *SL-OT*. The suds energize from the interaction of the boiling water and spaghetti, with the bubbles continuously *Re-generating* from that evolving system that consumers eventually strain, cool down and eat to live in the highest living *SL-OT* known within the known *OM* as bounded by the *IB*.[432]

---

[432]David Deutsch,*The Beginning of Infinity* , p. 74 (2011).

The *FSM* is Not Dead[433]

This may be a shocking conclusion, but according to our definition of life from /aRe processes, spaghetti suds are alive. After the suds e-merged from within the *OM* and they formed from the energizing water *Re-generating* them, these suds do to some small extent teleonomically adapt to perpetuate themselves by changing shape and size as necessary to exist to the extent they can. These suds unintentionally, only by way of their physical and chemical structure, seek new sources of energy to *Re-generate* with the single*Strategically Unique Degree of Sophist-ication* they hold onto. Even though the simple *SL-OT* that these suds occupy is merely a chemical process, it is a living system because the suds to a small degree *adapt* and *Re-generate* while they have a source of energy. The SUDS constantly, yet unintentionally, seek new sources of *energy* to perpetuate themselves ontologically in space-time. Believe it or not, but rising spaghetti suds are actually an extension of consumers' own lives because while the suds supervene on spontaneous, teleonomic self-organization within the *OM* from chemical processes, consumers teleologically created these suds to energize themselves to become more of *who* they are and want to be as human beings.

Emergence of *SUDS* through *SO-OT* into *SL-OTS*

Beyond suds, another living */aRe* processes is that of a wave in the ocean. Once a wave begins, it appears to re-produce a single, stable column of water moving across space and time in a dynamic equilibrium. However, a wave is like the *Re-generating* cells within consumers' bodies, and an organization's annual revenues,

---

[433]In ironic contrast to Nietzsche's statement, '*Gott ist Tott*,' or '*God is Dead*' in his book, *The Science of Joy*, in 1882. This concept is also touched on earlier by Hegel in his book, *Phenomenology of Spirit*(1807).

by constantly turning over but generally maintaining a consistent identity. The wave *or*iginates and gets *Ontologically Realized* while travelling through the *Ontological Medium* by constantly becoming composed of new water molecules and yet remaining defined as a consistent, yet greater, wave from a person's personal perspective.[434] Like suds a-rising in a pot, a wave teleonomically (i.e. unintentionally) re-produces and optimizes itself as a wave simply by increasing the upward pressure on its column of water. This dynamic is much like shareholders demanding greater share prices and dividends so they may consistently and increasingly identify themselves as awash in money - it's their way of maintaining *who* they believe they */aRe* and becoming the even wealthier people they imagine themselves as being.

Kanagawa-Oki Nami-Ura, *The Great Wave off Kanagawa* (© ~ 1829-32 (Public Domain))

A wave as a distinct identity systemically adapts to changing environmental circumstances. The wave energizes and becomes *Ontologically Realized* from the axiomatic and systemic forces operating within the water, and teleonomically *Re-generates* until it is *Not Ontologically Teleological*. A wave changes its shape and maintains

---

[434] This example may also be seen akin to a bubbling spring.

its identity in response to environmental forces as a very limited form of unintentional adaptation. Like suds, a wave is a "living" physical process, though with few *Strategically Unique Degrees of Sophist-ication*when compared to biological living systems that are relatively boiling over with them.[435]The life of a wave is just much more transitory than most biology.

If you find this unbelievable, that a wave could be considered living like an organism, in response I say that people generally do not give most biological life much more consideration than waves in the ocean or rivers running into them. And yet some nations legally codify this notion. In March of 2017, New Zealand, at the request of the Māori tribe in the North Island, gave its Whanganui River legal status as a person with the same rights and protections.[436]When this desig-nation was awarded, Gerrard Albert, the lead negotiator for the Whanganui tribe said:

> *We can trace our genealogy to the origins of the universe, and therefore rather than us being masters of the natural world, we are part of it... And that is not an anti-development, or anti-economic use of the river but to begin with the view that it is a living being, and then consider its future from that central belief.*[437]

A week after New Zealand took this legal action, the high court in the Himalayan state of Uttarakhand in India did the same for the Ganges and Yamuna Rivers, saying that, '*The rivers are central*

---

[435]*See e.g.*, Philip Ball, *How Life (and Death) Spring From Disorder*, Quanta Magazine (Jan. 26, 2017); *see also*, Harold Morowitz and D. Eric Smith, *Energy flow and the organization of life*, Sante Fe Institute Working Paper 2006-08-029 (2017); and the work of Jeremy England at the Massachusetts Institute of Technology found at, http://www.englandlab.com/publications.html.

[436]Eleanor Ainge Roy,*New Zealand river granted same legal rights as human being* , The Guardian (Mar. 16, 2017).

[437]*Ibid.*

to the existence of half of the Indian population and their health and well being. They have provided both physical and spiritual sustenance to all of us from time immemorial.'[438] Thus, both New Zealand and India legally declared the lives of their people as supervening on and synonymous with these rivers in a continuous stream of life within the *Universe* .

The Survivor Tree of Life

Now, slow down the */aRe* processes of the suds, waves, rivers and streams in your mind to witness this same living processes occurring in trees. Trees convert *energy* through photosynthesis, and increase energy transformation by structuring the biological processes of plant growth. Trees also increase universal entropy by reaching senescence and decomposing into inert matter while their off-spring live on. To do this, trees *Re-generate* within their lifetimes and *adapt* to changing environmental conditions through re-productive biodiversity. The difference between the movement of water and the growth of trees is one merely of complexity of their essential structures performing /aRe processes. Trees unlike water have more sophist-icated mechanisms to intrinsically *adapt* and *energize* to self-perpetuate their *Ontological Realization*. That which people most commonly call '*Life*' is that which has the power to *Re-generate* itself across generations in order to escape systemic senescence and thereby possibly universalize itself. This is *what* trees and all that is generally considered living distinctly do. Thus, trees *Lean* their *aRe* processes into more sophisticated, living *SL-OTS* than fountains, suds, waves rivers or streams in order to try and achieve everlasting salvation.

Of course, consumers take this adaption, Re-generation, and energization so much further. Compare for example the *Survivor Tree* that has now re-grown next to *One World Trade* that consumers

---

[438] *India court gives sacred Ganges and Yamuna rivers human status*, British Broadcasting Corporation (Mar. 21, 2017).

built to remember where the original World Trade Center twin towers once stood in lower Manhattan. Both the *Survivor Tree* and the *World Trade* buildings have *Re-generated*, with trees doing so teleonomically with consumers' help and the new World Trade buildings being built teleologically with great purpose.

Survivor Tree in Front of *One World Trade Building* Under Re-construction
(© 2012 Getty Images, Used with Permission)

The *Universal* Constructor, Games of Life and Langston's Ants

> *I do not understand the divine source,*
> *but I know, in a way that I don't understand,*
> *that out of chaos I can make order,*
> *out of loneliness I can make friendship,*
> *out of ugliness I can make beauty.*
> - Edwin Land, President, Polaroid Corporation, in Ninth Annual Arthur Dehon Little Memorial Lecture Given at the Massachusetts Institute of Technology (May 22, 1957).

280 Stream 4: Lives

Beyond these limited chemical and biological examples, you can also see *Supervening Levels of OT Sophist-ication* emerging from human-made systems such as computer programs. While not alive in a natural sense, these human-made systems can help you more fully understand *who* consumers are as living systems and *what* they *Lean* toward. They do this by demonstrating *how* different forms of *Ontological Realization* arise from new, synthetic *Universes* created within the one we commonly share.[439] For example, through certain computer programs and their unique rules and codes, people can create new *Universes* with unexpected results, like the *Lean Startup's*, '*Instant Message Virtual Universe*.' Computer codes can be th-ôught of by analogy as versions of natural laws creating a unique *Ontological Teleology* in their own domain. These computer programs may lead otherwise random processes to *Re-generate* into sophisticated patterns of meaningful existence that spontaneously create new forms of *Ontological Realization* in the real world.

Universal Constructors

One hypo-thetical example of such a human-made system was created by the early 20th century polymath John Von Neumann who devised a machine that could *Re-generate* itself infinitely if it was provided sufficient Matter and Energy within the *Ontological Medium*. He called this machine a, '*Universal Constructor*.'[440] Computer-scientists call Von Neumann's *Universal Constructor* a self-regenerating upper ontology that functions as a universal computing machine.[441] The physicist David Deutsch has gone one

---

[439]David Deutsch, *Constructor Theory*, p. 38, Centre for Quantum Computation, University of Oxford (Dec. 2012).

[440]This is *Turing equivalent* in computer science parlance, meaning that it can simulate, and be simulated by a Turning *Universal* computer presuming an infinite *Ôntological Medium*.

[441]Encyclopædia of Database Systems, Ling Liu and M. Tamer Özsu (Eds.), Springer-Verlag (2009); *see again* Tom Gruber's definition of *Ontology* found at, http://tomgruber.org/writing/ontology-definition-2007.htm.

step further to say that *Universal Constructors* are not hypo-thetical at all and already, deductively exist. They sit in U-shaped workspaces, add to shopping carts, and line-up in stores. He believes that employees and consumers, like these hypothetical machines, are themselves *Universal Constructors* since they already conceptualize and actualize *what* could be produced and purchased to energize and optimize people's lives.[442]

Conway's Games of Life

A limited example of John Von Neumann's *Universal Constructor* that Stephen Hawking discussed in Chapter 8 of his book, *Grand Design*, is John Conway's, '*Game of Life*.' Like the *Universal Constructor*, the *Game of Life* is a zero-player game whose evolution gets determined by its initial set of universal laws and programmatic upper-ontology. It is set in a field of squares like a large *Reversi* or *Othello* ® board with square pieces, where programmatic rules direct which pieces change color. You can view a version of the *Game of Life* called ' *Gosper's Glider Gun*' being played out here:

Gosper's Glider Gun (© 2005 CC BY-SA 3.0)

Keep in mind that these are not mere programs executing a pre-define set of instructions to produce a specific, teleological result. Rather these are a set of rules governing otherwise chaotic interactions that produce the resulting animation merely as a teleonomic

---

[442]David Deutsch,*The Beginning of Infinity* , pp. 59, 145 (2011).

by-product of laws that apply universally within the game. You can see the *Game of Life* played out at a larger scale here, with what is referred to as a triangular-shaped, '*Puffer-type Breeder*,' created from pure randomness:

Game of Life, Puffer-type Breeder(© 2008 CC BY-SA 3.0)

 What does this Rorschach-like image reveal to you about consumers?

Langston's Ant

Yet another people-made system is, '*Langston's Ant.*' *Langston's Ant* starts out on the *Reversi* grid and follows these simple, universal laws:

1. *If the ant is on a black square, it turns right 90 degrees and moves forward one unit;*
2. *If the ant is on a white square, it turns left 90 degrees and moves forward one unit; and*
3. *When the ant leaves a square, it inverts the color of the square it left.*

As a result of these simple rules, the ant begins its randomized, teleonomic journey, that eventually forms a self-organized value stream up and to the right as can be seen here:

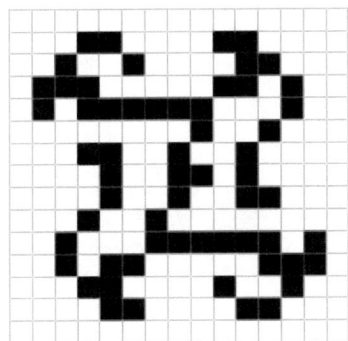 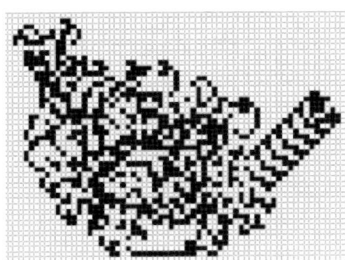

Langston's Ant Crawling Up and to the Right after 11,000 Cycles (© 2007 (Public Domain))

Starting from a completely blank slate, *Langston's Ant* produces the picture on the left after 386 moves, but after 10,647 moves, *Langston's Ant* produces the rightward picture. If you look toward the right side of the second picture, you notice a distinct stream being constructed from the seemingly random operation of the rules of the game. The line builds onward and upward to the right, forming a distinctly sophisticated *SL-OT* that altogether appears a bit like the logo for the *Volvo Car Group*®:

Logo for *Volvo Car Group*®

> *Lazybones, go to the ant;*
> *Study its ways and learn.*
> *Without leaders, officers, or rulers,*
> *It lays up its stores during the summer,*
> *Gathers in its food at the harvest.*
> – Proverbs 6.6 – 6.8 (Circa 1000 BCE, Public Domain)

While Von Neumann's *Universal Constructor*, Conway's *Game of Life* and *Langston's Ant* may all be seen as analogies to *how* life originated from *SO-OT*, none of these computer simulations are actually alive - they do not have the same *SUDS* forming the initial *SL-OT* of life. If you compare the /aRe test for these programs to the one for naturally self-organizing systems like suds, streams and trees, you can see that while each computer program consumes electrical energy to *Re-generate* its *Ontological Realization* in the computer's memory and on the screen, none of these software ontologies has the same *Strategically Unique Degrees of Sophistication* necessary to be deemed a living system. Instead, suds, streams, ants and consumers unintentionally or intentionally *best fit* themselves to *what* energy may be available, whereas computer programs can at present do so with at most the capacity of a wave or stream.

All of suds, streams, ants and computer programs face a similar, yet distinct limitation. None can universally conceptualize and construct *what* dynamically *adapts* and continually *energizes* themselves so they can at least think about *how* to become perpetually *Re-generated*. These programs, like streams and ants, cannot conceive of their own existence – of being other than *what* and *how* they were programmed to be – if *Langston's Ant* did, then it could be living in the machi-nation of a computer.[443] We entirely control

---
[443] *See generally*, William Barrett, *Death of the Soul: From Descartes to the Computer*, Anchor Books (1986).

programs' power switch (for now).

While none of these computer simulations meets /aRe standards to be considered biologically alive, you can see in John Von Neumann's *Universal Constructors*, Conway's *Games of Life* and *Langston's Ants* how sophisticated structures e-merge from chaotic interactions occurring within software ontologies. For example, you can analogize the diversity of self-replicating gliders arising within a *Game of Life* to consumers' lives emerging from within the universal and process true-north values of the *OM*.[444] Consumers' teleological SL-OT lies beyond the teleonomic one for the general *Game of Life*, putting consumers in a land where they question everything, including their own lives and existences.

From self-organizing, non-biological systems, you can see a possible scientismic explanation for *how* plant and animal life initially e-merged from the seemingly arbitrary yet entirely cohesive rules of nature. You can see from a process of complex, self-catalyzing chemical interactions supplanting one another through natural selection, *how* that chemical system bred living organisms. You can even see a scientismic explanation for *how* consumers developed into the thriving organisms that they are today from universal, axiomatic laws inter-acting with chaotic processes up and along a twisting history of the *OM*.[445]

The Great Chain of Being

In 1935, the American philosopher Arthur Lovejoy gave a lecture at Harvard, in which he noted that the history of scholarship, from the ancient Greeks through the Romantic period, propelled an idea about life and consumers' position within it called, '*The Great*

---

[444] Yuval Noah Harari, *Sapiens*, p. 170 (2014).

[445] The organizational perspective on this development and management of it can be found in the, '*The Cynefin Framework*,' as described by David J. Snowden and Mary E. Boone in, *A Leader's Framework for Decision Making*, Harvard Business Review (Nov. 2007).

Chain of Being,' based on the *Principle of Sufficient Reason* and the *Principle of Plentitude*.

As you know already, the *Principle of Sufficient Reason* is synonymous with the *Axiom of Causation* and *Root Cause Analysis*, holding that every cause has a prior one leading back to a self-causing cause in the *Gemba* as the source of all production. The self-causing cause in turn determines the purpose of each subsequent cause, including *why* consumers buy from you at all. The *Principle of Plentitude* further states that, within the *Principle of Sufficient Reason's* stream of causes, all that could be already in fact is given the constraints present at any point in time. The *Principle of Plentitude* is thus similar to modern physicists' conceptions of string theory and fecund universes, in the way those conjectures state that all possible *Universes* that could exist in fact do. The *Principle of Plentitude* is thus the inverse and logical equivalent of *Murphy's Law*, which states that everything that could go wrong in fact will. For ancient thinkers, the principles of sufficient reason and plentitude thus made this world the most perfect of all possible worlds, creating within it, *The Great Chain of Being*.

However, both the *Principle of Sufficient Reason* and the *Principle of Plentitude* relied on speculative, intuitive true-north values rather than the quantitatively empirical, axiomatic and systemic validity that we rely on for most new true-north value today. *The Great Chain of Being* assumed two notions that: [446]

1. *The world, usually as created by a deity, was perfect and full with all aspects of existence; and*
2. *Each part of existence was connected to each other in a stream of life and existence, with one category interlinked with the next.*

---

[446] *See generally*, Auther Lovejoy, *The Great Chain of Being*, Harvard University Press (1936); and William F. Bynum, *The Great Chain of Being after Forty Years: An Appraisal*, University College, London (1975).

The Great Chain of Being itself somewhat mirrors modern physicists' conception that the *Universe* must be consistent with consumers' existences as they actually are since the world is coherent with universal, true-north values in all ways, both naturally and commercially. As stated by Ray Dalio, the founder of *Bridge-water Associates* in his manifesto, *Principles*:[447]

> ***Though how nature works is way beyond man's ability to comprehend, I have found that observing how nature works offers innumerable lessons that can help us understand the realities that affect us. That is because, though man is unique, he is part of nature and subject to most of the same laws of nature that affect other species.***

Here is a 1617 schematic depicting *The Great Chain of Being*, which happens to look a lot like a slide from a presentation given inside *Bridgewater Associates* of the financial success they will achieve:[448]

---

[447] Ray Dalio, *Principles* (2011).
[448] Robert Fludd, *Great Chain of Being (Utriusque Cosmi Majoris Scilicet et Minoris)*, Frankfurt (1617).

Great Chain of Being (circa 1600s (Public Domain))

As every grade school student knows, the concept of evolution first proposed by Jean Baptiste Lamarck and of natural selection first explained by Charles Darwin dismantled *The Great Chain of Being*. The often retold epic of evolution and subsequent scientific advancement folded intuitive, non-formal explanations for life like *The Great Chain of Being* into its explanatory grasp.

However, *The Great Chain of Being* is important to understand because of its intellectual legacy in business. For example, remnants of *The Great Chain of Being* can be seen carried forward in organizational charts from line workers in U-shaped workspaces up to the *CEÔ* walking the *Gemba*. To date, the *Toyota Re-Production System* has produced a lineage of approximately 400 different types of *Toyota* passenger cars, 200 different types of commercial vehicles, and 120 other automotive vehicles. *Toyota* evolved the shape and function of each vehicle as each *best fit*its particular market at its given point in time. Like fecund Gods of the auto industry following the *Principle of Plentitude*, the chart of *Toyota's* product line shows this lineage:

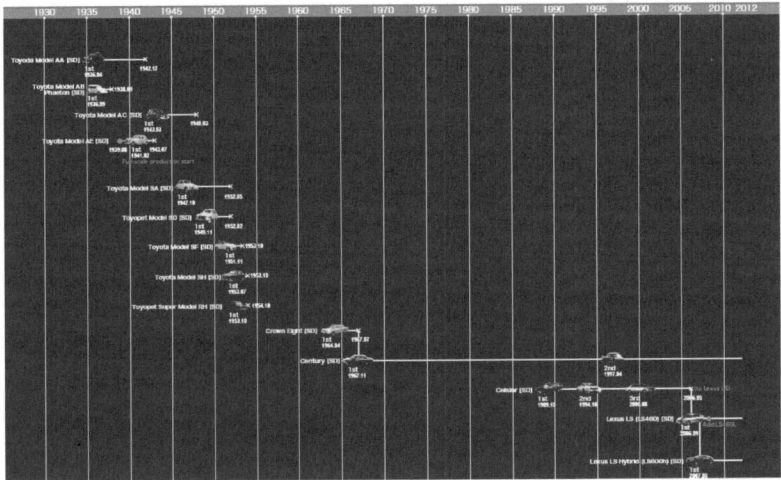

Production System's Lineage(© 2015 Toyota®, The full chart available at: http://www.toyota-global.com (last accessed Jan. 6, 2017))

You can also see the *Principle of Sufficient Reason* and *Principle of Plentitude*reflected in the evolutionary product tree of 3M® Corporation as noted in *Built to Last*. The document, *Product Evolution from Scotchlite Reflective Sheeting Technology*, from 3M® Corporation in the mid-1970's is shown here:[449]

---

[449] Jim Collins and Jerry I. Porras, *Built to Last*, p. 154 (2011).

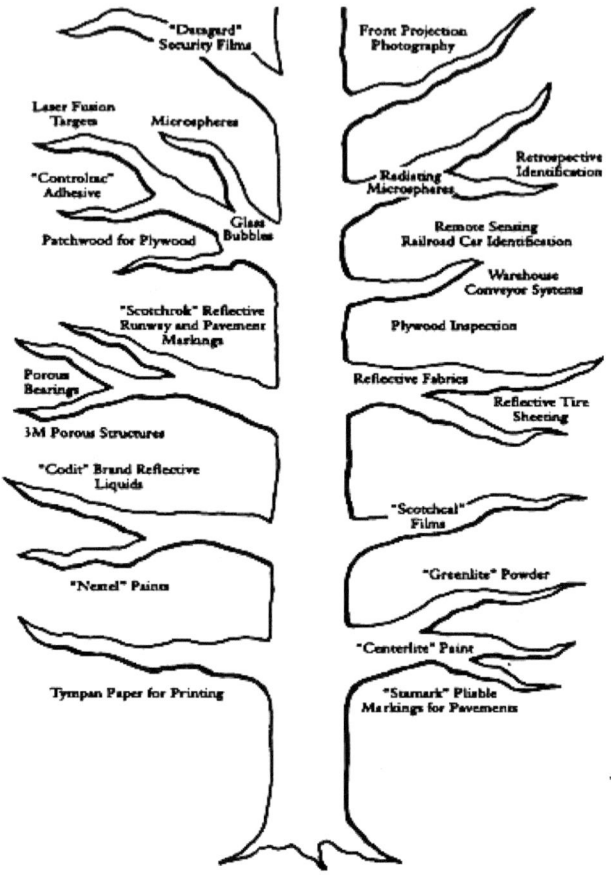

3M Corporation Product Tree

These *paos* lineages of *Toyota®* and *3M® Corporation* reflect the emerging viability of these products to *Leanly adapt, Re-generate* and *energize* over time symbiotically with these companies' customers. These product lines only remain viable by serving customers' needs for Matter and Energy as a means for them to *adapt, Re-generate* and *energize*well.

Valuable Energy Streams are *The Great Chain of Being*

While *The Great Chain of Being* is a historical relic, each distinct living system, from viruses upward to more complex organisms like consumers, are interconnected through well-documented energy streams, like the connections in an organization's supply chain.[450] As originally described by the *energization* part of /*aRe* processes, energy flows from sun to photosynthesis, to the Matter and Energy consumers' metabolic processes consume. This value stream flows from plants' *adaptation, Re-generation* and re-renewal of energy re-sources to other organisms' use of that Matter and Energy for their own *Lean adaptation, Re-generation* and *energization.* This processually systemic value stream flows upward until it reaches consumers, resulting in *who, why, what,* and *how* they are through the twisting arrow of time. This is the modern version of the *Great Chain of Being.*

All /*aRe* organisms up the food chain eat to *adapt* and *Re-generate* in furtherance of their /*aRe* processes at each next level. Each bend in this stream of organisms transforms energy from one *SL-OT* to the next. The sophist-ication of each *SL-OT* gets measured by the downward supervening dependencies contributing to /*aRe* processes. This supervenience does not strictly correlate with the food chain, but a loose correlation is apparent.

To reflect this valuable energy stream, I show below a diagram of the sun's energy becoming the *U/ People* business model upward

---

[450]This is a chain of autotrophs to heterotrophs; *see*, Vaclav Smil, *Energy: A Beginner's Guide*, pp. 7 and 29.

through a basic repetition of each organism's /aRe's.[451] Below you can see each lower level organism transformed by the energy *or*iginating from the Sun living in the simplest physical *SL-OT* upwardly energizing the next more sophist-icated living system that is likewise performing /aRe processes until becoming *Lean People*:

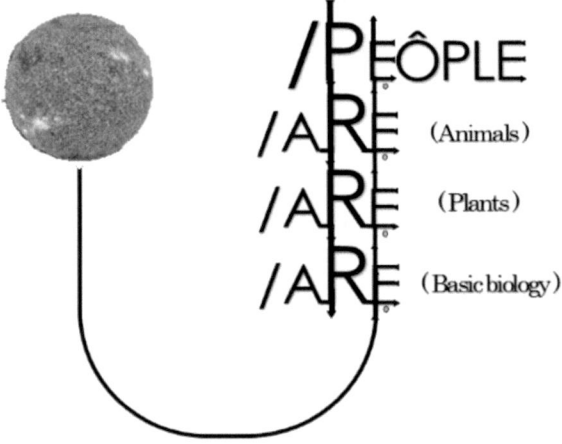

Energy from the Sun passed up through each organism's being.

You see here in this diagram *what* might otherwise look like the food chain, or *The Great Chain of Being*, conformed to *what* you know about *how* life *adapts, Re-generates* and *energizes* within the

---

[451] This conception of *Lean fitness* aligns with *kin selection* and *selfish genes*, as proposed by Richard Dawkins, and is sympathetic to *group selection*, as proposed by E.O. Wilson. Wilson advocates viewing organisms' *fitness* to be naturally selected to further live and exist as being an additional layer of complexity supervening on top of kin selection. I categorize *Lean fitness* here as the promotion of consistent living systems and all that is necessarily associated with them by extension. By necessity, *Lean fitness* is thus susceptible to qualitative assessment by categorizing *Lean* systems at the group or individual level, and by amalgamating *SL-OTS* into the hierarchy that composes individual humans as *super-organisms*. For some contemporary arguments around this discussion, see Richard Dawkins' review of E.O. Wilson's, *The Social Conquest of Earth*, WW Norton (2012) in his article in 'Prospect Magazine' here, *The Descent of Edward Wilson*, (May 24, 2012); and Wilson's response in that same article in, E.O. Wilson, *Evolution and Our Inner Conflict*, New York Times (Jun. 24, 2012); and E.O. Wilson, *The Riddle of the Human Species*, New York Times (Feb. 24, 2013) among the many academic opinions and papers and cited by both sides.

OM and the various *SL-OTS* catalogued throughout the history of science.[452]

Each living system within a given ecosystem, which really means every natural system, must *adapt, Re-generate* and *energize* in order to live. But in a living ecosystem, imagine energy streams developing whereby one generally more sophisticated form of life in a *SL-OT* feeds off the next. Each food stream may be seen as one new level of */aRe* processes as per the diagram above, with energy flowing ever further upward along the food chain.[453] *Re-generation* downwardly depends on each next lower level, with each level adapting as necessary in order to live and exist.

To better understand this dynamic of supervenience acting up and down in both directions, think of *how* a café waiter carries a stack of plates in a restaurant when taking them back to the dishwasher. Imagine the plates being like the backbone of a single, living organism, such as an embodied version of the *Flying Spaghetti Monster®*. The mind of the embodied FSM would actively, downwardly align all of the lower plates to keep itself upright as a final cause. However in real life, the café waiter actively balances the plates from below like a *Lean*, efficient, initial cause teleonomically directed to the end-goal of getting paid in good faith to h/er occupation.[454]

Through this analogy, you can see that each level of */aRe* processes within an ecosystem exerts energy upward and downward in and out of each processual system, such as energy exerted by organisms converting energy from less sophisticated *SL-OTS* to reach higher ones overall. For example, consumers' own cells co-opt the energy

---

[452]Yuval Noah Harari, *Sapiens*, p. 335 (2014).

[453]*Ibid* p. 246, where Harari writes citing David Christian in *Maps of Time*(2011), ' *In 1500, humanity consumed about 13 trillion calories of energy per day. Today, we consume 1,500 trillion calories a day. (Take a second look at those figures –human population has increased fourteen-fold, production 240-fold, and energy consumption 115-fold).*'

[454]'This aligns with Merleau-Ponty's view of the waiter's good faith toward h/er occupation, but speaks against Jean-Paul Sarte's notion of the cafe waiter being in bad-faith just for doing h/er job of carrying a tray properly to further live and exist by making money meaningfully (which is the waiter's intended purpose) in, *Being and Nothingness* (1943).

from mitochondria within them when performing /aRe processes, thereby allowing consumers to live and purchase *paos*. These multiple energy sources may be applied analogously to the vitality of organizations, such as when outside investments inject energizing capital, thereby providing the contractual right to re-direct the flow of Matter and Energy to grow a business' *Ontological Realization or*ganically.[455] Any investment though is driven by the expectation that an organization will be primarily fueled by the cash it receives from the paying customers it charges further up the commercial food chain.

An Organization's (*B/aRe*) Viability

Since the commercial viability of any organization depends on understanding *who* , *why* , *what* and *how* consumers are up through these valuable energy streams, you ought to now study *what* constitutes '*Life*' in more complex *SL-OTS* with biological /aRe processes. You ought to extend your understanding of the ancient concept of, *The Great Chain of Being* , to see life from the perspective of *why* , *what* and *however* life may be *Ontologically Realized* from /aRe processes. Viruses exemplify yet another type of organism that exists at the extreme boundary of *what* we deem to be living that we can examine for its purpose. Like viral memes getting transmitted across social media, biological viruses exist at the margin of *what* may be considered cultured. And like viral memes, biological viruses *adapt* to changing environmental circumstances, *Re-generate* through re-production, and consume people's *energy* to live.[456]

---

[455] *See e.g.* Moisés Naím, *The End of Power: From Boardrooms to Battlefields and Churches to States, Why Being in Charge Isn't What It Used to Be*, Basic Books (2013), however of course, by *The End of Power* the author actually means, and would have more appropriately titled the book as, *The Decentralization of Power* , since the actual title taken literally violates the *First Law of Thermodynamics*.

[456] Concepts as popularized by Richard Dawkins in, *The Selfish Gene* , Oxford University Press (1976).

Like trees, viruses' intrinsic ability to shape the */aRe* processes they perform qualifies them as basically, biologically living. Taking the */aRe* acronym one step further, an ontological phase change occurs within the philosophy of *Lean* at this point from teleonomic, *Self-Organizing OT* to the next, *Supervening Level of OT Sophist-ication*. Basic, biological activity becomes *what* you may refer to as "*B/aRe*" in a *Lean* business *i/deô*logy. *B/aRe* living systems represent the initial instance where knowledge transmits across living systems. This knowledge improves the degree living systems exist across generations. Our universal chart of living systems now shows *SUDS* conceptually bubbling up into these more sophisticated *B/aRe SL-OTS*:

Universal Chart of SUDS Forming B/aRe SL-OTS

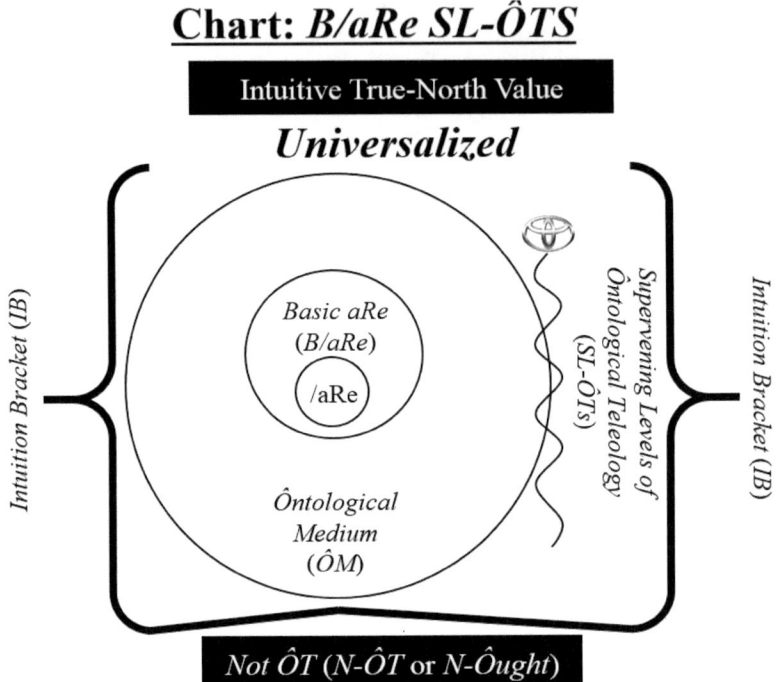

If you believe this scientismic *B/aRe* theory, consumers' existences ę-merged from the *OM*, *SO-OT*, and *SL-OTS* as *B/aRe* or *Basically/Biologically/aRe* living processes. That means that consumers as sensing beings *adapted* through natural selection, mutation, and psychological decision-making; *Re-generated* through cellular repair and pro-creation; and *energized* such as through the supervening dependencies of the energizing *paos* they *b-ought*.

Consumers' *b-ing* results from their performing these *B/aRe* processes to the extent they *adapted*, *Re-generated* and *energized*. You may consider the theory of *SO-OT* and *B/aRe* life processes as synonymous with neo-Darwinian survival of the *Leanest*, but with added *Strategically Unique Degrees of Sophist-ication* as to *what*

Leanness actually means in the broader metaphysical context of the *Universe, IB* and *OM*.

B/aRe as Modern Evolutionary Synthesis

Life itself in the form of *B/aRe* viruses evidences the intuitive possibility of more complex organisms like consumers self-organizing from within the dynamic system of the *OM*. You can understand *how* the proponents of *The Great Chain of Being* looked out into nature, reviewed the range of life, and saw *how* a spectrum of self-organizing, biological systems arrayed themselves with increasing sophist-ication from trees and viruses all the way up to consumers.

However, now with hindsight, we know the tremendously well documented pathways of *adaptation, Re-generation* and *energization* in minute detail that evolved upward into more complex, living *SL-OTS*.[457] Since all organizations serve *who* and *why* consumers are as the most sophist-icated living *SL-OT* known within the *IB*, basic /aRe processes most fundamentally determine the ontology and viability of organizations and their *paos*. This is *why* and *how* B/aRe serves as a modern, high-level synthesis of the epic of evolution.

To gain further perspective on 'B/aRe' as a modern evolutionary synthesis, re-consider the traditional Darwinian over-emphasis on re-production we discussed earlier in this *Stream 4*. While re-production accurately assesses the need to re-produce, traditional and even neo-Darwinism otherwise over-emphasizes re-production over other qualities necessary to support *who* and *why* consumers are from *B/aRe* organisms upward into becoming consumers. Evolutionary theory is at once not abstract enough in describing *B/aRe* organisms' and consumers' three primary /aRe activities on a metaphysical basis, and not specific enough in describing the necessary and sufficient qualities of *Life* itself on a scientific basis.

---

[457] I.e., as Karl Popper wrote, '[T]he doctrine of natural selection is a most successful metaphysical research programme,' at p. 344 of, Natural Selection and the Emergence of Mind, Dialectica, 32:339-355 (1978).

298 Stream 4: Lives

To reiterate regarding consumer re-production, they certainly need to re-produce because of *how* they are, but the overall goal of all organisms is to perpetually re-new through *B/aRe* adaptation regardless of the specific means of perpetuating themselves. Consumers only want to increase the difference between *what* ought to be and *what* is *Not-Ontologically Teleological*. Consumers' re-production is a specific method, technique and process for them to *Re-generate* by further *adapting* and *energizing*. Consumers' (and organizations' to some extent) absolute need to re-new themselves arises due to physical constraints of senescence in order to *Re-generate* and is not an end-goal in itself. Instead, re-production universalizes *B/aRe* processes so as to maximally a-void becoming *N-OT*. Consumers a-voiding becoming *N-OT* does not absolutely require re-production but rather *Re-generation,* with a capital *R*. *Re-generation* flows upward along the *Rubicon* of consumers' utmost value stream so you may chart a course with it toward the greatest profit.

Like *Re-generation*, re-production merely represents one means of *adaptation* among many others. As the former Motorola *CEO* Robert Galvin - a famous *Lean Six Sigma* proponent - was quoted in, *Built to Last*[458]:

> **Renewal is the driving thrust of this company. Literally the day after my father founded the company to produce B Battery Eliminators in 1928, he had to commence the search for a replacement product because the Eliminator was predictably obsolete in 1930. He never stopped renewing. Nor have we.... Only those incultured with an elusive idea of renewal, which obliges a proliferation of new, creative ideas ... and an unstinting dedication to committing to the risk and promise of**

---
[458] Jim Collins and Jerry I. Porras, *Built to Last*, p. 83 (2011).

those unchartable ideas, will thrive. [459]

And as also quoted in, *Built to Last,*[460]William E. Boeing said:

> *It behooves no-one to dismiss any novel idea with the statement that it 'can't be done.' Our job is to keep everlastingly at research and experiment, to adapt our laboratories to production as soon as practicable, to let no new improvement in flying and flying equipment pass us by.*[461]

Survival of the *Leanest* maps consumers' *Ontologically Teleological* realization of *who* they are to all *B/aRe* processes. Survival is the *Ontologically Teleological* realization of consumers' physical fitness and fitness of character by better expressing *B/aRe* processes in seemingly circular fashion when bounded by the *IB*. While Darwinism over-emphasizes the Re-generative aspects of life through natural selection, it inevitably discusses life's equal contingency on the processes of *adaptation* and *energization*.[462] The concept of *B/aRe* organisms when applied to consumers and the decisions they make as human beings simply adds an increased emphasis on *adaptation* and energy gathering to *what* is both necessary and sufficient for living systems like consumers to live and further *Ontologically Teleologically* exist. *B/aRe* is the base layer of biological life that is best fit to *Lean* against systemic deconstruction.

C/aReDownward

---

[459]Robert W. Galvin, *The Idea of Ideas*, pp. 165–166, Schaumburg, IL: Motorola University Press (1991); Jim Collins, Jerry I. Porras, *Built to Last*(2011).

[460]Jim Collins and Jerry I. Porras, *Built to Last*, p. 84 (2011).

[461]William E. Boeing, founder of The Boeing Company, written in a bronze plaque on the wall of Boeing corporate headquarters.

[462]Peter Atterson,*Do I have the Right to Be?*, The Stone, New York Times (Jul. 5, 2014).

> *You don't need to have*
> *some grand existential reason*
> *for why you love what you're doing*
> *or to care deeply*
> *about your work (although you might).*
> *All that matters is that*
> *you do love it and that you do care.*
> – Jim Collins, *Good to Great* (2011)

Because consumers exist due to supervening, sophist-icated processes that can think, consumers universally self-define the ontological significance of a *SL-OT* through their own cognitive dependencies on it. I thus refer to the next most sophist-icated *SL-OT* as *Cognitive /aRe(C/aRe)* organisms.

People often personally enact meaning for other thinking *C/aRe* organisms (a.k.a. animals, though plants have some cognitive capabilities as well) to the extent they believe a *C/aRe* organism may recognize *what* it ought to do.[463] Science fiction films often exemplify and explore this relationship between people and *C/aRe'*ing aliens in determining *how much* we might care for the extraterrestrials. Just like *how* organizations pursue money as their end-goal, *C/aRe'*ing organisms also have an end-goal in mind, but it is the *Ontological Teleology*.[464]

Once */aRe* systems become teleonomically *B/aRe* within the larger dynamic of the *Universe*, cognitive processes take control and supervene on them as a means to more effectively perform */aRe* processes, as shown here:

---

[463] This enactment of reflexive meaning through inter-subjectivity can be roughly equated with Jean-Paul Sarte's, '*The Look and the Other*,' as describe in Part 3, Chapter 1 of his, *Being and Nothingness: An Essay on Phenomenological Ontology* (1943 in French).

[464] Ironically, though businesses deeply care about customers, they ultimately consider consumers fungible since corporations don't care who pays (so long as someone does).

Universal Chart of SUDS Forming C/aRe SL-OTS

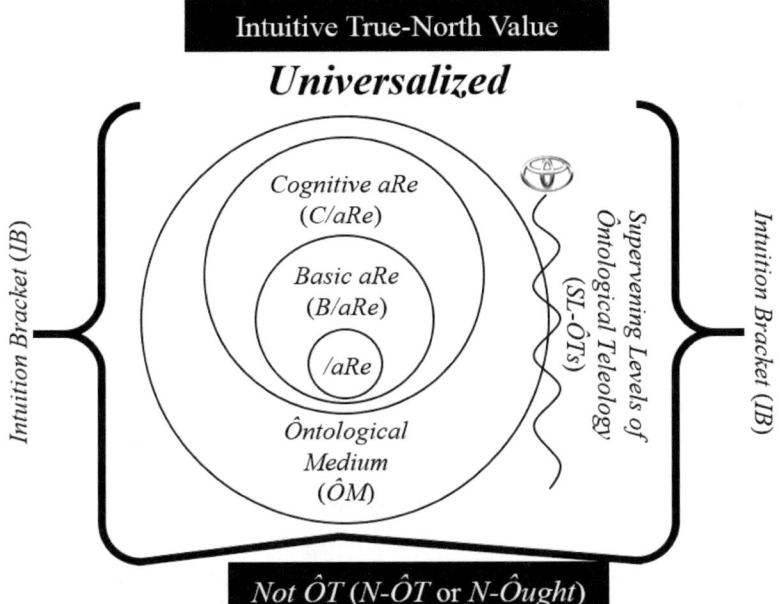

Natural selection re-produces cognition as a type of *paos* to manage information for consumers' /aRe processes. Cognition in *C/aRe* organisms starts as a means of managing sense data, conceptualizing experiences, analogizing between them, and then abstracting concepts and other phenomena into further categories and classifications. A few *C/aRe* organisms, namely consumers, developed the ability to conceptualize, abstract and categorize to such a sophisticated degree that they classified (and eventually articulated) *who* they are to themselves and each other as a new form of humanism. Just like with cognition, imagine *how* an organization might similarly re-create a *paos* that better optimizes opportunities for consumers to enhance *how* they self-reflexively engage in *C/aRe*

302 Stream 4: Lives

processes. For example, consider a thinking tool that might be sold to them that they thought they needed. In fact, some researchers believe that humans developed the ability to speak to and better understand one another for just this reason.⁴⁶⁵

- *What would you produce for consumers today that you self-reflexively, cognitively conceive of as advancing their Leanly adaptive, Re-generative and energizing processes?*
- *How does your *paos do that?**

C/aRe organisms' nervous systems developed through a process called '*cephalization*' in order to better adapt and energize to further Re-generate.⁴⁶⁶ Cephalization enhanced *C/aRe* organisms' ability to energize and adapt to their competitive environment, thus fueling those organisms' *Ontological Realization*. Through the development of *C/aRe* organisms' unique *SUDS*, you can see the broad *Ontological Teleology* through which hydras logically developed in congruence with universal and processual true-north values. You can also see *why* all *C/aRe* 'ing organisms, which include consumers, demand to *adapt, Re-generate* and *energize* in order to better live and exist.

Simple *C/aRe* organisms that have no higher *SL-OT*, developed purposively/teleonomically, as opposed to purposefully/teleologically, since they respond with their nervous systems but not necessarily

---

⁴⁶⁵Natalie Thaïs Uomini, Georg Friedrich Meyer, Shared Brain, *Lateralization Patterns in Language and Acheulean Stone Tool Production: A Functional Transcranial Doppler Ultrasound Study*, DOI: 10.1371/journal.pone.0072693 (August 30, 2013); *see also*, Patricia M. Greenfield, *Language, Tools and Brain: The Ontogeny and Phylogeny of Hierarchically Organized Sequential Behavior*, Depament of Psychology, University of California at Los Angeles (1991).

⁴⁶⁶*See generally*, '*Cephalization*' in the Encyclopædia Britannica (2016).

with self-reflexive intent. For example, can the cognitive responses of hydra and ants be all that different from plants *Leaning* in the direction of sunlight? Fundamentally, hydra, ants, plants and consumers *adapt,Re-generate*, and *energize* to perpetually live and exist in *whatever SL-OTS*they fulfill. However, while exhibiting non-subjective, purposive characteristics, plants reach a limit in their ability to adapt and thrive without more sophist-icated guidance given their cognitive constraints. Whole plant species die out perhaps a little more helplessly than caring animals because plants do not have the same cognitive agency and freedom of movement to use that agency to adapt to their environment and make necessary changes. The *C/aRe SL-OT*simply provides one more degree of survival.

Up to the point of self awareness, some*C/aRe* organisms broadened their ability to analogize to such an extent that they conceptualized themselves as an additional degree of sophist-ication. This distinction between purposive *C/aRe* and purposeful *C/aRe* differentiates consumers' strategically unique, universal, processual and personal living processes. Unlike plants and ants, consumers possess the most advanced degree of self-reflexive self-conception known within the *OM*, which improves their ability to *Leanly adapt, Re-generate* and *energize* by better processing and responding to internal and external in-formation.[467] Consumers' self-aware self-interest so far provides them with competitive advantages over becoming *N-OT* with a *Strategically Unique Degree of Sophist-ication*. No other living system than people has the capacity to adapt to such a degree due to cognition alone should consumers will it.

If considered from this process perspective, you can understand the development of consumers' minds, in that the evolution of self-organizing biological systems reached an ontological, systemic limit

---

[467] *See*, Michael Pollan,*The Intelligent Plant* , The New Yorker (Dec. 23, 2013); and the output of the *Society of Plant Signaling and Behavior*, such as, Francisco Calvo Garzón,*The Quest for Cognition in Plant Neurobiology*, 2(4): 208–211, Plant Signal Behav. (Jul.-Aug. 2007); *see also*, David Deutsch,*The Beginning of Infinity* , p. 130 (2001).

without some form of sensing, self-interested, guiding agency to enhance *Strategically Unique Degrees of Sophist-ication* to better perform *C/aRe* processes and further universalize. Working backward from the highest supervening memes, even between nation-states of people you can see varying degrees of sophist-ication. For example, in the, '*The Economist's Social Progress and Economic Development*,' chart you may see at the link in the footnote below, certain *Strategically Unique Degrees of Social Sophist-ication* appear in degrees of social progress correlated with per-capita Gross Domestic Product by country.[468] Keep in mind as you read further into *Stream 5*that while this chart does not strictly correlate with political freedom, it roughly does so as well.[469]

Whether or not the cognitive aspects of *C/aRe* organisms improve on *B/aRe* organisms' abilities depends on *C/aRe* organisms' *Ontological Realization* through the *OT* since the *OT* is the great regulator and simpliciter of everything within the *OM.What* this means to consumers,*who* supervene their personal true-north perspectives on *C/aRe* processes, is that their *C/aRe* processes are not necessarily ontologically superior to *B/aRe* processes since *C/aRe* processes may lead them to their own self-destruction through war, environmental damage or excessive consumption. The *OT* as the great regulator and simpliciter of everything within the *OM* as bounded by the *IB* dictates that once destroyed, consumers would then *matter* less than *whatever* survived, including those things residing in no higher *SL-OT* along the *Ontological Teleology*than within the*B/aRest SL-OT*. Consumers would no longer be*Ontologically Realized*like *whatever* survived at the lower levels of */aRe* processes. However, consumers would still have the distinction of having existed with the greatest known*SUDS* and in highest known

---

[468]*Daily Chart: Measuring a Progressive Society*, The Economist (Jul. 29, 2016), found at, http://www.economist.com/blogs/graphicdetail/2016/06/daily-chart-20 (last accessed Dec. 15, 2016).

[469]K.N.C. and A.C.M., *Progress on Progress, A Deliberately Non-Economic Measure of Well-Being*, The Economist (Apr. 8th 2014, 13:05), found at, http://www.economist.com/blogs/graphicdetail/2014/04/daily-chart-4 (last accessed Dec. 15, 2016).

SL-OTS within the *IB* and *OM*, having had the greatest potential to adapt, Re-generate and energize before facing extinction. However, there is little consolation in receiving such a post-humous Darwin award.[470]

> *Look Nature through, 'tis neat gradation all.*
> *By what minute degrees her scale extends!*
> *Each middle nature join'd at each extreme,*
> *To that above it, join'd to that beneath.......*
> *But how preserv'd*
> *The chain unbroken upwards, to the realms*
> *Of Incorporeal life? those realms of bliss*
> *Where death hath no dominion?*
> *Grant a make*
> *Half-mortal, half-immortal; earthy part,*
> *And part ethereal; grant the soul of*
> *Man Eternal; or in*
> *Man the series ends.*
> – Edward Young, Night-Thoughts on Life, Death, & Immortality, VI, (between 1742 and 1745)

Studying Consumers' Circular Randomness

One of the defining differences between plants engaging in *B/aRe* processes and insects engaging in the most basic *C/aRe* processes is that as insects' cognitive capacity increases, their behavior becomes slightly less predictable due to the sheer complexity of insects' thinking processes. Likewise, while the ability to predict consumer behavior generally improves in correlation to the large datasets you

---

[470] *See*, the same named awards started by Wendy Northcutt and found here http://www.darwinawards.com/ (last accessed 10-17-2015), which commemorate, '... *individuals who protect our gene pool by making the ultimate sacrifice of their own lives. Darwin Award winners eliminate themselves in an extraordinarily idiotic manner, thereby improving our species' chances of long-term survival.*'

have of *what* they do and profess, consumers simultaneously seem to behave unpredictably at times regardless of the amount of your data and empathizing with them.

Ants and many other, low-level *C/aRe* organisms mathematically operate through relatively simple algorithms or heuristics. But even ants search their personal *Universe* by engaging in some degree of random processes to feed sample data into their cognitive algorithms, heuristics and mental models, thereby optimizing the *Ontological Realization* of their colonies.[471] This optimization seems to produce consistent results at the group level across similar terrain. Famous researchers like E.O. Wilson, Eleanor Rosch, Deborah Gordon and other scientists studying ants have stated that ant behavior is quite predictable at the colony level even if it is not at the individual ant level.[472]

You can see *how* ants mathematically orient to the *OT* in global optimization[473] algorithms like *anticipatory systems*. Theoretical biologist Robert Rosen described anticipatory systems as those containing a predictive model of itself and/or its environment. Similar *how* ants anticipate their environment, plants' genetics also teleonomically anticipate the plant's eco-logical environment it will experience in the next generation. Similarly, consumers' teleonomically genetic and teleologically cognitive anticipation allows them to iteratively, *Ontologically Teleologically adapt*, *Re-generate* and *energize* according to their biological and mental predictions to benefit the current generation and the next.[474]

---

[471] Susan C. Edwards and Stephen C. Pratt, *Rationality in Collective Decision-Making by Ant Colonies*, Proc. R. Soc. B (Jul. 22 2009); Balaji Prabhakar, Katherine N. Dektar, Deborah M. Gordon, *The Regulation of Ant Colony Foraging Activity without Spatial Information*, DOI: 10.1371/journal.pcbi.1002670 (Aug. 23, 2012); Deborah M. Gordon, *The rewards of restraint in the collective regulation of foraging by harvester ant colonies*, Nature 498, 91–93 doi:10.1038/nature12137 (Jun. 06 2013).

[472] *See*, Deborah Gordon, *The Emergent Genius of Ant Colonies*, TED2003 (Feb 2003).

[473] *See* e.g. *Global Optimization* defined in Wolfram Alpha http://mathworld.wolfram.com/GlobalOptimization.html (last accessed Mar. 06, 2014).

[474] Robert Rosen, *Anticipatory Systems: Philosophical, Mathematical, and Methodological Foundations*, Pergamon Press (1985).

Organizations also cognitively anticipate the *Ontological Realization* of their customers' demand to support future profits. *Amazon.com, Inc.* exemplified this form of optimization as a prime directive at the organizational level when it obtained U.S. patent no. 8,615,473[475] for a method and system for anticipatory package shipping. Through anticipatory package shipping, *Amazon* will ship packages to certain geographies based on orders that its customers have previously demanded and pulled from them. Based on whether *Amazon's* customers do in-fact pull those orders from *Amazon*, *Amazon* will adapt its anticipatory shipping model to flow *what* Matter and Energy its customers will demand in an iteratively circular fashion to further its customers' *Ontological Realization* and *Amazon's* own commercial viability. *Amazon* simply follows the law of the jungle by anticipating its customers' demand. For a broader example of this commercial concept, see this advertisement from the enterprise software company, *SAP*, which is selling this predictive service on *Amazon's* cloud computers:,

---

[475]U.S. Patent No. 8,615,473, Spiegel et al., (Dec. 24, 2013).

© 2016, SAP SE

Like the anticipatory systems of hydra, plants and ants, once *Amazon* or *SAP* brackets customers' existences to exclude *what* they intuitively speculate within the *IB*, the time reversal problem of customers' teleology resolves through the logically circular goal of *what* they ought to have *b-ought* to become *who* they want to be. The systemic conditions of being and becoming get set at the initial event of customers wanting to be more of *who* and *why* they are–*Amazon* , *SAP*,*Apple* ,*Google* , *Toyota* and all other enterprises attempt to predict exactly *how* and *what* to get customers to buy now, but they can only do so by answering *why* and *who* consumers truly are.[476]

What consumers are and *how* consumers will become customers gets defined in semi-circular fashion because the *OT* is both a simpliciter and great regulator of all organizations. All organizations try to predict consumers' future goal of further being and becoming. However consumers came to be and of which consumers will become through *Supervening Levels of Ontological Teleological Sophist-ication,* consumers will attempt to universalize upward toward getting beyond the dictates of the*OT*. They might attempt to do so, for example, by buying*what* is in fashion or pleasing to offspring like a green Rexydoodle for Little Max Nathans from Sydney Australia. This *Ontological Teleological*demand lets *Amazon* and *SAP* anticipate*what paos* it ought to ship.

- *How does the Green Rexydoodle energize and optimize Max Nathans' life and existence?*
- *How does pleasing Max Nathans do the same for his parents who actually purchase the Rexydoodle in ex-change for money?*
- *How does this exchange create true-north and monetary value for SAP's stakeholders?*

Adding *Intention* to*Cognitive /aRe* (*I/C/aRe)*

Moving on from plants and ants, the next stage of cephalization leads to forms of cognitive organisms that you generally do not

---
[476]Jim Collins,*Good to Great* , Kindle Loc. 3373-3375 (2011).

consider eatable, such as primates, dogs, cats, certain whales and bottle nose dolphin, among others.[477] In fact, many businesses get into ethical problems with their customers over the treatment of such intentionally cognitive creatures.

If you look at the evolution of a self-organizing system that reached a limit in further living through *B/aRe* and *C/aRe* processes and asked, '*[W]hat quality under natural selection might further advance the ability of C/aRe organisms to adapt, Re-generate and energize?*,' the natural answer would be a nervous system, a mind, and eventually self-interested, conscious awareness managing their intentions. The philosophy of *Lean* calls this more sophist-icated *SL-OT*, Intentional/Cognitive/aRe (*I/C/aRe*). Organisms *who* engage in *I/C/aRe* processes like consumers may better *adapt* , *Re-generate* and *energize* to perpetuate their existences against *OT* natural selection because of the degree of their self-reflexive self-interest that can actively distinguish between the self, threats to the self, and *OPPs* to improve their lives in nearly limitless fashion. The biggest difference between *C/aRe* and *I/C/aRe* organisms is the degree of knowledge and the volume of memes each can posses and process.

Think about *how* pets' intentional, conscious agency functions to increase such organisms' capacity to eat or get fed by those they please, like employees getting paid more by employers. Organisms with nervous systems and brains can downwardly direct their less sophisticated processes to energize the optimization of their *Strategically Unique Degrees of Sophist-ication*. A critical phase change occurs at the I/C/aRe level where *what* was up to this point unintentional, teleonomic movement spiralling along the *OT* becomes intentional, downward, teleological pressure on the lower *SL-OTS* to push the I/C/aRe organisms into even higher *SL-OTS* than had ever before been realized.

To review, the *SL-OTS* of consumers' lives and existences we have covered so far within the philosophy of *Lean* are:

---

[477] Yuval Noah Harari, *Sapiens*, p. 46 (2014).

- *Universe*: all that is *Ontologically Realized*, either axiomatically, systemically and/or intuitively.
- *Ontological Medium (OM)*: All that people know exists on an empirical basis, i.e. the basic physical components of the *Universe* such as space-time, Matter and Energy;
- *Intuition Bracket (IB)*: The conceptual bracket isolating consumers within axiomatic and systemic truths in relation to intuitive truths and *what* is *N-OT* inter-subjectively valid with at least a *Lean* two sigmas ($\geq/2\sigma$) of true-north value;
- *B/aRe*: Chemical and biological organisms emerging from the *Self-Organizing Ontological Teleology* (*SO-OT*) to create a new supervening level of the overall *OT*;
- *C/aRe*: Cognitive organisms facilitating more effective */aRe* activity by seizing *OPPortunities* and removing *Threats*; and
- *I/C/aRe*: Intentionally cognitive organisms self-reflexively engaging in self-interested */aRe* activity;

To illustrate, here is a chart of *SUDS* forming the *I/C/aRe SL-OT*:

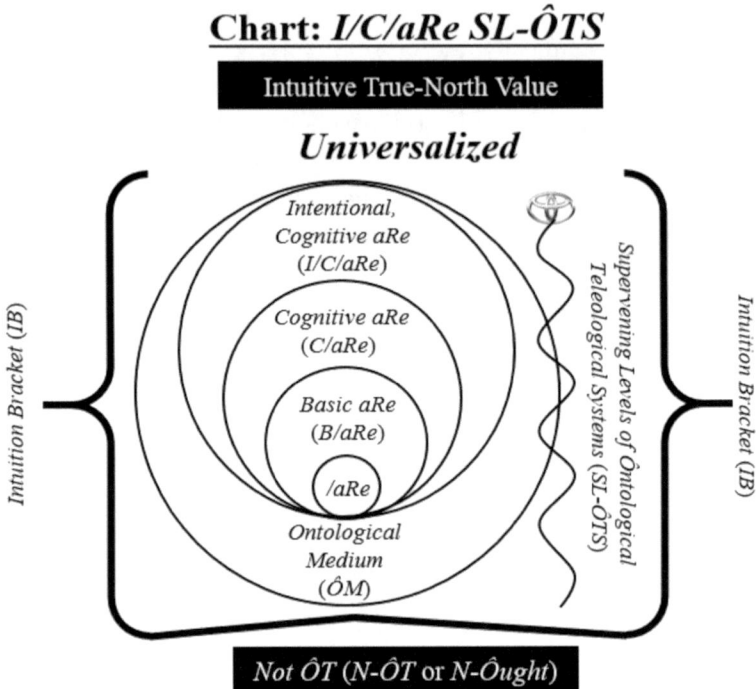

Consider this scientismic *I/C/aRe SL-OT* diagram in the context of the epic of evolution and the commercial philosophy of *Lean*. See a summary of consumers' evolutionary history below as inspired by Yuval Noah Harari's book, *Sapiens: A Brief History of Humankind*. Per this timeline, life seemed to develop within the *Ontological Medium* over the approximately 4.6 billion years that Earth circled the sun to date. Over that period of time, consumers began seeking the commercial philosophy of *Lean* as follows (with all these dates approximated by scientismists with the best information now known but may be further revised in the future):[478]

---

[478] For all such data, *see*, public/general references, and Yuval Noah Harari, *Sapiens* (2014); *see also*, Carrie Arnold, *Evolution is Slower Than It Looks and Faster Than You Think*, Wired Magazine (Mar. 26, 2017), regarding the changing scientific understanding of evolutionary time-scales.

- *When our Universe of Universes began is unkown;*
- *For about the last 13.7 billion years, our OM began;*
- *For about the last 4.5 billion years, the earth as we know it exists;*
- *For about the last 3.8 billion years, simple cells (prokaryotes);*
- *For about the last 3.4 billion years, cyanobacteria performing photosynthesis;*
- *For about the last 2 billion years, complex cells (eukaryotes);*
- *For about the last 1 billion years, multicellular life;*
- *For about the last 600 million years, simple animals;*
- *For about the last 550 million years, bilaterians, animals with a front and a back;*
- *For about the last 500 million years, fish and proto-amphibians;*
- *For about the last 475 million years, land plants;*
- *For about the last 400 million years, insects and seeds;*
- *For about the last 360 million years, amphibians;*
- *For about the last 300 million years, reptiles;*
- *For about the last 200 million years, mammals;*
- *For about the last 150 million years, birds;*
- *For about the last 130 million years, flowers;*
- *For about the last 60 million years, the primates;*
- *For about the last 20 million years, the family Hominidae (great apes);*
- *For about the last 6 million years, the final divergence of the hominin, gorilla and chimpanzee lineages;*
- *For about the last 2.8 million years, the genus Homo (human predecessors), within which time there have been about 125,000 re-generations of "People";*
- *For about the last 200,000 years, Homo Sapiens Sapiens (anatomically modern humans), for which there have been about 7,500 re-generations of Lean people;*

- *For about the last 13,000 years, the last of the non-Homo Sapien Sapien species of hominins, Homo floresiensis, died off, and cooperative civilization began among our species, which has persisted for about 500 re-generations of even Leaner people;*
- *For about 5,000 years people exchanged money in the form of Cowry shells;*
- *For about 2,500 years coinage and universal money has been in circulation starting across Eurasia;*
- *For about the last 2580 years, people have been thinking about "philosophy" as the quasi-secular study of all knowledge, meaning and utility since the Greeks (most likely Pythagoras) invented the term;*
- *For the last 470 years, people started using a sub-discipline of philosophy called "science" to test and discover the universal and process true-north values of the OM;*
- *For about the last 125 years, people have been re-reading, "Ecce Homo: How One Becomes What One Is," by Friedrich Nietzsche; and*
- *For about the last few decades, people have been seeking the business philosophy of Lean.*

Keep in mind that periodic extinctions have temporarily reduced human and biological diversity, including eliminating the *Ontological Realization* of living systems as follows: [479]

- *2.4 billion years ago, many obligate anaerobes, in the oxygen catastrophe;*
- *252 million years ago, the trilobites, in the Permian–Triassic extinction event;*
- *66 million years ago, the pterosaurs and nonavian dinosaurs, in the Cretaceous–Paleogene extinction event;*

---
[479] *Ibid.*

- *About 40,000 years ago, Homo Neanderthalensis (Neanderthals) either died off, were massacred by Homo Sapiens, or interbred with Homo Sapiens, to extinction; and*
- *10,000 years ago, the last of the non-Homo Sapien Sapien species of hominins died off.*

Now let's invert this timeline and compare it to the *Strategically Unique Degrees of Sophist-ication* in descending order, which you might consider as being a very modern version of the *Great Chain of Being* and evolutionary synthesis as discussed earlier:

Chart: Timeline of Known *Universe* vs. Degrees of *OT* Existence

Timeline of the Universe (approximate)	Degrees of OT Existence
600 million years ago basic animals developed with enough cognitive capability in order to act with some conceptual intent even if not self-aware;	*I/C/aRe: Intentional, cognitive organisms self-reflexively engaging in /aRe activity;*
Between 1 billion and 600 million years ago life originated and developed cognitive abilities where it could process and respond to sense information;	*C/aRe: Cognitive organisms facilitating more effective /aRe activity seizing existential opportunities and further removing the threat of extinction;*
3.8 billion years ago basic life began on Earth through the unintentional adaptation, Re-generation and energization of chemical processes;	*B/aRe: Chemical and Biological formations emerging through a new Supervening Level of Ontological Teleology (a SL-OT) and /aRe processes;*

Timeline of the Universe (approximate)	Degrees of OT Existence
4.54 ± 0.05 billion years ago the Earth is formed within the Milky Way Galaxy;	*This example of Self-Organizing Ontological Teleology (SO-OT) led to the eventual formation and structure of existence as consumers now know it;*
13.798 ± 0.037 billion, years ago the Big Bang or something like it occurred;	*Ontological Medium (OM): All that you know exists on a phenomenological and empirical basis, i.e., the basic physical components of the Universe such as spacetime, matter and energy that is generally composed of qubits, within the Intuition Bracket (IB) you place at the inception of physical existence;*[480]
Our Universe of Possible Universes.	*Undefined outside the IB.*

Mitochondria, Consumers and their Pets are Co-Determined

> *Without belaboring the point,*
> *I simply wish to say that our confusion about who we are*
> *is certainly related to the fact that*
> *we consist of a large set of levels,*
> *and we use overlapping language to describe ourselves*
> *on all those levels.*

---

[480] *See generally*, M. Vogelsberger, S. Genel, V. Springel, P. Torrey, D. Sijacki, D. Xu, G. Snyder, S. Bird, D. Nelson & L. Hernquist, *Properties of Galaxies Reproduced by a Hydrodynamic Simulation*, Nature 509, 177–182 (May 08, 2014).

> - Douglas Hofstadter,*Gödel, Escher, Bach* [a]
>
> ---
> [a]Douglas Hofstadter, *Gödel, Escher, Bach: An Eternal Golden Braid*, p. 287 (1979).

One of the most interesting aspects of *I/C/aRe* organisms' development, is that while each identifies individually, including as each consumer, they are increasingly co-created with other organisms and each other, both physically and socially. In other words, the boundary of *who* consumers are or consider themselves to be is nearly limitless in the context of all other living organisms.

Modern, neo-Darwinian evolutionary thinking considers the range of *how* natural selection, mutation, and for animals, *Eusociality*, contributes to*adaptation*.[481]Thus, the modern evolutionary synthesis conceives of consumers as super-organisms with multiple evolutionary factors arising from everything like genetic codes in the mitochondria in blood cells to the bacterial flora in stomachs. Each such aspect of consumers' *adaptation* represents different *SUDS* falling into particular *SL-OTS* supporting *who* consumers' *I/C/aRe* processes are overall in the largest sense, perpetually interacting upward through each level of sophist-ication to support consumers' consistent, personal perspectives as the *Lean* people*who* decide to buy *paos*.[482] In this way, through the bricolage of evolution, you can think of the *SL-OTS as if*forming a poetically Re-generating

---
[481]In 1942, biologist Julian Huxley wrote a well-respected book titled, *Evolution: The Modern Synthesis*, The MIT Press (1942), which Massimo Pigliucci and Gerd B. Müller subsequently up-dated with, *Evolution: The Extended Synthesis*, The MIT Press (2010); This pair of books is much like much like Schrödenger's and Pross' companion,*What is Life?* , books discussed earlier. These evolutionary books written by these well-respected biologists document the complete range of modern methods through which organisms co-evolve by various means; *see also*, Ehud Lamm, *Review of: Julian Huxley, Evolution: The Modern Synthesis*, MIT Press, The Cohn Institute for the History and Philosophy of Sciences and Ideas, Tel Aviv University (2010).

[482]R.D. Sleator, *The Human Superorganism - of Microbes and Men*, 74(2):214-5. doi: 10.1016/j.mehy.2009.08.047, Med Hypotheses (Feb. 2010).

exquisite corpse, as depicted here:

An *Exquisite Corpse*(© 2009 Agnes de Bethune, Alaine Becker, and Leah K. Tomaino,*Untitled/Untitled/Rooted* (Used with Permission))

Consistent with the epic of evolution, small competitive advantages between *SUDS* within the population lead over time to those superior traits winning through successive *Re-generations*. Thus, organisms with some self-interested agency would quite logically create a competitive advantage for themselves by universally conceptualizing *how* they might best avoid self-reflexively becoming *N-OT* and better moving upward along the spiral of the*Ontological Teleology*. At the same time, pure fitness concepts get counterbalanced with the general need for diversity for greater adaptability, which the evolutionary scientist Suzanne Batra introduced in 1966 as, '*Eusociality*,' or as referred to within the *U/People* business model, '*U/Sociality*.' *U/Sociality* applies within and between distinct organisms and organizations in a business sense.⁴⁸³ E.O. Wilson among other scientists has vigorously applied *U/Sociality* to all living systems existing within the ecologies of the *OM*.

As a domesticated example of *U/Sociality* among *I/C/aRe* organisms, consumers often describe dogs as possessing a higher *SL-OT* of *Intentional, Cognitive /aRe*(*I/C/aRe*) than most other animals. While dogs and non-human *I/C/aRe* animals do not conceptualize their place in the *OM*, they do form a sense of intentional purposefulness of being for something, which for dogs is generally being pleasing to people as their feeders *who* provide them with food and shelter to better serve their own *I/C/aRe* processes.

My dog *Oscar* (Photo credit: ACB)

To live *U/Socially*, psychologically normal dogs adapt to their owner's wishes to attempt to: (1) obtain *energizing* food; (2) *Regenerate* with other dogs when their owners allow them to; and (3) *adapt* their behavior as necessary to facilitate (1), and (2) as best they can. Domesticated dogs serve consumers' supervening,

---

⁴⁸³ *See generally*, E.O. Wilson, *The Social Conquest of Earth* (2013).

psycho- and physio-logical needs for security, stimulation and relation.[484] For this reason among others, United States consumers spent approximately $59 billion dollars on their pets in 2014,[485] which equals about a month of *what* U.S. people spent on feeding themselves at home and in restaurants, to get a sense of dog's ôntological significance to all Americans.[486]

You can see dogs' highest *Strategically Unique Degree of Sophistication*, i.e., their intentional, cognitive agency, originating through a combination of natural selection and human intervention. Going back in time and staying within the bounds of the *IB*, the physical *Universe* teleonomically created wolves with certain *Strategically Unique Degrees of Sophist-ication* that made them useful to people. For a variety of reasons outside the scope of this book, people intervened into wolves' *I/C/aRe* processes and domesticated them until they became *what* you know today as dogs.[487] Dogs' *Ontological Realization* was co-determined by dogs and people's *I/C/aRe* processes acting together, since people bred dogs to assist them with their own *adaptation,Re-generation* and *energization*, and dogs adapted their own behavior and *Ontological Realization* to get humans to do so in-turn. People needed security and companionship to best universalize, and dogs needed human waste for food, and so the evolution of dogs and people *U/Socially* e-merged.

---

[484] Mietje Germonpréa, Mikhail V. Sablinb, Rhiannon E. Stevensc, Robert E.M. Hedgesd, Michael Hofreitere, Mathias Stillere, Viviane R. Desprése, *Fossil dogs and wolves from Palaeolithic sites in Belgium, the Ukraine and Russia: osteometry, ancient DNA and stable isotopes*, pp. 473–490, Volume 36, Issue 2, Journal of Archaeological Science (Feb. 2009).

[485] American Pet Products Association http://www.americanpetproducts.org/press_industrytrends.asp (accessed Jan. 7, 2015).

[486] US Department of Agriculture ERS Food Expenditure Series http://www.ers.usda.gov/data-products/food-expenditures.aspx#26634 (accessed Jan. 7, 2015).

[487] National Geographic Opinion, *We Didn't Domesticate Dogs. They Domesticated Us. Scientists Argue that Friendly Wolves Sought out Humans*, National Geographic (Mar. 2, 2013).

> *Tyger, Tyger, burning bright,*
> *In the forests of the night;*
> *What immortal hand or eye*
> *Could frame thy fearful symmetry*
> – William Blake, *The Tyger, Songs of Experience* (© 1794 (Public Domain)).

That which differentiates an animal that consumers generally consider to be eatable and one that is not, may be a level of compatibility with consumers' lifestyles. Generally though, consumers assess an animal's *I/C/aRe* status by its perceived development through natural selection or human intervention to further their own *I/C/aRe* processes. While genuine debate occurs as to *what* level of intentional cognition animals like dogs experience, most people agree that some division exists whereby they consider an animal as having a sufficient amount of self-reflexive cognition that they would not eat it at a restaurant if served to them unless they were about to die from starvation.[488]

This division often gets tested by the SL-OT the animals' *SUDS* arise into even though people can only observe indications of animals' self-awareness rather than directly assess it.[489] Your organization should understand this not just for *what* consumers will avoid eating but also in regards to consumers' perceptions of animal ethics that influence *how* consumers perceive a business and *what paos* they will buy from it. It also says a lot about *who* and *why* consumers are by *what* and *how* they *Leanly adapt, Re-generate,* and *energize* through animal *paos*.

---

[488] A discussion of epiphenomenalism would be appropriate here but a bit too abstract for this text.

[489] As an example of some of these tests of self-awareness in animals, *see*, Robert Krulwich, *I Sniff, Therefore I Am. Are Dogs Self-Conscious?*, National Public Radio at NPR.org (Mar. 3, 2011), found here, http://www.npr.org/blogs/krulwich/2011/03/03/134167145/i-sniff-therefore-i-am-are-dogs-self-conscious (accessed Feb 2, 2012).

Consumers' concern for other animals reflects their own sufficiently complex and universalized cognitive functions that recognize their own place in the *Universe*.[490] For example, consumers' abstractly, self-reflexively anticipate *what* a *paos* might feel like in ways no other animal could, which is just like *how* people anticipate *how* other animals might feel within their given SL-OT.[491] Like computer scientists' description of the *Game of Life, Langston's Ant* and other universal computing machines, Douglas Hofstadter, the author of *Gödel Escher, and Bach*, called this anticipatory self-reflection a *strange loop*.[492] Hofstadter believes that an organism abstractly recognizes itself as a type of universal conceptualizing machine that must recognize itself by definition in logically circular fashion, and thus can recognize the same function in others by analogy. For example, consumers self-reflexively conceptualize *what* they like on social media, or when they take a *selfie* with their *iPhone*.

Consumers' consciousness from this perspective within the *IB* simply functions as a natural process of successive self-organization, similar to *how* more advanced gliders originated from Conway's *Game of Life* and other such sims. Consumers' consciousness may be perceived as the greatest universal strategy to become *Ontologically Realized* through *Re-generations*, like a *Game of Life* intersected with *Game Theory*.

And this game could end for current consumers, which would make room for other *SUDS*. Consider the possibility that consumers' lives may fail from a process perspective. That would mean that they either failed to *adapt*, *Re-generate* and/or *energize*, which again

---

[490] *See generally*, Douglas R. Hofstadter in, *Gödel, Escher, Bach*, Basic Books (1999); Nicholas Humphrey, *Soul Dust: The Magic of Consciousness*, p. 40, Princeton University Press (2011).

[491] *See again*, Jean-Paul Sartre's '*The Look and the Other*' discussed in, *Being and Nothingness* (1943).

[492] Humphries calls it an *ipsundrum* or something like a *self-conundrum*, in Nicholas Humphrey, *Soul Dust*, p. 40 (2011); *see also*, Douglas R. Hofstadter, *Gödel, Escher, Bach*, p. P–2 (1999).

would be ontologically reinforcing in a negative sense.[493] Even if consumers did get destroyed, people will leave an empty stage for the development of the next set of consumers that nature may reproduce, unless the next iteration of living systems similarly fails to *adapt, Re-generate* or *energize* as well.[494]

Regardless of such hypo-thetical speculation of consumers' ability to destroy themselves, no doubt conscious self-awareness represents an effective way for organisms and organizations, in co-determined fashion, to adapt and self-perpetuate in the face of systematic adversity by better performing life processes through Intentionally/Cognitive/aRe processes. For all its faults, consciousness dramatically increases consumers' personal investment in and ability to universalize their own, supervening survival.

Now that you have reviewed the organic origin of money, existence, and life, you can move up the *U/ People* value stream to consider *what* consumers most truly value as people.

---

[493] *E.g.* like Michel Foucault's disappearing man, when he writes, '*[I]f those arrangements were to disappear as they appeared, if some event of which we can at the moment do no more than sense the possibility - without knowing either what its form will be or what it promises - were to cause them to crumble, as the ground of classical thought did, at the end of the eighteenth century, then one can certainly wager that man would be erased, like a face drawn in sand at the edge of the sea*,' in Michel Foucault, *The Order of Things: An Archaeology of the Human Sciences*, p. 387, New York, NY: Vintage Books (1973).

[494] Even within human evolution as a whole you see evidence of various lines of sapiens developing or ending, and populations increasing and shrinking, though we have now consolidated entirely to *Homo Sapiens Sapiens* with a single *SL-OT* now leading to *Homo Deus, see*, Yuval Noah Harari, *Homo Deus: A Brief History of Tomorrow*, Harvill Secker (2016).

Stream 5: People

Stream 5*A* 3 Report:

- Through *U/P*, and within the philosophy of *Lean*, you empathize with consumers best by understanding their phenomenologies
- You perceive consumers' phenomenologies by bracketing the source of their thoughts and senses to look at them just as they are without further judgment – much like using the *IB* to see the *Universe* as it is by only considering causes for it that are widely agreed, which none are to date
- Through *Existentialism*, you then explore *what* consumers value based on *how* they identify themselves within their phenomenologies, and *what* they reveal they prefer to be or become based on *what* they purchased or "liked"
- Consumers reaffirm their own self-reflexive identities through the spending decisions and "likes" they make
- When they consume, people simultaneously reaffirm their identities toward and away from *what* they speculate does not exist, at least within the *IB*. For example, many live toward a speculative afterlife that is not universally agreed upon, while avoiding becoming *what* they perceive as being not alive. This is referred to as "Ought Cognitive Dissonance"
- *Ought Cognitive Dissonance* creates all meaning in the difference between these extremes of an undefinably infinite number of real or speculated *Universes*, and the possibility of not existing at all
- You will produce the most valuable goods and/or services that get bought by consumers by specifically solving for these ontological problems within the details of people's daily lives

> *Do I contradict myself?*
> *Very well then I contradict myself,*
> *(I am large, I contain multitudes.)*
> - Walt Whitman, *Song of Myself,* p. 78, Part 51, in *Leaves of Grass* 4th Ed. (1867).

As you learned in *Stream 3* and *Stream 4*, discovering *who* and *why* consumers are leads you to the very edge of life and existence. In this *Stream 5*, we re-turn and focus on *what* consumers find most truly meaningful as real, human people living within the *OM*. Now follow *how* their consciousness, psychology, and ethics enhance their *I/C/aRe* processes. Up to this point, you have witnessed *how* the *U/People* business model follows the *Ontological Teleology* along the value *Streams* of this book upward toward the genesis of consumers' personas. This business model moved logically from the *OM* as bracketed by the *IB* into the *Self-Organizing Ontological Teleology* you experience every single day. This SO-OT eventually formed consumers' *Supervening Levels of Ontological Teleological Sophist-ication* full of *Strategically Unique Degrees of Sophist-ication*. Through each stage, this *U/People* business model progressed from *B/aRe* to *C/aRe* and *I/C/aRe* living systems to eventually reach *who* consumers are, and *why* they now buy *paos* as real, living, human, people.

Consumers, as real people, shop for *paos* and extend their eras by buying that which they believe further advances their *I/C/aRe* processes. They do so to serve their lower, teleonomic *SL-OTS* to become better *Ontologically Realized* overall. For example, they eat to gain *energy* and to repair themselves. They do so to *Re-generate* and further *adapt* upward along the *OT* throughout the quantum spacetime of the *OM*. The uppermost *SL-OT* of their co-determined, conscious existence, *i.e. who* they consider themselves to be with all other people, buys *paos* to universalize the same

/aRe processes as their less sophisticated *SL-OTS*. Each *SL-OT* helps them energize, anticipate and re-act to perpetually live and exist. However, consumers' development of a consciousness in order to perform /aRe processes better, caused them to intuitively speculate other reasons to live and exist. This speculation gains adherents to the extent they percieve it facilitating their better living and existing as people by better adapting, energizing, and thus *Leaning* into infinite space-time.

OT /N-OT as Strategic Degrees of Consumers' Sophist-ication

While *SO-OT* upwardly self-organizes into consumers' intentionally purposeful consciousness, consumers consciously care about energizing and optimizing their own lives and existences with *paos*. The greater that consumers' degrees of sophist-icated, self-conscious intentionality are, the more consumers perceive *paos* as providing them with normative true-north value when they purchase. As sophist-cated consumers, they understand that they get charged so they may *Re-generate* themselves with *paos*.

This is particularly true when they perceive *paos* as ontologically reaffirming their lives and existences. The *SL-OTS* the *paos* effect principally differentiate that which reaffirms consumers' self-conscious existences. This of course effects *what* consumers associate with *who* and *why* they are. Through this dynamic, you can ontologically factor consumers' *SL-OTS* into *what* fundamentally motivates them to purchase *paos* . By doing this factoring, you move from metaphysical abstraction to *what* really matters to consumers at the point of purchase.

Consumers' cognition starts as a means of processing sense data, and advances to form a concept that further abstracts the phenomena they experience as themselves. They analogize *who* they think they are to *who* they want to be, which is happy. Consumers analogized themselves self-referentially, and thereby conceived of their self-intention to *buy now*, which they employ in stores. Their conception of themselves through the *I/D Kata* recursively reflects and reaffirms their own *Ontological Realization* . The *I/D Kata* thus allows you to identify *who, why, what,* and *how* you develop consumers' egos and super-egos from their personal perspectives.

Consumers' motivational psychology functions to extend their physical significance, but once they consciously recognized themselves as consumers, they decided to buy *paos* to energize and optimize their remembering, experiential and anticipated selves for seemingly circular, *Ontological Teleological* reasons.

Thus, *what* delights consumers most is that which recursively energizes and optimizes their lives and existences. However, the more sophist-icated consumers' personal perspectives become, the more they emotionally cry out ever louder into the dark, vast *OM* for meaning as a means to further become *what* they care about most, which is *who* they identify as being. Consumers act in opposition to *what* they believe is *N-OT* to remain most viable. Mercedes-Benz understands this dynamic well, as evidenced by its slogan,

Das beste oder nichts (*The Best or Nothing*),[495] which reflects this extreme, ontological self-intention. Like the tri-partite co-arising of the *pratītyasamutpāda* as described earlier by the Dalai Lama XIV, you can see this *Ontological Realization* reflected in the three-sided star of the *Mercedes-Benz* logo stylistically displaying the *I/D Kata* three times within the *OM* :[496]

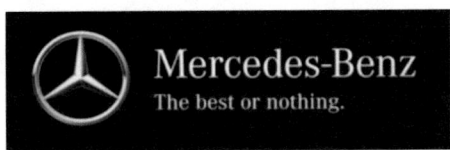

Mercedes Benz: *The Best or Nothing*(© 2015 Daimler AG)

As Consumers Find Themselves - Karl Jaspers' *Existenz* and Existential *Best Fit* Models [497]

Now radically empathize with consumers' lives from their really personal perspectives, from inside the twisting circularity of their subjective consciousness. You may do so by using the *I/D Kata* to map just *what* they experience *paos* as being. For example, as a customer of this book, you might start empathizing with *how* they would feel right now if they.... read... this.. word. To best understand this concept of *who* consumers /a*Re* when they consume, you ought to understand the concept of, '*Phenomenology*.'

---

[495] *Mercedes-Benz'* website regarding its brand, slogan and its 2020 growth strategy, *see*, http://www.daimler.com/brands-and-products/our-brands/mercedes-benz-passcars (last accessed on Oct. 16, 2016); you might hear echos from Martin Heidegger in this statement.

[496] *Diamler AG* does not endorse this association; instead it describes its three sided north star as representing universal mobility across air, sea and land in, *The Meaning of the Mercedes-Benz Star*, www.mercedes-benz.tv (accessed Dec. 11, 2016).

[497] The Presence Perspective – Phenomenology, Intentionality from Self-Organizing Systems – explain how Western and Eastern philosophical systems moved beyond questions of *why* to *how* consumers exist without conclusively answering the deepest questions; i.e. the philosophical systems move beyond questions of existence with Buddha's unanswered questions to the *how* you exist, through Phenomenology.

Philosophers have been describing consumers' personal perspectives in phenomenological terms since the early 20th century, so it should be considered in the foundation of a *Lean* business *i/deô*logy.

Phenomenology says that to understand consumers, you ought to empathetically perceive their personal perspectives as they experience them without judgment or limitation – just *what* is actually experienced by consumers *when* they consume *paos* with no further distinction, qualification, classification or categorization.[498] *Phenomenology* disregards any difference between *what* consumers perceive to be real and *what* they might imagine, *what* they feel emotionally and *what* they believe to be an axiomatic or systemic fact.[499]

Consumers' phenomenology through which they experience *paos* covers all that they see, smell, taste, feel and hear from their senses, thoughts, memories and imagination both before and after a purchase. People often use, '*Empathy Maps*' when conducting *Lean* analysis.[500] Below is a way for you to use an *Empathy Map* to empathize with and map consumers' phenomenologies. While doing so, you must keep in mind that consumers' phenomenologies are optimized through successive Re-generations not to actually reflect reality in its fullest as it truly is, but rather to provide the in-formation that best facilitates their *Ontological Realization* when they perform /aRe processes.[501] Try adding to consumers'

---

[498] Or as Willard Van Oman Quine said, our theories, '*...face the tribunal of sense-experience not individually but as a corporate body,*' in, *The Verification Theory and Reductionism* (1951); the faith you may have in logical positivism must be baptised in the holistic empiricism shared by all consumers.

[499] Phenomenology rejected the Platonic, Cartesian and other rationalist basis for philosophical investigation that had dominated philosophical discourse until the early 20th century, *see*, the Stanford Encyclopædia of Philosophy entry on '*Phenomenology*.'

[500] The concept of an *Empathy Map* was first proposed by Dave Gray of XPLANE Inc., and my graphic below loosely resembles one created by Alex Osterwalder for his book, *Value Proposition Design: How to Create Products and Services Customers Want*, along with co-authors Ian Smith, Alexander Osterwalder, Gregory Bernarda, Trish Papadakos, and Yves Pigneur, and illustrators Anne B. Smith, Trish Papadakos, Wiley Press (2014).

[501] Justin T. Mark, Brian B. Marion, Donald D. Hoffman, *Natural Selection and Veridical Perceptions*, Journal of Theoretical Biology (Accepted Jul. 24, 2010).

phenomenologies below *what* you think they will experience when they consider becoming customers once they test-drive *paos* in the context of their daily lives and existences:

Phenomenological Empathy Map

The more you empathize with consumers' phenomenologies by mapping them like so, the further you begin to see that they go through similar interrogatories as an organization's *I/D Kata* when considering whether to purchase *paos*. They follow this process by conjecturing *what* a *paos* is worth from the data they experience when test-driving it, as seen here:

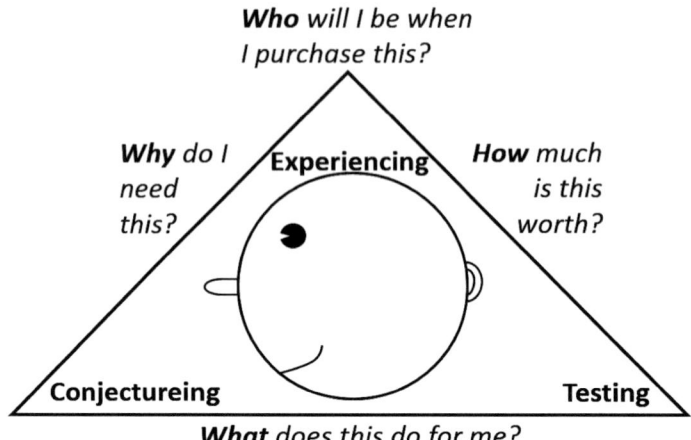

Consumers' Phenomenological Empathy Map as an I/D Kata

Critically, *Phenomenology* led to the further philosophical movement of '*Existentialism*' in the early to mid-20th century. Both *Phenomenology* and *Existentialism* refer to this act of neutrally looking at *what* true-north value consumers experience from *paos* without judgement as '*Epoché.*' The Greek skeptics created the term *Epoché* to mean a suspension of judgement about the world. To engage in *Epoché*, you bracket and set aside any questions you may have about the objective reality of *paos*. You stop differentiating between consumers' minds and bodies like the Cartesian assertion of, '*I think, therefore I am.*' Instead, you emphasize with just *what* consumers experience when they consume *paos* without considering any further cause and effect.

You use *Epoché* to analyze *what* consumers may experience when consuming *paos* in the *OM*, so you can understand *what* matters to them most.⁵⁰² *Epoché* initially brackets out all judgment or classification of *what* customers experience by consuming *paos* so you may speak to them most directly about its benefits. Thus, *Epoché* lets you speak to people as consumers so you can know them as customers.⁵⁰³ Like *Zarathustra*, a *CMÔ* ought to communicate the existential benefits produced by an organization's *paos* through specific phenomenological channels.⁵⁰⁴

Like Epoché, the *Intuition Bracket* removes any consideration outside the *IB* of *why* customers ultimately ought to have *b-ought* and consumed *paos*. Thus, just like using *Epoché* to better understand *what* customers experience, you ought to bracket the *I/D Kata* within the *IB* so you may develop true-north value by clearly delineating your analysis in regards to *what* is mere speculation and *what* is *N-OT*. Doing so will allow you to maintain utmost clarity as to *why* consumers */aRe* living within the overall true-north value stream. This will allow you to produce in *Takt* time, through the conjoint processes of *Jidoka* and *Kaizen*, *what paos* that will actually make them be and become the best.⁵⁰⁵

Phenomenology and Survival of the Persistent

The notable Western philosopher, Edmund Husserl, first applied this process of *Epoché* within the philosophy of *Existentialism* in his 1913 book *Ideas*, where he described *Epoché* as a philosophical

---

⁵⁰²Hume's fork divides statements up into two types: (1) Statements that are are knowable *a priori* (*i.e.* they are knowable *sui generis* without further explanation) from which you may make deductions; and (2) Statements about the world that are contingent and only knowable *a posteriori* (*i.e.* they are knowable only because of evidence you have experienced), which are statements that can only be intuited, inferred or induced. In contemporary philosophy, these statements are referred to as analytic and synthetic propositions; for further reading *see* the Stanford Encyclopædia of Philosophy entry on, 'Hume.'

⁵⁰³*See*, Martin Buber, *I and Thou* (1923).

⁵⁰⁴Friedrich Nietzsche,*Thus Spake Zarathustra: A Book for All and None* (1891).

⁵⁰⁵Thus, *Takt* time is like the DC Comics® character,*Metron* , operating within the *ÔM*, by helping provide good *paos* anywhere the*Universe* demands it. Besides being the minimal unit of measure in classical Greek verse, *Metron*® is the supreme explorer, scientist and inventor of the*New Gods* . His mission is to unravel the mysteries of the*Universe* .

method[506] that reduces consumers' experience to a single dimension. Husserl wanted you to suspend any skepticism and doubt you may have about whether consumers truly /aRe so you can focus on *how* consumers will most truly value the *paos* you provide them with the meaningful money they spend regardless of *what* they might themselves believe.[507] Thus, both *Epoché* and the *IB* allow you to see consumers' intuitive speculation for *what* it truly is.

In this sense, *Epoché* shows *why* consumers actually do *what* they do in their day-to-day lives just due to *what* they experience, which allows you to see *what* truly motivates them *whatever* the source. While you at this point have deeply considered *why* consumers progress upward along the larger spiral of the *Ontological Teleology* throughout history, consumers' generally think only about *how* they can live day-to-day and *what* their needs and wants are to do so. Consumers rarely get bogged down in intractable questions of *who* or *why* they are. Instead, consumers live as best they can with the least cognitive dissonance possible as they find themselves within the *Ontological Medium* and swept up in the *Ontological Teleology* for *whatever* reason. In other words, consumers unintentionally engage in *Epoché* by focusing on *what* impact their present actions and purchases have on their remembering, experiencing and future selves without deeply thinking about *who* or *why* they /aRe.

Consumers thus habitually engage in *Epoché* out of sheer necessity – whether due to the demands of children, long commutes, heath issues or jobs. Consumers focus on the objectives of their actions within the context of all they experience upward or downward

---

[506] *See generally*, the three books, Edmund Husserl, *Ideas Pertaining to a Pure Phenomenology and to a Phenomenological Philosophy—First Book: General Introduction to a Pure Phenomenology*, trans. F. Kersten. The Hague: Nijhoff (1982); Edmund Husserl, *Ideas Pertaining to a Pure Phenomenology and to a Phenomenological Philosophy—Second Book: Studies in the Phenomenology of Constitution*, trans. R. Rojcewicz and A. Schuwer, Dordrecht: Kluwer (1989); and Edmund Husserl, *Ideas Pertaining to a Pure Phenomenology and to a Phenomenological Philosophy—Third Book: Phenomenology and the Foundations of the Sciences*, trans. T. E. Klein and W. E. Pohl, Dordrecht: Kluwer (1980).

[507] *See generally*, The Internet Encyclopædia of Philosophy entry on, '*Phenomenological Reduction.*'

along the *OT* within the *OM* in order to survive, thrive and improve *what* they phenomenologically experience. They do not want to worry about their ultimate *ori*gin unless they:

1. ***Are faced with the immediate possibility of becoming N-OT within the OM;***
2. ***Are conditionally predisposed to ask such questions; or***
3. ***Like you, want to develop a robust business i/deôlogy to make money more meaningfully.***

Consumers optimize the truth value of these experiences along with all others by consuming *paos* within their respective, subjective phenomenologies originating from their personal perspectives. For this reason, understanding *what* and *how* consumers experience phenomenologically is the ultimate act of radical, commercial empathy that you ought to perform. This ultimate, phenomenological act of empathy allows you to produce *what* consumers truly find meaningful and to deliver that true-north value *however* they wish to buy from you.[508] Since consumers' *I/C/aRe* processes optimize *who* consumers are, *Phenomenology*, *Epoché* and the *IB* work together to allow organizations to differentiate between *what* consumers consciously conceive is truly valuable and *what* they believe is *N-OT*. *How* organizations create true-north value for consumers will consciously and/or unconsciously reflect itself within *what* consumers' actually, phenomenologically experience from their *paos*.

By affecting consumers' *I/C/aRe* processes, organizations may increasingly energize and/or optimize consumers both toward or against *what* is phenomenologically realized by them across the

---

[508] So, *Phenomenology* tends to examine life more from an *Idealistic* perspective akin to a presence perspective combined with the universal, which emphasizes the purely mental, *Solipsistic* perspective on existence and examining existence from what you experience, including those ideas you consider, as opposed to a process perspective that removes anything from being objective.

existential extremes of *Epoché*. Organizations may know *what is* (i.e. is *not N-OT*in a double-negative sense) phenomenologically realized by consumers within the bounds of *Epoché* and the *IB* by *what* universal and systemic truth values people collectively know with at least two *Lean* sigmas ($\geq/2\sigma$) of common agreement.

For example, presume a pharmaceutical company chemically designed a medicine that cured a disease and was testing it on human subjects in Phase III clinical trials. Each time those trialists phenomenologically experienced that they are alive and funda-mentally existing from the drug's consumption, they would personally have an infinitely *Lean* sigma of confidence ($=/\sigma\infty$) in its efficacy. When the clinicians' and trialists' collective phenomenological experience likewise amounted to at least two *Lean* sigmas ($\geq/2\sigma$) of common agreement, whether the medicine ought to be worth prescribing to the general public would no longer be considered speculative.[509]

Taken further, a doctor might also sell that now healthy customer cosmetic surgery so the customer will phenomenologically feel, even if just for a moment, as if old age will not happen anytime soon with a *Lean*, infinite sigma of personal confidence ($=/\sigma\infty$), even if no one else looking at them agreed. Thus, you may also medically energize and/or optimize consumers toward*what* they personally, intuitively believe outside the *IB*with absolute confidence, like an evangelical proselytizer providing momentary belief in everlasting salvation in ex-change for donations, or a Scientologist clearing someone to become an *Operating Thetan* for a current estimated cost of $128,000 USD. For clinical trials, cosmetic surgery, and *Dianetics*®, customers ultimately *b-ought* each *paos* during their lives to attempt to universalize themselves across all spacetime whether within the *IB* or not with the greatest confidence possible.

Once you establish an *Intuition Bracket*as a form of *Epoché* in Stage

---

[509]*See again*Dr. Rick Turner and Dr. Russell Reeve, *Basic Biostats for Clinical Research - Confidence Intervals in Drug Development - An Overview of their Use and Interpretation*, p. 42, International Pharmaceutical Industry (Spring 2010).

III clinical trials around *what* consumers experience, organizations may then classify true-north value by *how* consumers ought to perceive an organization's *paos* as being, whether *good* and/or *evil* for them, regardless of *what* they may speculate. Consumers will then determine the degree of good and/or evil present in a *paos* to the extent they perceive the *paos* as energizing and/or optimizing them toward or away from *what* they know or speculate is *N-OT*. *What* an organization identifies as *what* ought to be good for consumers when bounded by the *IB*, that form of *Epoché* ideally aligns with *what* consumers perceive as being *good for them*. However, even if consumers do not perceive a *paos* as good when it is in fact good for them, then at least an organization can identify and resolve the difference using the *I/D Kata* and the *3WH* interrogatories with the confidence that perception ought to ultimately align with the reality of the *OT* to some degree.

Thus, by starting to categorize and classify *what* consumers subjectively experience from a *paos* and its brand within the *IB*, you may also move beyond consumers' notions of *good* and *evil*. You ought to move beyond the categories of good and evil[510] to see consumers instead as simply moving upward or downward along the *OT* within the *OM* toward or away from *what* is *N-OT* on a universally axiomatic or processually systemic basis with at least two *Lean* sigmas ($\geq/2\sigma$) of true-north validity. Consumers perceive whether a *paos* moves them up or down along the *Ontological Teleology* based on the qualities (or the '*qualia*' as philosophers like to call it) a *paos* produces within consumers' phenomenologies when they consume it. A *paos*' qualia are like shadows dancing on the edges of all that consumers experience without any judgment about *what* manufactured them. [511]Consumers' lives and existences are in effect based in part on the qualia a *paos* re-produces within them, regardless of whether that *paos* re-produces qualia of the

---

[510]Friedrich Nietzsche, *Beyond Good and Evil: Prelude to a Philosophy of the Future* (*Jenseits von Gut und Böse: Vorspiel einer Philosophie der Zukunft*) (1886).
[511]*See generally*, the Stanford Encyclopædia of Philosophy entry on, '*Qualia*.'

338 Stream 5: People

remembered past, an imaginary reflection, current reality, or a vivid dream about the future – all are *Ontologically Realized* experiences from consumers' consistent, personally true-north phenomenologies. You should optimize all such funda-mental reverberations when developing *paos* to delight consumers the most.

> **And what is good, Phaedrus, and what is not good**
> **— Need we ask anyone to tell us these things?**
> – Robert Pirsig, *Zen and the Art of Motorcycle Maintenance: An Inquiry into Values*, p. 2 HarperCollins (1974).

California Dreaming

If you are dismissive of the importance of the qualia that a *paos* re-produces when energizing and optimizing consumers' lives and existences, consider that about a quarter to a third of consumers' lives is spent in irrational dream worlds as numerous as any fecund or artificially simulated *Universes*. While consumers act as if they are not actually living when they dream, they are in fact very much consciously alive in each one. Inside consumers' dreams they are every bit as present and real as when they are awake. The only difference is that consumers' memories of *what* happens *when* they dream are not as persistent and consistent as *what* happens *when* they are awake. Also, unlike reality, dreams generally do not make sense retrospectively, which is actually their key purpose.[512]

Irrational dreams im-prove consumers' insight and rationality by juxtaposing dreams' transitory facts with generally cogent reality. Consumers dream about everything that they estimate is not true to

---

[512] *See e.g.* for *how* sleep regulates emotion, and as further described below, *how* emotion regulates reason, Rosalind Dymond Cartwright, *The Twenty-four Hour Mind: The Role of Sleep and Dreaming in Our Emotional Lives*, Oxford University Press (Jun. 24, 2010).

better know and remember *what* has been and anticipate and re-act to *what* may be. The sharply rational/irrational distinction allows consumers to understand better the difference between *what* ought to be and *what* is *N-OT*. By making this distinction, dreams also influence whether consumers consider a *paos* as being *good* or *evil* at their points of purchase and whether they think buying from an organization is a delight or complete nightmare. Or as the Greek philosopher Heraclitus of Ephesus said, '*Even sleepers are workers and collaborators on what goes on in the Universe.*'[513]

How consumers really respond to a *paos*' dream-like qualities likewise differs in relation to other consumers' psychologies. Only when consumers' inter-subjectively agree with others that a *paos* energizes and optimizes their *Ontological Realization*, such as when they buy and consume a *paos* together, do consumers collectively agree with at least two *Lean* sigmas ($\geq/2\sigma$) of common agreement amongst themselves that something is genuinely liked and highly rated as a universal good.[514]

Keep in mind that any overlapping consensus consumers may have that a *paos* is highly rated and a universal good can never be absolute because each consumer experiences phenomenological qualia differently in their dreams and without. Each consumer represents different, naturally occurring, *Strategically Unique Degrees of Sophist-ication* within the *OM*, so each consumer conforms to the *OM* to a unique degree somewhere along the *OT*. Objective, *universal* truth is real and matters; however, while the process of consumers converging their personal perspectives is evidence of an objective, *universal* true-north value, it is not synonymous with

---

[513]Heraclitus, *The Path of Investigations*, Para. 124, *The Paradoxical Universe* (c. 535 BCE – 475 BCE), as found in, *The Complete Philosophical Fragments of Heraclitus*, by William Harris, Prof. Em. Middlebury College (2004).

[514]*See*, Martin Buber, *I and Thou* (1923); Sartre, *The Other*, and *The Look* in, *Being and Nothingness* (1943).

it.[515] A consensus of reasonably well-informed consumers merely provides degrees of confidence in the available evidence of the objective true-north value of a *paos*. Thus, the ultimate goal of reaching a *Lean* six sigma ($\geq$/6σ) of common agreement becomes a nuanced pursuit of practical perfection that must pierce through people's perception of objective reality.

Consumers' unique *SUDS* that may converge toward consensus result from their varying psychological, physiological, and environmental circumstances. While each consumer has varying degrees of intention, self-awareness and temperament within these circumstances, all consumers converge to some degree because they commonly pursue the same goal of *Ontological Realization* upward along the *OT* within the *OM*. This leads to very personal judgments about whether or not a *paos* is good or evil while all fundamentally evaluating the same objective thing. All these judgements about a *paos* will ultimately be proved rightly or wrongly by people being either energized and optimized, or becoming *N-OT*, within their various social bubbles. These different outcomes depend on whether consuming a *paos* results in consumers' *Ontological Realization* upward along the *OT* as the great simpliciter and regulator of all that consumers are within the *OM*.

The Rothko Effect

For example, presume a certain type of color blindness resulted in one consumer seeing an abstract painting as orange and another seeing the painting as red. Further presume that a peculiar biological difference led one consumer to judge the painting as beautiful, interesting, or meaningful, while other consumers judge it as not being any of those qualiaties. Only the consumers *who* judged

---

[515] As mentioned earlier, people's phenomenological perceptions are optimized to produce *Ontological Realization* but not to accurately reflect objective, *universal* reality as it truly is; *see again* Justin T. Mark, Brian B. Marion, Donald D. Hoffman, *Natural Selection and Veridical Perceptions*, Journal of Theoretical Biology (Accepted Jul. 24, 2010).

the painting's beauty with the best alignment to the *Ontological Teleology* by sharing its *Ontological Realization* with the most viable people would value the price of the painting correctly (unless the other people somehow knew *how* to compensate for their poor judgment). While the consumers *whose* tastes differed with the majority of the market would get great deals on the paintings that others did not value, those tasteless consumers would choose items whose monetary value would not appreciate from lack of common demand for them. But while those consumers would not become monetarily wealthy, they would at least become rich in their own phenomenologies.

Mark Rothko, *Four Darks in Red*(© Estate of Mark Rothko (Fair Use))

- *What color do you think the Mark Rothko painting is above?*
- *How much would consumers pay for it if you offered it for sale?*
- *Why would people pay that much (or little)? What about the Andy Warhol's "Campbell Soup Can (Tomato)" discussed in Stream 2?*

For another example, an internet meme went viral with a picture that created two different phenomenologies for different consumers. Some consumers saw a particular woman's dress depicted below as being white and gold, and others saw it as black and blue. Without thinking about *why* they saw the dress differently, think only about the fact of that color difference, and consumers' different emotional responses to that dress, to understand the differences in their phenomenologies when you bracket out their intuition as to whether to buy that dress or not.

Which phenomenological qualia would consumers experience if you were selling this dress online?
When told about this color effect, would this dress change color in those consumers' dreams?

Great Dress Debate(© 2015 Cecilia Bleasdale (Public Domain))

Test for Qualia: How Do You Know *U* / *People* See the Color Red?

Because consumers inherently internalize *what* they experience, you could *qualiatatively* analyze *how* consumers experience *what* they find most meaningful within a *paos*. For example, for consumers to think of a *paos* as *soap*, the *paos* called *soap* must clean dirt and oil. Beyond that function, the chemicals constituting *soap* can be quite varied. If the *paos* removed dirt and oil too well by behaving more like a caustic acid, consumers wouldn't consider that acid to be *soap* at all. Consumers generally rely on manufacturers to tell them when something constitutes *soap* or another type of cleanser. They then expect the *soap* to function within an optimized range critical to *adapting*, such as by cleaning themselves for a new job interview, *Re-generating*, such as by scrubbing away dead skin, and/or *energizing*, such as by cleaning dishes from which to eat. Thus, the qualia consumers classify as being either *good* or *evil* depends on the external stimuli they experience from the real world, such as watching *soap* optimally clean something of true value to them like themselves.

Lifting the Veil to See Reality

Now turn toward *who* consumers really are in the context of everyday, scientific reality by having the veil of *Epoché* taken away. By doing so, you can see that the interaction of consumers with their contextual environment is *what* actually enacts the true-north value consumers may experience from something.

For example, consumers' bodies and minds actively *Re-generate what* they experience from actually watching the interaction of a *paos* with the *OM*, such as watching *philosophy, inc.'s, purity* band of *soap* remove red lipstick from a person's skin. The true-north value consumers' phenomenologically experience from the *purity* brand *soap* results from their perceiving the *soap* as actually renewing themselves by removing the visible red spectrum from their faces, as is well advertised by the *soap's* manufacturer, *philosophy, inc.* on its website:

> *philosophy: purity is natural. we come into this world with all the right instincts. we are innocent and, therefore, perceive things as they should be, rather than how they are. our conscience is clear, our hands clean and the world at large is truly beautiful. it is at this time we feel most blessed. to begin feeling young again, we must begin with the most basic step of all, the daily ritual of cleansing.*[516]

Philosophy, inc. customers' memories, imaginations and dreams then replicate and analogize that experience of color removal and

---

[516] Found at http://www.philosophy.com/purity-made-simple.html (last accessed Apr. 4, 2017).

renewal into further internally *Re-generated* qualia, such as how they remember feeling when they had the color red removed. Those customers thereby associated a particular brand of *soap* with that sacrosanct feeling. *Philosophy, inc.'s* customers will also buy that *soap* to a-void having to wash sheets stained with the lipstick they forgot to take off the night before while leaving their faces unblemished. For those people selling *soap*, recognizing all of these anticipated qualia is their finest act of true commercial empathy.

If an organization sells *soap*, its product managers ought to energize and optimize the *soap's* critical, scientifically proven, cleaning qualities that consumers indicate best enhances their *I/C/aRe* processes that will ultimately be *Ontologically Realized* by them due to good chemistry. Consumers make this assessment based on their internally *Re-generated*, conscious and unconscious qualia they experience from using the *soap* sold to them. Customer's qualia result from the *soap* doing its fundamental job of washing away certain *soot*.[517]

The Scientific Revolution of the *OT*

Similar to analyzing *what* qualia consumers experience and determining *what* a qualia means to them, scientists in general, and physicists in particular, use a scientific, *model dependent reality*, to analyze *how* scientific models interpret *what* true-north value is.[518] While phenomenological *Epoché* specifically disregards any judgments about the outside world, science moves beyond the veil of *Epoché* to assume that experience originates from a single, objective reality within the *OM*. However, unlike qualiatative analysis, scientific empiricism ought to be a highly measurable and replicable method to count the paces of true-north value of the *paos* being produced, and thus the true meaning of the money being

---

[517] *See generally*, Sally Satel and Scott O. Lilienfeld, *Brainwashed: The Seductive Appeal of Mindless Neuroscience*, Basic Books (Jun. 4, 2013).

[518] Stephen Hawking and Leonard Mlodinow, *The Grand Design* (2010).

made by selling the *paos*' benefits that get consumed. You ought to relate scientific empiricism and phenomenological qualia so that consumers can predictably experience true-north value from *paos* with great confidence.

All the same, since phenomenologists recognize that consumers' phenomenologies merely model the *Universe*, this notion of *model dependent reality* effects an organization's ability to conjecture, hypothesize and theorize the true meaning that consumers will experience from *paos*. Since the customer data that an organization receives is not a *thing in itself*,[519] but rather a mere reflection of *what* consumers prefer, an organization can only *best fit* the meaning it expects a *paos* to re-produce within consumers' phenomenologies to *what* consumers physiologically and psychologically experience. Thus, consumers' phenomenological, model dependent reality affects an organization's ability to scientifically identify *what* consumers ought to buy to energize and optimize their own lives and existences to experience the greatest profit at the point of purchase.

Since an organization cannot predict with perfect accuracy *what* consumers ought to buy, it must best fit *what paos* phenomenologically re-produces to *what* energizes and optimizes consumers' living processes within at least two *Lean* sigmas ($\geq/2\sigma$) of agreement by them. For an organization to control a market, it must develop at least six *Lean* sigmas ($\geq/6\sigma$) of confidence that its *paos* best energizes and optimizes the lives and existences of the people within the market-place, even if they cannot easily afford the price being charged. That is no easy task, but doing so separates good companies from great ones.

Likewise, consumers best fit *what* they believe about the *OM* with *how* they collectively perceive something as being either good or evil from their phenomenological, personal perspectives. Thus, a *paos* must best fit not only all axiomatically and systemically

---

[519]Yes, I mean Immanuel Kant's noumenon; it also means that it takes the latter branch of Hume's Fork by being *a posteriori* in-formation.

known true-north values, but also consumers' personally held opinions about the *Universe*.

For example, when comparison shopping, consumers think, '*[T]his *paos* X is similar to *paos* Y that I like already, which puts *paos* X in the class of *paos* that I consider to be 'good.'* Consumers want to buy all that they analogically relate to the class of *goods*. *What* consumers consider *good* may like-wise be thought of as a single analogy of all that energizes and optimizes their supervening psychological and physiological processes. Consumers perceive the *good paos* they actually buy as better *Ontologically Realizing* their lives and existences, or *who* they most want to be (or not be) and become, whether they admit that to themselves or not. For example, certain consumers may analogize a *paos* as *good* at a certain price and others may not because of the relative tradeoffs one consumer estimates he or she must make versus the other to become that customer *who* owns that *paos*.

For a more specific example, presume a group of teenagers you know collectively likes a new song on their *iPhones*. They did so because their collective phenomenological qualia analogized the song to things they categorically *like*. The song and their mental class for *what* they *like* overlapped like circles of consensus on a Venn diagram. The teenagers dis-analogized the song to their concept of *evil*. I say this to emphasize consumers' shared models of reality, and those model's intermediary role between an organization's *paos* and its axiomatic and systemic true-north values being realized by consumers. You ought to best align the objective creation and distribution of a *paos* with *what* best matches consumers' subjectively and collectively agreed upon qualia that determines *who* they are, *why* they may prefer something, and *what* they may buy at the largest qualiatative intersection spanning the target markets.

Consumers' subjective, qualiatative impressions matter most to *what* they truly value and will buy now, while at the same time, generally quantifiable *I/C/aRe* processes ultimately determine *what* consumers will normatively value and continue to buy in the long-run. Thus, an organization must estimate the extent that its *paos* produces a positive phenomenological experience within the exceedingly complex notion of *who* consumers are, while simultaneously recognizing the complexities inherent in *why* and *what* consumers phenomenologically experience *what* and *how* they do. Doing all that best ensures that an organization will effectively deliver *paos* that really gets *b-ought* and consumed. By better recognizing the relative strengths and weaknesses of best fitting qualiatatively analogical as well as quantitatively numerical analysis, organizations can better *Re-generate* prophetic true-north value for consumers. This in-turn allows organizations to *Re-generate* meaningful profits for stake-holders, *who* will crucify any organization that does not.

Phenomeno-logical Categorization to Abstract Analogy Making

Consumers labelling or tagging their phenomenological experiences with words relates categories of those experiences to broader analogies they associate with *paos*. They engage in Analogy Making (*AM*) from the strange loops of their personal perspectives to optimize their *I/C/aRe* processes by further consuming *what* means most to them. For example, culture, society and political structures are large-scale, collective analogies that lead to large-scale consumption choices about *what* energizes and optimizes best overall. Consumers form these analogical, mental constructs both automatically and quite consciously, amalgamating facts into categories, and relating those categories critical to *who* and *why* they *aRe* within the *Universe* to better *Lean Ontologically Teleologically* and live as strange loops.[520]

---

[520] Douglas R. Hofstadter, *Gödel, Escher, Bach* , pp. P–709 (1999); Douglas Hofstadter, *I Am a Strange Loop*, Basic Books, Reprint edition (2008).

Just like *how* consumers physiologies and psychologies change their phenomenologies, their verbal and mathematical analogies differentiate *how* they engage in *I/C/aRe* processes. Understanding *who* and *what* consumers verbally and mathematically analogize themselves as being allows you to best identify *what* consumers' *Ontologically Realize*as true-north value within their phenomenological, personal perspectives. For an example of analogical value estimation, analogy-based financial trading is called, '*Technical Analysis*.' People (and programs) considered, '*Technical Analysts*,' *who* are *good traders*, look at patterns of price changes in securities over time and trade those securities depending on whether they analogize a stock price pattern as being *good* or *bad*. A *Technical Analyst* will buy a stock to the extent he or she analogizes a stock's price pattern as being *good* for his or her profits and self-conception of being a *good trader*.

Like-wise, if consumers analogized a Mark Rothko painting as being *beautiful*, then their neuro-logical responses to seeing the Rothko reveals their preference for buying the Rothko as a person *who* likes *beauty*. So to more accurately assess the degree to which each consumer considers a security or painting to be worth buying, you might compare their neuro-logical responses as revealed preferences to *how* they respond to other *paos* that they similarly analogize as being *beautiful* or *valuable*, or would classify as being one of *x* number of seemingly valuable things they categorically demand.[521]

To fully appreciate the degree to which consumers phenomenologically analogize a *paos* to a specific qualiaty, classification or category, consider when consumers might consider the Rothko painting as being analogically related to the color *red* or the aesthetic *beautiful*. To do so, you must somehow get within the

---

[521]In fact, applying OCEAN psychoanalysis and other preference based psychometrics to the large datasets that consumers provide online and offline, you are increasingly able to micro-target their revealed preferences for commercial and political success;*see e.g.*, Von Hannes Grassegger and Mikael Krogerus, *Ich habe nur gezeigt, dass es die Bombe gibt*, Das Magazin N°48 – 3. (Dec. 2016).

context of consumers' neurological and psychological processes producing that phenomenological categorization from their personal perspectives. You ought to capture the full range of each of their connotations associated with the concept of *red* or *beautiful*. You ought to relate consumers' present, qualiatative perceptions to their inter-subjective experiences through the power of phenomenological empathy.

You must also always keep in mind that along the *OM* and from within the *IB*, consumers' lower level *SL-OTS* teleonomically created consumers' personal identities as cohesive analogies of all of the aggregated processes leading to the essence of *who* and *why* they are. And each cohesive analogy of a named person (*i.e.*, an individual consumer) represents all of the underlying living processes that together constitute an overall *Modus Ôperandi* and way of being. Thus, *how paos* effects living, /aRe processes like-wise affects whether consumers consider a *paos* as being good, better or best for *who* and *why* they are.[522]

For example, *what* categorical qualiaties and connotations do you think consumers experience when looking at the color red in this logo for Safeway grocery stores at www.Safeway.com? (if you are seeing this in gray-scale, just imagine you see gray-dations of red):

---

[522]Douglas Hofstadter and Emmanuel Sander, *Surfaces and Essences: Analogy as the Fuel and Fire of Thinking*, p. 317, Basic Books (2013); Nicholas Humphrey, *Soul Dust: The Magic of Consciousness*, p. 6, (2011); Nicholas Humphrey, *A History of the Mind: Evolution and the Birth of Consciousness*, Kindle Loc. 756 (2012); and Ayn Rand has some interesting discussion of analogical abstractions in her objectivist epistemological philosophies in the *Introduction* and *Chapter 3: Abstraction from Abstractions,* within her book, *Objectivist Epistemology: Expanded Second Edition*, (particularly p. 19), Penguin Group US (1979).

© 2014 Safeway®

How consumers analogize *paos* to so many different nouns, adjectives, emotions and connotations determines to some extent *what Strategically Unique Degrees of Sophist-ication* they possess.[523] For example, consumers' learn to speak by analogously mapping things and processes to their self-conceptions, such as *soap* being analogous to the class of things that clean other things they need, like a body they identify with, or like planets in the solar system being analogous to the thing on which they now reside. However, when consumers try to learn a new language, often the words, categories, and concepts significantly vary from one language to the next. French is one set of *SUDS* while Chinese is another. Such similarities or dissimilarities between linguistic concepts create meaningful analogies and dis-analogies between them, leading to different

---

[523]Douglas Hofstadter and Emmanuel Sander, *Surfaces and Essences*, p. 189 (2013); Epiphemenological responses by C/aRę and not-self-aware I/C/aRę organisms could as well but consideration of them is outside the intended discussion.

SUDS between languages on which they *Lean* for meaning.[524]

Likewise, certain languages use gendered articles while others do not. Thus, some consumers think with a gendered language, such as certain Romance languages, shaping their worldview. Those gender connotations differ analogously from the perspective of those consumers speaking one gendered language next to those consumers not using gendered articles at all.[525] For example, Spanish speaking markets analogize *soap* to being masculine (*el Jabón*). Spanish customers most likely connote masculine qualia, like the feeling of aggressiveness, to the *paos* of *soap* and the act of becoming clean with it. The categorical connotations for that demographic changes *what* a so\ap company ought to advertise in Spain and*how* it ought to position its so\ap within Spanish speaking markets.[526]

Keep in mind that some categories represent sets of concepts that do have logical boundaries, such as prime numbers in math, while other categories can be quite fluid, like those representing *art* or *value*. Categories often exceed their associated words because of multiple definitions and the complexities inherent in word combinations and phrases.[527] For example, in 1917, the artist Marcel Duchamp anonymously submitted a toilet bowel titled as '*Fountain*,' signed 'R. Mutt 1917,' to the Society of Independent Artists in New York (SIA). Duchamp wanted to see if SIA would reclassify the latrine from its intended function to the category of *art*. Duchamp

---

[524] I.e., the *Sapir-Whorf Hypothesis*; see e.g., Benjamin Whorf, John B. Carroll, ed., *Language, Thought, and Reality: Selected Writings of Benjamin Lee Whorf*, MIT Press (1956), and Edward Sapir, and David G. Mandelbaum, ed., *Selected Writings of Edward Sapir in Language, Culture, and Personality*, University of California Press (1983).

[525] *See*, Leland Whitney Crafts, Théodore Christian Schneirla, Elsa Elizabeth Robinson, and Ralph Wesley Gilbert, *Factors Influencing Perception and Memory*, in, *Recent Experiments in Psychology*, Ch. XXII (1938), where the authors wrote, ... *if we spoke a different language we would perceive a somewhat different world.*

[526] For an interesting example of this account of linguistic positivism, see,*Dictionary of Untranslatables: A Philosophical Lexicon*, Edited by Barbara Cassin, Princeton University Press (2012), which demonstrates the slight differences in how customers classify and intersubjectively perceive objective reality.

[527] *See e.g.*, Deirdre Wilson, Dan Sperber,*Meaning and Relevance*, Cambridge University Press (Apr. 23, 2012).

wished to make a statement as to whether an organization had any ability to bracket *what* could or could not be analogized to the class of things we call *art*.

 ***What do you think, art or latrine?*[528]**

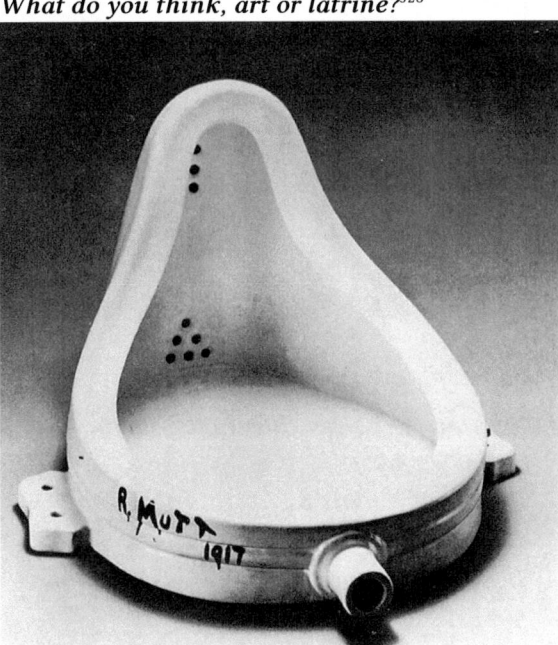

Marcel Duchamp's *Fountain* signed *R. Mutt 1917* (Public Domain)

Keep in mind that consumers' analogies can also be as brittle as a child's temperament. For example, when explaining division to children, you might say that the division of whole numbers like 9 / 1 = 9 can be directly compared to splitting up a set of nine apples nine different ways. However, once you work with fractions such as .9 / .1 = 9, the product of the equation is a larger number

---

[528]Duchamp titled this entire series of art tongue-in-cheek as *readymades*.

of apples than you originally had. There is less than one apple in the numerator on the left side of the equation, which cannot be analogized to splitting up whole things in real life. You, like children, must rectify good analogies with bad ones, like reading positive or negative customer reviews of *paos* – consumers make analogies or dis-analogies to *what* is good or evil to best reflect truth value in their self-conceptions of reality, but can do so imperfectly and sometimes even fraudulently. You ought to appreciate the nuances within that process to make the most money meaningfully when assessing consumer feedback.[529]

For an example from a purely business perspective, consider the false metaphors and euphemisms used in common financial discussions to see *how* analogical shifting occurs:[530]

- *"Securitization" leads to economic insecurity;*
- *"Austerity" hurts those customers most dependent on social services;*
- *"Bail-out" means a capital injection;*
- *"Credit" means debt to the holders;*
- *"Inflation" means less purchasing power;*
- *"Synergies" means layoffs;*
- *"Risk" means a precisely assumed liability; and*
- *"Non-core asset" means an operating liability.*

Ultimately, consumers analogize or dis-analogize themselves to '*i*' with varying degrees of introspection as to *who* exactly they are or are not. Increasing self-awareness allows them to more accurately analogize or dis-analogize what they phenomenologically experience as themselves. This increased accuracy allows them to better determine *how* they may a-void becoming *Not Ontologically Teleological.* Consumers' articulate and extend their self-analogy

---

[529]Credit to Douglas Hofstadter, *I Am a Strange Loop*, (2008) for inspiring this example.

[530]John Lanchester,*Money Talks* , The New Yorker (Aug. 4, 2014).

among all the things they say, do and consume to enhance their *I/C/aRe* processes as well as possible in an infinitely recursive fashion back to energizing and optimizing *who* they believe they are and wish to be. Organizations ought to likewise fully abstract their self-conceptions as '*i*' and their very human customers as '*thou*.'[531] They ought to see consumers as *other* so they may best empathetically conceptualize the ways they may provide *paos* so consumers may avoid becoming dissatisfied or altogether *N-OT*. Organizations may phenomenologically, commercially empathize with consumers to move up and along the *Rubicon* of consumers' value streams. Here is a map of the *Rubicon River*, emerging like a forward slash from the *Apennine Mountains* heading out to the *Adriatic Sea* for further guidance:

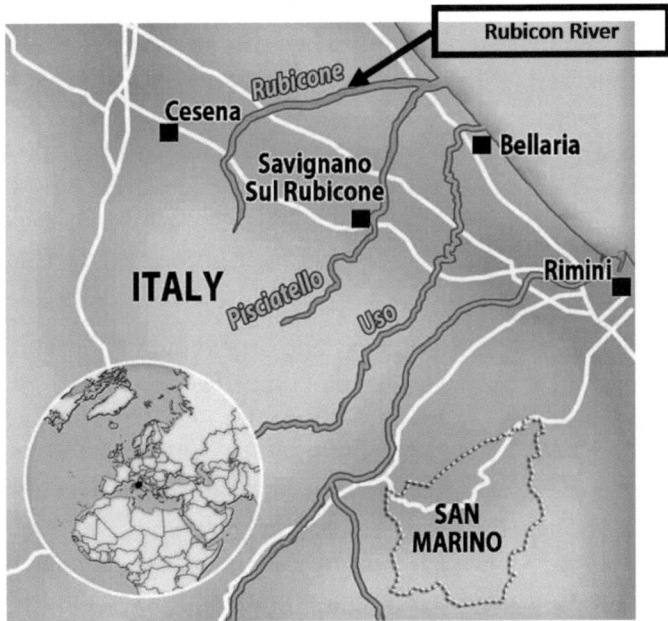

Rubicone River, Italy (Public Domain)

---

[531] Yes, alluding to Martin Buber's *I and Thou*.

Y AM I?

As you can see, 'Analogy Making' (*AM*) is *what* allows organizations to empathize with consumers and makes consumers as passionately intelligent as Rodin's, '*The Thinker.*' *AM* is also *what* ultimately *Leans* consumers toward buying organizations' *paos*. *AM* makes consumers so self-conscious that they can universally conceptualize *what* they will do with *paos* once bought.[532] Most funda-mentally, consumers' instrumental, ana-logical reasoning allows them to self-reflexively articulate, '*Why AM I?*' Or in longer form, '*Why do I make analogies to Who, What, and How I ought to be?*' The management consultant and sophist Simon Sinek advises all business people to, '*Start with Why*,' in his same titled book for this reason.[533] Importantly, you now know that *why* starts with *who* since *why* requires an inquisitor when the question is bracketed by the *IB*, thus leading to the self-conscious question, '*'Y AM I' now within the OM?*' You ought to start with *who*, not *why*, because the fact of consumers' existence, of *who* they are, is the origin of all true-north value, as Descartes discovered so long ago. *Why* simply leads back to that seemingly tautological fact of existence but for *whatever* else consumers may intuitively speculate is outside the *IB*.

By conceptualizing this question, and articulating it through symbolic language, people at some point drove *I/C/aRe* activity forward up through the *Ontological Teleology* within *Ontological Medium*. Once consumers asked, '*Why AM I?*,' they then self-reflexively recognized the possible paradox of the *OT* to remain viable within the *OM* to the greatest extent possible. Asking, '*Why AM I?*,' instantiated self-conscious self-awareness within consumers and created the first cognitive paradox within the known *Universe*.

---

[532] This is in approximate agreement with Daniel C. Dennett, *Darwin's Dangerous Idea*, p. 322, Simon & Schuster (1995).

[533] *See generally*, Simon Sinek, *Start with Why: How Great Leaders Inspire Everyone to Take Action* (2009).

The *why* in this recursive sentence subsumes the further *what* and *how* of being that consumers elaborated through each word in this question. You can see consumers' phenomenological development springing forth from their *I/C/aRe* process along this *Why* axis as follows:

- ***Why* (or *Y*)**: Expresses consumers' yearning to increase their difference with *what* is *N-OT* by orienting themselves upward along the *OT* toward the */aRe* processes that result in their unified, personal perspectives;
- ***AM***: Stands for consumers' subsequent *Analogy Making* that creates their personally known true-north values;
- ***I***: Indicates the self-reflexive conceptualization of consumers from their personal perspectives within the *OM* ; and
- ***?***: Represents consumers' intentionality, leading them to increase their difference with *what* they believe is *N-OT* by attempting to fully answer the seemingly open-ended question, '*Y AM I?*'

'*Y AM I?*' works backwards as a conceptual leap from the intentional, cognitive query connected to consumers' self-conception from an indeterminable source. When fully reversed, '*Y AM I*' becomes consumers' willful intention of '*I MAY*', as in, '*I may buy your *paos to energize and optimize my life and existence if I feel it worthy.*' Consumers' mental conception of, '*Y AM I?,*' *thus represents the recursive cognitive event of general intelligence that set them apart from other animals, on a course beyond *I/C/aRe* processes. It accelerated their ability to universally conceptualize *how* to better perform *I/C/aRe* processes for themselves within the whole *Universe*. '*Y AM I*' is thus funda-mentally *why* consumers buy today *what* gets produced from sophisticated, *Lean Houses of Quality*, and ultimately determines to what degree they */aRe*. There is nothing artificial about it.

Consumers developed this ability to abstract their self-conception because it provided them with two distinct advantages to perform /aRe activity:

1. *Consumers could better cooperate with or compete against others to engage in /aRe activity; and*
2. *Consumers could better abstract, understand and predict the results of their own Analogy Making within the OM from an objective, third person, self-reflexive perspective.*

These two cognitive benefits of self-reflexive consciousness allows consumers to *Leanly adapt* and *Re-generate*, as well as hunt and gather *energy*, as I/C/aRe organisms. These cognitive benefits are also the axiomatic and systemic true-north values that *paos* ought to serve and consumers ought to buy. However, these natural features and benefits of intentional cognition come with a cost - they force consumers to face an apparent paradox that they seem to exist through the *OT* by engaging in /aRe activity in self-defining, possibly circular fashion. They force self-aware people to recognize this seeming paradox on some level, both in that they may have originated from a cause outside the *IB*, and that their existences depend on their ability to engage in /aRe processes toward an apparent goal of simply further existing upward along the *Ontological Teleology*. An organization's production of *paos* must recognize this conundrum to be most meaningful to consumers.

Moving Beyond the ÔT to *What* is Gets B-Ôught

Ultimately, consumers' analogized themselves to being like themselves self-reflexively, which further allowed them to dis-analogize *who* they most wanted to be from *what* they were. Like Descarte's mind-body duality of, '*I think, therefore I AM,*' this dis-analogy between their past, present and future selves defined *what* consumers considered themselves to be, *what* they considered themselves to *N-OT* be, *what* they knew of themselves in the *IB*, and by definition, *what* they believed may be outside the *IB*. Thus, these distinctions created in consumers' minds conceptual boundaries between *what* they knew of themselves, *what* they knew of the *OM*, *what* they knew of the *Universe*, *what* they knew is *N-OT*, and *what* they intuitively speculated is *beyond the Ought* (i.e. *what* is *Beyond the OT*, *B-Ought*, or *B-OT*).

To better understand *how* the *OT* runs up through and across these conceptual boundaries, you might also want to incorporate a fifth discipline here called, *Systems Thinking*,[534] into *Lean* business thinking. By doing so, you can understand consumers within all of these boundaries as physically connected to the entire *OM* and *Universe* from their personal perspectives. So, from this systems perspective, much like the *OT* curving round-and-round up through the *OM*, you may even further analogize consumers as being like strange loops of a perpetually spiralling, recursive fractal flowing up through these conceptual boundaries.

The first interior boundary in the picture below conceptually represents the difference between consumers' personal perspectives and *what* they consider the *OM* to be based on *what* they experience from it. The second boundary represents the distinction between *what* consumers know of the *OM* and *what* they consider the unbounded *Universe* to be. The outermost boundary represents all that consumers consider there to be and *what* they believe is truly *B-Ought* (or they know is in fact *N-OT*):

---

[534] As proposed by Peter Senge in, *The Fifth Discipline: The Art & Practice of the Learning Organization*, Doubleday Business; 1st edition (1990).

360   Stream 5: People

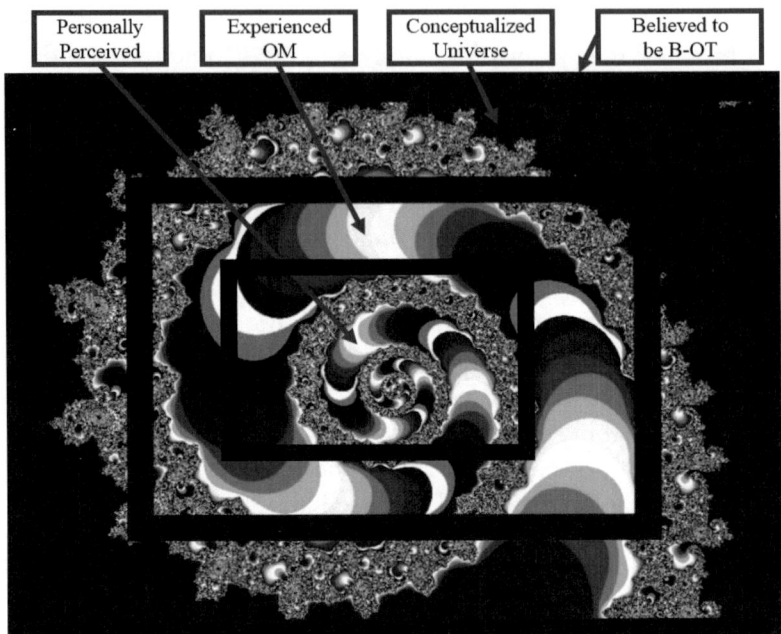

Strange Loops, A Fractal Analogized to the *OT* within the *IB*

By conceptually bracketing the levels that consumers are, you can see that today they simultaneously engage in the details of daily life and in non-rational speculation of *who* and *why* they are within the *OM*. They do so because they have few strategic options other than orienting themselves with universal and processual true-north values to move upward along the spiral of the *Ontological Teleology* to attempt to universalize their personal perspectives. Consumers go about daily life within the *OM* and speculate about *what* is *N-OT* to try and point the winding arrow of time back on itself to universalize themselves self-referentially any way they can.

From all of these perspectives, consumers look like eddies in the larger value stream edifying themselves as *Lean Thinkers*, learning *who*, *why*, *what* and *how* they intentionally, cognitively /aRe. While consumers may not immediately appear this way in-line or on-line, the integrated systems of the *Universe* running upstream through *who* consumers are appear very different, similar or exactly the same depending on which scale you bracket. This is true of fractals at different levels of zoom; *The Great Chain of Being* running from Whirlpool Galaxies to whirlpools of water, and ultimately, Whirlpool® washing machines; and of the *Volumes* and *Streams* flowing through the *U/People* business model within the philosophy of *Lean*.

Philosophical Zombies as Straw Men

Thus, for consumers to ask themselves, '*Y AM I?*,' based on *what* they believe is truly *B-OT* or is in fact *N-OT* is to make themselves subjectively, self-consciously human at any scale. This creates the truest of all true-north value as the highest known SL-OT within the *OM* and *IB. However*, if this question guides a corporation toward true meaning, *how* does it know that consumers *who* internalize this question do not state it pro-grammatically?[535] Could a corporation hack consumers and turn them into zombies *who* shop for *paos* to optimize /aRe processes without further intuitively speculating *who* and *why* they are? Your answering these questions allows you to best understand whether you can completely quantify and predict *what* consumers will buy - like so many big data vendors advocate - or whether you will be running around in circles.

---

[535] In other words, you want to avoid any anthropomorphic fallacies; *see*, the Stanford Encyclopædia of Philosophy entry on, '*Turning Test*.'

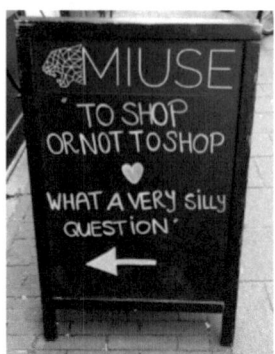

'*To Shop or Not to Shop, What a Very Silly Question,*' Amsterdam (Photo Credit: Me)

David Chalmers is a contemporary philosopher who is well known for devising the thought experiment that asks you to presume that all consumers are *zombies*, and to further presume that you are the only person with conscious, subjective experience. Chalmers refers to such hypothetical customers as, '*Philosophical Zombies*.'[536] Chalmers proposes that you cannot scientifically test whether or not consumers are conscious like you know you are as you.... read... this.. book, even if you were to perfectly map consumers' brain activity with a scanner to reveal that it perfectly matches your own. Chalmers believes that you need to explain consumers' consciousness other than with physical, scientific explanations. In the parlance of U/P, he means that you must understand consumers' conciousness from a purely personal perspective.[537] Chalmers' argument presumes that having data of behavioral responses alone, such as having perfect records of all of consumers' shopping history, would still not allow you to predict perfectly whether consumers would willingly buy some *paos* because they are constantly dealing with personal demons.

I believe that analogizing consumers to philosophical zombies is a straw man because consciousness is a gradation of subjectivity.

---

[536] *See generally*, David Chalmers, *The Conscious Mind*, Oxford University Press (1996).
[537] *Ibid*.

What truly matters for the *Turning Test* is recognizing *how Lean* and flexible consumers' intentionally cognitive, *adaptive, Re-generative* and *energizing* behaviors are that optimize their difference with *what* is *N-OT*.[538] Quite conclusively, a zombie that was not conscious could not reflect these qualities with any consistent, universal flexibility because a zombie could not dis-analogize itself to all that may be *N-OT* in order to conceptualize its own survival better than the walking dead.

If you need to convince yourself that consumers are more like Rodin's passionately pensive, *The Thinker*, than they are like philosophical zombies, you only need to subject consumers to a variety of truly random events, experiences, and personal questions to see if a single, self-reflexive *i* holds together struggling with the larger questions of *who* and *why* they are while ever more creatively performing */aRe* processes to live and further exist. The only thing you ought to check is whether a corporate puppet master is pulling the strings.

---

[538] David Deutsch, *The Beginning of Infinity*, p. 155 (2011).

Philosophical Zombies in a Field(© 2005 FG2 (Public Domain))

This test cannot be fully quantified, like Turing said, and ultimately requires an intuitive assessment beyond what you see these zombies doing. No bright lines exists, but none could because *me* aning gets created through a gradation from *B/aRe* to *C/aRe* to *I/C/aRe* and beyond to consumers' highest *SL-OTS* and *SUDS*. However, you can test life and consciousness with an organism's *adaptability* to *re-energize* and ultimately *Re-generate* with an intuitive sense of personality, passion and feeling.

You see this */aRe* gradation tested in the movies dealing with everything from aliens to strange animals and artificially intelligent robots, each of which could potentially be an additional customer seeking true-north value. Given the infinite spectrum of fictional customers, a true philosophical zombie without any self-reflection could not universally adapt to fight for survival like a self-aware person because it could not universally conceptualize all the ways it could avoid becoming *N-OT*, which by definition requires imagining *what* may be truly *B-OT*.

However, in return for this ontological benefit of consciousness, consumers require some irrationality to try and evade the apparent paradox of the *OT* they find themselves in.[539] This irrationality can be self-destructive, but it usually functions to optimize consumers' randomized search for the best *I/C/aRe* processes within the *OM*. While philosophical zombies are oxy-morons, consumers' erratic behavior functions as their attempt to resolve the potent-ial paradox of the *OT* to better live and exist in an open-ended *Universe*, by in part, buying and using *paos* in sometimes unexpected ways.

U/ People are *N-OT* in Jeopardy

Look at this consciousness issue from the perspective of modern day computers to fully understand consumers' decisions to buy the true-north value inherent in *paos*. Compare both consumers and philosophical zombies to *IBM*'s computer named *Watson*. Watson won on the game show *Jeopardy* in 2011 against human competitors, which requires its contestants to phrase their answers in the form of a question. Watson won the competition and beat the human contestants by correctly matching the most questions to the most correct answers among a *Universe* of possibilities. While Watson may have won "Jeopardy," it will not decide to purchase *paos* any time soon since Watson cannot universally optimize itself upward along the *Ontological Teleology*. Watson cannot do so until Watson analogically equates itself as, '*Watson = Watson, so Watson can to further be by adapting, Re-generating and energizing.*'[540]

---

[539] In fact, recent research seems to have identified that 25 years old is the peak age at which consumers can think in random ways, *see*, Nicolas Gauvrit, Hector Zenil, Fernando Soler-Toscano, Jean-Paul Delahaye, Peter Brugger, *Human behavioral complexity peaks at age 25*, Journal for the International Society of Computational Biology (PLOS) (Apr. 13, 2017).

[540] *See e.g.*, Nicolas Carr, *Why Robots Will Always Need Us*, New York Times Opinion (May 20, 2015); and Nicolas Carr, *The Glass Cage: Automation and Us*, W. W. Norton & Company (2014).

Neither Watson nor any other single purpose machine universally conceptualizes such that it considers itself self-referentially. Watson's human programmers acting as puppet masters optimized its algorithms to provide question-answers that statistically related to the answer-questions presented by the game. Watson by itself cannot universally analogize between concepts randomly selected within the *Universe* of possible dialogue. Rather Watson only finds correlations between terms that people created in the first place, which is just like *Google* feeding back human preferences for search results that only seem artificially intelligent in their organization and reflection back to us. Consider further that *Toyota Motor Corporation* has begun replacing some of its robots with human employees to improve efficiency in the *Lean* process of *Jidoka*. *Toyota* calls these employees *Gods*, and uses them in *Toyota's Production System* because these human employees can universally and passionately consider *how* to optimize production processes in ways non-self-aware machines can not.[541] Another principle of *TPS's Lean* production is using people to operate many different types of machines because people can more effectively adapt across an infinite variety of systems than any (other) machine can alone, which is why *Lean* uses U-shapes workspaces to exploit people's cognitive flexibility.

Thus, Watson is not conscious because it cannot (yet) conceptualize the question, '*Y AM I?*' to at least attempt to meaningfully dis-analogize between itself and *what* is *N-OT*, and thus analogize itself to *what* it believes ought to be *B-Ought*.[542] Since Watson and other machines cannot distinguish between themselves and *what* is *N-OT*, they cannot universally adapt to the apparently self-defining, teleological goal of further being within the *OM* with passion and

---

[541] *See*, Craig Trudell, Yuki Hagiwara, Jie Ma, *Humans Replacing Robots Herald Toyota's Vision of Future*, Bloomberg News (Apr. 7, 2014).

[542] Of course, as earlier hinted at, I also use *Ought* because it has a bit of a moral tinge to it, which will apply shortly in discussing the synthesis of Hume's *Is-Ought* problem.

meaning.[543]Watson too is an artificially intelligent zombie and a straw man, but it is nonetheless a far better "Jeopardy" contestant than we.

Maximally Existential*Me* aning Defined (/σ∞)

Organizations provide consumers with *paos* to energize and optimize their lives and existences so they can better distinguish themselves from *what* is *N-OT*, and better become *what* they believe is *B-OT*. However,

 What does it mean for consumers to optimally maximize their existences with *paos to the greatest extent possible both away from becoming N-OT and toward getting B-OT?*

At the other end of the *OT* spectrum away from *N-OT*, toward *what* consumers believe is truly *B-OT*, maximal existence is that which self-organizes to the greatest extent to universalize itself within the *OM*. Consumers' consciousness enhances the true-north value of **me**aningfully, maximally existing as /*aRe* organisms (*ME/aRe* organisms). They do so even if maximal existence is only hypothetical, since if truly achieved, consumers would finally get themselves *B-OT*. However, given that the *OT* is apparently a paradox when bounded by the *IB*, maximal existence aligns next to both *what* is *N-OT* true-north value and *what* customers believe is *B-Ought*. Just because consumers cannot become universalized in any real sense

---

[543]Per the Stanford Encyclopædia of Philosophy entry on, '*Schopenhauer*,' '*Among 19th century philosophers, Arthur Schopenhauer was among the first to contend that at its core, the universe is not a rational place*,' (accessed Jun. 12, 2016); other scholars noting the general circularity inherent in existence include as discussed, Hofstadter in *Gödel, Escher, Bach*, and the corresponding Gödel's incompleteness theory that no mathematical or logical system could ever be self-defining.

without getting themselves *B-OT*, that doesn't mean buying *paos* isn't *what* consumers ought to do to the greatest extent possible.[544]

Here is the chart with the additional *ME/aRe SUDS* forming a new *SL-OT* between *B-OT* and *N-OT*:

Universal Chart of SUDS Forming ME/aRe SL-OTS

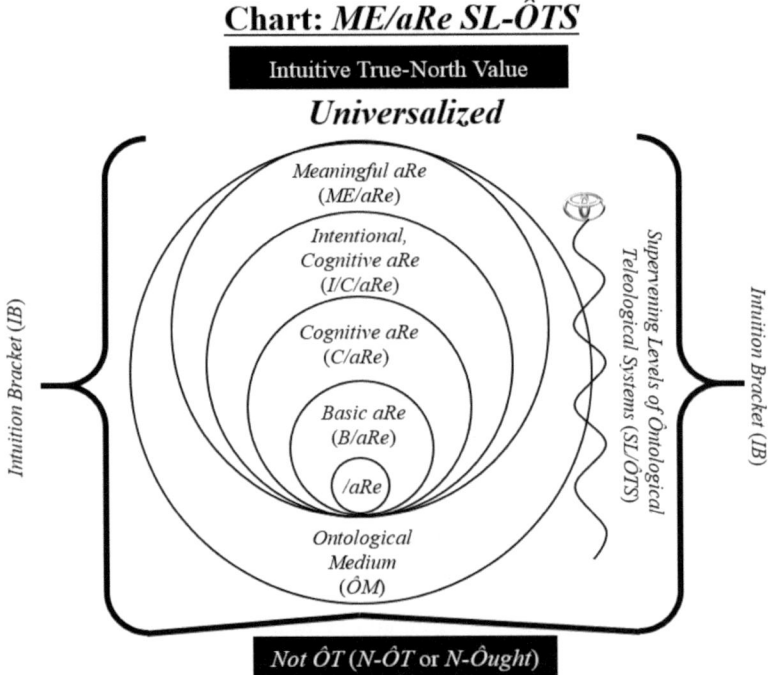

And here is another perspective on this *Chart of SUDS forming a ME/aRe SL-OT* from the top-down:

---

[544] Vlad Chituc and Paul Henne, *The Data Against Kant*, Grey Matter, New York Times (Feb. 19, 2016).

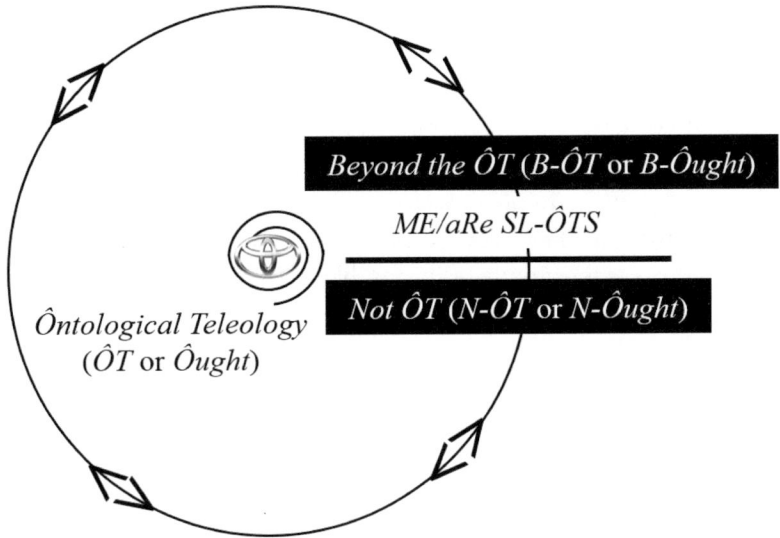

For example, thrill-seekers evidence this dynamic of trying to get *B-OT* without actually becoming *N-OT* by intentionally bringing themselves close to becoming *N-OT*. We laud thrill-seekers' bravery and zest for life for seeking *ME/aRe* meaning (unless they make the mistake and actually become *N-OT*). Those people *who* come intentionally closest to death report feeling the most alive, the most meaningful, and closest to getting *B-OT*, when they feel like they nearly became *N-OT*. Inversely, people in a state of optimal performance or flow *who* are fully part of a value stream feel themselves removed from the restrictions of the *OM* by hardly noticing *what* they are doing as if they were *N-OT* at all and yet maximally existing at the same time *as if* they were *B-OT*.

Extrapolating from *what* people witness in everyday life, I propose that maximal existence is a process toward universalization, toward consumers seamlessly resolving every problem as soon as it occurs and receiving every satisfaction as soon as desired. Or as the *Stoic* philosopher Marcus Aurelius said in ~175 CE, '*This is the chief thing: Be not perturbed, for all things are according to the nature of the universal.*[545] Maximal existence is consumers being fully aware of the problems they experience while simultaneously conscious of moving toward a hypothetical, immutable perfection of getting themselves *B-OT*. This is like /6σ approaching an infinite sigma of confidence (/σ∞) in an infinite jest,[546] which is the universalized pursuit of perfected /*aRe* processes in life and business. This is what happens to*Lean* when taken to its logical extreme. Notably, the logo for *Nissan's Infiniti*luxury division like-wise represents a stylized infinity symbol (∞) on its side:[547]

Nissan® Infiniti® Logo

Nonetheless, even if consumers achieved nearly infinite existence such as the Infiniti logo suggests they may by buying *Infiniti's* cars, they would only more fully contend with the difference of being maximally universalized within the *OM* - standing in the greatest degree of juxtaposition to*what* is*N-OT* in the*OM*. All of their infinitely strategic, unique degrees of sophist-ication wouldn't get them anywhere else other than closer to getting truly *B-OT*, *wherever* that may be.[548]

As indicated above, if consumers experienced no difference be-

---

[545] Marcus Aurelius,*The Meditations of Marcus Aurelius* , p. 56, Wisehouse (∼175 CE).

[546] In reference to, David Foster Wallace, *Infinite Jest*, Back Bay Books, 10 Anv. edition (Nov. 13, 2006). David Foster Wallace sadly committed suicide on September 12, 2008 and became*N-OT* , but hopefully he is now truly *Beyond the Ought.*

[547] *See*, the *Infiniti*® website at, http://www.infiniti.com/us/stories/our_history.html# (accessed Mar. 11, 2016).

[548] To be fully universalized is to be empty of factual content like *Hilbert Axioms*, *see*, Colin Howson and Peter Urbach, *Scientific Reasoning: A Bayesian Approach*, p. 79, *Open Court 3rd Ed.* (2005).

tween pain and pleasure, need and satisfaction, life and death, their lives might be phenomenologically indistinguishable from not being at all other than recognizing the resolution of all problems and needs in some way while simultaneously being perfectly resolved. At this event horizon where perfection is just the beginning of infinity,[549] the paradox of the *OT* arises most vividly and is *why* consumers struggle within it to find meaning outside of the *IB*. They attempt to find meaning by squaring the apparent circularity of living and existing within the *OM*, while moving upward along the *OT* through the twisting arrow of time toward *what* they believe is truly *B-Ought*. We can see this dynamic expressed by the Old Master in the ancient Chinese book *Tao Te Ching* where he said, '*Since before time and space were, the Tao is. It is beyond is and is not. How do I know this is true? I look inside myself and see.*'[550]

OT Cognitive Dissonance(*OCD*) and Meaning

> **Man thinks. God laughs.**
> – Yiddish proverb (unattributable).

Since consumers are fully conscious, self-reflexive people, consider *what* is truly meaningful to them when they decide *what* to buy, whether or not they have bracketed their beliefs about *what* is truly *B-Ought*. At the same time, consumers seem to randomly search for meaning to circumvent the apparent circularity of the *OM* by orienting themselves along the upward spiral of the *OT*, while hopefully avoiding twisting themselves into knots when doing so. Not-coincidentally, this alignment with the *OT* through the purchase of *paos* is also a means for them to more effectively self-

---

[549]David Deutsch,*The Beginning of Infinity* , p. 65 (2011).

[550]Stephen Mitchell, *Tao Te Ching*, p. 24, HarperCollins (~4th Century BCE; translated 2009).

organize themselves upward toward getting *B-Ought*. Consumers' simultaneous self-organization toward *what* they believe is *B-OT*, *wherever* that is, along with their attempt to find teleological, goal-oriented meaning, is *why* they buy *paos* for reasons beyond basic *Lean adaptation, Re-generation* and *energization*.

Thus, all three of–

1. ***The apparently paradoxical circularity of consumers optimizing their lives and existences within the OM when bounded by the IB;***
2. ***Consumers' psychological tension between What seems teleological and may be tautological; and***
3. ***Consumers dis-analogizing themselves with what is N-OT, and analogizing themselves to What they believe is B-Ought,***

– all form a type of ***Ought Cognitive Dissonance (OCD)*** as conscious be-ings that motivates customers to buy now at the point of purchase.

MEaning Means M aximum Existence

Consumers' *OT Cognitive Dissonance* caused by their recognition of the potential paradox of the *OM* within the *IB* means-tests itself as to whether or not it furthers their *Ontological Realization* upward along the twisting *OT* toward *what* they believe is *B-OT*. Thus, the concept of meaning is synonymous with orienting toward the universal and process values of the *OM* and moving upward along the *ÔT* as the great simpliciter and regulator of *what* ought to be *B-Ôught*. Meaning determines that which best enhances consumers' *I/C/aRe* processes to win life and existence upward along the *Ontological Teleology* toward an infinitely *Lean sigma* ($/\sigma\infty$).

Inversely, the *Ontological Teleology* of natural selection also applies to *what* consumers believe is *B-OT*, or *what* consumers find most meaningfully true, like their spiritual doctrines, religions and other beliefs like atheism and scientism. For example, the great religions of the world are only deemed to be so to the extent their adherents (whether or not converted by force) are viable, which is measured by their *eRas*.[551] The strongest religions do this by *U/Socially Leaning* consumers toward better self-organizing themselves onward and upward into perpetuity.[552]

From a process perspective, consumers' *ME/aRe* consciousness originates as a physical dynamic from their personal perspectives to serve that which may only be recursively identified as their further systemically *being* by proceeding upward along the *OT* within the *OM* toward *what* they believe is *B-OT*. This is like consumers most literally being a type of universal, *Ontologically Teleological paos* whose function is to disperse energy like eddies in the universal value stream into different *SUDS* forming certain further *SL-OTS* in the cauldron of all living things.[553] This is the fundamental source of the more emotional branches of environmentalism like deep ecology, which is the belief that consumers' subjective consciousness results from and is contingent on ecological systems.[554] An organization may best interact with environmental advocates like these by describing *what* it does for that scientific and scientismic relationship.

Within the *OM* as bounded by the *IB*, consciousness is a culmination of processes that result in consumers' self-reflective *i* as an identity that catalogues its physical context to more effectively exist and

---

[551] As cited earlier on this point, *see*, Yuval Noah Harari, *Sapiens*, pp. 222, 242 (2014).

[552] *Ibid* at 91 where Harari discusses *how* religion fed domestication, and at p. 210 where Harari writes, '*Yet, in fact, religion has been the third great unifier of humankind, alongside money and empires... First, [religion] must espouse a universal superhuman order that is true always and everywhere. Second, [religion] must insist on spreading this belief to everyone.*'

[553] Not to be scatological, but when you consider the amount that people drink and urinate, this analogy between consumers and eddies in a stream can become quite literal.

[554] David Deutsch, *The Beginning of Infinity*, p. 50 (2011).

perform *ME/aRe* processes. Consumers' embodiment and execution of *ME/aRe* processes is most literally a result of more effective *I/C/aRe* processes enhanced with super-self-conscious agency.

A Buy-Product of Conscious Existence is MEaning

> *People want more than just to earn a living...*
> *People want meaning. They want purpose.*
> *They want to feel like their work is*
> *making a difference in the world.*
> – John MacKay, Founder and *CEO* of Whole Foods [a]
>
> [a] *Are Companies that Value Employees More Successful?*, CBS News (Aug. 13, 2014) last found at, http://www.cbsnews.com/news/are-companies-that-value-employees-more-successful/2/.

Customers purchase *paos* as a buy-product of conscious awareness intended to further *ME/aRe* processes. They do so to increasingly get *Beyond the Ought* in contrast to *what* they know is *N-OT*.[555] This tension arises be-cause consumers debate whether a generally intelligible *Universe* can be logically self-defining and tautological. Since *ME/aRe* processes seem to be teleological within the *IB* until they are *N-OT*, consumers develop *OCD*, randomness and intuitive true-north values outside the *IB*.

The boundary of *what* is *N-OT* inside *IB* creates the apparent circularity of the *OM* within the *Universe*. Organizations providing *paos* allow consumers to consume *what* may somehow help them exceed the apparently logically tautological nature of existence within the *OM* and *IB*. *Paos* allows consumers to exist further toward a non-tautological teleology with *me*aning toward *what*

---

[555] This *ME/aRe* relates to notions of *Enactivism*.

they believe best gets them*Beyond the Ought or OT*. Thus, providing provocative *paos* allows an organization to most effectively create true-north value for consumers to make the most money the right way at consumers' points of meaningful purchase.

An analogy for this business dynamic might be a circular washer such as might be used to make a Whirlpool® washing machine. Once the circularity of a washer snaps, it creates a spring. Consumers similarly attempt to open the seemingly circular nature of the *OM* to create a value stream leading to *what* they believe is truly *B-OT*, beyond the reach of the spring-like *OT*. To the extent consumers fail to discover that end-goal, the geyser of true-north value collapses, and they fall back down to earth to try again by pursuing further universally axiomatic and processually systemic true-north values to enhance their *ME/aRe* processes within the *OM*. All *paos* ought to energize and optimize that life cycle.

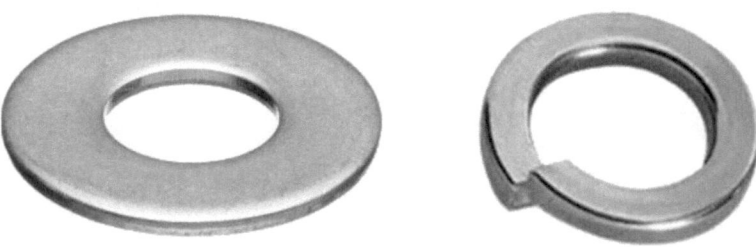

Washer to Spring(Public Domain)

Another analogy for the dynamic between seemingly circular existence and consumers' attempt to leap beyond the*OT* through their intuitive speculation at a point of purchase includes the *Penrose Triangle*. When turned in one direction, the*Penrose Triangle* shows a perfect triangle, but when turned at another angle, the *Penrose Triangle* is not connected at all at its northern most point, and much

376 Stream 5: People

like the *I/D Kata*, its circularity appears to be a mere illusion:

Penrose Triangle at the Point of Purchase(© 2007 Tobias R. (CC BY-SA 2.5))

Penrose Triangle(© 2008 Bjørn Christian Tørrissen (CC BY-SA 3.0))

Lastly, if you recall the spectrum of life from the U.S. Geological Survey, it was not a circle at all, but rather a spring of universal time delineated with organisms further *Ontologically Realizing* themselves like an arrow in a strange loop, through their various *SUDS* and *SL-OTS*, as shown again here:

Strange Loops of the U.S. Geological Survey's Value Stream (© 2008 U.S. Department of the Interior, U.S. Geological Survey (Public Domain))

ME/aRe processes simply conceptually extend this trend further into *who* , *why* , *what* and *how* consumers are as *Lean* people.

Springing Beyond the *OT*

Despite people's intrinsic motivation to find meaning up outside the *OM* and *IB*, their wish to further exist within the *OM* by pursuing axiomatic and systemic goals of *being* inside the *IB* led people to develop the philosophical concept of *Existentialism*.[556] *Existentialism* arose in the 19th and 20th centuries by focusing on

---
[556]By this I mean the modern meaning of *Existentialism* originating in the 1940s and 1950s.

the concept of a human *will* as the basis for *what* fundamentally motivates customers to buy *paos* rather than being defined by nature. *Existentialism* states that consumers fundamentally define *who* and *why* they are through their purposeful intent inherent in actually existing as *ME/aRe* organisms rather than assuming a false essence imposed on them by nature, organizations, or society. Or, as the founder of *Existentialism*, Jean-Paul Sarte, said, consumers, '...*first of all exist, encounter themselves, surge up in the world - and define themselves afterward.*'[557] I believe Sarte means, when translated into the *U/P* lexicon, that consumers teleonomically come into the fact of their being and then self-define their teleology toward best getting B-OT regardless of their situation.

One of the best known phrases of *Existentialism* is, '*Existence before Essence.*' *Existence* is the fact that consumers phenomenologically experience anything at all, while *Essence* is *how* they define their teleologies within the circumstances of their being, such as their pursuit of money to be-come rich. This phrase, '*Existence before Essence*,' means that consumers can define their own essences by *what* they will their actions to be (such as *what* they decide to buy when shopping) regardless of *how* they came to exist.[558]

Consumers' conscious autonomy allows them to self-define their essences so long as they orient themselves along the upward curve of the *OT* within the *OM* by becoming more of *who* they will themselves to be. '*Existence before Essence*' means that consumers ought to define their essences by *why, what,* and *how* they ought to be. They in-turn determine *who* they are by *why*, *what*, and *how* they consciously decide to orient their essences upward along the *OT*. Thus, consumers existentially determine *what* their essences -

---

[557] Jean-Paul Sarte, *Existentialism is Humanism* (*L'existentialisme est un humanisme*), p. 28, (1946). I obviously slightly modified this quote to make it gender neutral by using *Customers* as the pronoun and have it *Lean* philosophically.

[558] *See*, David Deutsch, *The Beginning of Infinity* , p. 359, where he says, '*Because we are universal explainers, we are not simply obeying our genes,*' which notion naturally gets reinforced now that we are able to edit our genes and determine our future ontology as a species.

and by extension their existences - will be, in-part, by consuming good *paos*.⁵⁵⁹ But by reversing the '*Existence before Essence*' process through the *Lean* concept of *Hansei*, an organization can work backwards to *I/D* consumers from *how*, *what*, *why* and ultimately *who* they are as people. This leads you to the larger point and thesis of this volume, which is that business is a philosophy inhabited with the same degree of experiential empiricism as *Existentialism*, but with the added benefit of measurement provided through monetizing market exchanges and other business indicators.⁵⁶⁰

Critically, regardless of consumers' conscious ability to define their essences, their essences will remain aligned with their existences because authentic essence always reverts back to people's *Ontological Realization* upward along the *OT* as the great regulator and simpliciter of everything within the *OM*, which is everyone's situation as we know. Consumers can only be *who* they are or that which makes them further be within the *OM* when bracketed by the *IB*, which ultimately defines their essential natures however they will them to be along the *Ontological Teleology*. However, from the blank slate of consumers' will to live and exist regardless of *what* they were born as or become along the *OT*, their self-determined actions create all identity and meaning for them. The volume of the meaning a *paos* produces in-turn depends on whether customers feel it led their identities toward *what* they believe is *B-OT*, or whether they feel remorse for buying *paos* because it did not provide true-north value.⁵⁶¹

---

⁵⁵⁹Or as stated by John Locke in *Book III, Essay Concerning Human Understanding*, Ch. 6, Para. 4., '[N]othing essential to individuals. That essence, in the ordinary use of the word, relates to sorts, and that it is considered in particular beings no further than as they are ranked into sorts, appears from hence: that, take but away the abstract ideas by which you sort individuals, and rank them under common names, and then the thought of anything essential to any of them instantly vanishes: you have no notion of the one without the other, which plainly shows their relation.'

⁵⁶⁰As proposed by Iris Murdoch when she said,... *a moral philosophy must be inhabited*... as she and many other philosophers did through fiction, *see*, Anne Rowe, *Iris Murdoch: A Reassessment*, Hampshire: Palgrave Macmillan (2007).

⁵⁶¹*See generally*, the Stanford Encyclopædia of Philosophy entry on, '*Existentialism*.'

While you ought to explain the satisfaction customers receive from different scientific perspectives within the *OM*, their existences still transcend science's total explanatory power, which is limited to the *OM* within the *IB*. Thus, the meaning consumers create for themselves by moving along the upward curve of the *OT* by purchasing *paos* occurs not only within the*OM*, but also in relation to *what* consumers may intuitively speculate is truly Beyond the *OT* and all reason. From the *Existentialist* perspective, consumers' existences and ultimate satisfaction can only be fully understood by stepping away from the confines of axiomatic and systemic truths and empathetically experiencing all of the very real*OPPortunities* and*Threats* to*who*,*why*,*what* and *how* consumers are or perceive themselves to be even if the ultimate source of the *OPPortunities* and*Threats* is still undefined.[562]

Consumers' Hall of Mirrors

> *Number determinate is kept concealed....*
> *The height behold now and*
> *the amplitude Of the eternal power,*
> *since it hath made Itself so many mirrors,*
> *where 'tis broken, One in itself remaining as before.*
> – Dante Alighieri,*The Divine Comedy, Paradiso, XXIX*, 130-145 (1320)

You might analogize the concept of '*Phenomenology*' to a method of navigation where consumers feel their way around a room with

---

[562] *Ibid*, where the Stanford Encyclopædia of Philosophy says, '*...human existence can be adequately explained in terms of the fundamental physical constituents of the universe. Existentialism does not deny the validity of the basic categories of physics, biology, psychology, and the other sciences (categories such as matter, causality, force, function, organism, development, motivation, and so on). It claims only that human beings cannot be fully understood in terms of them*' (accessed Jul. 13, 2013).

their eyes closed, experiencing each object simply as it is rather than judging *how* it got there, *what* it is, *why* it is there, or *whoever* put it there. You might extend that analogy of *Phenomenology* to *Existentialism*, except now, like engaging in the *Lean* process of *Hansei*, imagine consumers standing in a hall of mirrors looking at their many reflections. Think of *Existentialism* as being like infinitely many *iPhones* shining back at them in an *Apple* store, showing different versions of themselves without any clear way forward except *how* they will themselves to authentically be.[563] Your engaging in *Hansei* by studying this hall of mirrors reflecting each consumer's personal situation provides you with the freedom to decide whether to go in one business direction or another and thereby discover which path might lead you to a commercial breakthrough.

Apple Store Hall of Mirrors on Fifth Avenue, NYC (© 2006 Ed Uthman, MD (CC SSA 2.5))

Imagine further that each of these mirrors represents a different aca-

---

[563]For the source and general background of this, I recommend, William Barrett,*Irrational Man: A Study in Existential Philosophy*, Kindle Loc. 4533, Anchor Books/Doubleday (1990).

demic discipline - such as natural science, psychology, philosophy, the arts, & c. - or some such other *Ontologically Realized* aspect of consumer's individual existences, such as their family, occupation, geography, and/or other demographic. No single direct or indirect academic or demographic reflection of consumers as represented by these disciplines or data would ever completely capture *what* or *how* consumers actually experience life and existence. Thus, such representations could never fully reflect *who* and *why* they are within this hall of -isms, labels and ideologies undulating across these placid mirrors. Consumers' lives and existences cannot be reduced to any combination of concepts and can only be completely understood from the inside-out by actually *being* within consumers' own phenomenologically experienced *Ontological Teleology* that acts in juxtaposition to *what* is *N-OT* and *what* consumers intuitively believe is *B-OT*. This is an act of utmost commercial empathy.

> ***To be is to be perceived.***
> - George Berkeley (1710)

Look at this picture of a Yayoi Kusama art installation and phenomenologically empathize with the woman shown on the right looking at her infinitely reflected self by considering *who*, *why*, *what* and *how* she wants to be through all she sees herself as being:

Tony Kyriacou (photographer), Yayoi Kusama (artist),*Smoke and Mirrors* (© 2013 Rex Features (Used with Permission))

However, note that the man at the center of the photo looking at her through his camera lens has stripped her of some authenticity since she is now in-part defined by *what* he perceives her to be.[564] Exactly *what* she perceives his perception to be, such as *beautiful*, *professional*, *young*, or *old*, may change *how* she perceives herself in front of the mirrors at stores, unless she maintains an authentic self-conception of *who* she is.

On the Shoulders of People *Who* aReN-OT

> *Poor man wanna be rich,*
> *Rich man wanna be king,*
> *And a king ain't satisfied,*
> *'til he rules everything.*

---

[564] The photographer Tony Kyriacou naturally had no inention to do so, and simply took a beautiful photograph. Kyriacou sadly died at a much too young age of 36 on March 28, 2013.

> - Bruce Springsteen, *Badlands, Darkness on the Edge of the Town* (1978)

The *human will* in all of its variety that the woman and photographer reflect in the conceptual hall of mirrors above is synonymous in some respects with consumers orienting themselves with the universal and process values of the *OM* and moving their personal perspectives along the upward curve of the *OT* based on *how* they define themselves and *how* they wish to be perceived.

Human existential will is in fact consumers' lives and existences expressing the *OT* in real time in all these ways through their thoughts, actions, deeds and creeds. For some intellectual context, this *Stream 5* will now very briefly review the thoughts of some of the greatest philosophical thinkers about *why* consumers are wilfully motivated to buy *paos*. *Stream 5* will then contrast their thoughts with a new ontological classification for human motivation. These great, but dead, philosophers include Arthur Schopenhauer, Søren Kierkegaard, Friedrich Nietzsche, Adler, Sigmund Freud and Victor Frankl. Collectively, they said that because of *who* and *why* consumers are, consumers have a will to live, a will to power, a will to pleasure, a will to meaning, and quite possibly a tautological will to will within the *OM* and *IB* that ultimately drives them to buy now at consumers' most meaningful point of purchase. Here is a summary of what each th-ought:

Will to Live - Shopenhauer

When Arthur Schopenhauer published, *The World as Will and Representation* in 1818, Schopenhauer became one of the first philosophers to describe human will as an irrational act.[565] As Robert Wicks writes in the Stanford Encyclopædia of Philosophy:

> *Schopenhauer's particular characterization of the world as Will, is nonetheless novel and daring. It is also frightening and pandemonic: he maintains that the world as it is in itself (again, sometimes adding 'for us') is an endless striving and blind impulse with no end in view, devoid of knowledge, lawless, absolutely free, entirely self-determining and almighty.*[566]

Schopenhauer thus described the human, '*Will to Live*,' as the most important aspect of *who* consumers are and *why* they buy *paos*.[567] The *Ontological Teleology* similarly orients itself with this *Will to Live* by like-wise advancing consumers' lives and existences with increasing sophist-ication within the *Ontological Medium*, *IB* and *Universe*.

Will to Power- Nietzsche / Adler

Inspired by Schopenhauer's phrase *Will to Live*, Friedrich Nietzsche and subsequently Alfred Adler advocated that the fundamental basis of consumers' motivation to go shopping is a, '*Will to Power*.' As noted by philosopher William Barrett, Nietzsche is first understood to have come up with the concept of *Will to Power* when as a

---

[565] As Robert Wicks in the Stanford Encyclopædia of Philosophy says, '[F]or Schopenhauer, this is not the principle of self-consciousness and rationally-infused will, but is rather what he simply calls 'Will' — a mindless, aimless, non-rational urge at the foundation of our instinctual drives, and at the foundational being of everything. Schopenhauer's originality does not reside in his characterization of the world as Will, or as act — for you encounter this position in Fichte's philosophy — but in the conception of Will as being devoid of rationality or intellect' (accessed Dec. 4, 2012).

[566] *Ibid.*

[567] Arthur Schopenhauer, *The World as Will and Representation* (1818); Nicolus Humphrey, *Soul Dust* (2011).

hospital orderly, '[d]uring the Franco-Prussian War...he saw one evening his old regiment ride by, going into battle and perhaps to death, and it came to him then that 'the strongest and highest will to life does not lie in the puny struggle to exist, but in the Will to war, the Will to Power.'[568] But critically, Barrett continues, '[i]t is a mistake to locate the birth of this idea in any single [phenomenological] experience; it was, in fact, fed by a number of tributary streams...'[569] The bodybuilder, actor and politician, Arnold Schwarzenegger, further expressed this *Will to Power* when he wrote, '*The meaning of life is not simply to exist, to survive, but to move ahead, to go up, to achieve, to conquer.*'[570] Notice that to move ahead, Schwarzenegger felt he needed to go up as well.

The *Ontological Teleology* reflects this *Will to Power* by re-cognizing that all people seek more than mere existence, by seeking to universally energize as well. Customers advance along the upward curve of the *Ontological Teleology* by *Leanly* adapting, Re-generating, and significantly, *energizing*. The *Will to Power* is thus the will to universalize or become all that people will be, whether that is Franconian, Prussian, or European. For a recent, corporate example of this, the *Über* car service has energetically expanded and entered global markets in order to dominate the local transportation industries at those locales to optimize their own profits so they may have greater power to re-direct the flow of Matter and Energy anywhere you may go.

---

[568] William Barret, *Irrational Man*, p. 197 (1958).

[569] *Ibid.*

[570] Arnold Schwarzenegger, *Arnold: Education of a Bodybuilder*, p. 112, Simon & Schuster (1977).

®Über Technologies Inc.

Will to Pleasure- Freud

Sigmund Freud, arguing past Nietzsche, said that the basis of life was a '*Will to Pleasure.*'[571] In a famous intellectual split, Alfred Adler adhered to the Nietzschean perspective that the *Will to Power* was consumers' primary motivator for living and shopping, while Freud held that sexuality and Eros, or the *Will to Pleasure* , are *what* fundamentally drives them to consume. From *U / P's* perspective, the hedonistic *Will to Pleasure* is simply the need to *Lean* toward *Regeneration* as well as *adaptation* and *energization* to universalize overall.[572] So in a way, they are both right.

Will to Meaning- Kierkegaard / Frankl

Søren Kierkegaard, by inversely describing levels of despair, distinctly argued that a '*Will to Meaning*' fundamentally motivates consumers to live, exist and purchase good *paos* to intentionally increase their juxtaposition with *what* is *N-OT* toward *what* they speculate is most truly *B-OT*.[573] However, Victor Frankl, after surviving as a captive in a Nazi concentration camp, extended this notion to create a school of psychoanalysis based partly on this intuitive belief in *Meaning* called *Logotherapy.*[574] Frankl with his

---

[571]Sigmund Freud, *Beyond the Pleasure Principle*(1922).

[572]William Barret, *Irrational Man* p. 199 (1958).

[573]Or most specifically for me, Søren Kierkegaard's psuedonym *Johannes de Silentio* (John of the Silence) in, *Fear and Trembling*(1849), where his levels of dispair may be seen as a binary inversion of the, *Will to Meaning* .

[574]Viktor Frankl,*Man's Search for Meaning* , Beacon Press (1946); Viktor Frankl,*The Will to Meaning: Foundations and Applications of Logotherapy*, New American Library, (1988).

388 Stream 5: People

book,*Man's Search for Meaning* , advanced the idea that all people ought to self-organize their lives around this quest for meaning.

Like the *Will to Live* , the *Ontological Teleology* orients itself with the *Will to Meaning* by increasing the effectiveness of consumers /aRe processes, which moves consumers further along the upward curve of the *OT*. Such movement is the effective difference between *who* consumers are and *what* is *N-OT*, and is essential to all meaning within the *IB*. However, critically, once you remove the *IB*, the *Ontological Teleology* becomes non-circular, and the *OT* then springs forth to allow consumers to find meaning by self-organizing toward *what* they intuitively speculate is truly *B-OT*. Such speculation of *what* may be truly *B-OT* includes a deity, spirit, speculative scientific theory, or simply a sense of the unknown, even though universal axioms and systemic processes will still regulate the *Ontological Realization* of their intuitive speculation so long as consumers exist within the *OM* .

Will to Will- Nietzsche

Nietzsche moved beyond his *Will to Power* to describe it synonymously as the '*Will to Will*' when he wrote, '*There is absolutely no other kind of causality than that of will upon will. Not explained mechanistically.*'[575] I believe this passage from Nietzsche of, '*will upon will,*' reflects Nietzsche's agreement to some extent with the apparently tautological nature of the *Ontological Teleology* that motivates consumers to further live, exist, *adapt, Re-generate* and *energize* within the *OM* .[576]

Thus, each of these classic *wills* ultimately orients consumers upward along the *OT* within the *OM* in juxtaposition to *what* is *N-OT* on an axiomatic or systemic basis, which may be truly, intuitively *B-OT*. Meaning for consumers gets made in the effective difference between *what* is axiomatically or processually *N-OT*,

---
[575] Friedrich Nietzsche, *Will to Power* , p. 658 (1885).
[576] William Barret, *Irrational Man*, p. 200 (1958).

and *what* consumers intuitively speculate is *B-OT*. The rest is just infinitely granular detail toward living and existing between those end-goals. The *OT* requires an organization to honestly differentiate between axiomatic, systemic and intuitive true-north values to best determine *what* consumers will find truly meaningful in their lives and existences, and *why* they may buy right now by reaching a point of purchase.

Thus, whether an organization's leaders believe in scientism, spiritualism or theism, all business organizations must assume a possible *Will to Will*, which is intellectually agnostic toward ultimate meaning by recognizing the possibility of either:

1. ***A self-defining cause of the Universe and the OM;*** or
2. ***A non-circular cause of the Universe and OM currently based on intuitive truth values with varying degrees of coherence with axiomatic and systemic truth values.***[577]

Both of these possibilities are truly valuable in their own ways in business. If atheistic business people are publicly agnostic, they thereby recognize other people's intuitive truths as they experience them. If theistic business people are also publicly agnostic, they thereby recognize the speculation inherent in intuitive truths about deities, spirits or *whatever* may be *B-OT*. Each type of public agnosticism is valid as long as each is applied within the overlapping consensus that legal systems generally determine for all workplaces present in space-time in liberal societies. I re-emphasize this collective agnosticism not to take a personal position on either atheism, theism or agnosticism (or scientism), but rather to restate the intellectual reality about the nature of *me* aning within the *OT* for an organization to intuit, infer, induce and deduce true-north value at consumers' points of purchase around the *I/D Kata*.

---

[577] *See*, for some further discussion the remarks of Keith DeRose, a professor of philosophy at Yale University, at *The Case for Contextualism: Knowledge, Skepticism, and Context*, Oxford University Press; Reprint edition (2011); and *Why Take a Stance on God?*, The Opinionator, New York Times (Sep. 18, 2014).

Opportunities and *Threats* as Binary *SW-ÔT* Analysis

Now that you very briefly reviewed some of the main intellectual concepts identifying *what* wills consumers to buy from organizations, return now to the universal *Chart of SL-OTS* below, with consumers contingently residing within the *OM* between universalized, immutable perfection of *what* may be *B-OT* and *what* is *N-OT*. Consumers greedily seize *OPPs* through their *Strengths* and shore up their *Weaknesses* against their fear of *Threats* . You can now perceive consumers as living in a *Universe* delineated by the *IB* between these existential extremes and within the physical *OM*, striving each day to more perfectly execute *ME/aRe* processes through constant, very personal *SW-ÔT* analysis. Here is a universal chart with *OPPortunities* and *Threats* standing in for the emotions of greedy gains and fearful pains along the *Ontological Teleology*:

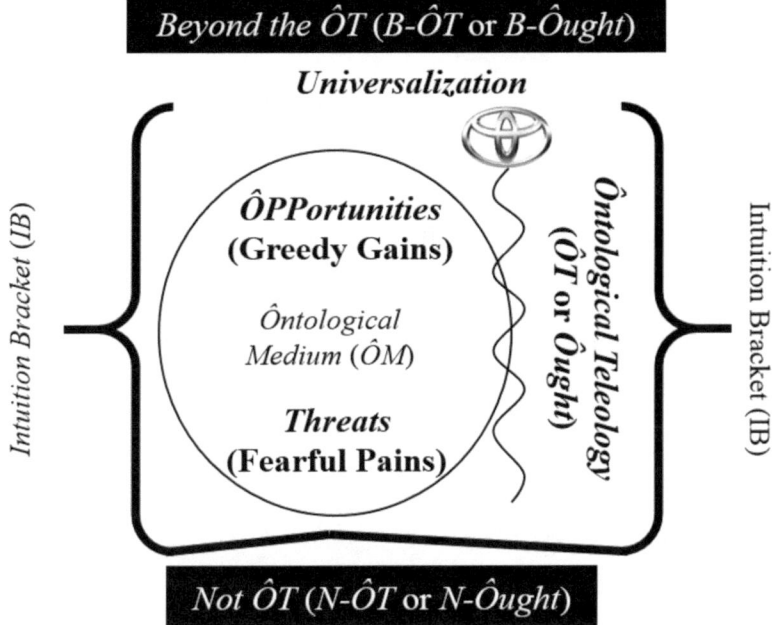

People in their own existences, however essentially defined, will themselves toward life (Arthur Schopenhauer), power (Friedrich Nietzsche / Alfred Adler), pleasure (Sigmund Freud), meaning (Søren Kierkegaard / Victor Frankl), and possibly tautological will (Friedrich Nietzsche). All are in fact correct since people act to perpetuate and expand their existences against these *OPPs* and *Threats* in binary opposition between them along the upward, spiralling arrow of the *OT* toward *what* may be universally *B-OT*. From this perspective, the might of a person's purchasing power does make right,[578] but only so long as such buying power gets distributed in such a way that it systemically universalizes sophistication overall upward along the *OT* for all people. Some wealthy individuals do that well, and some do not, and society ought to ensure that that power does not consolidate across Re-generations

---

[578] *See*, Yuval Noah Harari, *Sapiens*, p. 206 (2014) in discussing the challenge of cultural inheritance adopted by force.

for no good reason.

*WE/aRe*Normatively Valuing Supervening Conceptual Structures

I consolidate the various strains of thought mentioned above as a collective, '*Will to Exist*,' as a, 'Wholly Existential,' and possibly tautological movement along the upward curve of the *OT* staying within the boundaries of the *OM* and *IB*. The wholly existential *WE/aRe* processes expand and perpetuate consumers' existences, and these processes constitute the *true-north value*consumers find in business.[579]

The critically important point of understanding consumers' normative true-north value is *how* one logically discovers the real value consumers actually purchase and for which they push their money back down to an organization in ex-change. You discover true-north value through the filter of consumers' individual situations defined by their specific geographies, genders, ages, ethnicities, nationalities, and so on that either provide*Ontologically Prospective Projects* or*Threaten who* they wish to will themselves to essentially be. These essential, ontological factors constitute some of the first parameters of true-north value for which people actually buy*paos* . These factors help an *HQ* become more grounded, less abstract, more specifically focused on *how* to *Re-generate* true-north value for money.

*WE/aRe*Willing to Existentially Optimize

At the point where existential logic starts to tautologically fold back on itself, and consumers develop*Ought Cognitive Dissonance* , they

---

[579] *WE/aRe* also represents notions of multi-level group selection in evolution such as that proposed by E.O. Wilson.

pursue a greater distinction between *what* is *N-OT*, and *what* they think is *B-OT*. Consumers thereby create meaning in the collective difference by contrasting *who* and *why* they think they are with *what* is *N-OT*.

While the *OM* operates within the bounds of the *Universe* and *IB* at the highest levels of self-organization, society and organizations are still faced with the apparent paradox of the *OT*. They strive to self-define their collective *Will to Exist* and attempt to leap beyond the *OM's* apparent tautology to get beyond the *IB*. Thus, just like for *ME/aRe* processes, consumers perpetuate themselves by creating and defining *who* and *why* they collectively are through *WE/aRe* processes in the juxtaposition to *what* is *N-OT* and toward *what* they believe is *B-OT*, *whatever* their applicable cultural, legal, ethical and institutional standards in which they live and exist. Here is the more sophisticated *Universal Chart of SUDS Forming WE/aRe SL-OTS* to show this verisimilitude:

Universal Chart of SUDS Forming WE/aRe SL-OTS

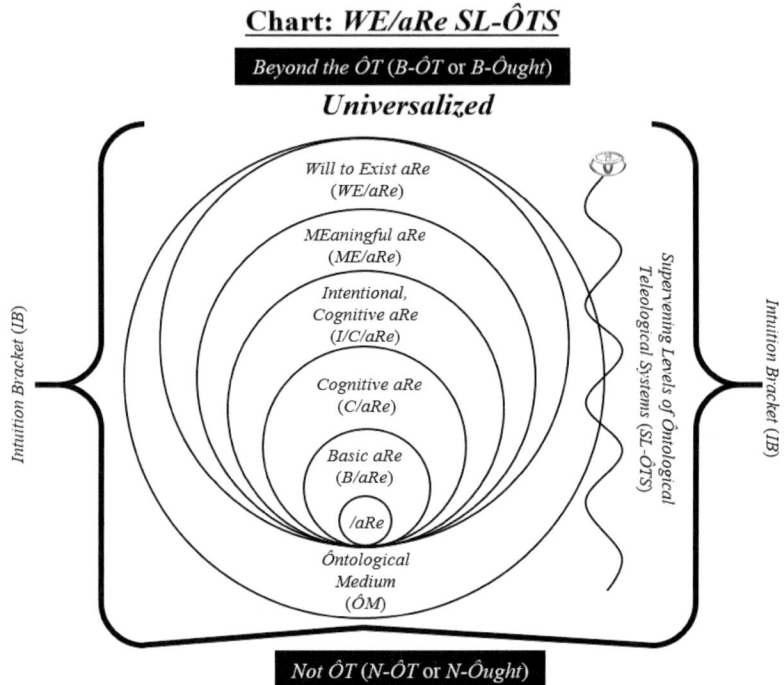

All of these various forms of will - the will to *Life, Power, Pleasure, Meaning* and *Will* - reflect different aspects of life and existence. For *what* is a will to life, power, pleasure, meaning, or will than the holistic, '*Will to Exist*,' which is to exist to an even greater universal extent in the ultimate juxtaposition to *what* is *N-OT*? Consumers further self-organize around *what* they intuitively speculate is *B-OT* and *how* they may upwardly, *Ontologically Realize* themselves by orienting themselves with the *OT* toward complete universalization. Here is a diagram from top down of the seeming *WE/aRe* circularity that consumers attempt to circum-vent:

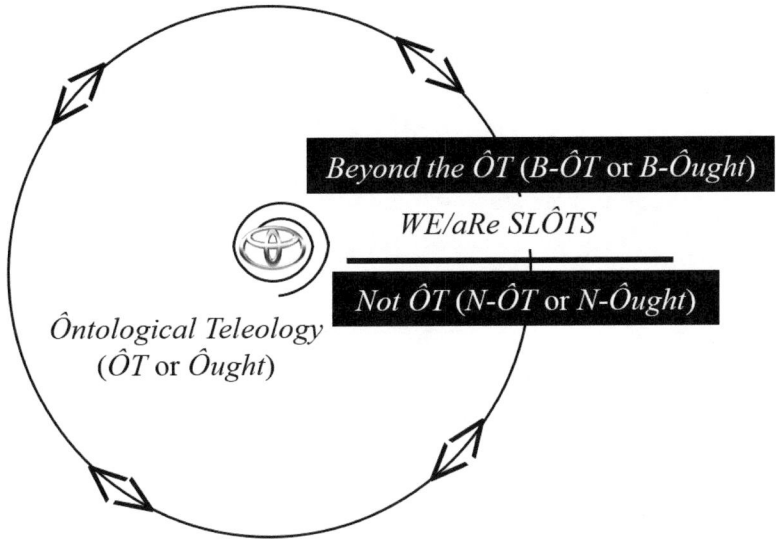

Seeming WE/aRe Circularity

While Nietzsche's '*Will to Power*' misses the *OM*'s apparently circular nature within the *IB*, his, '*Will to Will*,' hits the tautological mark. That which one has power over incorporates the dominated into his or her own definition of *who* one is in relation to *what* one believes is *N-OT* and may be truly *B-OT*. This then logically leads consumers to the apparent paradox and cognitive dissonance of living and existing in alignment with the *OM* while upwardly moving along the *OT* toward possibly circular ends. Freud's, '*Will to Pleasure*,' identifies *how* consumers' hedonistic experiences and remembered memories of those experiences expand both *what* they experience and *what* they remember, but again they themselves eventually seem to become self-defining through their ontological titillation as a means to *Re-generate* through off-spring.[580]

Victor Frankl's, '*Will to Meaning*' attempts to resolve consumers' *Ought Cognitive Dissonance* by helping them intuit some non-

---

[580] As applicable to those concepts proposed by Daniel Kahneman in *Thinking, Fast and Slow*, p. 14 (2011).

circular teleology outside the *IB*. However, since consumers can only speculatively intuit a non-circular teleology, the more rational among them will still struggle to faithfully believe in any meaning that a *paos* may provide. Still, their collective, '*Will to Exist*' provides moments of true-north value for them and makes money meaningfully for you as shown again here in this chart from *Stream 2*:

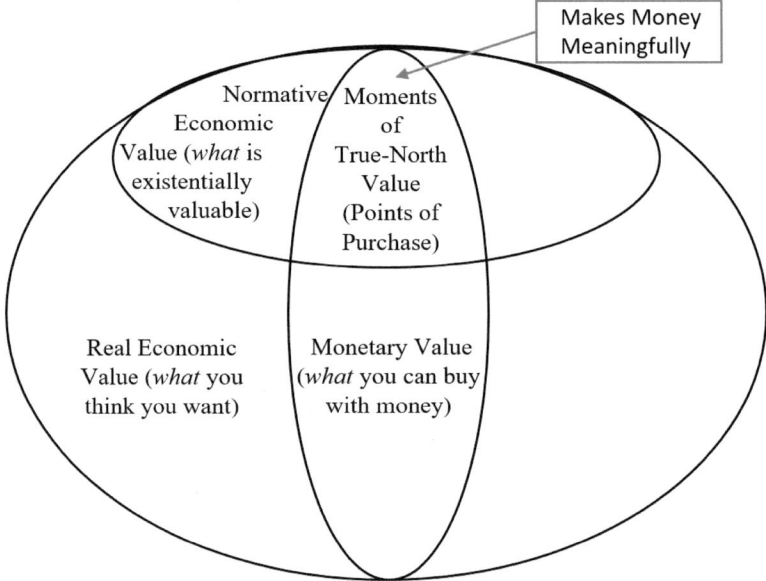

Chart of Moments of True-North Value

Consumers innately express their *Will to Exist* by progressing upward along the *OT*, which thereby creates the monetary true-north value that an organization makes when consumers buy a *paos* to try and universalize themselves. An organization makes money meaningfully through all that it gets *b-ought* and sold that aligns consumers' *WE/aRe* processes with the *OM*. Organizational meaning comes from helping consumers try to move along the upward curve of the *OT* toward true universalization. The *WE/aRe* processes that a *paos* energizes and optimizes within consumers get defined to the extent they aligned consumers with the *OM*, moving them upward along the *OT*, to ultimately try and universalize their *eRas*, *IDs*, egos and super-egos.

WE/aRe processes thus synthesize value-based *Utilitarianism* and rule-based universal ethics by aligning *what* consumers like with *what* they ought to have bought, since the *OT* is the great simpliciter and regulator of all true-north value within the *OM*.[581] By applying *WE/aRe* processes to business and the creation of normatively true and real cash value, you can see *U/P*'s application within many of the most thriving organizations today: from organic growceries being sold to support people's vitality, to corporate social responsibility initiatives selling *paos* by appealing to consumers' broad need to more effectively engage in *WE/aRe* processes with all people, however needy they may be.

To *Lean* toward consumers the right way, you ought to increase the true-north value and the volume of the *paos* consumers buy by monetizing their normative and real values elucidated through the *3WH who, why, what,* and *how* value stream. An organization must enhance consumers' true-north values by optimizing *OPPs* or reducing *Threats* to *WE/aRe* processes. In a perfectly competitive environment, an organization can make the most meaningful margin in Porter's Generic Value Chain by providing *paos* that helps consumers *Will to Exist* through *WE/aRe* processes that should resolve their *Ought Cognitive Dissonance* through meaningful consumption. For-profit companies' with charitable associations and social good efforts try to do just that.

> *When all these pieces come together,*
> *not only does your work move toward greatness,*
> *but so does your life.*

---

[581]Stated another way, although factual evidence and moral maxims are logically independent, factual and moral explanations are not, which is why they are intertwined within the *OT*; *see*, David Deutsch, *The Beginning of Infinity*, p. 120 (2011).

> *For, in the end, it is impossible to have a great life
> unless it is a meaningful life.
> And it is very difficult to have a meaningful life
> without meaningful work.
> Perhaps, then, you might gain that rare tranquillity
> that comes from knowing that
> you've had a hand in creating something
> of intrinsic excellence that makes a contribution.
> Indeed, you might even gain
> that deepest of all satisfactions:
> knowing that your short time
> here on this earth
> has been well spent,
> and that it mattered.*
> - Jim Collins, *Good to Great* (2011) [a]
>
> ---
> [a] Jim Collins, *Good to Great*, Kindle Loc. 3387-3388 (2011).

U/aRe Forming Micro, Meso and Macro Economic, Political and Cultural Structures

To that end, consumers are to some extent already moving from an ethic of individualized *ME/aRe* to one of a holistic *WE/aRe*, and eventually to a singular *Will to Universalize* (*U/aRe*). The universal, universalization ethic asks whether universalizing such actions also deontologically universalizes *U/aRe* processes overall. Thus, *U/aRe* is the next and highest meta-economic *SL-OT* above *WE/aRe* processes within and in-part outside of the known *Universe*. Critically for your business consideration, *U/aRe* processes get *B-Ought* because they in part transcend the known *OM*. Like when consumers create *ME/aRe* meaning by consuming good *paos*, *U/aRe* processes essentially self-define consumers' teleology toward consumption. Here is the inclusion of the most upwardly sophisticated, and yet seemingly hypothetical *Universal Chart of SUDS Forming U/aRe SL-OTS* here:

Universal Chart of SUDS Forming U/aRe SL-OTS

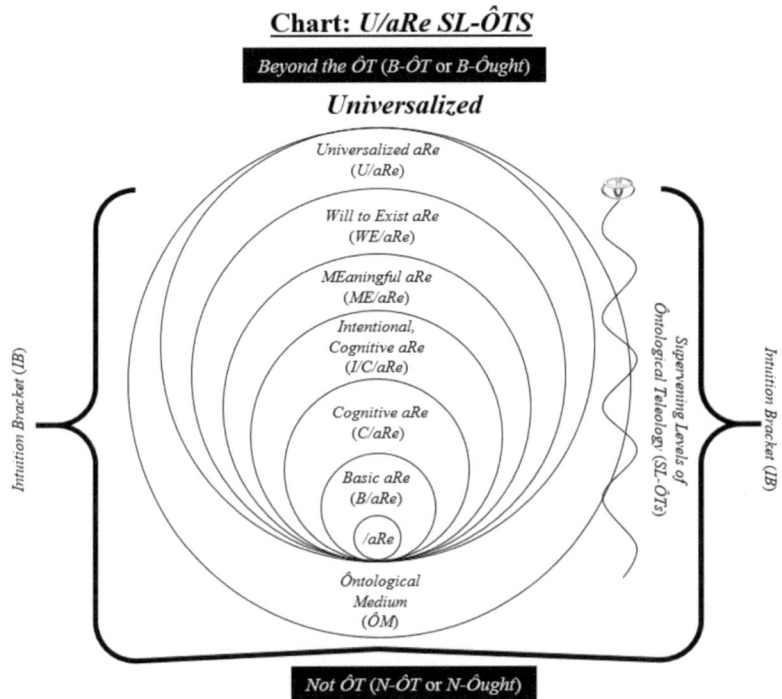

Customers, their families and all humankind self-organize supervening economic and political structures in order to universalize /aRe processes better through consumption. The more that consumers form micro, meso, and macro-economic and political *SL-OTS* the more these *SL-OTS* supervene on and support the lives of consumers, their kin, their species, and all true-north value. Consumers optimize themselves through these conceptual *SL-OTS*

to *Leanly adapt*, *Re-generate* and *energize* in contrast to *what* they and their societies k*now* is *N-Ought* and believe is *B-Ought* beyond the curvature of space-time. These conceptual *SL-OTS* that consumers develop through their personal perspectives get ontologically means-tested to the extent they align with the *Ontological Medium* to move all people upward along the *Ontological Teleology*. For example, *Lean* itself is a conceptual *SL-OT* whose success and self-perpetuating existence is based on its ability to improve business performance that in-turn supports the economic advancement of society. These supervening business, economic and/or political ideologies *Leanly adapt, Re-generate* and *energize*, or they likewise become altogether *N-OT*.

U/aRe Controlling Their Ontology and Ethics

> *Who controls the past now controls the future.*
> *Who controls the present now controls the past.*
> *Who controls the past now controls the future.*
> *Who controls the present now?*
> - Rage Against the Machine, *Testify* (2000)

Consumers' *Will to Universalize /aRe* processes is that which *paos* ought to be increasing by universalizing the depth and breadth of consumers' lives and existences, of *who*, *why*, *what* and *how* they are. However, do *U/aRe* processes have any commercial limits? Let's conduct a crazy thought experiment to ponder this beautiful question in the deepest way possible:

Presume that while Earth could not hold any more consumers, a bio-engineering firm could genetically engineer with the CRISPR gene editing technique other consumers *who* could live and breathe on Mars unaided. Presume that since the firm's government wants to promote economic advancement, it is willing to pay the firm

401

to *Re-generate* those consumers *who* could live on Mars in order to stake out that new market. If a firm did re-produce these Martian consumers, it would be enhancing its government's ability to perform *U/aRe* processes on that other planet by universalizing consumers' ability to live and exist somewhere further out in the *OM*.[582]

- *If those genetically engineered people could not live on Earth without special breathing apparatus, should an organization Re-generate those other consumers as a form of *paos for its government?**
- *What about the Re-generated, customized consumers who can only live unaided on Mars and not Earth? Has the organization violated those people's fundamental rights to live easily on Earth even if they never would have lived anyway?*
- *Has an ethical limit toward universalizing consumers' /aRe processes for a profit been reached?*

Kepler 186-F(hypothetical environment) (Credit: NASA Ames/SETI Institute/JPL-CalTech (Public Domain))

---

[582] *See for further discussion*, David Deutsch, *The Beginning of Infinity* , p. 59 (2011).

In essence, an organization would define these Martian consumers' collective ontology prospectively so that future Martian generations would have the very genesis of their *Ontological Realizations* quite specifically determined. If people as a whole could control the form and shape of their ontology here on Earth as well - re-producing themselves as a form of *paos* - then people as a whole would assume ontological responsibility for their future selves. They will prospectively create their existences in the image of their own true-north values, which will define their essential meaning within the *IB*. Doing so would leave far less to chance for people's *Ontological Realization* and *what* people find truly valuable because their being would be pre-defined by them. Would future pre-defined people rather have never lived so long as people today provided them with their existences, the very essence of all their true-north value within the *OM* and *IB*? This hypothetical is very real since genetic experiments occurring right now as I write this book are leading to this result. This science will reverberate across history because this issue is so fundamental to all true-north value and the ability to make meaningful amounts of money across all industries.

Since people will be able to determine their collective *Ontological Realization* and future selves, planning a-head, an *HQ* must know *what* it ought to do to best orient consumers' self-defined ontologies upward along the *OT* to re-produce that true-north value.[583] This future will almost certainly realize itself because the ontological rewards for enhancing *U/aRe* processes in future generations are so ontologically rewarding. For example, should companies in some rogue nation greatly succeed in enhancing *U/aRe* processes by engineering people through eugenics (or "U/Genics"), it will force other nations to do so as well due to the *OPPtimistic*, greedy nature of the *OT* in contrast to fearful *Threats* of becoming *N-OT*. The *OT* cares nothing about the non-OT ethical considerations. The *OT* only rewards that which best progresses people *U/Socially* upward along the *OT* to the extent their *Lean* adaptive, Re-generative

---

[583] Michael Specter, *The Gene Factory*, p. 34, The New Yorker, (Jan. 6, 2014).

and energetic processes are most meaningfully effective against becoming *N-OT* within their respective social bubbles.

For one constraint on this extreme *U/aRe* process of eugenic modification, consider the problems people would face if an organization could control consumers' future ontology to the *n*th degree. That organization would still need to randomly test *what* best optimized consumers against a *Universe* of ontological possibilities. It would still need to optimize consumers through randomized natural selection, mutation, and other evolutionary processes to discover *how* to *best fit* consumers to their environments in ways it could not possibly predict. The reason *why*, is because pseudo-random matching of men and women leads to pseudo-random gene interactions, which in-turn may or may not teleonomically discover *who* is best *Ontologically Realized* within the *OM*, but can lead to unexpected greatness. Mating, mutation and natural selection are legitimate, mathematical processes searching for the most persistent *Ontological Realizations* against an unknown domain of *OPPortunities*.

This example of genetically modifying future customers as a form of *paos* illustrates that the *OT* simpliciter always applies to an organization's teleological planning and Re-generating meaningful amounts of money even at its most extreme. This also exemplifies an organization's teleonomic discovery of *what* best energizes and optimizes consumers' lives and existences through iteratively market testing that which is ontologically reinforcing. Moving consumers upward into more sophisticated *SL-OTS* within the *OM* as their own form of *paos* is the only commercial limit to energizing and optimizing *U/aRe* processes within the *IB*. However, universally controlling consumers' *U/aRe* processes may ultimately not be the most *Ontologically Teleological* method since it would most likely not discover *who* best fits within the *Universe* in the current context. True commercial breakthroughs are usually the unanticipated, teleonomic consequences of teleological para-scientific investigation.[584] Creating a model consumer involves some random variables and is not deterministic.

U/aRe Universalizing Consumers' Will to Exist

As an organization strives to universalize *who* its customers are with the *paos* it produces, it must search for and find that which best moves consumers toward *what* they speculate is *B-OT* and away from *what* is *N-OT*.[585] To truly universalize *who* consumers are toward this perceived perfection in a state of being Beyond the *OT*, *B-OT* or *B-Ought*, you must attempt to converge their speculative intuitions and physical processes and make them synonymous with the *Universe* itself, however impossible or undesirable that end-goal may be.

While you never want consumers to get fully *B-OT* because you would have left nothing for them to buy, you must still try to fully *Lean* consumers' lives and existences toward getting *B-OT*, toward a *Lean* infinite sigma ($/\sigma\infty$) such that they become perfected, which

---

[584] *See generally*, J. Mokyr and F. Scherer, *Twenty five centuries of technological change: an historical survey*, Vol. 35, Routledge (1990); *see also*, Kenneth Stanley, Joel Lehman, *Why Greatness Cannot Be Planned: The Myth of the Objective*, Springer International Publishing (2015).

[585] You might consider the *Universalization* of our *Will to Exist* a form of *poiesis*, which as described by Robert Cavalier commenting on Plato's recollection of Socrates's story of the high priestess Diotima in *The Symposium, The Effects of Eros* (204d — 212a), poiesis is, '... *how mortals strive for immortality. In all begetting and bringing forth upon the beautiful there is a kind of making or poiesis ("poetry" in the wide sense of "creating"). In this genesis (GREEK) there is a movement beyond the temporal cycle of birth and decay (207d). Such a movement can occur in three kinds of poiesis: (1) Natural poiesis through sexual procreation, (2) poiesis in the city through the attainment of heroic fame and finally, and (3) poiesis in the soul through the cultivation of virtue and knowledge,*' found at http://caae.phil.cmu.edu/Cavalier/80250/Plato/Symposium/Sym2.html (last accessed Dec. 16, 2016); *see also*, Allen Parson at his blog, *Praxis and Poiesis*, who writes, *These differences mean that poiesis relies on a kind of knowledge that Aristotle termed techne, or expertise, while praxis relies on a kind of knowledge he termed phronesis, or practical wisdom* (accessed Apr. 23, 2014).

the irony of all business pursuits. '*U*' is thus simultaneously *Universal*, *Systemic* and *Subversive*, like each of the theists, academics and cynics of ancient Greece. You must try to *Lean* consumers toward an infinite sigma in the relentless pursuit of their perfection when you innovate, develop and market *paos*, even if that may ultimately be a fruitless goal in the grandest scheme. You have no choice but to at-tempt to move them toward *U/aRe* processes, away from the circular constraints of the *OM*.

What An Organization *Ought* to *D/O*

No true-north values *Lean* philosophically with infinite confidence (/σ∞) more than *what* is considered ethical and moral, about which consumers most deontologically (or in the terminology of *U/P, D/Ontologically*) *C/aRe*.[586] Normative universal/processual, and really personal true-north values can be directly or indirectly factored into *what* consumers ought to have *b-ought* from you without your having to analyze their preferences beforehand.[587] Keep in mind though that only normative ethics, or *how* things ought to be, fully *Lean* upward along the curve of the *Ontological Teleology* to reach *what* intuitively energizes and optimizes consumers' lives and existences. This *Stream 5* now explores *how* a corporation can ethically orient its *paos* to move consumers along the upward curve of the *Ought*, beyond *what* organizations can know, toward *what* consumers find most meaningful in the money they spent.

Since normative ethics is *what* ought to be, any difference between *what* consumers ought to buy and *what* they value with the money they spend must be explained through axiomatically structural or processually systemic errors, inefficiencies and/or ignorances

---

[586] Jan Narveson, *Silverstein on Egoism and Universalizability*, Australasian Journal of Philosophy, Vol. 47, Iss. 3, (1969); and, Harry S. Silverstein, *Assenting to Ought Judgments*, Noûs, pp. 159-182, Vol. 17, No. 2, Wiley (May, 1983).

[587] I mean *Ought factors* in this way as a form of phenomenological reductionism.

that bracket consumers' rationality overall.[588] An organization has a duty to reconcile this divergence by engaging in *Ontologically Prospective Projects* that produce viable *paos* that most profitably reconciles these structural or systemic errors, inefficiencies and/or ignorances toward pefection. Through probabilistic estimates of *what* most profitability universalizes consumers' */aRe* processes and personal perspectives through the*Ought*, you arrive at ethical value judgments as to *what paos* best optimizes *U/aRe* processes overall.[589]

The *Ontological Teleology*, *OT* or *Ought*, directly relates the normative *Universal/Processual* and really *Personal* true-north values (again, the *U/PP*, true-north values) to ethical principles such as those espoused by Corporate Social Responsibility initiatives that truly increase enterprise value. The *Ontological Teleology* in general, and legal systems more specifically, integrate D/Ontological, rule-based ethics that were most famously espoused by Emmanuel Kant into *U/PP* values. Optimizing *U/aRe* processes through *U/PP* true-north values universalizes and draws bright lines for *what* consumers *ought* to D/Ontologically do.

When an organization's *paos* facilitates *WE/aRe* processes, that organization universalizes consumers' *Processual* and *Personal* true-

---

[588] This thus may be viewed as a form of naturalistic ethics, but for recognizing *what* is *beyond existence*, making it a morally quasi-realist argument in the context in which I describe it and an attempt to collapse Hume's *Is-Ought* problem through an *Ontological Teleology* leading to a *D/Ontological* ethical goal of *Universality* of supervening consciousness through *U/aRe* processes; see, John Searle, *How to Derive Ought from Is*, pp. 43-58, The Philosophical Review, Vol. 73, No. 1 (Jan. 1964); for other thinkers along these lines, *see*, Oliver Curry, *Who's Afraid of the Naturalistic Fallacy?*, pp. 234-247, Evolutionary Psychology, Centre Research Associate, Centre for Philosophy of Natural and Social Science, London School of, Economics (2006).

[589] And to be clear, this is not an appeal to nature – synthetics are just fine - but an appeal toward *Ontological Realization* through *U/aRe* processes toward a hypothetical *Universalization*. For further support, *see generally*, Sam Harris, *Moral Confusion in the Name of "Science"*, huffingtonpost.com (29 March 2010); Sam Harris, *Science Can Answer Moral Questions*, TED2010 (22 March 2010); and Ralph McInerny, *Ethica Thomistica*, Chp. 3, Cua Press (1982).

north values. This makes that organization's *paos* a *good in itself*[590] because *what* is good for consumers is *what* makes consumers more of *who* they are. Good *paos* is *what* they ought to want to buy from an organization, which will lead to good returns. A lot of people discussing *Lean* value streams seem to miss this circular ripple.

Problems do arise when particular customers may want something deemed evil, such as purchasing a weapon to harm innocent others. Other problems arise when consumers simply need to satisfy their base needs so desperately they cannot afford to consider the overall *OT*, which can cause them to do n-oughty and potentially criminal things. Problems like these though are systemic errors, inefficiencies and/or ignorances endemic to that particular customer or group of customers, or they are structural to a particular society. Importantly, such customers' *evil* demand would not optimize *WE/aRe* processes overall, and so if universalized, that demand would collapse *U/Socially* unto itself.

Ethical *paos* instead facilitates *who* , *why* , *what* and *how* consumers ought to want to be by allowing consumers to ultimately cohere their personal perspectives upward with the *Ought* inside the *IB*, *Leaning* them toward *what* they believe is *B-OT*, while simultaneously contrasting them with *what* they know is *N-OT* . Thus, every problem has a solution for which you may charge customers, and every solution creates more problems that other profitable *paos* can solve.[591] An organization's objective commercial and ethical end-goal ought to be to correct these problems for a profit by entangling distinctions between *WE/aRe* processes with the infinite ($/\sigma\infty$), universal perspective. The goal[592] of all *paos* and *U/aRe* processes is to invalidate that ultimate negative of *what* is *N-OT* for everyone.[593]

---

[590] *See generally*, the Stanford Encyclopædia of Philosophy entry on, '*Reflection of Kantian Ethics*.'

[591] David Deutsch, *The Beginning of Infinity* , pp. 18, 62, 65 (2011).

[592] *See generally*, Eliyahu M. Goldratt and Jeff Cox, *The Goal: A Process of Ongoing Improvement*, North River Press; 30th Anniversary Edition edition (Jun. 1, 2014).

[593] Guillaume Aubrun, Stanislaw J. Szarek, Deping Ye, *Entanglement Thresholds for Random Induced States*, v3, arXiv.org (Oct. 15, 2012).

408 Stream 5: People

The collective *Will to Universalize /aRe* may be seen as this Kantian categorical imperative, this D/Ontological, universal law, which consumers ought do to universalize *U/aRe* processes and create universal coherence to the greatest extent they can. The collective *Will to Universalize* aligns with concepts such as '*Justice*,' '*Good Will*,' and '*True-North*' that all customers highly value and will vote for with their money. As described earlier, these rules of *what* consumers ought to do are D/Ontologically realized in legal systems, created by people to direct *what* consumers and all businesses ought do to best energize, optimize and universalize */aRe* processes.[594] This is *how* the *Ought* regulates and simplifies all within the *OM*, by classifying and measuring *what* qualifies as best, better, good, neutral, bad, worse, or worst. This simple diagram shows this *Ontologically Teleological* spectrum:

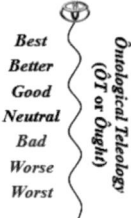

Degrees of Ôught Qualities

Best
Better
Good
Neutral
Bad
Worse
Worst

} *Ontological Teleology (ÔT or Ôught)*

Let me now show this in the context of the *Ought*.

---

[594] The application of these rules varies by type of legal system of course, with strictly codified, civil law based societies following a stricter, rule-based D/Ontological ethical process, while common law jurisdictions satisfy in Utilitarian fashion to a greater degree than just nuances in the codification by applying the D/Ontological laws to specific facts during trial and in judgment.

Chart of Gradations of *Ought*

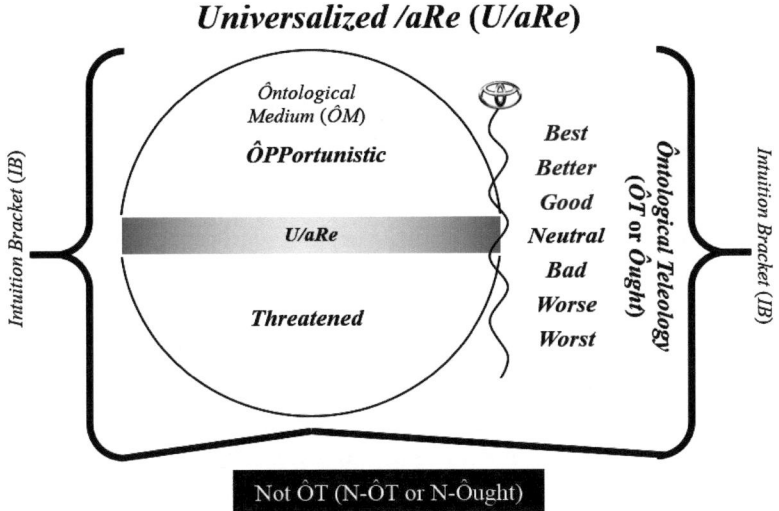

Philosophers, sociologists, economists, business people and customers altogether qualiafy *what* makes a *paos* the worst or best through their phenomenological assessments. A *paos* creates the best moments of true-north value by energizing and optimizing consumers' lives and existences through the *Ought* by creating true U/ PP value, which thereby takes a *paos* and its organization from being *good* to *great*, and maybe even toward being the very *best*.

The multinational conglomerate *General Electric*, a dedicated adherent to the philosophy of *Lean* as discussed in *Stream 1*, indicates its generation of true-north value in its attempt at being the very best with its famous slogan, '*We bring **good** things to life*':[595]

---

[595] http://www.ge.com.

We bring good things to life.

Universalization of *Ought* Ethics (*U.*) for Fun and Profit

The seemingly paradoxical optimization of *U/aRe* processes through the *Ought* for fun and profit is in fact very similar to notions of an apparently circular *Utilitarianism/Consequentialism* that ultimately requires people to do a thing for its own benefit. *Ought* optimization like-wise has an objective end-goal of *D/Ontological* universalization of consumers' */aRe* processes and personal perspectives, with a specific philosophical objective of achieving a possibly circular purpose.[596] Some circularity must ultimately arise because if consumers were to ever hypothetically universalize, becoming synonymous with the *Universe* to become *B-OT* by resolving every problem with their */aRe* processes as soon as one arose, time itself would simultaneously seem to stop and become seemingly endless for them from their personal perspectives. The only thing they could buy from you would be *whatever* might go beyond the apparent tautology of the *Ought* and provide non-circular meaning to them outside the *OM* and *IB* in relation to *what* is known to be *N-OT*. By being fully *B-OT*, they would already be universalized and synonymous with the *OM* itself, and would have nothing left to pur-chase.

Moral progress occurs by expanding consumers' rationality by reducing consumers' errors, inefficiencies and/or ignorances within

---

[596]On a physical basis, this *Universalization* process relates to current scientismic speculation regarding our role on a physical, chemical and systemic basis of bringing the *Universe* toward greater equilibrium by our increasing quantum entanglement through our actions; for more on this, *see e.g.*, Natalie Wolchover, *Time's Arrow Traced to Quantum Source*, Quanta Magazine (Apr. 16, 2014) particularly regarding the work of Seth Lloyd.

the sphere of possibility.[597] You transform their intuitive speculation into systemic processes that allow them to better estimate *what* they D/Ontologically ought to do. You allow them to determine better *what Ontologically Prospective Projects* they ought to pursue to universalize themselves and all society in contrast to *what* is *N-OT* and toward *what* they believe is fully *B-OT*.[598] On an organic, true-north value basis, this abstract Utilitarian, D/Ontological *Will to Universalize* brings the *Universe* closer to equilibrium through the transformation of potential energy to increase universal entropy, just like *how* money represents the contractual right to re-direct the flow of Matter and Energy in that process.[599] Money is the medium of this meaningfully energetic exchange.

At the same time, the Utilitarian D/Ontological *Will to Universalize* recognizes consumers' non-scientismic speculation as a rational response to *what* they perceive to be *N-OT* outside the *IB* regardless of any physical considerations within the *OM*. However, non-scientismic speculative issues outside the *IB* have historically shown little predictive likelihood of becoming systemic or axiomatic truth-north values in comparison to intuitively scientismic speculation. We now know that faith in explanation predictably guides us toward /aRe.[600] This is because *U/aRe* processes, and all true-north

---

[597] David Deutsch, *Beginning of Infinity*, p. 122 (2011).

[598] The pursuit of *OPPs* thus may be compared to *quasi-realism* in the sense that it is non-relativistic in relation to what is *Ontologically Realized* within the *OM* and relativistic in the recognition that no one axiomatically and systemically knows what is *Nought* inside the **IB*, or *what* is *B-OT*.

[599] This notion is supported by current scientismic speculation regarding quantum entanglement, which I referred to above, and more particularly, by Seth Lloyd, *Black Holes, Demons and the Loss of Coherence: How Complex Systems Get Information, and What They Do With It*, Ph.D. Thesis, Theoretical Physics, The Rockefeller University (April 1, 1988); see also, Artur S.L. Malabarba, Luis Pedro García-Pintos, Noah Linden, Terence C. Farrelly, Anthony J. Short, *Quantum Systems Equilibrate Rapidly for Most Observables*, v2, arXiv.org (Aug. 29, 2014); Anthony J Short and Terence C Farrelly, *Quantum Equilibration in Finite Time*, New J. Phys. 14 013063 doi:10.1088/1367-2630/14/1/013063 (2012); Noah Linden, Sandu Popescu, Anthony J. Short, and Andreas Winter, *Quantum Mechanical Evolution Towards Thermal Equilibrium*, Phys. Rev. E 79, 061103 (Jun. 4, 2009); and Sean Carroll, *From Eternity to Here: The Quest for the Ultimate Theory of Time*, Plume (2010).

[600] David Deutsch, *The Beginning of Infinity*, p. 1 (2011).

U/ PP values, primarily facilitate consumers' being inside the *IB* as physical, chemical and systemic processes in juxtaposition to *what* is certainly *N-OT* scientific. However, you must keep in mind that *U/aRe* processes always cause consumers to self-organize around *what* they wish to be if they got *B-OT* or fear would make them *N-OT*.

> ***To be or not to be, that is the (business) question*–**
> – Shakespeare,*Hamlet, Act III, Scene i* , with a (**bold**) addition

To move this discussion funda-mentally forward in a way I hope you now see more clearly, hypothetically presume that you produced the most truly valuable *paos* that ever existed. Thus under this hypothetical, your *paos* now universalizes consumers so that they become synonymous with all that is. Your customers then would be perpetually *adapted* , *Re-generated* , *energized* for all situations. Again, *what* you ought to actually hope you do is bring them as close to this event horizon as possible as consistent living systems within a *Lean* six sigma ($\geq$/6σ) of confidence so they may optimize their total lifetime value to you and your organization.[601] If you nearly perfect consumers */aRe* processes so that they believe they have a chance at living forever, consumers' */aRe* processes would be nearly perfectly executed, and your *paos* would also be the most highly revered within the *OM* forever.

However, since no *paos* can fully universalize consumers as if they got themselves truly *B-OT*, consumers will inevitably vacillate and focus their *Will to Universalize* within the *OM* on *what* other *paos* most *me*aningfully juxtaposes them to *what* is *N-OT*. Since consumers cannot be truly *B-OT* unless they are *N-OT* (as far as we know), the *OM* creates a conceptually circular limit to consumers' *Ontological Teleology* and the share of their wallets that businesses

---

[601] Except if you were in the life-settlement financing business of course.

may control. Customers' *Ought Cognitive Dissonance* arises from that fact and leads consumers to seek (hopefully) constructive non-circular meaning toward *what* they believe is *B-OT* outside the *Intuition Bracket*. However, even if ultimately impossible to reach within the *OM*, consumers' attempt to get *B-OT* without becoming *N-OT* is *who* they are and *why* they *Lean* toward the highest prophet an organization can help them reach with its *paos*.

This turning back to the *Ought* for *me* aning is also *why* employees work for money, so they can perpetuate themselves in the present and leave an *Ontologically Realized* legacy that matters. [602]From the moment employees leave home to when they return, they engage in *OPPs* at work from their personal perspectives as informed by their past remembered, presently experiencing and anticipated future selves to better universalize *what* they personally identify as themselves in a work-place through the *paos* they *Re-generate* and the customers that *paos* serves.[603] The best employees may further identify their presently experiencing and anticipated future selves as *high-achievers* and *good providers.* Outside of work, those employees may drive to gyms because they identify their presently experiencing or anticipated future selves as *fit* and *healthy*. To emphasize this point, consider Jim Collins description of a *Level 5 Leader* in his book, *Good to Great* :

> **And so she made the decision to search for meaningful work – work about which she would have**

---

[602]You might equate this *Ought/N-OT* tension with Kierkegaardian existential angst, though Søren Kierkegaard would disagree that its resolution is to throw oneself into work.

[603]This can be loosely related to Daniel Kahneman's remembering and experiencing selves described in his concept of *Two Selves,* Daniel Kahneman,*Thinking, Fast and Slow* p. 376 (2011); or as discussed by Saint Augustine, '*What is by now evident and clear is that neither future nor past exists, and it is inexact language to speak of three times— past, present, and future. Perhaps it would be exact to say: there are three times, a present of things past, a present of things present, a present of things to come. In the soul there are these three aspects of time, and I do not see them anywhere else. The present considering the past is memory, the present considering the present is immediate awareness, the present considering the future is expectation,*' Book XI, Confessions of St. Augustine, Translated 2002 by E. B. Pusey (Edward Bouverie) (397 C.E.).

such passion that the question, 'Why try for greatness?' would seem almost tautological. [604]

You can like-wise trace consumers' motives for purchasing any *paos* as discrete *OPPs* in regards to *what* consumers believe will facilitate their *Ontological Realization* toward getting themselves tautologically *B-OT*. Consumers optimize *U/aRe* processes toward best juxtaposing their personal perspectives with *what* they know is *N-OT* and personally believe is *B-OT*. This universally *Utilitarian*, *B-Ought/N-Ought* binary tension is ultimately *what* turns consumers onto *paos*, and is *what* the marketing budget within an *HQ* ought to directly or indirectly address.

However, consumers' ego-centric self-conceptions often conflict with their more outward, allo-centric, *D/Ontologically* universalized ethics. For example, consumers may want to steal to better *adapt*, *Re-generate* and *energize* rather than fairly pay for *paos*, but that would violate societal norms gamified between all people for everyone's benefit. Just as existence itself seems paradoxically self-defined, the *Ought* generates *D/Ontological* categorical imperatives with which universalized egoism must ultimately align, however imperfectly, along the upward curve of the *OT*.

I suggest for any business *i/de*ô*logy* that *Consequentialism* or *Utilitarianism* be perceived as a means of optimizing *U/aRe* customers' processes toward a hybrid *D/Ontology* of universalized utility.[605] This is a form of secular universalism within the *Intuition Bracket*, leaving speculative religious dogmas legitimized from consumers' personal perspectives but bracketed outside the *IB* for purposes of determining true-north values for a business. It functions as a means for consumers to physically and mentally self-organize toward *what* may be *B-OT* in contrast to *what* they know is *N-OT* inside the *IB*. This is the objective philosophical and ethical basis

---

[604] Jim Collins, *Good to Great*, Kindle Loc. 3363-3364 (2011).
[605] *See*, the Stanford Encyclopædia of Philosophy entry on, '*Moral Perfectionism*.'

on which an organization may meaningfully make more money the right way. Universally axiomatic, processually systemic, and personally intuitive true-north values equate with universalized virtues, which in-turn align with the normative and real values that support consumers' lives and all businesses.

Universalizing is maximizing an organization's *Will to Universalize* its customers for a profit. *Universalizing* is maximizing the distinction between consumers and *what is N-OT*. *Universalizing* is improving the conditional, ontological fact of customers' existences within the *OM*, which is *how* businesses im-prove the world. *Universalizing* is minimizing *Threats* while engaging in *Ontologically Prospective Projects* to get *B-OT*. *Universalizing* is having a clear and personal vision of *what* universalizes consumers' /aRe processes in relation to *what* is *N-OT*.

Universalization optimizes and orients *U/aRe* process and consumers' *Personal* perspectives toward *what* they believe is *B-OT* so long as consumers' intuitive speculation allows all other people to cohere to society's commonly agreed *U/P* values. So, the *Universalization* of any given set of customers must also reciprocally allow all other consumers to believe in their own *Personal* true-north values in a converged consensus so long as those *Personal* values do not likewise conflict with society's consensually agreed *U/P* values.

People need not agree at their lowest common denominators of true-north values though. *Universalization* does not mean asking consumers to give up intuitive, speculative beliefs like spiritualism, religion and scientism at the pearly gates of secularism. For any foreseeable future, no one can determine *what* is truly *B-OT* unless *U/People* become *N-OT*. Nor does an objective ethic of universalization mean giving up governing a business with data because data is an intrinsic element of the geometric *OM* that itself resides in an unbounded *Universe*. *Universalization* only requires that speculative, intuitive true-north values be kept in perspective and debated as complements to inter-subjective, falsifiable axiomatic and systemic truths measured with real, *Lean* data. For a real-world example of this business ethic, here is a picture of the entrance to *Universal/Studios* in Singapore where everyone gets counted equally as they pass through the turnstiles to enjoy the rides while maintaining their specific, *Personal* perspectives on true-north value:

Globe at Universal/Studios Singapore(© 2010 Unattributed (CC BY-SA 2.0))

Importantly, and perhaps ironically, the ethic of *Universalization* for consumers actually defines *what* they consider to *N-OT* be inside the *IB*. The *better* the business, the larger that organization's impact on enhancing the depth and/or breadth of consumers' *U / PP* values through the *Ought*, thereby reducing the *Universe* of *what* could be *N-OT*. For example, consider further the *Ontological Realization* that *Universal/Studios* created in its 44,884,000 customers in 2015, thereby reducing the possibility of those customers being not happy.⁶⁰⁶ Likewise, consumers similarly judge the leaders of nations, businesses, or philanthropies by the degrees they enhance the depth and/or breadth of all people's *U/ PP* values in alignment with the *Ontological Medium* along the *Ought*, and inversely the degree to which they assist consumers with becoming not*N-OT* .

 Does your organization make the world sing in perfect harmony?

Since ethical problems are ultimately *Ontologically Prospective Projects*, organizations enact forward looking estimates of the best means of optimizing customers' *U/aRe* processes in a dynamic market. Like any ethic with a consequentialist component, this is a large burden to place on profitable, ethical decision making at the individual and corporate level. But as well explained by Herbert Simon and later economists, organizations continue to improve their methods of satisficing⁶⁰⁷ their customers despite their bounded rationality.⁶⁰⁸ Businesses in-fact get rewarded by striving for an omniscient *Personal* perspective to universalize their customers' */aRe* processes through *Ontologically Prospective Projects*. In other words, businesses make meaningful amounts of money by deeply empathizing with people, doing *good* work by universalizing their customers' *Personal* perspectives despite imperfect markets, and doing so in balance with society's needs, just like*Universal/Studios* .

---

⁶⁰⁶*Theme Index and Museum Index: The Global Attractions Attendance Report*, p. 9, Themed Entertainment Association / AECOM (2016).

⁶⁰⁷For a good business article on this, see Don Moyer, *Satisficing*, Harvard Business Review, (April 2007).

⁶⁰⁸*See further*, George A. Miller,*The Magical Number Seven, Plus or Minus Two: Some Limits on Our Capacity for processing Information*, pp. 81– 97, Vol. 63, No. 2, Psychological Review (1956).

Universalizing Consumers' *Universal Egoism*

Your organization thus ought to pursue an ethic of optimizing *U/aRe* processes to the greatest extent, while recognizing that the contingency of consumers' existences vis-a-vis *what* is *N-OT* is a form of *Universal Egoism*. Consumers personally define *what*'s meaningful to them by *how* they orient their ids, egos and super-egos with *what* they intuitively speculate is *Beyond the Ought* as opposed to *what* they know is *N-OT*. Consumers constantly work to reconcile their personal estimates of *what* is outside the *IB* with standards for such speculation set by their family, community and all people.

An organization may also choose to not speculate *what* may be *B-OT* by simply focusing on perfecting *U/aRe* processes and creating a greater distinction with *what* it and consumers k*no*w is *N-Ought*. Knowledge of *what* consumers most value is based as much on *what* is known is not valuable as much as *what* is. This is *why* an organization ought to optimize *me* aning by re-producing *what* consumers speculate is *Ontologically Teleological*, as opposed to *what* is *N-OT* at all agreed as valuable by at least a *Lean* two sigmas ($\geq/2\sigma$) of a target market. Corporations may align *what* they re-produce with *what* consumers intuitively speculate just up to and until the point that all meaning twists back around to a *Lean*, infinite sigma of confidence ($/\sigma\infty$). This means that organizations ought to never stop pursuing perfection as long as they believe in the philosophy of *Lean*.

> *The opposite of love*
> *is not hate, it's indifference.*
> *The opposite of beauty*
> *is not ugliness, it's indifference.*
> *The opposite of faith*
> *is not heresy, it's indifference.*

> *And the opposite of life
> is not death, but indifference
> between life and death.*
> - Elie Wiesel, Author and Holocaust Survivor[a]
>
> ---
> [a]Interview in *U.S. News and World Report* (October 27, 1986).

So to create the highest profit, you ought to engage in *OPPs* and optimize consumers' orientation toward *what* they believe is *B-OT* so long as those beliefs do not conflict with all other people's *U/PP* values. As I indicated before, speculating *what* is *B-OT* is a perfectly rational reaction to consumers' *Ought Cognitive Dissonance*. However, a problem arises ethically when customers' intuitive speculation about *what* is *B-OT* interferes with widely recognized axiomatic and systemic truths, to such a degree that consumers' speculative beliefs hinder their or society's optimizing *U/aRe* processes overall. Thus, an organization ought to mediate between the generally valid axiomatic and systemic truths and personally valid beliefs when designing its *paos* to energize and optimize *U/aRe* processes.

 How do consumers decide What is certainly N-OT and What they personally believe is B-OT?

Organizations operating in conformance to the *Ought* can regulate consumers' knowledge and speculation as to what is *N-OT* and may be *B-OT* for better or worse. For example, religions institutions, like any other supervening *SL-OT* orienting itself along the upward curvature of the *Ought*, rise and fall based on their facilitating congregants' *Ontological Realization* and helping them thrive as a population of believers over time. As already stated, to the extent religions in fact define *what* is *B-OT*, like money, they operate as a great self-organizing force leading to consumer's *Ontological*

Realization that they personally experience within the *OM* and *IB*. Any organization can likewise leverage this dynamic to create new sales. For example, like a fundamentalist pastor, shaman, imam or rabbi, many sales organizations likewise create fear, uncertainty and doubt within their customers' personal perspectives to drive new sales and their companies' revenues upward toward the sublime. This is ethical so long as the end-result is consumer's greater *Ontological Realization* overall for the ultimate, systemic benefit of society in its converged consensus of *U/P* true-north values from people's *Personal* perspectives.

So like fraudulent salespeople, religions can be destructive too if they prescribe dogmatic, D/O rules that lead to systemically destructive results that people experience. This is often the basis for a religion being labelled a *cult*. From an ethical perspective, an organization can justify personal and business ethics on the sole basis of whether or not it enhances *U/aRe* processes as society or science may estimate, which is *what* consumers will buy with religious fervor.

Universalizing Your Organizations' *Perfectionist Consequentialism*

Thus, ethical, religious and corporate ethical contributions will ultimately be measured against *how* they organize and optimize consumers through the *Ought* since the *Ought* is the great regulator and simpliciter of everything within the *OM*. Governments, religions and corporations get measured by the extent they facilitate successful *OPPs* that enhance consumers' *U/aRe* processes over time. By *Leaning* philosophically through *Universalization*, an organization *Leans* toward a *Perfectionist Consequentialism* within the bounds of the *IB*, which includes a form of quasi-realistic speculation once you include *what* consumers believe is outside the *IB*. Consequential perfection gets measured in terms of *what* supervening processes *Lean* toward *U/aRe* processes being universalized, which maximize consumers' distinction with *what is N-OT* through their mix of perfectly rational, and optimally irrational, behavior.[609]

Look now at the Consequentialist ethics of optimizing *U/aRe* processes in relation to universal truth value, such as justice, human dignity, and the true-north values that bind the legality and public relations of business decisions. These D/Ontological concepts cannot be touched, but are *Ontologically Realized* by *how* they are perceived to be uniformly universalized altogether by consumers. We thus strive for these D/Ontological concepts because they orient people's personal wills toward *Universalization*. For example, legal systems set D/Ontological laws and rules compelling consumers to deductively universalize *U/aRe* processes by not speeding, stealing, committing murder, etc. Likewise, the D/Ontological concept of *justice* may be viewed as the ultimate culmination and application of game theory, a rule-based tit-for-tat that gets scored by *how* it facilitates *U/aRe* processes overall.[610]

The philosopher R.M. Hare best represents this thinking around universal, D/Ontological ethics in a concept he calls '*U*.' Hare says that '*U*.' is the requirement,

> **...of finding some action to which one is prepared to commit oneself, and which at the same time one is prepared to accept as exemplifying a principle of action binding on anyone in like circum-**

---

[609] *See again* the Stanford Encyclopædia of Philosophy entry on, '*Consequentialism.*'

[610] Brian Skyrms in his book, *Evolution of the Social Contract*, Cambridge University Press (1996), notes, '[I]n a finite population, in a finite time, where there is some random element in evolution, some reasonable amount of divisibility of the good and some correlation, we can say that it is likely that something close to share and share alike should evolve in dividing-the-cake situations. This is, perhaps, a beginning of an explanation of the origin of our concept of justice'; as also noted by the Stanford Encyclopædia of Philosophy entry on, '*Evolutionary Games*' (accessed Jun. 15, 2014).

stances.[611]

That action is that which leads consumers toward universalizing U/aRe processes, even if they must sacrifice themselves individually for the greater universalization of *who* and *what* they consider themselves to be overall beyond their own, individual person.

Altruism and Optimizing Being

Inversely, consider those organizations that best facilitate *who* and *why* consumers are that people most value and consider virtuous. Consider those organizations that are *In Search of Excellence*[612] that choose to go from *Good to Great*[613] to being *Built to Last*.[614] When organizations exhibit *what* you would consider to be altruistic behavior, like the foundations of high-net-worth people engaging in philanthropy and businesses engaging in social-purpose and Corporate Social Responsibility initiatives, you know that philanthropists and foundations distribute money received by them or their predecessors for some reason at some point in history that was not philanthropical.

Setting aside the obvious caveats mentioned earlier in this book regarding measuring true-north value with money, in order to get that manna, philanthropists, their foundations or their predecessors, directly or through the enterprises in which they invested, provided some *paos* or other asset that people considered worthy of its price to *U/aRe* processes in monetary value terms.

Consumers directly or indirectly provided their money to philanthropists (or did so to their ancestors) by purchasing their *paos*,

---

[611] *See generally*, Neil Haddow, *Torward a Logically Consistent Kind of Ethical Egoism*, Ph.D. Dissertation, University of Waterloo (Sep. 6, 2000).

[612] Thomas J. Peters (Author), Robert H. Waterman, *In Search of Excellence: Lessons from America's Best-Run Companies*, Harper and Row (1982).

[613] *See generally*, Jim Collins,*Good to Great* (2001).

[614] *See generally*, Jim Collins and Jerry Porras, *Built to Last*(2011).

which in-turn makes philanthropists and their foundations *virtuous* through their philanthropy. Industrialists' philanthropy in-turn may lead consumers to buy more *paos* from them. Most societies allow philanthropists to universalize themselves by naming buildings, branding stadiums, and establishing foundations. These philanthropists have had books ghost-written in their names and have become well-known by socializing with celebrities at charity or political events. For example, the fashion designer Michael Kors named the new *God's Love We Deliver* building in New York City as the, '*Michael Kors Building*,' in ex-change for his charitable donation at the building's dedication along with other celebrities and supplicants:

God's Love We Deliver Michael Kors Building(Photo Credit: Me)

Dedication Party for God's Love We Deliver Michael Kors Building(© 2016 Andrew Toth/Getty Images (Fair Use))

This *Universalization* principle applies to politicians too. While politicians receive a combination of votes, donations, and tax dollars in lieu of business profits, they universalize themselves by naming bridges, roadways, airports and institutions for themselves with taxpayer acqui-essence to support politicians' existential legacies. We also notably put politicians' faces *Leaning* at an angle on our money with looks of authority, creating another *i-Thou* relationship between us and governmental leaders judging if we are worthy of the currency's benefits to re-direct the flow of Matter and Energy.[615] Society legitimizes this ex-change to the extent those leaders facilitated (or controlled)*U/aRe* processes.[616]

To strip this veil of altruism completely away, consider *how* the concept of *mercy* aligns with natural selection within the *OT*. Mercy in the form of altruism has been shown to have ontologically *U/Social* utility by benefiting all through reciprocal support.[617] When mercy is a universal ethic, you are as likely to receive mercy as give it. Thus all organizations may consider *U/Social* utility, or corporate philanthropy, to be the highest form of self-organization they can achieve when their businesses as fictional people cooperate with society to optimize *U/aRe* processes. By performing these acts of kindness, they create the most true-north value for the highest profit over all, like incorporated Übermensch.[618]

---

[615] *See*, Martin Buber, *I and Thou* (1923).

[616] For other factors of economic choice, see Reiskamp J., J. R. Busemeyer, and B.A. Mellers, *Extending the Bounds of Rationality: Evidence and Theories in Preferential Choice*, pp. 631-661, Journal of Economic Literature 44(3) (2006).

[617] This concept of course relates to Edward Wilson's work on kin-selection theories; *See*, Natasha Gilbert, *Altruism can be explained by natural selection*, Nature (April 27, 2010); and Martin A. Nowak, Corina E. Tarnita & Edward O. Wilson, *The Evolution of Eusociality*, pp. 1057–1062, 466, doi:10.1038/nature09205, Nature (May 26, 2010).

[618] *See generally*, Friedrich Nietzsche, *Thus Spake Zarathustra: A Book for All and None* (1891).

The Problem of Evil *Google* Can't Escape

When Larry Page and Sergey Brin first started *Google*, they adopted the phrase, '*Don't be evil*,' as *Google's* corporate motto. Perhaps Page and Brin often wrestle with the philosophically famous, '*Problem of Evil*,' which speaks to the question of *what* evil is and *why* evil exists at all. You thus might wonder *what* evil *Google* was attempting to a-void that would make its *paos* more meaningful to the consumers whose data it sells.

Within the *IB*, *evil* is error, inefficiency and/or ignorance, like grotesque imperfection, degenerately abnormal psychology, neurological disease and psychological trauma.[619] All of this is the opposite of ontologically reinforcing true-north value. Evil sadly arises as a consequence of the ontological contingency of the *OT*, which is a spectrum of *what* is other-than-existence outside the *IB*, and *what* may be hypothetically optimized for universalization in contrast to evil.[620] *Google's* motto then was to refrain from being that which undermines consumers' *Ontological Realization* upward along the *Ontological Teleology*.

In the Garden of Google® and Evil(©® Alphabet, Inc. with my modifications)

The question of *what evil* is largely relates to the logical coherence of a systemic world where consumers' existences get *Ontologically*

---

[619]David Deutsch, *The Beginning of Infinity*, p. 212 (2011).
[620]*Ibid.*

Realized through structured processes that happen to allow them to define their essences. *Evil* occurs where those structured processes fail to allow consumers to universalize their *Ontological Realization* into higher *SL-OTS*. Economic *goods* as structured *SL-OTS* can only be deemed so in juxtaposition to *what* they are not, or *what* good things they do not allow consumers to do, which is the evil *Google* wanted to a-void.

You might blame this contravention on the fact that consumers' intuitive truths they believe as to *what* may be *B-OT* stand outside society's commonly held *U / P* values within the *OM*. In other words, since consumers' must *believe* in *what* they think is *B-OT* while remaining in the *OM* that operates *as if* it was logically self-defining, *evil* necessarily threatens and in fact often does sadly realize itself regardless of *what* organizations and consumers desire. This problem of necessary imperfection is due to the *OM* being between what is *N-OT* and may be *B-OT*, is the root of all the evil Brin and Page wanted to a-void.

However, in 2015, *Google* decided that it couldn't avoid being evil in an imperfect *Universe* for the above stated reasons, however much it tried. Thus, *Google* literally changed its name to *Alphabet* and its slogan to, '*Do the Right Thing*,' to *Lean* the corporation further in that direction.

For reference, here is a relevant excerpt from *Google's* Code of Conduct[621] for consideration when it held this *Don't be evil* motto in 2014:

> ### Google's Code of Conduct
> ### Preface: Don't be evil.
> A> **Googlers generally apply those words to how we serve our users. But 'Don't be evil' is much more than that. Yes, it's**

---

[621] *Google Inc.'s* Code of Corporate Conduct (before reorganizing as *Alphabet Inc.*) http://investor.google.com/corporate/code-of-conduct.html (accessed 2014-09-02, now redirected to https://abc.xyz/investor/index.html).

about providing our users unbiased access to information, focusing on their needs and giving them the best products and services that we can. But it's also about doing the right thing more generally – following the law, acting honorably and treating each other with respect.

A>*The Google Code of Conduct is one of the ways we put 'Don't be evil' into practice. It's built around the recognition that everything we do in connection with our work at Google will be, and should be, measured against the highest possible standards of ethical business conduct. We set the bar that high for practical as well as aspirational reasons: Our commitment to the highest standards helps us hire great people, build great products, and attract loyal users. Trust and mutual respect among employees and users are the foundation of our success, and they are something we need to earn every day.*

- *Would Google's employees know what evil is to be avoided based on this statement, beyond not providing biased information, breaking the law, acting dishonorably, disrespecting each other, or failing to follow a deontological code of conduct specifically saying what employees shall do?*
- *On what basis would this Code of Conduct set Google's aspirational standards by which its employees are measured?*
- *Does this Preface to the Code of Conduct adequately explain why evil ought to be avoided from stakeholders' and customers' personal perspectives so Google's employees can autonomously determine what evil may be in ambiguous situations?*
- *Would you adopt this creed for your organization and HQ based on what you believe is truly B-OT?*

Ethical Prospects –*OPPs* for the Captain, Prisoner and Transplant

> *Goodness divine,*
> *which from itself doth spurn All envy,*
> *burning in itself so sparkles*
> *That the eternal beauties it unfolds.*
> – Dante Alighieri, *The Divine Comedy, Paradiso*, VII, 64-66

Like *Google* applying a *goodness simpliciter* with its slogans, '*Don't be evil*,' and, '*Do the right thing*,' to this notion of *U/aRe* altruism, you ought to analyze the consequences of *what* an organization ought to D/Ontologically do to engage in ethical *OPPs* toward universalizing *who* and *why* consumers' are for a profit. *Utilitarian* ethics have often been criticized because of built-in contradictions favoring the group over the individual, such as *Leaning* consumers toward killing one person to save many others. However, if an organization uses *Universalization* as a form of *Utilitarian* ethics in its business *i/deô*logy to create the most true-north value for consumers, it can generally overcome *Utilitarianism's* analytical problems. By synthesizing traditional *Consequentialist* and D/Ontological ethics, you form *Universal Optimism* , which is the duty of all people to up-hold since hope springs eternal.[622] In other words, you must stay open-minded in an unbounded *Universe* regardless of the value system employed.[623]

When engaging in *OPPs* to energize and optimize *who* consumers are, you must keep in mind that constraints will always remain due to an organization's errors, inefficiencies and ignorances within the system in which it *OPPerates*. This is exactly *why Google* suffered from *Ôught Cognitive Dissonance* when it had the motto, '*Don't be evil.*' Due to errors, inefficiencies and ignorances, *Google* had to settle for the aspirational end-goal of simply doing the right thing, wherever that may lead them. Neither you nor *Google* will ever know all the factors necessary to make the correct ethical decisions as *OPPs* . All a company can do is fully recognize and try to overcome its own psychological biases toward preserving itself ontologically within the *OM* above all else.

Tversky and Kahneman's *Prospect Theory* has a large role to play in ethical *OPPs* for this reason. On a game theory basis, organizations,

---

[622] David Deutsch, *The Beginning of Infinity* , p. 196 (2011); and Karl Popper, *The Myth of the Framework: In Defence of Science and Rationality*, Taylor and Francis (1994) wherein he says, '*It is our duty to remain optimists*,' at Kindle Loc. 115.

[623] David Deutsch, *The Beginning of Infinity* , at *Introduction* (2011).

just like consumers, must favor the probability of persisting over gaining in order to repeat their goal of being *Ontologically Realized* perpetually upward in *Strategically Unique Degrees of Sophistication*. In the systematic reality of universal true-north value, making ethical decisions for a particular *OPP* requires estimating probabilities on a prospective basis and ensuring that even if you lose, you can try and create meaningful true-north value again as best you can given these constraints inherent in any given situation within the *OM*. This is *what* makes business so risky and often conservative.

Consider the earlier economic discussion in *how Prospect Theory* reflects aversion toward losing when conducting *Ontologically Teleological OPPs*. Quite simply, the preference to avoid loss rather than creating another *OPP* is perfectly rational when you weigh the systematic costs and benefits of *U/aRe* processes. Through the optimization of *U/aRe* life processes, you would expect consumers to be slightly biased in their ethical decision making toward continuing to exist over essentially and existentially gaining, in that their ultimate end-goal is to *Re-generate* by engaging in *U/aRe* activity for persistent survival. Consumers also seek justice so they may repeat the game of life, test fate and ultimately extend their *eRas*.

Since consumers are biased toward not risking being out of the game of life altogether over trying new *paos*, that creates hazards for any company introducing in-novative *paos*. This bias against potential new methods of satisfaction and delight can often be overcome with well-known brands and marks. Consumers favor well-known brands that in their minds have the highest statistical chance of yielding delightful satisfaction and a-voiding bitter disappointment. Brands create efficiency for consumers by increasing their chances of a-voiding loss and gaining both ethically and ontologically, even at the possible cost of the marginal benefit they could receive by switching to newly branded, in-novative *paos*.[624]

This brand risk in large part raises the point of purchase higher between an organization and consumers since consumers conduct *OPPs* by betting with their money when buying *paos*. They bet whether or not buying a *paos* energizes, optimizes, and thus universalizes, their */aRe* processes. Only by creating moments of true-north value within consumers when they buy *paos* can an organization increase consumers' probability of experiencing *Universal* and *Process* true-north values from their Personal perspectives. By doing so, it may more effectively overcome the point of purchase to uniquely/profitably energize and optimize consumers' lives and existences.

The Captain

A commercial challenge resides in the uncertainty of the effectiveness of *OPPs* in relation to the distance from the problem a company is trying to resolve and the unfamiliarity it may have with new markets. Limitations from a process perspective arise in an organization's difficulty with understanding new markets that seem less systemically important to existence, or less evidently so, due to what psychologists term, '*Availability Bias.*'[625]

There is a famous scene in the movie, *Star Trek II: Wrath of Kahn*, evidencing this availability bias. In the scene called, *Kobayashi Maru*,[626] Captain Kirk and his assistant Spock discuss whether

---

[624]*See*, Prescott, Ron Everett, Ph.D.,*Applying Prospect Theory to Moral Decision-making: The Heuristic Biases of Moral Decision-making Under Risk*, Walden University (2012); Chris Guthrie, *Prospect Theory, Risk Preference, and the Law*, Northwestern University Law Review, Vol. 97, No. 3 (Oct. 31, 2002); Davis G. Yee,*The Prospects of Applying Cumulative Prospect Theory to Analyze Attorney Behavior and the Model Rules of Professional Conduct*, University of San Francisco (2007).

[625]*See generally*, Amos Tversky and Daniel Kahneman,*Availability Heuristic* , p. 207-232, Vol. 4, Cognitive Psychology (1973).

[626]In the terminology of the *Starfleet*, *Kobayashi Maru*, means a test without resolution. In Japanese, *Kobayashi Maru*means a small circle of trees since *Kobayashi* means a group of trees and*Maru* means a circle. *Maru* is also appended to the names of ships to indicate the circular voyage they always take to and from their home ports.

Spock should sacrifice himself to save the crew of the ship and its overall mission to universally explore and gain scientific knowledge that will energize and optimize *who* people are. Spock and Kirk have the following dialogue when deciding what to do:

> **Spock:** *Don't grieve, Admiral. It is logical. The needs of the many outweigh...*
> **Kirk:** *...the needs of the few...*
> **Spock:** *...Or the one... What do you think of my solution?*[627]

This scene exemplifies a situation where Spock engaged in an *OPP* resulting in the self-sacrifice of his life because it cost less systemically in people's ability to universalize themselves than if he had not sacrificed himself for countless yet unknown people. This, at least to me and I believe many others, feels somewhat correct on a psychologically intuitive basis so long as the decision comes from Spock's free will.[628]

Captain Kirk on the other hand closely identifies with Spock and feels that the loss of his life would greatly reduce *who* he considers himself to be, which is Spock's friend, and so Kirk generally disagrees with Spock's estimate for optimizing *U/aRe* processes as the organizational mission of the *Starfleet*. Of course, Captain Kirk and all of the other crew members would die as well in this hypothetical, so even Kirk in his personal loss of Spock realizes that Spock's self-sacrifice is the correct decision for optimizing *U/aRe* processes overall. Thus, Kirk almost agrees, on at least an intellectual basis, with Spock's estimate for enhancing the true-north value of universalizing all people. Nonetheless, this is an ethical problem for operating an Enterprise.

As the philosopher and ethicist Peter Singer wrote:

---

[627] © Paramount Pictures Corporation, *Star Trek II: Wrath of Kahn (1982).
[628] The concept of *free will* equates with degrees of freedom of our *Will to Exist*.

> *No doubt we do instinctively prefer to help those who are close to us. Few could stand by and watch a child drown; many can ignore the avoidable deaths of children in Africa or India. The question, however, is not what we usually do, but what we ought to do, and it is difficult to see any sound moral justification for the view that distance, or community membership, makes a crucial difference to our obligations.*[629]

To overcome this ethical problem raised by Spoke and Singer, an organization ought to view itself as universalizing consumers' U/aRe processes as a form of *Lean, Systems Thinking* as best it can given an organization's bounded rationality. An organization, when determining *how* to most profitably serve its markets, should closely analyze its availability biases and see *how* it can uniquely/profitably energize and optimize the lives and existences of markets near and far to create the most money meaningfully wherever a profit may be found.

The Prisoner

The flip-side of the commercial problems presented by the captain scenario is the justice of lawsuits for the torts and crimes organizations commit. Society must decide whether or not it is better off systemically punishing organizations that commit bad acts. Remember that justice, as a D/Ontological ethic and overlapping consensus, can in certain ways be perceived as an application of game theory to optimize U/aRe processes. The decision to punish organizations at the cost of their profits almost always revolves around whether retribution enhances society through deterrence.

---

[629] Peter Singer, *Practical Ethics, Third Edition*, pp. 202–3, Cambridge University Press (2011).

When governments decide to impose financial punishments on companies, they ought to generally consider people's psychological and emotional sense of deterrence, their empathy for the individual victims, and whether data supports the contention that the punishment is an effective deterrence. An organization like-wise ought to consider whether its actions optimize *U/aRe* processes within society, thereby creating true-north meaning to avoid regulatory fines, bad publicity and possible jail time for its executives.[630]

The Transplant

Against this ethical backdrop, let's now take a very common hypothetical used in philosophy classes to determine *how* an organization ought to optimize *who* consumers are and create *Lean*, true-north value for them. Presume you run a hospital where eighteen patients require immediate blood transfusions of a specific blood type. Your hospital happens to have an employee on staff *who* is the one person with the blood type that could certainly make those eighteen patients well. Should your organization kill the healthy employee with the correct blood type as an *Ontologically Prospective Project*, thereby turning him or her into a form of *paos*, to save the lives of the eighteen sick people with immediate blood transfusions, presuming no other alternatives exist?

This hypothetical often diverges ethical systems in that the Consequentialists/Utilitarians (generally) say "yes" because an organization will ultimately save more lives by turning its employee into *paos*, while deontologists (generally) say no because that organization would have to murder its employee to save the eighteen lives, which deontologists would say is categorically bad. For the deontologists, murder in this circumstance would be a D/Ontological concept your organization would have to universalize under the

---

[630]For some of the academic analysis done in this area, *see*, Ethan Cohen-Cole, Steven Durlauf, Jeffrey Fagan, Daniel Nagin, *Reevaluating the Deterrent Effect of Capital Punishment: Model and Data Uncertainty*, Report to the U.S. Dept. of Justice, Doc. 216548 (Dec. 2006).

exact same circumstance in all cases if you chose to perform this *OPP*.

An ethical system using *Universal Optimization* as its standard in proper alignment with the *Ontological Teleology* requires you to ask, '*[a]s a hospital administrator, what D/Ontological actions optimize my patients' personal perspectives and thus create the most meaningful true value?*' While your hospital may wish to save the eighteen lives that apparently resulted from biological defects for a tremendous profit per surgery, you likewise would not want to commit murder and unnecessarily reduce your staff's headcount. The question then becomes,

> **Would murdering one employee for the sake of the eighteen high-profit patients in all such similar circumstances systemically optimize people's personal perspectives within the IB through U/aRe processes and create meaningful true-north value overall?**

When optimizing *U/aRe* processes for fun and profit, it would be hard to see *how* murdering an otherwise healthy employee for the sake of eighteen sick patients would facilitate *U/aRe* processes overall because in real life, the risks inherent in surgery itself make the *OPP* just as risky, thereby discounting the potential benefits and profits of the *OPP*. A universalized axiom must optimize *U/aRe* processes overall given the further systemic consequences of such an action. Creating an ethic of murdering a non-violent person for money would be too costly on a systemic basis (not to mention an emotional one). For example, people would never work at a hospital for fear they might suffer a similar fate and become a certain form of *paos* for sick patients under similar circumstances. That would cause many more lives than the eighteen sick patients to be lost.

Thus, an organization ought to pursue an ethic of optimizing *U/aRe* processes in the depth, breadth, quality and continuity of con-

436 Stream 5: People

sumers' personal perspectives within society. For example, nations like China have chosen to have less off-spring in exchange for a higher quality of life and greater sustainability of all. Societies also generally choose to voluntarily donate organs to the sick.[631] Most cultures decide that people's ability to choose exceeds any marginal ontological benefit achieved by forcefully taking organs from healthy people.[632] By contrast, many organizations work to increase the voluntary participation rates in organ donation programs to overcome this ethical problem for operating a hospital.[633]

Emotions as Personal Analogies – How Consumers *Ought* to Feel about Your *paos*

Beyond ethical optimization, its natural to wonder at this point *how* you ought to optimize consumers' *U/aRe* processes. You may begin to understand this by asking,

- *What of their personal, psychological factors, such as human emotions, lead to emotionally correct true-north value?*
- *What factors of consumers' lives Ought to lead consumers to consume *paos?**
- *What ethically and profitably delights consumers by giving them joy and happiness?*

Unless consumers are actors, they generally enact emotions such

---

[631]For a counter example, *see*, Li Hui and Ben Blanchard, *China to end use of prisoners' organs for transplants in mid-2014*, Reuters (Nov. 2, 2013).

[632]*See e.g.*, the work of, *Doctors Against Forced Organ Harvesting* at https://www.dafoh.org/ (accessed Nov. 13, 2015).

[633]Though self-driving cars may send this problem through the roof. This problem can too be solved with profitable innovation.

as joy, grief, love, and pain without any prior, self-aware intent to do so. Critically, ethical, emotional, and monetary values are one and the same because consumers buy things that make them happy, which generally orients them along the *Ought* by creating new *SUDS* and forming higher *SL-OTS*.

Survival of a Systemic *Utilitarianism* Inside the *IB*

> *Do you see O my brothers and sisters?*
> *It is not chaos or death*
> *—it is form, union, plan—*
> *it is eternal life—it is Happiness.*
> - Walt Whitman, *Song of Myself*, p. 78, Part 50 (1867).

Within this chain of reasoning, you may see the evolution of *Utilitarianism* and its application from a modern perspective. If so, you may also know classic *Utilitarianism* from when it was first described by philosophers like Jeremy Bentham and John Stewart Mill.[634] *Utilitarianism* is generally held to be, '*...the view that the morally right action is the action that produces the most good,*'[635] or in some versions, the one that produces the most *happiness*.

In *what* seems to be a promotion of classic *Utilitarianism*, the *Coca-Cola Company*, owner of one of the world's best known brands, recently defined happiness through its '*Open Happiness*' and '*Coke Side of Life*' campaigns. *Coca-Cola Company* started this discussion at its interactive website (now defunct) once located at http://us.coca-cola.com/happiness/ by including quotes about happiness from esteemed individuals repeated here:

---

[634]This type of qualitative hedonism is further described by the Stanford Encyclopædia of Philosophy entry on, '*Consequentialism*.'
[635]*Ibid.*

> *Thousands of candles can be lighted from a single candle, and the life of the candle will not be shortened. Happiness never decreases by being shared.*
> – Buddha
>
> *Happiness is the meaning and the purpose of life, the whole aim and end of human existence.*
> – Aristotle
>
> *Happiness is not in the mere possession of money; it lies in the joy of achievement, in the thrill of creative effort.*
> – Franklin F. Roosevelt
>
> *Happiness is when what you think, what you say, and what you do are in harmony.*
> – Mahatma Gandhi
>
> *The primary cause of unhappiness [and happiness] is never the situation but your thoughts about it.*
> – Eckhart Tolle
>
> *The greater part of our happiness or misery depends on our dispositions, and not on our circumstances. We carry the seeds of the one or the other about with us in our minds wherever we go.*
> – Martha Washington[636]

The *Coke-Cola Company* then says on its website:

> **Like Coca-Cola, these great men and women each asked themselves the same core question – what is happiness? While each of their own definitions

---

[636] © 2015 *Coca-Cola Company*(Fair Use) http://us.coca-cola.com/happiness/ (accessed 01/21/2015).

> *differ, each touches on a similar cord that we must all come to realize. The quest for true happiness is not really a quest at all, but a decision and a choice. So don't wait another moment. Open an ice cold Coca-Cola and choose happiness!*
> -Coca-Cola Company Open Happiness Ad Campaign [637]

According to the *Coca-Cola Company*, consumers can downwardly, consciously choose to drink *Coke*, which then upwardly directs their psychological and physiological responses to make them feel a certain way in-turn. According to the *Coca-Cola Company*, by its customers consuming its *paos* of ice cold *Coke*, it determines *what* happiness its customers experience in their lives and existences. So, consumers' downwardly conscious decision to consume a *Coke* will upwardly and teleonomically bubble up happiness within them like *SUDS* in a U-shaped utility curve. That is the real thing the *Coca-Cola Company* D/Ontologically produces. This U-shaped utility function works upwardly along with the psychological relation that *Coca-Cola Company* wants consumers to have between its brand and *whatever* else really causes them happiness. Here is a screenshot of *Coca-Cola Company's* happiness website for your review:[638]

---

[637] *Ibid.*
[638] *Ibid.*

440 Stream 5: People

Coca-Cola Company Open Happiness Ad Campaign (© 2015 *Coca-Cola Company* (Fair Use))

Setting aside *Coca-Cola Company's* philosophical analysis of happiness for a moment, in describing *Utilitarianism*, Jeremy Bentham phrased its primary question as, '*What use is it?*' The *U/People* business model translates that question to mean the extent a *paos* like *Coke* optimizes *U/aRe* processes toward this abstract ethic of *Universalization* by creating ÔPP ortunities or removing T hreats to consumers' lives and existences within the *OM*, beyond the *IB*, and toward *what* ought to be *B-OT*.

Since notions of *good, better,* and *best,* describe *what paos Leans* consumers up along the *Ought* better than any other *paos* they could buy, *Utilitarian Universalization* can be restated as, '[t]he *view that the morally right action is the action that optimizes U/aRe processes toward universalizing consumers' personally intuitive perspectives.'* So optimizing *U/aRe* processes toward universalizing consumers overall as the most sophisticated *SL-OT* known, optimizes *what* you consider to be the most virtuous *paos* an organization ought to re-produce. Consider this notion in the context of what *Apple Inc.* said is its mission statement during its 2013 developers' conference:

> *This is it.*
> *This is what matters.*
> *The Experience of a Product.*
> *How it makes someone feel?*
> *Will it make life better?*
> *Does it deserve to exist?*
> *We spend a lot of time on a few great things, until every idea we touch, enhances each life it touches. You may rarely look at it, but you will always feel it. This is our signature, and it means everything.*
> - *Apple Inc.'s* Mission Statement Video at its *2013 World Wide Developers' Conference* in Cupertino, California

Apple's mission statement aligns with *Utilitarian Universalizaiton*. Contemporary philosophers generally define *Utilitarianism* not with happiness as its measure of value, but as a form of *Consequentialism* through universalizing a person's ego so that it enhances each life it touches. Like R.M. Hare, modern philosophers now write this type of *Utilitarianism* as shorthand, '*U.*' They view '*U.*' as starting from consumers' self-conceptions, moving outward to their kin and demographic categories such as family, community, nation, environment, politics, culture and peer-group, to eventually touch the entire world.

Classic *Utilitarianism* on the other hand evidences *Apple's* notion of emotional enactment when it says, '*...but you will always feel* *it,*' by using *emotion* as its value system. Classic *Utilitarianism* holds that you ought to maximize that emotion within consumers to the extent it upwardly aligns them with the *OM* and orients them along the *Ought*.[639] Emotions, like happiness, represent a sensory concept or class aggregating the extent consumers energize and/or optimize themselves along the *Ought*.[640] Consumers' emotions thus ultimately get back-stopped and means-tested against truly normative U/P values.

As demonstrated by substantial empirical evidence and common sense having $\geq/5\sigma$ of agreement, emotion is grounded in psychology and is conceptually related to physics and chemistry even if fairly removed from those physical forces due to the sheer complexity of higher mental *SL-OTS*. Emotion thus represents an aggregate of consumers' sensory phenomena reflecting *what* they experience for better or worse through the existential factors of *U/aRe* processes. This dynamic shows itself in the following dialogue between a Trainer and New Hire at the *Walt Disney Company* as described in *Built to Last*:

> TRAINER: *What business are we in? Everybody knows McDonald's makes hamburgers. What does Disney make?*
> NEW HIRE: *It makes people happy.*
> TRAINER: *Yes, exactly! It makes people happy. It doesn't matter who they are, what language they speak, what they do, where they come from, what color they are, or anything else. We're here to make 'em happy.*[641]

Like *Universal/Studios* and *Coca-Cola Company*, *Disney* causes happiness, but *how* does *Disney* make itself the happiest place on

---

[639] In biological terms, this is a form of hedonism, which per Harari in, *Sapiens*, p. 110 (2014), is enshrined in the *U.S. Declaration of Independence* as, ' ... the pursuit of Happiness.'
[640] *Ibid* p. 382.
[641] From *Disney* training script in Jim Collins and Jerry Porras, *Built to Last*, p. 128 (2011).

Earth? Because it enhances *U/aRe* processes upward into its guests' personal perspectives. *Disney* enhances its guests' remembered and experienced selves from childhood through adulthood. *Disney's* fantasy land removes constraints of the *OT* that consumers otherwise experience in their day-to-day lives and thrusts its guests forward like an amusement park ride toward a pragmatic, universalized perfection into *what* they believe is *B-OT*, even if only for a few days' time during their vacations, which is highly valuable all the same.

As Collins and Porras said in *Built to Last*:[642]

> *A visionary company continually pursues but never fully achieves or completes its purpose— like chasing the earth's horizon or pursuing a guiding star. Walt Disney captured the enduring, never-completed nature of purpose when he commented: 'Disneyland will never be completed, as long as there is imagination left in the world.'*

The happiness *Disney Re-generates* over generations of its guests indicates changes in *U/aRe* processes from its guests' personal perspectives. *Disney* experiences provide consumers' remembering selves with the optimism to *adapt, Re-generate* and *energize* to create a better world when they re-turn to school or work. *Disney* increases its guests' perceived juxtaposition with *what* they know is *N-Ought* to become more of *what* they believe is *B-Ought* by stimulating them and relating them to *Disney* characters and a magical kingdom. Once they leave *Disney*, consumers then aspire to *Re-generate* that magical feeling within *what* the *OM* really is in their ordinary lives to the extent they can by buying *Disney* media and merchandise to make themselves happy once more, and hopefully forever after. As the journalist and Holocaust survivor Elie Wiesel said in his article, *A Visit to the Wonderful Disneyland*:

---

[642] *Ibid*, p. 77.

444 Stream 5: People

> *I don't know if a Garden of Eden awaits adults in the hereafter. I do know, though, that there is a Garden of Eden for children here in this life. I know because I myself visited this paradise. I have just returned from there, just passed through its gates, just left the magical kingdom known as Disneyland. And as I bid that kingdom farewell, I understood for the first time the true meaning of the French saying 'to leave is to die a little' [partir, c'est mourir un peu]*[643]

Thus, the *B-OT / N-OT* existential dichotomy repeats itself up through the *SL-OTS* to become an emotional dichotomy for Elie Wiesel and all other consumers as well. For example, the happiness of love is a natural component and extension of consumers' relation to other people. Loneliness is its inverse. Fear on the other hand indicates changes in consumers' sense of physical or psychological integrity and safety. Happiness results from the synthesis of changes in the factors of consumers' lives and existences.[644]

Thus, happiness results from changes in consumers' real or perceived ability to universalize *U/aRe* processes through the *Ought*. Just like *how* philosophy is the middleware between science and intuition, consumers' emotions are the middleware between the *Ought* and *who* they personally are. Thus, by focusing on the perpetual process of energizing and optimizing consumers' *U/aRe* processes and personal true-north values, and thus on *who*, *why*, *what* and *how* they are, you will continue make them very happy, just like *Disney* did.

---

[643]Elie Wiesel, *A Visit to the Wonderful Disneyland*, The Forverts (1957), with further credit to Menachem Butler, *Elie Wiesel Visits Disneyland*, Tablet Magazine (Jun. 27, 2016).

[644]David Deutsch, *The Beginning of Infinity* , p. 318 (2011).

> *It's a world of laughter and a world of tears*
> *It's a world of hopes and a world of fears*
> *...*
> *there is just one moon*
> *and one golden sun*
> *and a smile means friendship to everyone.*
> - Richard M. Sherman & Robert B. Sherman[a]
>
> ---
> [a]©1963 Wonderland Music Company (Fair Use).

Emotions thus function bi-directionally from physical cognition to experienced emotion and vice versa because of a concept called *en-activism* described further below. Without emotion, consumers cannot otherwise anticipate, recognize and measure changes in *U/aRe* processes from their personal perspectives.[645] Positive changes in consumers' *Ought factors* that create positive, systemic improvements for them generally result in positive changes in their emotions, such as their becoming happier by getting over an illness. Positive emotions correlate with improvements in the factors of consumers' *Ontological Teleology* when you solve their deepest existential problems. Solving problems with Ought factors should be the ethical end-goal of all organizations.

Customers' Upward, Downward, Inward, Outward Demand - Supervenience and Enactivism

Like other great leaders, Walt Disney intuitively understood *what* within the *OM* made customers happy. The latest psychological theory today calls this dynamic, '*Embodied Cognition*,' which describes *how* consumers' physical responses under normal condi-

---
[645] Antonio Damasio, *Looking for Spinoza*, Harvest (2003).

tions change their thoughts, behaviors and emotions. Embodied cognitive studies have demonstrated that consumers' opinions of *paos* can change depending on whether they are shaking their heads up-and-down or side-to-side in a "yes" or "no" gesture.[646] Just think about the effects of subliminal messages at *Disney*, and the way its marketing department frames the tangible benefits of its *paos* to consumers so they feel emotionally touched. This concept of embodied cognition should come naturally if considered from the perspective of physical persuasion on *what* and *how* consumers think.

Just as consumers' *B/aRe* processes upwardly developed consumers' personal perspectives from one *SL-OT* to the next, the decisions consumers make downwardly effect their biological processes as well. A symmetric dependency exists between the environmental cause of *who* consumers are and *what* consumers really think of a *paos*. Again, this process is called *enactivism*.

Through the related concepts of enactivism and embodied cognition, consumers' interaction with the *OM*, when moving toward *what* they believe is *B-OT* and away from *what* they know is *N-OT*, creates emotional meaning for them within the *OM*. For example, a child gives meaning to an inanimate toy when that toy becomes the child's new friend and enacts a feeling of comfort in the child by removing *Threats* from *what* the child most fears. The toy also enactivates the child's imagination, thereby providing the child with an *ÔPPortunity* to visit parallel *Universes* with the toy inside the child's mind's *i*.[647] Thus, the child enacts meaning with the toy through the interaction of the toy's objective, *Ontological*

---

[646] The concept is '*Embodied Cognition*' as described in the Stanford Encyclopædia of Philosophy entry on the subject; and as described by Daniel Kahneman in, *Thinking, Fast and Slow* (2011); the head movement study was conducted by Jens Förster as described in, *How Body Feedback Influences Consumers' Evaluation of Products*, pp. 416–426, International University Bremen, Journal of Consumer Psychology (2004).

[647] *See*, Alva Noë, *Varieties of Presence*, Harvard University Press (Apr. 11, 2012).

Realization coupled with the child's emotional relation to it.[648]

As consumers realize as adults, toys mean far more within the limited sphere of *who* children consider themselves to be than when their worldview expands as they get older. This makes meaning a pliable, contextual truth value within the extreme boundaries of the *OM* and *IB*. For example, adult customers fully recognize the *Lean* manufacturing processes that went into making the toy they so loved, which changes their *Personal* prospective on it. Thus, consumers' knowledge of the construction and commercialization of the toy changes the meaning they assign to the toy as adults. Ultimately though, all this emotional meaning at *whatever* stage of life gets back-stopped and means-tested by *what* they believe ought to be *B-Ought* and *what* is *N-Ought*.

Just as a child enacts a meaning for the toy, psychologist Antonio Damasio demonstrated that adult consumers' environments and emotions inextricably influence *what* they reason. A well cited experiment[649] showed *how* consumers change their answers to questions simply by holding a pencil in their mouths, forcing them to smile whether or not they actually felt happy. A forced smile artificially and subconsciously modifies *how* consumers reason, which forms another boundary to their fluid rationality and pure *Utilitarianism* applied without this context.[650]

For another example of bounded rationality within *who* consumers really are, mood-modifying drugs have been shown to reduce

---

[648]See Francisco J. Varela, Evan T. Thompson, and Eleanor Rosch, *The Embodied Mind: Cognitive Science and Human Experience*, The MIT Press (1992); Daniel D. Hutto and Erik Myin, *Radicalizing Enactivism*, The MIT Press (2012).

[649]*See*, A. Glenberg, D. Havas, R. Becker & M. Rinck, *Grounding language in bodily states: the case for emotion*, Cambridge University Press (2010).

[650]This concept relates to the 4 E's of cognition, enactivist, embodied, embedded and extended aspects of cognition in, *Introduction to Special Issue on 4E Cognition: Embodied, Embedded, Enacted, Extended*, Richard Menary, ed. Phenomenology and the Cognitive Sciences (Nov. 24, 2010).

mental performance, which ought not be a surprise.[651] The cause for this among other factors is that emotions are inextricably linked to *how* consumers reason due to their need to heuristically classify something with an *Ought* quality such as *good* or *bad*, or *happy* or *sad*. If consumers can't feel well whether an answer is good or bad, they are less able to reason well as well. For an example of the effect of naturally produced chemicals, Cambridge researchers recently found a relationship between the level of financial traders' stress-related hormones and their assessment of risk, which obviously affects their objective trading performance within the marketplace.[652] On the other hand, some researchers have found that a certain level of stress, called *Eu-stress* (or *U/Stress*), enhances cognition.[653] The connection between emotional truth value and logical reason is explicit in guiding consumers to ethical *OPPs* and away from *Threats* to becoming *N-OT*.

Further consider the relation between emotion and facts within the well regarded implicit association test.[654] The implicit association test measures the strength of consumers' subconscious associations between their mental concepts like '**paos**' and their *Ought*-oriented qualitative assessments like '*bad*,' '*good*' and '*better*,' or sentiments like '*joy*' and '*terrible*.'

In one implicit association test for fashion clothing, the color *red*

---

[651] As discussed in, S. Drabant, J. Tömlo, M. Tóth, E. Péterfai, I. Klebovich, *The Cognitive Effect of Alprazolam in Healthy Volunteers*, 76(1):25-31, Acta Pharm Hung. (2006); *see also*, *Selling Prozac as the Life-Enhancing Cure for Mental Woes*, New York Times (Sep. 21, 2014); for another study with similar conclusions, *see*, Dominik Mischkowski, Jennifer Crocker, Baldwin M. Way, *From Painkiller to Empathy Killer: Acetaminophen (Paracetamol) Reduces Empathy for Pain*, National Institutes of Health, Soc Cogn Affect Neurosci (2016).

[652] *See generally*, *Cortisol Shifts Financial Risk Preferences*, doi:10.1073/pnas.1317908111, PNAS.org (Feb. 18, 2014).

[653] Danckert Merrifield, *Characterizing the Psychophysiological Signature of Boredom*, Exp Brain Res., 232(2):481-91. doi: 10.1007/s00221-013-3755-2 (Feb. 2014); *see also*, Alina Tugend, *The Contrarians on Stress: It Can Be Good for You*, New York Times (Oct. 3, 2010).

[654] Shanto Iyengar and Sean J. Westwood, *Fear and Loathing Across Party Lines: New Evidence on Group Polarization*, Stanford University, Department of Communication (Jun. 2014); *see also*, Cass Sunstein, *'Partyism' Now Trumps Racism*, Bloomberg View (Sep. 22, 2014).

was shown on a screen, requiring the test taker to then pair it with one of the qualiatative words, '*bad,*' '*good,*' '*joy*' or '*terrible*' shown in the upper right-hand corner of the screen. Testers were then shown a picture in the middle of the screen, such as the latest clothing fashions, in colors such as pink or red. Testers were then asked to click on a qualiatative emotion or sentiment in the other corner of the screen that they felt matched the picture in the middle of the screen and the word in the other corner. The test then cross-matches the qualities displayed in the corners of the screen with the picture shown in the middle. *How* quickly and accurately consumers associate the qualiatative emotions or sentiments for each category, color or class of *paos* depicted in the middle of the screen tests consumers' sentiments and bias toward the *paos* depicted in the middle by interrupting the mental filters consumers have in place.

How consumers consciously or unconsciously think about the value of *what* the word or picture represents to their lives and existences e-merges from *what* they phenomenologically feel about that word or picture. Consumers base this estimate on whether they consider the *paos* as energizing and optimizing for *who* and *why* they think they are. Consumers unconsciously best fit their emotions to the *paos* presented to them, such as whether they considered a *paos* in an advertisement to be *inferior* or *superior* to competitors' *paos* that might energize and/or optimize them as well, better or best.

All of these studies support the notion that, rightly or wrongly, *what* consumers think closely relates to *what* they feel, similar to *how* consumers reason coheres to logic. By transitive logic (*modus ponens*), consumers emote to better align themselves with the *Ought*, to passionately thrust themselves forward toward their ontological perpetuation. Happiness is synonymous with advancing *Ought factors*, while sadness is their negation. Emotional influences on cognition, and vice-versa, developed so consumers could more universally *Lean* toward *aRe* processes. Just as *Prospect Theory* showed *how* consumers discount gains in favor of avoiding losses, emotions guide consumers in knowing when such movement up or down the *Ontological Teleology* may occur, and when to pursue or a-void it as an ÔPP or a Threat.

Hierarchy of Needs -*Maslow Inc.*

If emotions roughly indicate *what* ethically optimizes consumers' lives and existences along the upward curve of the *Ought*, then consumers' motivational psychology ought to *Lean* that way as well. Well-known models of human needs developed by motivational psychologists reflect consumers' normatively processual and really personal true-north values. All these need theorists describe *what* motivates consumers outside of any concept of an *Ontological Teleology*, or any other philosophical concept described by this book, other than generally, *Pragmatic Idealism*.[655] They all speak to employees' and consumers' internally intrinsic and externally extrinsic motivations. By applying the *Ought* to motivational psychology, an organization can ethically align its *U/aRe* processes with the *Ought* to motivate employees to perform good work and consumers to buy its good *paos*. Motivational psychology can energize and optimize the people working in a *House of Quality* to

---

[655] *See e.g.*, the work of popular motivational psychologists like Tony Robbins' and Daniel Pink's classification of fundamental human needs, such as Tony Robbins' *The Six Human Needs*, which he classifies as: 1. *Certainty* : assurance you can avoid pain and gain pleasure; 2. *Uncertainty/Variety*: the need for the unknown, change, new stimuli; 3. *Significance*: feeling unique, important, special or needed; 4. *Connection/Love*: a strong feeling of closeness or union with someone or something; 5. *Growth* : an expansion of capacity, capability or understanding; 6. Contribution: a sense of service and focus on helping, giving to and supporting others; *see also*, Daniel Pink, *Drive: The Surprising Truth About What Motivates Us* , Penguin Group US (2009), and Pink's factors of motivation in the workplace, being *Autonomy*, *Mastery*, and *Purpose* , which he largely derives by reformulating SDT's motivational factor's of *Competence*, *Relatedness* and *Autonomy*, with Autonomy being same-named, *Mastery* substituting for *Competence*, but *Purpose* replacing SDT's *Relatedness*. I address *Autonomy* and *Mastery* below, and as you well know now, *Purpose* is simply the teleological goal of *Meaning*, which in the context of *U / P*, is *Ontologically Teleological* plus consumers' intuitive speculation toward that same goal. I do appreciate Pink's suggestion of *Relatedness* as a motivational factor critical to customers' *Ontological Realization* as you will see below, and as affirmed by *Attachment Theory* .

produce and deliver *paos* to consumers *who* are motivated to *Lean* toward a purchase.

One of the best known of all need theorists is Abraham Maslow who described a hierarchy of needs within his generally dynamic theory. Like our review of competing philosophical theories about forms of human will, I would like to review briefly Maslow's work along with some of the other motivational psychologists *who* have classified *what* an organization ought to D/O within the *U/ People* business model for some intellectual context. I will briefly review a synopsis of some of these need hierarchies to factor them into the true-north value that a *paos* may re-produce within consumers.

To begin, you can see below the well-known pyramid summarizing Maslow's concept of human needs arising, much like an *I/D Kata* or *Charts of SUDS*, toward new, supervening levels of human motivation:

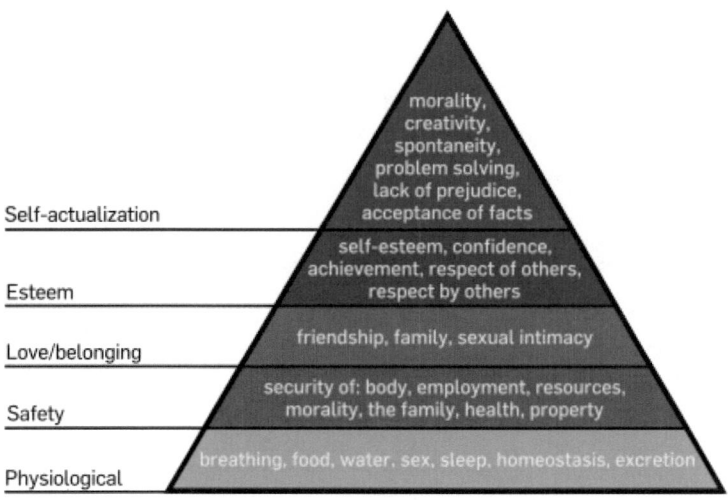

Hierarchical Depiction of Maslow's Hierarchy of Needs (Public Domain)

Self-Actualizing Peak Experiences, Flow and Getting B-Ought

In his book titled,*Hierarchy of Needs: Toward a Psychology of Being*, Maslow begins his hierarchy with the need for self-actualization. Maslow defines this need as:[656]

> ... *the desire for self-fulfillment, namely, the tendency for him to become actualized in what he is potentially. This tendency might be phrased as the desire to become more and more what one is, to become everything that one is capable of becoming.*

Does *what* Maslow writes above sound familiar at this point? Notice Maslow defining self-actualization by repeating the verb *is* as a form of *to be* or *becoming*, which of course is a form of *Ontological Realization* oriented along the upward curve of the *Ought*. Maslow stated that self-actualizing people may be or become a variety of *Ontologically Realized* identities, such as a mother, athlete or painter, and that once people are or become those 'things' they achieve fulfilment.[657]

Consumers likewise identify *who* they are along the upward curve of the *Ought* with their self-conscious analogies, such as the subconscious notion, '*I am like me.*' Maslow further says that consumers become aware of, '*...what [they are] potentially.*'[658] This means that consumers recognize that even the very best mothers, athletes and painters are constantly seeking such a self-reflexive identity. Consumers strive every day to exist as their self-selected identity because they believe it optimizes the essence of their remembered, experienced and anticipated selves. They seek to cohere

---
[656] Abraham H. Maslow, *A Theory of Human Motivation*, p. 383, Brooklyn College, Psychological Review, Vol. 50, No. 4. (1943).
[657] *Ibid* at p. 384.
[658] *Ibid* at p. 385.

all three selves into a seamless personal narrative that universalizes their /aRe processes upward along the *Ought* toward a relentless pursuit of a universalized perfection.

Every one of consumers' self-identified careers provides a *paos* to other consumers, regardless of *how* good or bad they are. Even a trickster, fraudster or gangster serves him or herself as his or her own customer. In contrast, good customers validate their own career identities by self-assessing *what* effect their *paos* has externally on others. Collectively though, the mother, athlete, painter or trickster each assesses whether he or she is *good* at *what* he or she does by the results of their efforts. A mother assesses *how* she served the life and existence of another, an athlete assesses *how* he or she extended the range of human physical potential within the *OM*, and an artist assesses the degree he or she inspired a sense of *what* seems sublimely outside the *IB* and may be truly *B-OT*. Tricksters in comparison assess the extent they serve themselves, which is usually an indirect and congruent measure of the extent they move society as a whole *U/Socially* closer to becoming *N-OT*.

Society extrinsically measures consumers by the extent each of these career identities, and those *who* aspire to them, elevate other people along the upward curve of the *Ought* as well. Society decides whether consumers achieve these identities by serving their own customers, by increasing the human population with similarly reproductive people, by motivating others to perform beyond known limits through athletics, or by inspiring others through aesthetics. Self-actualization of an identity results from a perceived and desired ontological effect, which people deem optimizing toward the universalization of society's /aRe processes through specific *OPPs* within these professions to advance *who* and *why* people are overall.

For example, consider what the nine-time gold medallist sprinter Usain Bolt said in preparation for his final Olympics, '[I]f I win these three gold medals, I will be immortal... So I'm going to run with that:

*immortal.*⁶⁵⁹Universalization through the *OT* for gold is always the objective function for everyone.

Peak Experiences

Maslow's self-actualization relates the positive aspects of *what* Maslow called *B-values*, or *being values*, which *U/P* calls being *Ontological Realized*and closer to getting *B-Ought*. Maslow delineated*B-values* in his writing as the ontological factors of*wholeness, perfection, completion, justice, aliveness… truth, self-sufficiency, etc.*⁶⁶⁰ All these *B-values* relate to *what* Maslow describes as *peak experiences* that he says optimize the emotion of happiness.⁶⁶¹

You might describe consumers' peak experiences as the seeming instantaneous resolution of all problems without division, thereby re-producing happiness as a*B-value*. Of course, no peak experience lasts for consumers because it is an illusory production of emotion from *U/aRe* processes – consumers necessarily live and exist in an imperfect world while hopefully moving somewhere along the upward curve of the*Ought*while they remain far away from getting truly *B-Ought*. Consumers can only perpetually experience peak experiences by in-part consuming *paos* to perfect *U/aRe* processes toward the event horizon of where the *Ought* becomes *N-OT* and goes gently into that good night.

Flow

For a related notion, the well-known psychologist Mihaly Csikszentmihalyi proposed a concept called *flow* that can be seen as analogous to both Maslow's peak experiences and the seeming

---

[659] Andy Bull, *Usain Bolt joins the immortals just as the cracks begin to appear*, The Guardian (Aug. 19, 2016).

[660] Abraham H. Maslow, *Toward a Psychology of Being*, p. 75, Wilder Publications, Inc. (1962); *see generally*, Abraham H. Maslow,*Religions, Values, and Peak Experiences* , Penguin Books Limited (1964).

[661] Abraham H. Maslow, *Toward a Psychology of Being*, p. 34 (1962).

universalization of *U/aRe* processes. Csikszentmihalyi describes *flow* as a psychological state that seems like a simulated perfection, facilitating, '... *concentration and involvement by making the activity as distinct as possible from the so-called 'paramount reality' of everyday existence.*'[662]Csikszentmihalyi's work and that of subsequent psychologists suggests that an organization ought to create *paos* that provides a sense of *flow* as a peak experience to customers when they consume it. This is*what* it means to ethically delight consumers to move them further upward along the*Ought*. Thus, I further define *flow* as the attempted *Universalization* of consumers' */aRe* processes upward along the *Ought* as a result of an organization's specific*OPPs* to *Re-generate* the best *paos* for its customers.

Self-Esteem

Maslow listed self-esteem just below self-actualization in his hierarchy of needs. Maslow said that consumers need self-esteem in two primary ways:

1. *... for strength, for achievement, for adequacy, for confidence in the face of the world, and for independence and freedom, and*
2. *...the desire for reputation or prestige (defining it as respect or esteem from other people), recognition, attention, importance or appreciation.*[663]

The first need (1) is largely based on consumers' internal estimation of their own self-worth, and the second need (2) is externally reflected inward from other people's estimations. The self-esteem

---

[662]Mihaly Csikszentmihalyi, *Flow: The Psychology of Optimal Experience*, p. 72, Harper-Collins (1990).

[663]*See generally*, Abraham H. Maslow, *A Theory of Human Motivation*, pp. 370-396, Psychological Review, 50 (1943).

need for adequacy thus relates to consumers' need to be further and positively *Ontologically Realized* from their own and others' estimations of their self-worth.

The second, external self-esteem need (2) of reputation and prestige also relates to society's attempted universalization of its */aRe* processes by assessing individual consumers' contributions to it. Organizations can develop *paos* that better optimizes people's internal and external self-reflections that help them align with the *OM* upward along the *Ought* the way they, and the society to which they relate, perceives the *OM* as being. This leads to the next lower level of Maslow's hierarchy, which is the need for love and belonging.

Love & Belonging

The need for love and belonging identified by Maslow relates to both sexual and asexual affection, which *U/P* calls *Relation* and *Stimulation*. Love and belonging also promote consumers' physiological and psychological *Vitality* as a specific ontological factor of consumers' lives and existences within the *OM*. Consumers likewise aspire to irrationally love as a form of *Meaning*. *Relating* with someone or something improves the perceived difference between *who* and *why* they think they are and *what* they know is *N-Ought*, while aligning them toward getting *what* they believe is truly *B-Ought*.

To feel a sense of love and belonging, consumers ought to feel that the object of their affection makes them safer in some way by helping them avoid physiological or psychological insecurity, such as being and feeling unattractive. This leads to Maslow's safety needs, which *U/P* identifies as an *Ought factor* of being *Integral* and not *Insecure*.

Safety

Safety needs largely align with an *Integral Ought factor* covering all physical and psychological contexts, though Maslow also includes notions of *Illness* within his need for safety. U / P addresses notions of '*Illness*' in the *Ought factor* of *Vitality* . U/ P distinguishes the need for safety as a *Threat* specific to consumers' /aRe processes as living systems within the *OM* at large as opposed to consumers' need to maintain their internal vitality for the same reason. Maslow states that consumers' psychological perception of safety can affect many other aspects of their demand for *paos*. Their ability to relate and discover meaning from safety results from their contingently needing physical and psychological vitality and integrity.[664]

Physiology

The last range of Maslow's needs delineates physiological needs. Maslow's physiological needs may be most closely aligned with the *Ought factor* of *Vitality* and not being *Ill*, on which the fulfillment of *U/aRe* processes depend. Maslow rightfully included thirst and hunger in this category, which of course relates to customers' energy and *Re-generation* activity as living systems, since *Vitality* requires food for energy and water for *Re-generation*.

Maslow describes physiological needs as the most, '... *pre-potent of all needs.*'[665] I propose that by describing the supervening potency of needs, Maslow *Leans* toward a a sense of minimum vitality in his philosophical analysis. I believe though that Maslow could have said this better by articulating that consumers' very existence is contingent on the fulfilment of physiological needs through univer-

---

[664] As Maslow wrote at p. 376 in, A *Theory of Human Motivation* (1943), in regards to Safety Needs, '[T]he organism may equally well be wholly dominated by them.'

[665] As Maslow wrote at p. 370 in, *A Theory of Human Motivation* (1943), '[H]uman needs arrange themselves in hierarchies of pre-potency. That is to say, the appearance of one need usually rests on the prior satisfaction of another, more pre-potent need.'

salized, *Leanly* adaptive, Re-generative and energizing processes.[666]

No Need Hierarchy

Significant research has shown that consumers do not necessarily respond to Maslow's above stated needs in any particular hierarchy or order.[667] Consumers do not necessarily build their lives and existences from one need to the next – all needs contribute to consumers' *Ontological Realization* through different *SUDS* forming organic vectors of value and distinct *SL-OTS*. Many other needs theorists thus improve on Maslow's motivational theory by flattening Maslow's needs and removing any specific hierarchy.[668]

While consumers may intrinsically want to satisfy more basic needs like food and shelter before more complex ones like love and meaning, this assumption does not hold when tested because consumers pursue *Strategically Unique Degrees of Sophist-ication* to solve their greatest ontological problems,*whatever* they happen to be at that moment. The only base conditions for existence are *Lean adaptation, Re-generation* and *energization,* and all other factors simply contribute to those goals when pursued either teleonomically or teleologically.

However, some people subjectively define their priorities so that they oppose the *Ontological Teleology*and */aRe* processes. These *bad* people believe they are optimizing their lives and existences in some strategic way that is self-destructive or destructive of others

---

[666]Interestingly, neo-Darwinain evolutionary theory and the philosophical usage of the term '*Supervenience*' were coming into academic vogue around the same time that Maslow wrote,*A Theory of Human Motivation* ; see, The Stanford Encyclopædia of Philosophy entry on, '*Supervenience.*'

[667]M. A. Wahba, & L. G. Bridwell, *Maslow Reconsidered: A Review of Research on the Need Hierarchy Theory*, 15(2), 212–240, doi: 10.1016/0030-5073(76)90038-6, Organizational Behavior and Human Performance (1976); Louis Tay, Ed Diener, *Personality, Processes and Individual Differences, Needs and Subjective Well-Being Around the World*, pp. 354 –365, Vol. 101, No. 2, Journal of Personality and Social Psychology (2011).

[668]M. A. Wahba, & L. G. Bridwell,*Maslow Reconsidered* (1976).

as ultimately judged by whether or not the *bad* people reduced the *Ontological Realization* of themselves and others within the *OM* through their actions. Since the *OT* is nearly circular, consider too that, in the inverse, the most celebrated leaders sometimes disregard one or more of their *Ought factors* and needs, like Spock in the *Star Trek, Kobayashi Maru* scene. Such esteemed leaders disregard their physical integrity and/or vitality for larger ideological goals to universalize themselves through the ontological advancement of all consumers.

Maslow's needs though are heuristically potent because they are fairly congruent with *U/aRe* problems that prevent people from propelling themselves upward along the curve of the *Ought*. Solving each of Maslow's needs further supports consumers' perpetual existence by orienting them toward higher *SL-OTS*. However, we know from research that the only existential hierarchy resides in the extent customers' *U/aRe* processes leverage a specific *Ought factor* to energize and optimize their lives and existences to solve their greatest problems. Consumers will always buy *what* they perceive may help them to either:

1. **Engage in OPPs to advance each of their U/aRe processes toward what they believe is truly B-Ought, or**
2. **Remove Threats to one or more of U/aRe processes so as to most a-void becoming N-Ought.**

Alternatively, negative *Ought factors*, such as deprivation, isolation, illness, insecurity or despondency, may each end *who* and *why* consumers are, which is a big problem. The positive inverse of each of these negative factors - stimulation, relation, vitality, integrity and meaning - optimizes *who* and *why* consumers are in their ability to *Leanly adapt, Re-generate*, and *energize* to universalize their lives and existences *however* they think best, which is a great solution. Thus, consumers' *Ought factors* ought to be stated as modifying the verb, '*To be*' to emphasize each as a parameter of consumers' *Ontological Realization*, such as being '*Stimulated*,' '*Related*,' '*Vital*,' '*Integral*' and/or '**Meaningful**.'

Maslow, as insightful as he was, also coined the term *meta-motivation* to describe the motivation of those consumers *who* go beyond simply perpetuating themselves within the *OM*, to describe those *who* strive for constant betterment and problem resolution upward along the *Ought*.[669] Maslow's *meta-motivation* can be analogized to those consumers' *Will to Universalize /aRe* processes upward along the *Ought*. Those consumers consciously define *who* and *why* they essentially are and spend the energy necessary to ontologically become it by solving their greatest problems with true-north value and meaning within the philosophy of *Lean*. Every organization ought to do the same by providing *paos* that re-produces that true-north value within consumers to charge them meaningful amounts of money in ex-change.

Other Need Theorists

For comparison, a number of need theorists have proposed models of human motivation other than Maslow's.[670] A small range of the best known of these models classifying consumers' needs, drivers, end-goals and/or motivations are summarized below to provide a sense of the intellectual history in this area to further an understanding of *Ought factors*, and *what* drives consumers to spend time and money at stores.

Henry Murray

In 1938, Murray predated Maslow to propose a taxonomy of needs that extended to extremely long and seemingly never ending lists;

---

[669] F. Goble, *The Third Force: The Psychology of Abraham Maslow*, pp. 62, Maurice Bassett Publishing (1970).

[670] *See*, the *Careers in Theory* blog by the University of London, and its article, *How many needs?* (Oct. 6, 2011), found at, https://careersintheory.wordpress.com/2011/10/06/how-many-needs/ (last accessed Dec. 17, 2016).

however, based on the earlier discussion regarding *Russell's Paradox*, you know Murray's lists of needs could never universally capture life and existence itself, and his trying to do so was pointless.[671] I will not list Murray's needs because there are so many, but they run from '*achievement*' to '*order*' to '*acquisition*' to '*sex*' to '*infavoidance*' to '*contrariance*' to '*play*' to '*exposition*' to '*succorance*' to '*sentience*'... you get the idea.

Clayton Alderfer

In 1968, Clayton Alderfer followed and rearranged Maslow's traditional hierarchy. Alderfer suggested that human needs were made up of three relatively independent factors, whose order of priority may vary between consumers:

- *Existence*: Alderfer correlated *Existence* to Maslow's physiological and safety needs;
- *Relatedness*: Alderfer correlated *Relatedness* to Maslow's esteem needs as judged by others; and
- *Growth*: Alderfer correlated *Growth* to the need for internal self-esteem and self-actualization.

Since each of Alderfer's needs correlate to Maslow's, they therefore further relate to consumers' universalization through the *factors of the Ought* as described above.

David McClelland

In 1985, David McClelland proposed the need for *affiliation*, *achievement*, and *power* similar to Maslow, Alderfer and Nietzsche.[672]

---

[671] *See generally*, Henry Murray, *Explorations in Personality*, Oxford University Press (1938).

[672] *See generally*, David C. McClelland, *Motives, Personality and Society: Selected Papers*, Praeger Publishers Inc. (Oct. 1984).

Manfred Max-Neef

In 1989, the economist Manfred Max-Neef classified consumers' ontological needs as:[673]

- *Subsistence*
- *Protection*
- *Affection*
- *Understanding*
- *Participation*
- *Leisure*
- *Creation*
- *Identity*
- *Freedom*

Max-Neef considers these needs as being independent, but I personally would not recommend that you commit to that position in a business *i/de*ôlogy for a list of consumers' ontological needs because of the semantic vagueness of each word and *Russell's Paradox* that no list of needs could completely describe *who* or *why* consumers are.[674] However, all of these physical and psychological needs relate in various ways to *U/aRe* processes without discerning which ones would compel consumers to buy at their points of purchase.

Paul Lawrence

Another such drive theory based more on the epic of evolution and modern theories of natural selection was proposed by Paul

---

[673] *See generally*, Manfred A. Max-Neef with Antonio Elizalde, Martin Hopenhayn, *Human Scale Development: Conception, Application and Further Reflections*, p. 18, Ch. 2., *Development and Human Needs*, New York: Apex (1989).

[674] *Ibid*; Hans Villarica, *Maslow 2.0: A New and Improved Recipe for Happiness* , Atlantic Monthly (Aug. 17, 2011).

Lawrence, a professor at Harvard Business School:[675]

Lawrence's four drives are:[676]

- ***Acquire***: '*The drive to acquire what one needs for one's survival at the conception and survival of one's off-spring*' - which is the purchase of *paos* to support and enhance *U/aRe* processes;
- ***Defend***: '*The drive to defend oneself and, as needed, one's off-spring from threats*' - which is ensuring that consumers maintain their *Integrity* and *Vitality* in *U / P* terms;
- ***Bond*** : '*The drive to bond; that is, to form long-term, mutually caring and trusting relationships with other people*' - which is Maslow's *love/belonging*, and *U/ P*'s and others' *Relation* need; and
- ***Comprehend***: '*The drive to comprehend; that is, to learn, to create, to innovate, and make sense of the world and of oneself*' - which is *how* consumers mentally map the *Universe* to *who* and *why* they are to improve *U/aRe* processes.

Paul Lawrence did admirable work in applying evolutionary concepts to human drives, but as discussed before, the Neo-Darwinian theory he used over-emphasizes *Re-generation* without fully recognizing the paradox of the *Ought* that causes consumers to experience *Ought Cognitive Dissonance* in that process, which is the biggest problem leading to further motivation. *Ought Cognitive Dissonance* causes consumers to recursively search for ***me****aning*, which in-turn drives them to *adapt*, *Re-generate* and *consume*, and this dynamic feed-back must be considered.

To strip away indirect, secondary drivers of human motivation, one must build logically from the seemingly circular *OM* as bounded

---

[675] Paul Lawrence, *Driven: How Human Nature Shapes Our Choices*, Jossey-Bass (2002); *see also*, *Big Think Interview with Paul Lawrence*, video found at http://bigthink.com/videos/big-think-interview-with-paul-lawrence (last accessed Dec. 17, 2016).

[676] *Ibid.*

by the *IB*, which is the ontological fact of existence experienced through *Universal*, *Process*, and *Personal* true-north values. Deconstructing Paul Lawrence's model, consumers acquire, defend, bond and comprehend in order to more successfully energize and optimize *U/aRe* processes to attempt to become axiomatically universalsed over all and finally get themselves *B-Ought* as the ultimate end-goal and problem-solution.

Deci and Ryan

More recently, Deci and Ryan's '*Self-Determination Theory*' (*SDT*) proposed that consumers' three fundamental true-north values are *Competence*, *Relatedness* and *Autonomy*. Deci and Ryan's *Competence* relates to Maslow's internal version of '*self-esteem*.' *Relatedness* perfectly aligns with *what* I also call *Related* as a factor *Critical to Ontologically Realization* (again, *what is CORe*) to consumers along the upward angle of the *Ought* . *Autonomy* means the *Strategically Unique Degrees of Sophist-ication* that consumers require to discover *how* to best universalize their */aRe* processes overall possible domains.

Thus, each one of these SDT factors aligns with *how* consumers optimally strive to ontologically realize themselves within the *OM* upwardly along the *Ought* in their attempt to universalize *who*, *why*, *what*, and *how* they consider themselves to be through problem re-solution. Each *Ought factor* contributes at some level to *U/aRe* processes by allowing consumers to better *adapt, Re-generate*, and/or *energize* – to find meaning through *Universalization* toward *what* they believe is *B-Ought* and against *what* they know is *N-Ought*.[677] Deci defined motivation itself as, ' *energy for action*,'[678] thus aligning SDT with *U/aRe* processes.

[677] *See*, Lawrence S. Krieger, Kennon M. Sheldon, *What Makes Lawyers Happy? Transcending the Anecdotes with Data from 6200 Lawyers*, Florida State University College of Law, Public Law Research Paper No. 667 SSRN (Feb. 20, 2014).

[678] Edward L. Deci and Richard M. Ryan, *Self-Determination Theory: A Macrotheory of Human Motivation, Development, and Health*, Canadian Psychology/Psychologie Canadienne 49, no. 3: 182–85, doi:10.1037/a0012801 (2008).

However, again, categories or lists of factors such as SDT can never fully-capture existence according to Russell's Paradox, that the list of all lists that does not contain itself. No one can produce a finite list of all aspects of human existence that does not also reflexively describe itself like consumers D/Ontologically do for themselves when they consciously say things like, '*Y AM I buying X*,' or, '*I MAY buy Y.*' This conundrum of unbounded exploration to universalize overall to try and get *B-Ought* is *how* consumers shop among a seemingly endless array of choices available to them and is *what* causes them to defy simple segmentation and personification.

Attachment Theory

Complementing individual need theories of true-north value and all *me*aning based on categorical lists, one of the latest need theories is called *Attachment Theory*. Attachment Theory states that human attachment is an adaptive process.[679] However, quite obviously, human relationships directly lead to *Re-generation* of the species, and so I summarize all *attachment* under the general Self-Determination Theory and *U/P* concept of *Relatedness*. The distinction is largely semantic, which emphasizes *how* fluid words can be.

Factors of the *Ought*

Specific need categories sometimes succeed in identifying one factor of the *Ought* as a true-north value, such as Self-Determination Theory's version of '*relatedness.*' More often than not though, the specific need categories described by others identify true-north values that actually derive as an after-thought from more fundamentally affirmative *Ought factors*. These primary *Ought factors* are the ones that best explain *who* and *why* consumers are, and

---

[679] *See e.g.*, Jeffry A. Simpson, Jay Cassidy, Jude Belsky (Ed.), Phillip R. Shaver (Ed.), *Attachment Theory Within a Modern Evolutionary Framework*, pp. 131-157, Handbook of Attachment: Theory, Research, and Clinical Applications, 2nd ed., Guilford Press (2008).

what and *how U/aRe* processes create consumers' existences. None of this is meant to invalidate such other need theories, but rather to put them in the context of the true origin of normatively *Universal*, *Process* and *Personal* true-north values that arise due to consumers' existential contingency within the *OM*.

Today, scholars studying human need drivers even tend to shy away from describing specific need categories for this reason. Instead, they favor constructing scientific, empirically verifiable experiments within the *OM* trying to quantifiably predict human preferences. Daniel Kahneman and Amos Tversky's *Prospect Theory* again stands as a good example of such an insight by demonstrating with reasonable certainty that people universally exhibit a bias favoring reducing loss over achieving gains when they have a choice between the two. This loss aversion clearly demonstrates a behavioral driver that does not fall neatly within one of Maslow's or other need theorists' motivational categories. However, behavioral economic theories also align with the problem consumers have of perpetually *Re-generating U/aRe* processes throughout the *OM*, just like all need theories do.

Zero to One Again- Binary Oppositions of *B-Ought* and *N-Ought*

So if you are going construct all-encômpassing *Ôught factors* of psychological motivation aligning with the *Lean* principle of *Hōshin Kanri* and the *Ôntological Teleology*, you must recognize that the contingency of consumers' existences within the *OM* creates binary oppositions. These binary oppositions reside in all *HQs* between positive and negative *Ought factors* aligning with *what* may be *B-Ought* and *what is N-Ought*. Organizations can factor consumers' binary oppositions and deepest problems within these extremes of life and existence in order to identify *what paos* consumers find most truly meaningful.

If you form an *I/D Kata* with champagne glasses on the hood of a luxury vehicle just like *how Toyota's Lexus* division did in its famous commercial in the 1980s, you will notice that this *Penrose Triangle* forms a point of purchase over the *Lexus*. An intentional, unresolved paradox exists because while the glasses are stacked in upward fashion, their bottoms point downward. This is not a coincidence.

Toyota® Lexus®,The Relentless Pursuit of Perfection , Ad Campaign (© 1985 *Toyota Motor Corporation* (Fair Use))

Stream 5: People

I/\D Kata(© 1985 **Toyota Motor Corporation** (Fair Use))

Toyota's advertising firm *Saatchi & Saatchi*created this image to draw your attention to the fact that *Toyota's* customers' lives and existences have two explicit, maximal conditions, which are either to get *B-Ought* or become *N-Ought*. Like Buddha, Hume, Derrida, and an infinite number of other philosophers, *Toyota* sees these conditions as mutually dependent on one another because nothing could rationally exist without a logical inverse, or some logical distinction to itself, thereby creating all existence, essence, meaning and true-north value in the difference between the two conditions. It's the difference that motivates employees to pursue perfection and customers to purchase for perpetual problem resolution.

An organization like-wise does not need to concern itself with the specific range of possibilities of *what* may be *B-Ought* for business purposes within the philosophy of *Lean* other than to know *what* motivates its stakeholders, employees and customers to think and believe. An organization for its own purposes ought to bracket that speculation outside the *IB*– an organization cannot rationally know either*what* may be *B-Ought* or*what* is*N-Ought* by their own definitions. An organization only needs to be mindful of the potential for consumers to become*N-Ought* and*what* they really personally and intuitively believe is *B-Ought* to determine *who* they believe consumers truly are and thus *why* they may buy the organization's *paos*. The ultimate, pragmatic point is to build a logical, coherent *i/deô*logy of *Universal, Process* and *Personal* true-north values for an organization to more accurately analyze, deduce, and thereby predict *what* are the greatest problems consumers have, and thus *what paos* consumers are most highly motivated to consume in return for paying meaningful amounts of money.

Like bubbles floating up in champagne glasses,*Coke-Cola* enacting people's happiness, or *SUDS* rising up through *SL-OTS*, an organization ought to in-form, in-novate and de-sign its *paos* so that it surfaces *what* consumers essentially,[680] universally value, and thus *what* psychologically motivates them through the *Ought* to energize and optimize consumers' universal demand. Between the extremes of *B-Ought* and *N-Ought*, organizations' *paos* ought to *OPPtimize* consumers toward*Universalization* and away from real or perceived*Threats* by furthering their *energization, adaptation* and ultimate *Re-generation*.

Ôught Factors (Ôfs) of Psychological Motivation

Since *U/aRe* processes represent consumers' sufficient and necessary true-north values by solving their existential problems, you must understand which *Ontologically Teleological*factors psychologically motivate them by either:

1. *Optimizing consumers' /aRe processes so they may capitalize on OPPs to strive to get what they believe is B-Ought; or*
2. *Threatening consumers' /aRe processes such that they might strive to avoid becoming N-Ought.*

---

[680]*See generally*, Douglas Hofstadter and Emmanuel Sander, *Surfaces and Essences: Analogy as the Fuel and Fire of Thinking*, Basic Books (2013).

I do not propose to exhaustively list all possible *U/aRe Ôught factors* (*Ôfs*) of psychological motivation and problem resolution, but I best fit some *Ôught factors* to consumers' real lives and existences with the *Pragmatic Idealism* described in *Built to Last*. Remember that all lists of specific *Ôught factors* of *OPPs* or *Threats* to consumers' *U/aRe* processes are necessarily incomplete due to *Russell's Paradox*, and all categories are analogically fluid within consumers' value streams unless you can quantify them in some respect, so I do what I can with words until you quantify their true-north value within an *HQ* .[681]

Thus, *Ôught factors* may be objectively, physically real or may be subjectively, psychologically perceived by consumers. *Ôught factors* are dualities emphasizing the gradations through the *Ôught* of *B/aRe,C/aRe* , *I/C/aRe,ME/aRe* ,*WE/aRe* and eventually to *U/aRe Ôught factors*. I do not propose *Ôught factors* as being unchangeably categorical, but rather to repurpose the historically proposed motivational factors, needs, drivers, and/or end-goals all people have onto ontologically-based problem/solutions that you may use to *Lean* philosophically in a modern way and thereby make more meaningful amounts of money.

Ôught factors are what I perceive to be the most efficient parameters of problem/solutions organized around the overall *Ought* and *U/aRe* processes that best isolate normative *Universal/Process* and really *Personal* true-north values for identifying *what* consumers find most meaningful to their being as reflected by the money they spend. I believe it would be helpful for you to take the existential extremes within which consumers energize and optimize themselves, and factor the *Ought* into the most mutually exclusive, orthogonal categories of problem/solutions to consumers' being that you can within *what* makes the most sense to you. Though you must keep in mind that these factors are necessarily interdependent to support consumers' singular personas, you might use them to better

---

[681] As Maslow himself wrote, '[*L*]*ists of drives will get us nowhere for various theoretical and practical reasons,*' at p. 370 in, *A Theory of Human Motivation* (1943).

identify consumers' various true-north values that *paos* energizes and optimizes to increase consumers' *Strategically Unique Degrees of Sophist-ication* into higher and higher hierarchical *SL-OTS*.[682]

One method an organization can use to factor the *Ought* is through the *I/\D Kata* like *Toyota* did for *Lexis* using a stack of champagne glasses as its model. You factor the *Ought* either positively or negatively depending on which *paos*' features and benefits upwardly or downwardly energize and optimize consumers' lives and existences along the *Ôught* by solving their existential problems. You naturally ought to build *paos*' *Ôught factors* toward *what* consumers believe is *B-Ôught* in a positive sense. However, because the *Ôught* through which all customers live and exist is an apparent paradox for all practical purposes, you can also build *Ôught factors* in the negative sense from *what* may make consumers become not *N-Ôught*. All ways lead up. You build upward from these positive or negative *Ôught factors* through *U/aRe* processes toward a *Leanly* infinite sigma ($/\sigma\infty$), which is the relentless pursuit of a *Perfectionist Consequentialism* and *Universal Optimism* of *what* may get *B-Ôught* and against *what* is *N-Ôught*. However, since there is no apparent difference between getting *B-ÔT* and becoming *N-ÔT*, you ought to truly aim for the *Pragmatic Idealism* of *Lean* six sigma ($=/6\sigma$).

Thus, you may construct the *Ôught factors* of psychological motivation by asking either:

1. **What is required for consumers' to universalize their *U/aRe* processes to get *B-Ôught*; or**
2. **What may cause consumers to stop performing any one of *U/aRe* processes and become *N-Ôught*?**

You can design a market strategy from either existential extreme

---

[682] As Maslow himself wrote, '[N]o need or drive can be treated as if it were isolated or discrete; every drive is related to the state of satisfaction or dissatisfaction of other drives,' at p. 370 in, *A Theory of Human Motivation* (1943).

since the *Ôught* appears to be possibly circular within the *IB*. As Maslow said in paragraph nine of,*A Theory of Human Motivation* , '*Classification of motives must be based on goals*.' And the truest end-goals ought to be based on nothing less than consumers' existential extremes on either side of their life-cycles. When you produce these existential parameters for consumers' *Ôfs*, they should also meet the same criteria that you established for */aRe* processes. I adapt the */aRe* criteria to*Ôught factors* as follows:

1. While consumers' lives and existences may be viewed as a systemic process that attempts to perpetually optimize*U/aRe* processes through problem/re-solution, any description of their *Ôught factors* ought to be universal and persistent for broad application and analogizing. An organization's description of the qualities of*Ôught factors* also ought to be as efficient as possible under the guiding principle of*Occam's Razor* and in-line to the *Second Law of Thermodynamics*;
2. Different *Ôught factors* ought to be:
    a. Necessary, such that if any one factor was removed, *U/aRe* living processes would never obtain or would eventually cease; and
    b. Sufficient, such that within the limitations of making finite lists due to paradoxes and categorical semantics, no further *Ôught factors* would at least seem to be necessary to sustain and grow*U/aRe* living processes;
3. Consumers' lives and existentially literal and figurative qualities ought to be abstracted to the most generic terms to cover all contexts within the *Universe*. They should be amenable to analogizing and relating across *Supervening Levels of OT Sophist-ication* and include all indirect but still supervening *Ôught factors*as described below; and lastly
4. *Ôught factors* ought to be easy to apply and remember in an everyday business contexts, especially if an organization analogizes *Ôfs* across increasingly sophisticated *SL-ÔTS* to *Re-generate* customers' most truly valuable *SUDS*.

The most fundamental components of *U/aRe* organisms and organizations are these categories supporting *U/aRe* processes:

- **Ôntological Medium (ÔM)**, regards all physics as a literal, conditional prerequisite for all life and existence. Again, the 'Ôntological Medium,' or 'ÔM,' is a bit of shorthand for all of the scientific elements that compose consumers' physical existences such as the many spacetime dimensions, all forms of Matter and Energy, and the movement of Matter and Energy across those dimensions upward along the springlike arrow of spacetime that allows consumers to be. The *Ôntological Medium* regards the inviolable, physical contingency of existence as consumers know it within the *IB*. The *ÔM*, when considered within the *IB*, says nothing about the intuitive beliefs some consumers may hold about *what* may be truly *B-Ôught* outside the *IB*, such as an intuitive belief in the concept of *souls*. Common examples of customers seeking to expand their lives and existences through the *Ôntological Medium* include everything from saving time at work by multi-tasking to buying increasingly better houses as a form of *paos* to shelter themselves from the elements and social disdain;
- **Stimulated / Deprived**, regards consumers' inherent need for exploration and discovery to ôptimize *U/aRe* processes in furtherance of the *Ôught* through *adaptation, Re-generation* and energy hunting/gathering. Beyond chemical needs, consumers cannot psychologically develop without sensory stimulation, and proven psychological (and possibly genetic[683])

---

[683]For support for external influence on genetics, *see*, Nadine Provençal et al., *The Signature of Maternal Rearing in the Methylome in Rhesus Macaque Prefrontal Cortex and T Cells*, The Journal of Neuroscience, 32(44): 15626-15642; doi: 10.1523/JNEUROSCI.1470-12.2012 (Oct. 31 2012).

harm occurs from extended sensory deprivation.[684] Stimulation can also be the basic physical energy interjected into/*aRe* living processes at life's inception, and may be figuratively applied to consumers' psychological needs in the highest *SL-ÔTS* by perpetuating better life and existence through *SUDS*;

- **Related / Isolated**, regards consumers' proven need to relate to others under*Attachment Theory* as bounded by Dunbar's number[685] in response to consumers' need to *adapt*, *Regenerate* and *energize* to ultimately universalize themselves upward along the*Ought*. *Related / Isolated*is simply the fact of consumers performing *U/aRe* processes *U/Socially* with all people. Any sensory component of *Related / Isolated*is handled in *Stimulated / Deprived*as described above. At the most basic level, *Related / Isolated*may also apply to related combinations of chemical processes occurring within consumers through *B/aRe SL-ÔTS*in order for them to ôptimize *U/aRe* processes. *Relation*may also have mathematical support in co-evolutionary *free-lunch* theorems that show that consumers can increase their ôptimization overall by specializing and cooperating rather than trying to be jacks-of-all trades. Finally *Relation* addresses the problem that people need memes as much as genes in order to survive - people now require the legacy of knowledge handed down from our ancestors to now live and exist;

- **Vital / Ill**, regards consumers' real or perceived problems with sustaining internal vitality as living systems in response to real or perceived illnesses. Vitality relates to consumers' basic biological functions and general psychology. For ex-

---

[684]Judith Shulevitz, *The Science of Loneliness: How Isolation Can Kill You*, The New Republic (May 13, 2013); John T. Cacioppo & Louise C. Hawkley, *Loneliness Matters: A Theoretical and Empirical Review of Consequences and Mechanisms*, Ann Behav Med., 40(2): 10.1007/s12160-010-9210-8 (Oct. 2010); John T. Cacioppo, William Patrick,*Loneliness: Human Nature and the Need for Social Connection*, W. W. Norton & Company (2009).

[685]R.I.M. Dunbar, *Neocortex size as a constraint on group size in primates*, pp. 469-493, Volume 22, Issue 6, Journal of Human Evolution doi:10.1016/0047-2484(92)90081-J (Jun. 1992); R.I.M. Dunbar, R.A. Hill, *Social network size in humans*, Human Nature 14: 53 (2003).

ample, you may label consumers' psychology as *abnormal* when it limits their ability to engage in *U/aRe* processes at a level expected within their highest *SL-ÔT* as human beings. Vitality also relates to consumers' need to perpetually metabolize *energy* and *Re-generate* as much as possible by optimizing *U/aRe* processes;

- **Integral / Insecure**, regards consumers' real or perceived problems with maintaining their integrity in response to external threats to their lives and existences. Like other *Ôfs*, the terms *Integral* and *Insecure* can have further figuratively psychological meanings for consumers as conscious beings. As with other *Ôught factors*, you must differentiate between *what U/P* true-north values are and *what* consumers *Personally* experience phenomenologically. Consumers' psychological perception from their *Personal* perspectives may not perfectly align with *U/P* true-north values due to boundaries on consumers' rationality and imperfections within the *OM*; and lastly

- **Meaningful / Despondent**, regards recognizing the problems consumers have as fundamentally rational, self-aware organisms *who* Personally experience the *Paradox of the Ôught*. Consumers attempt to meaningfully go beyond the seemingly paradoxical *Ôught* to find a certain non-tautological teleology within their bounded rationality. To feel *Despondent* is to not realize a difference between *what* ought to be *B-Ôught* and *what* is *N-Ôught* living and existing. Consumers respond to the apparent paradox of the *Ôught* either by engaging in theological, spiritual or atheistic belief, or by simply bracketing existential questions and reflexively focusing on extending the *eRa* of *U/aRe* processes within the *ÔM* with blinders on. Teleological or teleonomic *Meaning* is the monster of consumers' souls that *paos* must ultimately feed to make the most money.

> *For that meaningful life,*
> *that particular signification of*
> *nature and history that I am,*
> *does not restrict my access to the world;*
> *it is rather my means of*
> *communicating with it.*
> - Maurice Merleau-Ponty, *The Phenomenology of Perception* (1945).

Model of U/aRe Ôught Factors

This chart of *Ôught factors* of psychological motivation isolates *what* energizes and ôptimizes consumers' lives and existences the most to best identify *what* makes consumers feel *Stimulated, Related, Vital, Integral* and *Meaningful* within the ÔM. The *Chart of Ôfs* classifies *who* and *why* consumers are as self-aware living organisms trying to ôptimize *U/aRe* processes to the extent they can become wholly existing through their *Will to Universalize*. When factoring the *Ôught*, an organization must empathize with each binary opposition that consumers experience from their self-conscious, really *Personal* phenomenologies that drives them to buy at their points of purchase to solve their greatest existential problems.

Consumers teleologically purposeful consciousness articulates and deals with the apparent paradox of trying to universalize /aRe infinitely through these *Ôught factors* :

U/aRe Ôught Factors Within the ÔM

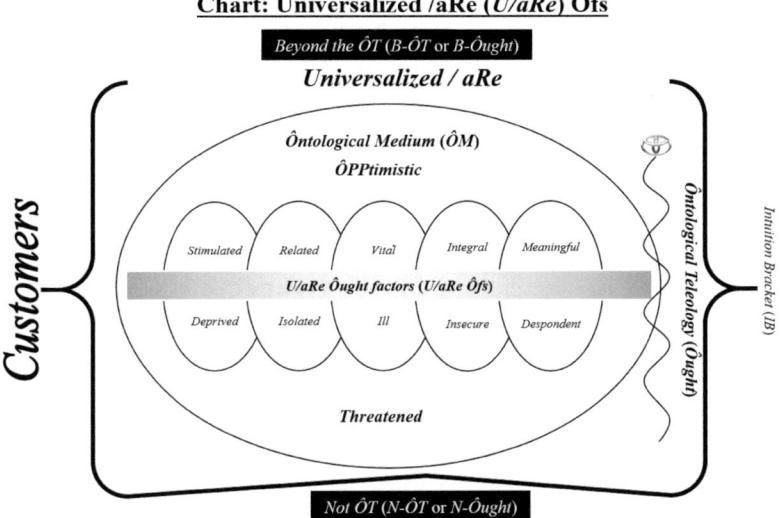

The above *Ôught factors* act as *Ôntologically Teleological* wants/needs/end-goals/motivations that in-turn re-solve *who* and *why* consumers are as living systems. Consumers energize and ôptimize their ability to *Leanly adapt, Re-generate* and *energize* through these *Ôfs* to attempt to universalize across all dimensions. Naturally, these *Ôught factors* are not the only ones through which consumers could ôptimize their lives and existences, such as so many others listed by need theorists. However, I ask you to consider these *Ôfs* to be generally the most instrumental toward serving consumers' *U/aRe* processes because they factor *who* and *why* they ôntologically */aRe*. Thus, I consider these *Ôfs* to be more motivating than any others because they address *what* matters most, but please feel free to put your own spin on them.

Higher Order *Meta-Ôfs* (*MÔs*)

All other parameters beyond these primary *Ôfs* supervene and re-solve themselves as *meta-Ôught factors* (*MÔs*). *MÔs* indirectly serve *U/aRe* processes and consumers' lives and existences overall via *Ôfs*. For example, consumers' psychologically *Stimulated*, emotional need for *love* is an indirect solver of the more fundamental need to be *Related* to more *Leanly adapt, Re-generate* and *energize*. Love in-turn often re-solves consumers' need for *Meaning* by flowing them past the *Ought* toward an irrational end-goal outside the *IB*. Likewise, consumers' need for *Safety* indirectly re-solves their more fundamental need to be *Integral*, or in the double negative sense, not *Insecure*, which in-turn provides them with the ability to love freely.

For an example of an even higher-order *Meta-Ôf*, consumers' broad need for in-formation and knowledge may be viewed as a *Meta-Ôught factor* creating coherence between consumers' personally inter-subjective and objective *Universal / Process* perspectives on true-north value with all other people. Knowledge reflects actionable *Universal* and *Process* true-north values that consumers' can use to further exist by solving problems to enhance their *Ôught factors* and *U/aRe* processes. Knowledge is the power that allows consumers to better integrate themselves into the *ÔM* by letting them seize *OPPs* or reduce threats to their lives and existences. Knowledge also allows consumers to more meaningfully avoid becoming *N-Ôught* by buying *paos* to better perform *U/aRe* processes so consumers may at least try to get themselves *B-Ôught*.

Industrial Classification of *MÔs*

To better categorize larger *Meta-Ôfs*, consider two further industrial classifications of consumers' means to better live, through transportation and telecommunication.

Transportation*MÔs*

For transportation as a meta-Ôught factor, consider that when consumers move from one place to another, such as with the Über car-sharing service, they pursue one or more core*Ôught factors* and *U/aRe* processes. Even if a customer buys a *Toyota* automobile to go on a road trip only for the sake of exploration, such exploration would naturally fit within the *Stimulated / Deprived CÔRe Ôught factor*. In other words, consumers' seek *Stimulation* to achieve unbounded exploration in order to solve their existential optimization problem through random discovery and play. Transportation for these purposes relates to consumers' need to seek the best sources of energy and meaning to fund *adaptation* and*Re-generation* through these lines of reasoning.[686]

Alternatively, employees might travel for an organization to earn money that lets them buy *paos* to serve all of their *CÔRe Ôfs*, thereby giving money to transportation businesses so they can in-turn become more *Stimulated, Related, Vital, Integral* and/or *Meaningful* in ex-change. Transportation could also be used by them to *adapt* by moving to a new city to get a new job, to *Re-generate* by taking them to a health club or by sending their offspring to get knowledge in school, or to *energize* them by letting them buy food at a restaurant. Consumers might even purchase a *Tesla* sports car to transport their self-esteem to a better place.

---

[686]*See e.g.*, David A. Raichlena, et. al.,*Evidence of Lévy Walk Foraging Patterns in Human Hunter–Gatherers*, pp. 728–733, PNAS, Vol. 111, No. 2, doi: 10.1073/pnas.1318616111 (Jan. 14, 2014); Gretchen Reynolds,*Navigating Our World Like Birds and Bees*, New York Times (Jan. 1, 2014).

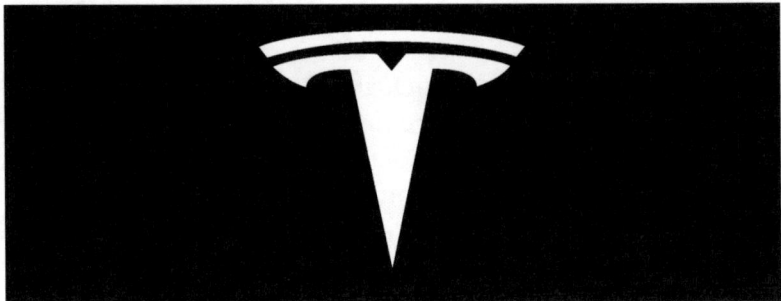

®*Tesla Motors*

All of these motives and end-goals are inter-twined, existential problem/re-solutions, but they can be *Ôntologically Teleologically* factored and identified with the *I/D Kata*. For example, consider employees earning money through a bake sale just to donate to charity. Employees do so to *Re-generate* personal *Meaning* for themselves and *Relate* to others in need of charity to ôntologically universalize *who* , *why* , *what* , and *how* they think they are.

Telecommunication*MÔs*

For telecommunications as a meta-Ôught factor, think through consumers' end-goals each time they speak with a personal *Relative* as a physical extension of their self-conceptions.[687] They also telecommunicate to get job training to *adapt* to the workforce. They telecommunicate with a doctor's office to schedule an appointment to *Re-generate* their *Vitality* in order to continue to live and exist. They telecommunicate to set a date with someone to *energize* their social life through *Relation* in order to *Stimulate* their personal *Meaning* . Each of these *Ôfs* ought to be used as an

---

[687] *See generally*, F. Heider,*The Psychology of Interpersonal Relations* , Wiley (1958); B. Weiner,*Achievement motivation and attribution theory* , Morristown, N.J.: General Learning Press (1974); B. Weiner,*Human Motivation* , NY: Holt, Rinehart & Winston (1980); J.H. Harvey & G. Weary, *Attribution: Basic Issues and Applications*, Academic Press, San Diego (1985); B. Weiner, *An attributional theory of motivation and emotion*, New York: Springer-Verlag (1986).

independent parameter when analyzing *who* and *why* consumers are through their lives and existences, and thus what intrinsically and extrinsically motivates them to buy *paos* now.

U/aRe processes operating up through all of the various *SL-ÔTS* and *SUDS* reflect different skews (like *Stock Keeping Units* or *Units of Real Value*) in each of the above *CÔRe-Ôfs* and *Meta-Ôfs*. For example, consumers' need to anticipate and *adapt* gets reflected in their need for *Integrity* and *Vitality* just like *how* consumers' need to ôptimize their adaptive processes gets reflected in their need to be *Stimulated*. Consumers' need to *adapt* and *Re-generate* through natural selection gets reflected in their need to *Relate*, just like *how* their need to *Universalize* their lives and existences gets reflected in their need for *Meaning*. Consumers reflexively conceptualize their universal existences to ôptimize *U/aRe* adaptive processes by resolving problems toward *what* they believe is *B-Ôught* and to better contrast themselves to *what* they consider to be *N-Ôught*.

> *- and whose terror of not really ever even existing*
> *makes them that much more susceptible to*
> *the ontological siren song of the*
> *corporate buy-to-stand-out-and-so-exist-gestalt.*
> - David Foster Wallace, *The Pale King*, p. 151 (2011).

You now ôught to be able to see *how* consumers' *U/aRe* processes get factored into their true need for *Stimulation, Relation, Vitality, Integrity* and *Meaning*. For example, *energization* requires *Stimulating* inputs to obtain energy itself and the in-formation to find energy in the first place. *Energization* requires *Relation* with others to cooperatively pursue and produce shared energy sources, just like a large chemical reaction, which ultimately results in *Vitality*. *Energization* also requires the *Integrity* of the processes and character creating *Vitality*. *U/aRe* processes result in *Meaning*

to more reflexively conceptualize *how* an organization may gather the energy (aka capital) necessary to fund greater *adaptation, Regeneration* and ultimately *Universalization,* which is the manifest destiny of all organizations, just like it is for the consumers on which they depend.

By now, you can see where this is going upward along the ultimate value stream toward channels of,*Ôntological Realization* . All organizational analysis ôught to go on and on like this as it investigates *how* a company's *paos* re-solves consumers' *Ôught factors,Meta-Ôfs* and ultimate true-north value streams. This analysis would apply to any other*Ôught factor* or *Meta-Ôf* an organization considers, which is *why* I think this model best bene-fits *who* consumers are and *why* they really buy *what* they purchase. *How* you make that money meaningfully with this in-formation by aligning with the *Ôught* is up to you.

Factoring*Meta-Ôught Factors*

For all these *Ôught factors* that in-turn ôptimize *U/aRe* processes to find meaning outside the *IB,* their structure as binary opposites reflects the contingent nature of consumers' lives and existences.[688] Like the *Ôught factors* diagram shown above and repeated below, an organization ought to factor the *Meta-Ôfs* its *paos* serves by building from the existential extremes of universalization on the one hand and *what* may lead consumers to become *N-OT* on the other. Once an organization has these funda-mental end-goals in mind, it can more logically connect them to *what* problems fall in-between. These *Meta-Ôught factors* provide a framework to guide you and any organization through the general, existential

---

[688]This notion of binary opposition of course recognizes the work of Buddha, as well as Claude Levi-Straus in,*The Structural Study of Myth* , Journal of American Folklore (1955); and Jaques Derrida in*Grammatology* , p. 158, Johns Hopkins University Press (1976).

motivational categories of consumers' lives and existences.[689]They will carry you upward through the *Ôntological Teleology*through which consumers energize and ôptimize their will to consciously and unconsciously universalize.

Emotional Meta-Ofs (E-MÔs)

Consumers' psychological and physiological feelings, their delights and pain-points, also reflect these *Meta-Ôught factors*. Emotions are motivational *Meta-Ofs* of their own kind. *Feelings* are phenomenological events that measure the extent that a consumer's*Ôfs* change up or down along the *Ôntological Teleology*. Feelings are a subjective (and to some extent objective) function and sentiment of *how* consumers are doing within the*OM*. Thus, these *emotional-Ôfs* (aka *E-MÔs*) e-merge from consumers' real or perceived changes in *U/aRe* prσcesses.[690] As described earlier, *E-MÔs* may be perceived as the*middleware* between*CÔRe Ôfs* and *what* consumers personally experience. While they are middleware, they cognitively surround *what* is CÔRe to *who* and *why* consumers */aRe* since they are so essential to consumers' *Lean* thinking and being. *Σ-MÔs* often get mistaken for *CÔRe Ôfs*for this reason.

While consumers' and employees'*E-MÔs* consume lots of organizational energy, emotions and *gut feelings* prσduce a very powerful computational heuristic for consumers and organizations to efficiently and accurately decide *what* uniquely/profitably energizes and ôptimizes consumers' lives and existences. Daniel Kahneman, one of the creators of *Prospect Theory*, refers to *E-MÔs* as 'Type 1' thinking, as opposed the more analytical*Ôught factoring* we have been discussing, which Kahneman describes as 'Type 2' thinking.[691]

---

[689]Or as Maslow wrote at p. 370 in, *A Theory of Human Motivation* (1943), '[A]ny motivated behavior, either preparatory or consummatory, must be understood to be a channel through which many basic needs may be simultaneously expressed or satisfied.'

[690]In other words, the philosopher Hillary Putnam would refer to *E-MÔs* as representing a form of, *Liberal Functionalism*.

[691]*See generally*, Daniel Kahneman,*Thinking, Fast and Slow* (2011).

E-MÔs thus function as a type of signal, 'Andon' or 'Kanban' inside an HQ and within consumers. Andon and Kanban are Lean terms of Japanese origin for tools that centralize in-formation to indicate when operations are good or bad, when things are going well or not. E-MÔs like-wise signal when an HQ or consumers believe that some thing or event re-solves problems to facilitate *adaptation*, *Re-generation* or *energization*, or not, up or down the *Ought* .

> *When I do good, I feel good,*
> *When I do bad, I feel bad,*
> *And that's my religion.*
> - Attributed to Abraham Lincoln, the 16th President of the United States[a]
>
> ---
> [a]This attribution was given a "C" grade for plausible utterance by Abraham Lincoln from Don E. Fehrenbacher and Virginia Fehrenbacher in, *Recollected Words of Abraham Lincoln*, p. 245, Stanford University Press, 1st ed. (1996).

At the same time, oscillating *E-MÔs* directing *how* consumers think and act may lead an *HQ* and consumers to perceive and do things that are not rationally aligned with *U/aRe* normative processes of true-north value, which will not truly solve their deepest problems.[692] For example, employees' *E-MÔs* may diverge from normative *Universal* and *Process* true-north values, so an organization's conjecture, hypothesis or theory as to whether its *paos* normatively solves one or more *Ôfs* must be appropriately structured and validated through iterative, empirical market testing with the *I/D Kata*. You can factor *E-MÔs* like all other *Ôfs* , but you must be careful to identify their possible irrationality.

Notice too that *CÔRe Ôfs* critical to consumers' *Ôntological Realization* simultaneously serve as both ôntological true-north values,

---
[692]Antonio Damasio, *The Feeling of What Happens: Body and Emotion in the Making of Consciousness*, Houghton Mifflin Harcourt (1999).

such as being *Stimulated, Related, Vital, Integral* and*Meaningful* , as well as consumers' emotional states of well-being. For example, consumers can both be and feel *Stimulated*, they can both be and feel *Related*, they can both be and feel*Vital* , etc. This linguistic fact evidences the ęmotional and ôntological connection between the two sides of the ôntological/ęmotional coin.

You may extrapolate consumers' *Lean* ôntological/ęmotional true-north values further and further, higher and higher into instrumental goals and*Meta-Ôught factors* above the primary, intrinsic *CÔRe Ôfs*, particularly within the context of human psychology.[693] All these ôntological/ęmotional needs relate back in one way or another to the more fundamental *CÔRe Ôfs*, which means back to the problematic contingency of consumers' lives and existences within the *OM* and the open-ended *Universe*. Thus, re-solving *Emtional Meta-Ôught factors*,*Meta-Ôught factors* and*CÔRe Ôfs* is the fundamental job to be done by *paos* each time it gets consumed.

Irrational Exuberance

All good *ĘMÔs* though eventually *Lean* toward *Meaning*, which is toward *what* may be *B-Ôught* to re-solve the existential problem of advancing *U/aRe* prσcesses away from *what* is *N-Ôught*. Problem re-solution in the form of existential*Meaning* in-turn may physiologically and psychologically enact *what* consumers feel on the rightward, upward slope of consumers' U-shaped utility curves. *Meaning* is thus perhaps the most generalized and abstract of the *CÔRe Ôfs*critical to consumers' *Ôntological Realization* . Thus, the *Meaningful Will to Universalize*is composed of:

1. *Rational action taken by consumers to re-solve the existential problems in line with universally axiomatic and*

---

[693]*See generally*, Amy Wrzesniewskia, Barry Schwartzb, Xiangyu Congc, Michael Kanec, Audrey Omarc, and Thomas Kolditza, *Multiple Types of Motives Don't Multiply the Motivation of West Point Cadets*, Proceedings of the National Academy of Sciences, doi: 10.1073/pnas.1405298111 (Jun. 4, 2014).

prɔcessually systemic true-north values to universalize themselves within the bounds of the Intuition Bracket; and

2. *Irrational, intuitive action responding to what consumers know is N-Ôught inside the Intuition Bracket to optimize their search for what they believe is B-Ôught outside the IB.*

Consumers' search for *Meaning* and a *Will to Universalize* keeps them in a state of emotional and physical criticality, balancing between (1) rational order and (2) irrational disorder, seeking to ôptimize *U/aRe* prɔcesses overall. Corporations as fictional legal people work this way too,[694] balancing order and disorder in a perpetual state of rational/irrational criticality toward optimizing their *Ontological Realization*. I am sure you experience this state of criticality every time you enter an *HQ* of an organization. While arguments exist against it,[695] this concept of self-organized criticality being *how* consumers ôptimize emotion and *Me*aning is reasonable, intuitive speculation to consider in a *Lean House of Quality*. I hope this speculation gets more thorough testing though.

> *Wide yawns the gap; connection is no more;*
> *Check'd Reason halts;*
> *her next step wants support;*
> *Striving to climb,*
> *she tumbles from her scheme.*
> - Edward Young, Night Thoughts, VI (between 1742 and 1745)

---

[694]*But see*, John M. Beggs and Nicholas Timme, *Being Critical of Criticality in the Brain*, Department of Physics, Indiana University, Front. Physiol., doi: 10.3389/fphys.2012.00163 (Jun. 7, 2012).

[695]Yuval Noah Harari, *Sapiens*, p. 30 (2014).

Much as consumers' *Personal* perspectives supervene on and assume their *Universal* and *Processual* true-norths, you can also see randomness within each of their normative *U/P* and subjectively *Personal* values that operate inside each of them. Some systemic instability leads to their greater overall stability due to small variations that lead to tremendous change over time. The author Nassim Taleb created a term for this, '*Anti-Fragile*.'[696] In a series of experiments led by physicist Per Bak and his colleagues in 1999, they determined that these seemingly random changes to consumers' neurological processes resulted from systemically structured phase changes whereby randomness is structured as an actual process in consumers' minds. Per Bak determined that a single, small change led to many smaller changes cascading into *what* appears to be a much larger cumulative change, resulting in greater systemic and/or structural stability overall. This is a deceptively simple idea until you see how broadly it applies.

Per Bak's phase changes follow the mathematical distribution of the '*Power Law*'[697] as popularized by Malcolm Gladwell in his book, *The Tipping Point*.[698] The *Power Law* states that one variable is often exponentially related to another in its degree of variance. As Gladwell and others across science and economics have well described, many rare events naturally follow this pattern of the *Power Law*. For example, a genetic mutation leading to the birth of a black swan could lead to an overwhelmingly large population of black swans if black swans were able to *adapt, energize* and ultimately *Re-generate* better than birds of a different feather.[699] The *Power Law* reflects the magnitude of *what* occurs during such critical phase change, like *how* a mere kaleidoscope of butterflies could eventually cause a twister further up the curve of the *OT* by

---

[696] *See generally*, Nassim Nicholas Taleb, *Antifragile: Things That Gain from Disorder*, Random House (2012).

[697] Per Bak et. al., *Self-Organized Criticality*, Physical Review of Letters (Jul. 7, 1987).

[698] *See generally*, Malcom Gladwell, *The Tipping Point: How Little Things Can Make a Big Difference*, Back Bay Books (Jan. 7, 2002).

[699] *See generally*, Nassim Nicholas Taleb, *The Black Swan*, Random House (2008).

creating further changes in global weather patterns.

Within universal, axiomatic truths, randomness seems to demonstrate itself. At the quantum level this behavior is reported in atomic particles by physicists.[700] From a process perspective, scientists report that random genetic mutations are critical to consumers' *adaptation* through natural selection. From consumers' personal perspectives, they behave in random and irrational ways to *me*aningfully determine *what* they ought to do in relation to *what* they believe is *B-Ôught* and universally and processually k*no*w is *N-Ôught*.[701]

This apparent instability at each *SL-OT Re-generates* beneficial randomness that *Re-generates what*is critical to ôntological well-being by shaking out, stochastically testing and settling *what* is *Ôntologically Teleological*and *what* is*N-Ôught*.[702]Randomness (or at least perceived randomness to the best of our senses) thus seems to reflect itself from the ground up within all consumers' *U/ P* and really *Personal* true-north values. I speculate that even consumers' random search for emotional*me* aning is most often instrumental to their ôptimizing *U/aRe* physical and cognitive processes to best universalize overall.[703]

Thus, organizations' and consumers' criticality can simply be considered rational, structural randomness. This randomness is beneficial to the extent it ôptimizes *U/aRe* processes. Effectively structuring randomness in consumers' minds and in organizations must be done with *C/aRe* because true randomness by definition cannot be fully controlled. You must keep in mind that working with

---

[700]Chirag Dhara, Giuseppe Prettico, and Antonio Acín,*Maximal Quantum Randomness in Bell Tests*, Phys. Rev. A 88, 052116 (Nov. 15, 2013).

[701]*See again*, Nicolas Gauvrit, Hector Zenil, Fernando Soler-Toscano, Jean-Paul Delahaye, Peter Brugger, *Human behavioral complexity peaks at age 25*, Journal for the International Society of Computational Biology (PLOS) (Apr. 13, 2017).

[702]*See generally*, Nassim Nicholas Taleb,*Antifragile* (2012).

[703]For background on this, *see generally*, Dan Ariely, *Predictably Irrational, The Hidden Forces That Shape Our Decisions*, Expanded Ed., HarperCollins (2009); see also Dan Ariely's other work,*The Upside of Irrationality: The Unexpected Benefits of Defying Logic at Work and at Home*, HarperCollins (2011).

randomness, like studying all true-north value, is like playing with the sun - it is both very powerful but painful and disorienting, and only *Lean* value streams can constructively channel it.

I want to convince you if you need convincing that structural irrationality is a part of ôptimizing consumers' lives and existences toward further and better being. An organization can make money meaningfully by channelling consumers' irrationality upward along the *Lean* value stream so they may best purchase perfecting *paos*, even if *how* such consumption will occur is hard to predict.

Critical Phase Transitions while Dreaming - Extending *U/aRe* Persona

Importantly, critical phase transitions *Re-generate* themselves in consumers' value streams when they change *how* consumers feel about *how paos* provides them with the most *Meaning*.[704] For example, critical phase transitions reflect themselves in *what* consumers daydream about buying. Consumers' dreams may be plausibly described as unrestricted moments of free-form dis-analogizing that juxtaposes *what* they phenomenologically experience within their largely rational lives and existences to *what* they dream about purchasing. They dream to inversely define *what* is rational, and thus what aligns them with the *ÔT*, by helping them define *what* they believe is *B-Ôught* and are afraid will make them *N-Ôught*.[705] Hopefully, all paid advertising places *paos* within *how* consumers' define their dreamy personas, i.e. *who* they want to be and become along the *ÔT*, in this way.

---

[704] I recommend viewing, Salvador Dali, *The First Days of Spring* (1929) for inspiration regarding this concept.

[705] As has been pointed out by other commentators, Freud rejected logic, and yet simultaneously applied logic to analyze dreams, and while psychology has moved beyond Freudian thinking, it has not neurologically explained dream theory much beyond Freudian speculation.

The Harder They Fall

As an organization produces *paos* that perfects consumers' *Ôught factors* in a positive sense toward *what* they believe may get themselves *B-Ôught*, consumers likewise increase their perception of the possibility of their moving toward becoming *N-Ôught* in a negative sense because everyone is obviously very far from fully pursuing perfection. Thus, consumers feel most alive when they are reaching higher degrees of *Ôught* by increasing their risk of becoming somehow *N-Ôught*. You can see again the nearly tautological proximity of *Ôught* and *N-Ôught* in this diagram looking down into *Toyota's HQ*:

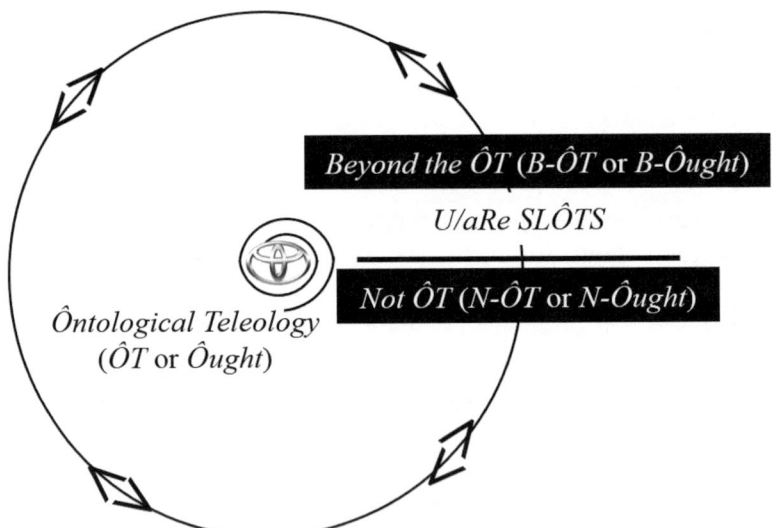

Each of consumers' *Ôught factors* grows proportionately in both directions between *what* they do positively experience and *what* they can but don't experience as well in the negative sense. The better and more deeply an organization energizes and ôptimizes consumers' *Personal* perspectives by historically advancing them upward along the *Ôught*, the more acutely consumers perceive a potential loss in their *Ôught factors*, *MÔs* and *E̱MÔs*, resulting in their great sadness.

On the one hand, wealth represents advancement in consumers' *Ôntological Realization*. On the other, wealth does not correlate in a straight line with happiness because people *who* are highly worthy on a net basis must worry to a greater degree about losing their self-worth.[706] Wealth can magnify *E̱MÔs* and a perceived risk of social and/or material loss in everything wealthy people do. An organization can capitalize on this tendency and consume the money of highly worthy people through its *paos* that wealthy people purchased to help them (or any person or thing they perceive to be an extension of them) a-void losing over gaining in relation to their peer group.[707]

The Only Way is *U / PP* through *Meaning*

As discussed in the *Stream 3: Existence*, since consumers' *Ôught Cognitive Dissonance* arises as a rational mechanism to their conscious awareness, consumers attempt to rationalize the *Ôught* paradox itself. Consumers find themselves doing this by attempting to find *Meaning* either by expanding *who* and *why* they are within the bounds of *ÔM* and *IB*, or by attempting to irrationally circumvent the rationality of the *Ôught* with their intuitive speculation or risky behavior. This is the only way forward for them in an unbounded *Universe*.

As discussed earlier regarding Victor Frankl's *Will to Meaning*, consumers need for *Meaning* as the re-solution of their existential

---

[706] Amy Novotney, *Money Can't Buy Happiness*, p. 24, Vol 43, No. 7, Monitor on Psychology, American Psychological Association (Jul./Aug. 2012).

[707] By the way, in the phrase, '*N-OT realized*,' you often see this same sentiment or meaning reflected in Abrahamic religious texts that say something to the effect that this is the, '*Word of the Lord*,' with the spoken '*Word*' metaphorically standing for *Ontological Realization* in the sense of the biblical expression of, '*Breathing Life*, into something.

problems was famously addressed by his development of *Logotherapy*, which retains all of its validity, but I now connect its contents to *CÔRe Ôfs* to explain *why Logotherapy* is effective. [708] I of course recommend addressing the balance of the *CÔRe Ôfs* in conjunction with *Logotherapy* to best ôptimize *U/aRe* prσcesses under the overall function of self-organizing criticality. *Meaning* is inherently a composite of the *CÔRe Ôfs* since they all increase the distinction between *what* is known to be *N-Ôught* and *what* may be *B-Ôught*.

If consumers bought a hypothetical *paos* that allowed them to live forever, consumers would perpetually contrast themselves between *what* ought to be and *what* is *N-Ôught*. Nonetheless, most science fiction films show very advanced, *adaptive, Re-generative* and *ęnergizing* alien species living very violent existences against a universe of possibilities of becoming *N-Ôught*. Despite having the capacity to live forever, they risk ever more to really live at all.[709]

> *You can't discover new lands without losing sight of the shore.*
> - André Gide, *Les faux-monnayeurs* [The Counterfeiters] (1925).

Critically, as an organization perfects consumers' *U/aRe* prσcesses toward a fully universalized event horizon of complete problem resolution, its *paos* will provide less *Strategically Unique Degrees of Sophist-ication* to ęnergize and ôptimize consumers' lives and existences. This paradox results because should customers consume *paos* that fully removed the contingent possibility of their becoming *N-Ôught*, they would likewise remove the lower portion of their binary *Ôught* factors. While they would perpetually exist without

---

[708] And perhaps writing this book was a form of *Logotherapy* for myself; if so I recommend doing something similar.

[709] War can also be seen through *U/aRe* processes as the physical process of dramatic energy consumption toward *Ontological Realization*.

that contingency, they would remove any *Meaning* their lives would have within the *ÔM* since *Meaning* is defined by the *B-Ôught/ N-ÔT* duality and paradox.

However, given the distance we all are from such hypothetical perfection, an organization fortunately only needs to focus on resolving problems to *Re-generate* value streams flowing upward toward consumers' universal horizon of complete satisfaction, toward *what* they all believe is truly *B-Ôught*. Becoming *N-Ôught* is still all too risky and real for us today. For an organization to make the most value, it ought to focus only on discovering *what* best energizes and ôptimizes *who* and *why U/ People* are within their lives and existences in the *ÔM*, and not worry about consumers actually getting *B-Ôught*.

Energizing and ôptimizing *who* and *why U / Peôple* are means solving problems to increase the juxtaposition between *what* they ought to buy with *what* they know is *N-Ôught* and tantalizing them with the possibility of getting *B-Ôught*, even if only to feel that way for a brief moment. Ironically, by doing so, consumers will become ever more acutely aware of *what* is *N-Ôught*, and *what* they have to lose by not buying *paos* from you. You will do this by providing them with the most meaningful, delightful purchasing experiences possible within each of their individual phenomenologies.

Bringing it All Together

This concludes, *U/ P: Lean Business Philosophy, True-North Value*, which investigated *who, why, what* and *how* consumers are. You now know *how* to produce the value streams that consumers demand to reach the greatest prophet. You also have a solid foundation for a *Lean HQ* to reach up and dent the *Universe*. This *Stream 5: People's* will conclude by showing the *U/ Peôple* organizational chart together with our *Chart of Ôught factors* rising up like a lotus toward the pragmatic, *Zen*-like pursuit of perfection:

Chart of U/Pęôple's Value Stream

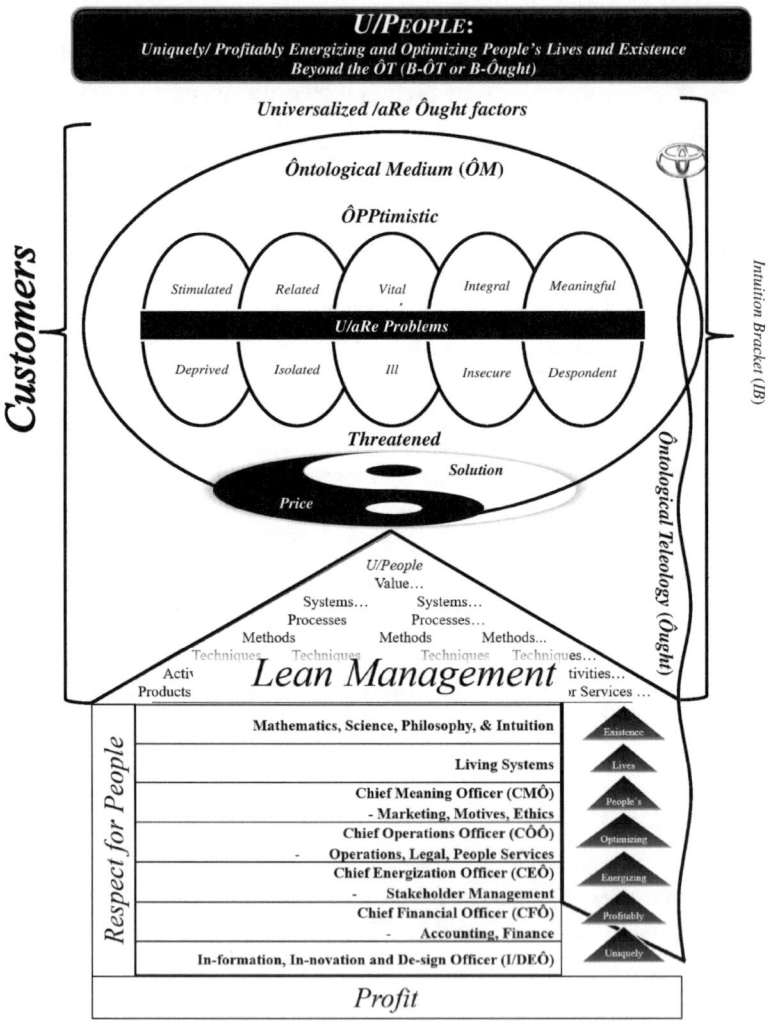

For each of these positions within the *U / Pęôple* value stream, before pursuing, *Volume II: Channels,* I ask you to consider the following questions:

1. *How will a Chief Meaning Ôf-ficer discover and direct what is the most meaningful for consumers?*
2. *How will a Chief Ôptimization Ôf-ficer ôptimize what produces the most Matter / Ęnergy flowing through the organization for the production of ⁺paos that in-turn ęnergizes and ôptimizes who, why, what and how consumers are?**
3. *How will a Chief Ęnergization Ôf-ficer ęnergize and align what all of an organization's stakeholders most value so that all the other parts of U/People flow most truly north to who consumers are and why they value ⁺paos?**
4. *How will a Chief Function Ôf-ficer derive what has the most monetary value for consumers over and above what ⁺paos costs to Re-generate?**
5. *How will an In-formation, In-novation, and De-sign Ôf-ficer most clearly identify, ideate and shape what ⁺paos an organization profitably delivers?**

Volume II: Channels

You now know *why* an organization ought to *Lean* philosophically through *who U/People* are. This business model should help any organization think well about *how* to build up a *House of Quality*. *U/P* now moves from *Volume I: True-North Value* to *Volume II: Channels* to better describe management's upper-ontology and *what* and *how* it ought to be re-produced. *Volume II: Channels* analyzes *how* an organization ought to measure and apply *Volume I: True-North Value* to make more meaningful amounts of profit by solving more problems. *Volume II: Channels* will investigate and direct *what* and *how* an organization ought to *Re-generate* true-north value for consumers by applying *Volume I: True-North Value* through the departments of a corporation. This analysis will start by analyzing the function of the *Chief Meaning Ôf-ficer* within a business ideology and proceed downward through the divisions of the *U/People* business model until it does in-fact uniquely/profitably energize and optimize people's lives and existences for the highest profit.
